TRIBES AND POWER

TRIBES AND POWER
Nationalism and Ethnicity in the Middle East

Edited by
Faleh Abdul-Jabar and Hosham Dawod

SAQI

To the memory of Hanna Batatu, a great thinker and a modest human being.

British Library Cataloguing-in-Publication Data
A catalogue record for this book is available from the
British Library

ISBN 0 86356 804 1

This edition first published 2003

Saqi
26 Westbourne Grove
London W2 5RH
www.saqibooks.com

Contents

Introduction   7

PART ONE
ARAB AND MUSLIM TRADITION: KINSHIP, TRIBE AND IBN KHALDUN
1. Agnatic Illusions: The Element of Choice in Arab Kinship   15
   Edouard Conte
2. Ibn Khaldun and Contemporary Anthropology: Cycles and Factional
   Alliances of Tribe and State in the Maghreb   50
   Pierre Bonte   50

PART TWO
TOTALITARIANISM AND TRIBALISM: THE BA'TH REGIME AND TRIBES
3. Sheikhs and Ideologues: Deconstruction and Reconstruction of
   Tribes under Patrimonial Totalitarianism in Iraq, 1968–1998   69
   Faleh A. Jabar
4. The 'State-ization' of the Tribe and the Tribalization of the State:
   the Case of Iraq   110
   Hosham Dawood
5. Tribalization as a Tool of State Control in Iraq: Observations on the
   Army, the Cabinets and the National Assembly   136
   Keiko Sakai

PART THREE
KURDISH TRIBES AND STATES: TRIBALISM, ETHNICITY AND NATIONALISM
6. Kurds, States and Tribes   165
   Martin van Bruinessen
7. Yazidi Tribes, Religion and State in Early Modern Iraq   184
   Nelida Fuccaro   184

Contents

PART FOUR
EMIRATES AND TRIBES: MAGHREB, ARABIA AND IRAN
8. A Few Reflections on 'Tribe' and 'State' in Twentieth-Century
   Morocco   205
   Kenneth Brown   205
9. Tribal Confederations and Emirates in Central Arabia   214
   Madawi al-Rasheed   214
10. The White Tent programme: Tribal Education Under Muhammad
    Reza Shah   234
    Farian Sabahi

PART V
TRIBES, COLONIALISM AND NATIONALISM
11. The Social Ontology of Late Colonialism: Tribes and the Mandated
    State in Iraq   257
    Toby Dodge
12. Tribes and Nationalism: Tribal Political Culture and Behaviour
    in Iraq, 1914–20   283
    Thair Karim

   Contributors   311
   Glossary   314
   Index   321

Introduction

A major characteristic of most anthropological and sociological research on the evolution and mutation of tribes in the Middle East has been the use of a lineal approach. Certain classic works on tribes have depicted an irreversible line of development, a continuum of the disintegration of tribes and tribal structures and the emergence of national societies with individualized citizens at its core. A similar view has tended to overwhelm the thinking of various elites – be they domestic, modernist, political or intellectual.

There have been many facets of modernity. These include the rise of large-scale modern organizations (from standing armies to a growing bureaucracy with advanced technologies of regulation and control); the growth of urban life (in the shape of large megalopolises with millions of faceless nomads severed from their primordial cords); the development of fast communications systems (aeroplanes, railways, cars, telegram and telephone lines unifying segmented spaces and ending their ancient solitude); the emergence of a modern, profit-oriented and contractual economy; the evolution of modern culture (with nationalism, trade unionism, liberalism and other ideologies, superseding or transforming traditional culture); and the implementation of ramified regulatory regimes and control systems. These and other facets of modernity serve to strengthen the omnipresence and omnipotence of the modern Leviathan, the central state or nation-state, and weaken pre-modern social organization and culture.

Yet the realities of the 1990s, and perhaps even earlier, provide ample evidence that in certain Middle Eastern countries the tribal factor has not only been strengthened but become decisively manifest. Tribal networks have not only endured but have taken new and varied forms. Modern 'socialist' or 'nationalist' elites bent on 'progress', or liberal monarchs with their eyes set on modernization, reinstated an already active tribal value system and deployed tribal networks in mobilizing allegiance or restructuring modern political and social institutions. Tribes, driven from nomadism to sedentary agriculture to urbanism in less than a century, mutated in terms of forms, structures,

7

leadership patterns, environment, and material or symbolic capital. But tribes were not passive entities; they retained their solidarity networks and value-systems, and held to their belief in: the ideology of fictive or real common lineage, a communality of interests, the reciprocity of obligations, common residence (in city or provincial town quarters) and the importance of marriages and alliances. The tribes' flexible response resulted in various elastic forms of group solidarity. These, in turn, provided spaces for social, economic, political and cultural action. These spaces have grown into a wide and complex area and this empirical reality raises many questions.

Why, in this day and age, are people inclined, constrained or even encouraged to regroup themselves into large domestic units or tribes (real or fictive)? What collective and individual interests link them that are reproduced through the tribal system? What is the meaning of the contemporary resurgence of tribalism at a time when the dominant discourse for over two decades has been couched in the language of world processes and globalization? What exactly is a tribe in various Middle Eastern contexts today?

For social scientists, societies are particular and their histories always singular – yet in many cases one can see the reproduction of comparable processes and patterns: Tribes and their chiefdoms recur in different epochs and also in different societies which have no contact with each other. One has only to look at the current socio-political map of Africa, Central Asia or elsewhere to see this repetition. But to acknowledge this is not to abandon standards of debate: if grand evolutionary theories are dead, it is still true that social structures and ways of life and human thinking have evolved in the course of history and will continue to do so. The issue is how to make the best possible reconstruction of this evolution and this history.

For more than 20 years there has existed a clear (negative) convergence between the grand paradigms: Marxism (in its Soviet and Third World versions), Liberalism and Modernism, to cite only three major ideological currents. By consistently underestimating the importance of all phenomena below the level of the State, these doctrines have been unable to register either the current tendency for kinship relations to become invested with political power (especially the higher levels of political power), or the new forms of local solidarity and the ethno-cultural differences between peoples that have developed.

The current proliferation of tribal phenomena is simply relegated to the old banal categories of tradition/modernity as mapped by the linear scale of progress. Yet (and without falling into the hyper-relativist postmodernism latterly so in vogue), there is much empirical evidence that the breakdown of the old social structures under the influence of modernization and globalization, has produced some unanticipated consequences. One major consequence is that diverse forms of tribal *'asabiya* (solidarity), and religious and ethnic linkages, have been reinforced rather than weakened.

In considering theories explaining the origin and character of the tribe, it is crucial to jettison the theme of their essentially archaic character, as in stark contrast to a 'modernizing rationalism'. In this approach all social change is reduced to the passage from the traditional to the modern, from the simple to the complex, from 'particularism' to 'universalism' (to rehearse the Parsonian repertoire). From this perspective, the tribal belongs to the 'particularist' or 'pre-modern' world; located on the side of the obsolete and hence, 'obstacle to change' or the result of 'incomplete modernization'. Thus preconceived at the start, the tribal seems of only minor interest to the theorist. In relation to the tribe, globalization gives a renewed stimulus to modernity and the modernist vision in peripheral societies. But at the same time, we are witnessing political and cultural levels moving in precisely the opposite direction to economic integration, via a process of segmentation. New nation-states appear and multiply, each seeking to affirm their identity and legitimacy, both ancient and modern. It is precisely here that we observe, at the infra-state level, a revivification of tribal sentiment (real or reconstituted) that irreparably undermines modernity's image of its own origin.

To examine the question of tribes and powers, a seminar was organized in March 1999 by our research group, ICF, in conjunction with the School of Politics and Sociology, Birkbeck College, London University. A host of anthropologists, sociologists, political scientists and historians took part in the seminar, presenting novel ideas and stimulating fruitful debate. The main contextual focus of this book is Iraq, the most under-studied society in the region. Other cases from Arabia, Morocco, Mauritania, Iran and (in the case of the Kurds) Turkey are studied with a comparative intent.

A general theoretical framework is offered at the outset of this book through an analysis of the meaning and forms of kinship bonds within Arab tribal traditions. As Edouard Conte comprehensively shows, illusions of agnatic kinship bonds notwithstanding, blood ties are often substituted by symbolic cognatic affiliations, or re-manufactured in various types of alliances. Pierre Bonte re-examines the logic of *riyasa* (chieftainship) as one fraught with fierce competition and structured hierarchy, whereby different segments are ranked inferior or superior to one another. He also questions the validity of the Khaldunian tribe-state cycle. Both these chapters define the general framework of kinship.

Several tribes acted as catalyst for civilization, creating the six great civilizations in world history. Most, however, lived through the proper or modified Khaldunian cycle of resisting, conquering or opposing city-states.

In industrialized times, however, a multitude of roles were assumed by tribes and supra-tribal confederations: some developed political structures and wielded central power as in Arabia, while others reached the threshold of such development but fell short of it. In many cases they were overwhelmed by mightier powers, which had themselves evolved out of a mixture of Bedouinism and puritanism – as the case of the Shammar principality in Hail, Arabia shows (al-Rasheed, chapter 9).

Tribes may also serve as markers of language-based ethnicity, as Bruinessen shows in the case of the Kurds in Iraq and Turkey (chapter 6), or of religious community, as Fuccaro shows in her study of Yazidi Kurds (chapter 7). They may, as Thair Karim contends, oppose the very logic of nascent nationalism (chapter 12), or, as we can deduce from Toby Dodge, they may get incorporated into the nascent nation state, only to then gradually dissolve (chapter 11).

The theoretical meaning of 'tribe' and state-tribe relations is debated by Kenneth Brown in the context of Morocco; while we (in our respective chapters), attempt to analyse the structure of the modern tribe within a broader perspective: the totalitarian state *vis-à-vis* tribes in Iraq (chapters 3 and 4). Here it is the sub-tribal, even sub-clan, formations, like the *fakhith*, thigh, *bayt*, house, *hamoula* or lineage, that is the unit of analysis. Keiko Sakai, on the other hand, analyses the tribal factor as an element of control in state institutions, the Army, the Cabinet and the Assembly (chapter 5). The tribal appears one factor among many others, excluding any mono-causality. But if any major conclusion is to be drawn it is that in the framework of the Middle East, tribes and powers stand to each other in different modalities, and these tend to defy any schematic typology.

This volume is the fourth of our project. The first was on Arab nationalism and was published only in Arabic; the second was on Post-Marxism and the Middle East; the third was on State and Religion, while the fifth deals with Ethnicity and State: the Case of the Kurds. These seminars would not have been possible without the support and assistance provided by various institutes and individuals, above all: the Department of Politics and Sociology at Birkbeck College, and the Centre for Middle Eastern Studies, SOAS. The number of individuals to whom we are indebted is indeed difficult to count. Nevertheless, special mention must be made of Sami Zubaida, Fred Halliday, Peter and Marion Farouk-Sluglett, Eberhard Kienle, Maurice Godelier, Kate Soper and Sarah Stewart, for their participation, support and interest in the ICF project.

We would also like to thank those who contributed to this project through editorial work and translation: Wendy Christiansen and Nadje al-Ali (the volume on state and religion), and also Beverley Brown, member of the editorial board of *Economy and Society Quarterly*, who provided the excellent translation and editing of chapters 2 and 4 of this volume. And one major debt we have is to the Iraqi community in London: we are grateful to both individuals and organizations for the altruistic willingness they have shown in supporting our work.

Faleh Abdul Jabar & Hosham Dawood

PART ONE

Arab and Muslim Tradition: Kinship, Tribe and Ibn Khaldun

Agnatic Illusions: The Element of Choice in Arab Kinship

Edouard Conte

While much is made of true descent by the Bedouin, they are in fact speaking of the validity of status connections, not of patrilineal consanguinity (Peters 1990: 46).

Arab kinship can hardly be reduced to its most noted feature, namely marriage between the children of paternal brothers, nor be accounted for by the rhetoric of endogamy and pedigree that envelops it.[1] Yet, both learned theories and Arabs themselves tend to stress the pre-eminence of agnation in what is, in effect, a cognatic system characterized by the marked asymmetry of gender relations.[2] This bias is part and parcel of the social practice that local agnatic ideology endorses, and has long led many observers of Arab societies, from within and without, to remain silent on the social and sociological relevance of the ever adaptable panoply of techniques used to sustain the illusion of agnation in situations where patrilineal kinship does not (but ideally should) obtain. Indeed, what would the tribe *(qabila)* be without these?

Drawing upon classical sources as well as contemporary ethnography, this chapter stresses the complementarity of these negotiated ties of closeness, which, I believe, it would be unfair to explain away as quaint manifestations of 'fictive kinship'. My argument is that the establishment of elective bonds of relatedness is a necessity in societies favouring a form of marriage between patrilateral parallel cousins which is not, if practised exclusively, reproducible from generation to generation without the adjunction of outside elements (Copet-Rougier, 1994), as here, discrete descent groups simply do not exist. In this context, if chosen, albeit structurally induced, relationships of proximity ensure subtle transitions and continuity between spheres of life, so it would be difficult to circumscribe these as individual or collective, private or public, domestic or political. Equally, pacts both generate and respond to the severance of existing ties, efficiently maintaining collective identities (tribal in particular) beyond the breaches of relations between close agnates that engender fission and segmentation. To a large extent, thus, 'the effective *qabila* is that of voluntary alliance, of brotherhood proclaimed, solemnly and in writing; sometimes temporary, sometimes lasting, it takes precedence over the ties of blood, which slowly fade from memory, as if to open the way to elective kinship' (Bédoucha 1994: 214).

'Blood': A Metaphor Abused

In describing bonds of social propinquity in Arab societies past and present, Western orientalists and anthropologists often rely on the metaphor of blood. When used uncritically, this seemingly 'natural' choice of words lead to confusion as to the idea of kinship and the root meaning of the term 'consanguinity'. In English, of course, this assimilation might appear self-evident, a mere reflection of elementary biological truths: indeed, the *Concise Oxford Dictionary* defines kinship as 'blood relationship' while, conversely, equating blood with 'race, descent, parentage'. Yet, to imply that speakers of Arabic always did and continue to share such an understanding can be termed, at best, a slip of the pen.

Following L. H. Morgan (1871), early anthropologists predicated the theory of kinship upon the ancient Roman dichotomy opposing *consanguinitas* and *affinitas*. Among western cultural historians and philologists, in turn, the Arabic term *nasab*, translatable as 'genealogy', 'descent in the male line' (but, alternatively, as 'affinity', 'relationship by marriage'), came to convey a misconception that surreptitiously passed from one generation of scholars to the next. Arabs do of course order generationally, through ascending 'chains' (*salasil*) or 'trees' (*shajarat al-nasab*), the names of their male ancestors, and the patrilineal representation of kinship ties is vested with enormous cultural and political weight. However, this mode of depiction does not imply that individual identity is transmitted through the 'vital fluid' blood. Agnatically conceived *shajarat al-nasab* differ in this regard from the cognatically conceptualized *arbores consanguinitatis* and *affinitatis* so eruditely elaborated by the European nobility and its princely houses (see Klapisch-Zuber 2000). Nor are the prohibitions stipulated by Islamic marriage statutes (*ahkam al-nikah*) informed by notions of shared substance identical to those reflected in the canon law applied by Christian clerics to determine prohibited degrees of consanguinity between would-be spouses and draft, where permissible, relevant dispensations (see Conte 2000, Ibn Taymiyya 1988).

Classical Arab physicians deal little with blood, which they classify, like their Greek predecessors, among the four cardinal humours *(al-akhlat)*.[3] In Arabic literary and legal sources, *dam* (blood) is not defined as passing on hereditary attributes: such transmission is mentioned in *hadith* collections either in terms of perceived resemblance between males or the acquisition of traits, morphological or psychological, through the mother's or wet nurse's milk.[4] Nevertheless, ideas of shared substance are by no means absent from Arab discourse. This is commonly illustrated by the use of the term *lahma* (meat, flesh) to designate kinship or the classification of tribal sections through metaphoric reference to body parts (e.g., *batn*, belly, or *fakhidh*, thigh). Yet, blood imagery has no claim to precedence.

Ambivalent, largely female in its origin and properties, *dam* appears either as the life-giving nutrient of the foetus or, alternatively, as a source of pollution *(haydh)*. Spilt, it is, equally ambivalent, either the medium of sacrifice, or a stain on the collective honour of its (necessarily male) protectors.[5] In contrast, blood flowing in the veins [6] is considered the seat of individuality, of soul, as signified in idioms referring to marks of character and personality. Still, a philologist no less distinguished than J. Wellhausen fell prey to the semantic code of the Wilhelminian era, making multiple references to *Blut* (blood) as the symbol of pedigree among those Arabs fortunate enough to claim credible genealogies, namely the free and the noble *(ahrar)*. He cites the possibility offered to the refugee to 'grow into the authentic blood' *(in das echte Blut hinein[zu]wachsen)* of his hosts (Wellhausen 1900: 4). Analogously, he defines true 'full-bloodedness' *(echtes Vollblut)* as deriving from the idealized eminence and parity of one's paternal and maternal ascendants *(mu'imm wa mukhwil)* (Wellhausen, 1893: 440). Although these are without doubt highly evocative for a European reader, these figures of speech are not congruous with Arab conceptions, according to which the notions of blood *(dam)* and descent *(nasab)* only partially overlap. The killer of a kinsman 'cuts the blood' *(yaqta'u al-dam)* and thereby 'cuts [the bond of) the womb' *(yaqta'u [silat] al-rahim)*, a term semantically closer to 'kinship' than *dam*. By contrast, the adopted son, elective brother 'enters into the blood' *(yadkhulu fi al-dam)* of an agnatic group into which he was not born. The implication, however, is not one of a fusion of substance, but of joint recognition by 'he who enters' *(dakhil)* and those who receive him, of co-responsibility to avenge the blood spilt of an elective agnate, of his ward, dependant or guest. *Diya*, translated as 'blood-money', refers not to *dam* as such, but rather to retribution required in *dima'* (plural of *dam*) or 'homicide cases'. Membership of a vengeance group and the sharing of blood-debt constitute the foundation upon which any pact of kinship rests.

The Orientalists' Anthropological Insights

Indispensable though the identification and critique of Orientalism has been for coming to terms with the heritage of colonial anthropology, it is to the perspicacity of classical scholars that we are indebted for showing how the fluctuating nature of genealogy and chosen forms of kinship were essential to the understanding of Arab social organization, past and present. In addition to W. R. Smith (1885), I refer here mainly to the work of 19th-century Germanophone philologists such as I. Goldziher (1889), O. Proksch (1899), J. Wellhausen (1884, 1893) or G. A. Wilken (1884), whose contribution to inter-cultural studies Edward Said (1978: 209) has, I believe, underestimated. At the time of Muhammad, writes Smith,

> the Arabs throughout the peninsula formed a multitude of local groups, held together not by any elaborate political organization but by *a traditional sentiment of unity, which they believed or feigned to be a unity of blood* (my emphasis), and by the recognition and exercise of certain mutual obligations and social duties and rights, which all united the members of the same group to one another against all other groups and their members (1885: 1).

According to the theory of Arab genealogists, Smith adds, 'the groups were all patriarchal tribes, formed, by subdivision of an original stock, on the system of kinship through male descents' (ibid.: 3).

In his 1899 work on vengeance, Proksch questions the adequacy of a theory of social organization that postulates the primacy of patrilineality with regard to the constitution of descent groups and the solidarity deriving therefrom *('asabiya)* (1899: 13–17). He observes that the range of effective co-responsibility in matters of retaliation *(tha'r)* and blood-money *(diya)* does not always correspond to the agnatically defined limits of the descent group or *hayy* in the classical sense of the term (Cf. Ibn Manzur, s.v. HYW; Smith, 1885: passim.). The bond between mother's brother *(khal)* and sister's son *(ibn al-*

18

khal), in particular, can prove most relevant in the settlement of feuds. This underlines the importance of the principle of *jiwar*, a 'neighbourship' that encompasses, beyond the scope of *nasab*, affinal *(sihr)* and uterine relationships *(silat al-arham)* (Proksch 1899: 26). Further, warfare and revenge are documented within the 'tribe' *(qabila)* or 'clan' *(hayy)*. Solidarity among their members cannot be determined through *nasab* (agnatic descent) only, without reference to the political, matrimonial or residential propinquity implied by links of *hilf, sihr* and *jiwar*, respectively.

Smith nonetheless stresses that the Arabs were not primarily concerned with 'genealogical correctness', i.e., with full congruence between 'chains' and 'trees' aligning fathers, brothers and uncles on the one hand and, on the other, effective descent (1885: 41). Their interest was in preserving the *qabila* through the generations. In this endeavour, some succeeded if one judges by the historical permanency and geographical stability of, for example, the Yemeni tribes studied by P. Dresch (1989). Genealogical deletions, drift and gaps notwithstanding, a key feature of Arab political organization remains that 'all members of a permanent guild or other social unity, at that time, are sons of that unity' (Smith 1885: 15). This flexible idea of corporateness reduces contingency in order to ensure continuity, albeit nominal. Such accommodation of time-scales depends to no small degree on the extensive classificatory use of the terms *ibn* (son), akh (brother) and *'amm* (father's brother) that strikes Western authors.[7] Indeed, the *umma* itself is styled as a community of 'brothers in faith'. Extreme semantic latitude is an essential conceptual tool in rendering subtle transitions between neighbourship, kinship and elective ties, without questioning outright the social and political pre-eminence of the principle of agnation. For this reason, it would be imprudent to attribute exclusively such figures of speech implying agnatic kinship to a propensity for hyperbolism.

Despite his culturally inappropriate usage of the term *Blut*, Wellhausen captured well the structural significance of the often slow transition from 'neighbourship' to 'brotherhood':

The native can grant a right of sojourn in his sib *(Sippe)* to the stranger; through his acceptance into the sib, the settler is made one of their own *(nostrificirt)*. Not only lone men but entire *sibs* and lineages can thus be absorbed; and in practice this occurs not seldom...but since ever more newcomers arrive, the distinction between the (external and inborn) elements prevails for ever. Kinship and neighbourship operate together to cement the tribe together; external ties are absent. Consanguinity *(Blut)* is the higher and stronger principle and neighbourship thus develops into brotherhood (Wellhausen 1900: 4).

Goldziher, for his part, coined the concept of *Afiliirung* to account comprehensively for modes of incorporation not based on pre-existing agnatic descent. Taken in this sense, affiliation *(intisab)* encompasses procedures ranging from the hierarchically established assimilation of the outcast or the oppressed through the granting of permanent asylum to the 'solemn pact that can replace common descent *(gemeinsame Abstammung)*' among equals (Goldziher 1889: 40). The precursors of anthropological theory thus insist, rather more than some of their functionalist successors, on the structural complementarity of filiation and affiliation, recognizing that the social predominance of descent through males should not be mistaken as implying that kinship can be explained in solely patrilineal terms. The Orientalists share this realization with the early doctors of Islam, who, on the basis of very different criteria and convictions, understood full well that in the Arab practice they sought to transform, there was no consanguinity without elective kinship and vice versa. The creation of the egalitarian and theocratic society the *ulema* advocated depended, in their view, on the dissolution of this link: in Islam, there is no genealogy, no pact; all are brothers in faith.[8]

The doctors of the Law, while accepting the pre-eminence of men over women as God-given (The Qur'an 4, 34), broke down kinship into three component aspects *(asbab al-qaraba)* and examined them in terms of their interrelations. The confrontation of their opinions reveals a number of 'creative ambiguities' (Conte 1994a: 146–53). The neutral generic term for kinship is *qaraba*, translatable by 'proximity' or 'propinquity', either social or spatial. *Qaraba* comprises three facets, namely *nasab*, comparable to descent, *musahara*, designating affinity, and *ridha'a*, suckling and the relations derived therefrom. The 13th-century lexicographer Ibn Manzur, author of the *Lisan al-'arab*, associates *qaraba* with *nasab*, meaning (agnatic) descent, while establishing a parallel between the related term *qurba* and that of *rahim*, literally 'uterus', designating (womb) kinship in the broadest sense. *Nasab*, as mentioned, denotes primarily filiation in the male line, yet also affinity. Ibn Manzur observes that it obtains 'especially in the male line' ... but not exclusively, as Lane too shows (1863–93, s.v. NSB). The term *nasib* (agnate and/or brother-in-law) refers either to 'consanguinity' or 'affinity', according to place and context. The *Lisan al-'arab* gives *sihr* (from which *musahara* is derived), understood, in principle, as 'affinity', as a quasi-synonym of *qaraba*. Are those bound by *sihr* in-laws (affines) or kin or both at once? In a society practising frequent cousin marriages, the question remains ever open, with each successive union modifying the situational (and genealogical) reference points of the two terms. Summing the situation up as neatly as possible, Ibn Manzur writes: 'One becomes the ally (or affine) *(ashara)* of a tribe by binding oneself to them and placing oneself under their protection in virtue of co-residence *(jiwar)*, consanguinity *(nasab)* or marriage *(tazawwuj)*' (s.v. SHR). Hence, one could hardly take issue with classical Arab authors for pretending that the *asbab al-qaraba*, the 'ties of propinquity' (one dare not speak of kinship) are as univocal as genealogies *(ansab)* portray them to be. Echoing Goldzhier's (1893) brief but pointed statement on 'the fiction of consanguinity among Oriental peoples', Peters (1990: 158) forcefully concludes:

> Essentially, agnation has little to do with kinship. Its bonds are political, and they bind together – for certain purposes only – a corporation of men conceptually endowed by the Bedouin with a fiction of kinship but among whom are included consanguineously unrelated males.

'Agnation,' he adds, 'is a denial of choice, and the enforcement of duties,' whereas 'affinity retains its frailty until the birth of children turns debt partners into kin' (ibid.: 160, 162). Thus, 'to speak of the principle of agnation conflicting with the principle of cognation or maternal origin is nonsense' (ibid.: 109).

The Many Roads to Adoption

The term 'adoption' has also been, albeit to a lesser extent than 'blood', a source of considerable ambiguity for the interpretation of Arab customary and Islamic law. The issue is frequently 'neutralized' by a perfunctory reference to the Qur'anic verse (33, 5) that cancels the tie of filiation between Zayd and his adoptive father Muhammad: 'Ascribe them to their (biological) fathers … If you do not know their fathers, then (let them be) your brethren in religion and your companions.' This made possible the Prophet's union in AH 4 to his father's sister's daughter, Zaynab, whom he had initially given in marriage to Zayd. Western authors have tended to interpret this decision as evidence that Muhammad was quite ready to do away with an old Arab tradition, *tabanni*, or filial adoption, on the sole and selfish grounds that he in turn to marry the attractive Zaynab.[9] However, Watt maintains that this allegation is 'an unjustified inference' (1962: 282–3). Indeed, whatever the specific circumstances of the incident may have been (ibid. 329–30), this breach of custom was a major element of the Islamic reform of personal status law; on this account alone, it warrants less anecdotal treatment than it has often received. Watt fittingly establishes a parallel between the abolition of full adoption and 'the rule which permits marriage with a stepdaughter provided the marriage with her mother has not been consummated' (ibid. see The Qur'an 4, 23–7). The point at issue in both instances is whether a set of marriages implies a deleterious 'encounter of substances', entailing what F. Héritier (1994) terms an 'incest of second order' *(inceste de deuxième type)*. Had Muhammad been the socially recognized father of Zayd at the time he married the divorced Zaynab, this could have been interpreted as creating an incestuous tie between the Prophet and Zaynab, and by repercussion, through Zaynab, between the Prophet and his 'son'. Analogously, a man who consummates marriage, whether simultaneously or successively, with a woman and her daughter by another man, would be viewed as entertaining an incestuous relationship with his stepdaughter, while at once creating a symbolically incestuous bond between mother and daughter through a shared spouse. In contrast, Wellhausen (1893: 441, n. 3) argues that, in a society where the status of *pater* in certain respects prevailed over that of genitor (see below), the people of Medina did not necessarily view the marriage to Zaynab as incestuous, rather as simply contradicting the new norms Muhammad himself had laid down. Both positions seem to have had their supporters, if one judges by differences in beliefs concerning the nature of body fluids (Ibn Manzur. d.: s.v. GHYL, Conte 1994b). Whatever the case might have been, Watt accurately concludes that the Islamic reform of personal status amounts to 'a general attack on fictitious – or should we say 'merely social' – relationships' (Watt 1962: 283). Expressed in modern terms: did Qur'anic law seek to make genealogy and biology congruent?

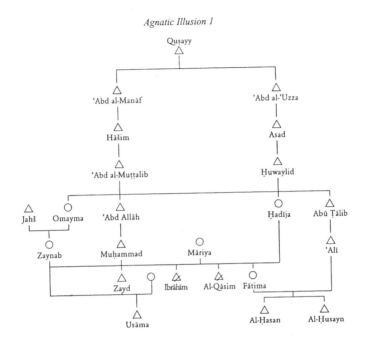

Agnatic Illusion 1

The wide-ranging implications of the restrictions placed by Islamic law on pacts of kinship become clearer when the marriage with Zaynab is considered not as an isolated incident, but in the context of Muhammad's union of 29 years with his first wife, Khadija, and his on-going, ever affectionate bond with Zayd and, later, with Zayd's son, Usama. This paradigmatic complex of relationships is, I would argue, of relevance to our understanding of often differing canonical and customary conceptions of kinship and marriage in modern Arab contexts, from which the elements of choice and accommodation are by no means absent. There persists a danger of grouping a broad and intricately interrelated set of Arab social practices, ancient and contemporary, under the vague heading of 'adoption', as today understood in European civil codes. 'Adoption' may of course be rendered by the classical *tabanni*, derived from the verb *tabanna*, meaning 'to take as a son' *(ibn)* by granting the beneficiary the right to bear his new father's name and to become his heir. In the Arab tradition, however, it must be stressed that the establishment of a father-son relationship is very much a reciprocal affair: *ista'bba*, derived from the noun *ab*, father, means to recognize someone as *pater*. The verb *idda'a*, which evokes the Latin *arrogare*, signifies 'to call someone and to regard him as one's son/father'. Yet, *da'i,* i.e., 'one who claims a relationship of a son to one who is not his father', designates the illegitimate as well as the adopted son, he who is rejected as well as he who is (or pretends to be) 'called'. Indeed, the *da'i* may be a *hajin*, the child of a slave mother, an *ibn al-zahira*, the abandoned child or orphan taken on and fostered through compassion or piety, or the son of a deceased or, in some cases, of a living agnate. *Istalhaqa* means to adjoin a person to one's pedigree or line of filiation *(nasab)*, to recognize paternity. The connotations of affiliation to a line of descent *(intisab)* and absorption into another agnatic unit *(indimaj)* are thus manifold. They should not be obscured in their semantic and historical diversity by reducing the process of adoption to the attribution of two legal rights (to bear a name and receive inheritance) denied in the Revelation. It should also be kept in mind that the Qur'an enjoins the believer to protect the orphaned and the weak:

> Worship God and do not join partners with Him, treat with kindness parents, kin, orphans, the needy, the client who is a relative *(jar dhu l-qurba)*, the client who is a stranger, the companion, the wayfarer and your slaves (4, 36).

The Revelation here plots the broadest of fields in which affiliation, alliance, aggregation and assimilation originate within and beyond the bonds of agnation. Muhammad the orphan[10] was deprived of both father and mother by the age of two, initially adopted by his father's father 'Abd al-Muttalib, who addressed him as 'my son', and finally, at his grandfather's death, taken under the protection of his father's brother Abu Talib (Ibn Hisham 1990, I: 173; Guillaume 1967: 73). Were not all these men of one name, sons of Hashim ibn 'Abd Munaf and heirs in the line of Quraysh? To view adoption and fosterage in the Arab tradition as individual matters would be largely erroneous.

It is said that Zayd ibn Haritha was born in a largely Christianized tribe of the Syrian marshes. He was acquired as a captive by Khadija bint Khuwaylid ibn Asad, a rich, aristocratic tradeswoman of Mecca who was to become, as is well known, Muhammad's first wife and the first convert to Islam. At the time of their marriage, Khadija was some 15 years older that the future Prophet (Watt 1953: 32–39), and his senior in genealogical terms. Their union, arranged at her behest, departed from a certain Arab ideal of male status and prerogatives in that it was monogamous, hypergamous (from Khadija's standpoint) and uxorilocal (*cf.* Smith 1885: 273–274).[11] Zayd was bestowed upon Muhammad by Khadija as a gift to her young husband. It is not ascertainable whether Zayd was released from bondage by his new patron when Muhammad married Khadija or later (Watt 1962: 282). Be this as it may, the process of adoption is portrayed as reciprocal and voluntary. Tribesmen of Zayd, visiting

Mecca, offered to procure ransom for him but the *da'i* preferred to remain with his adoptive father and be his freedman *(mawla)* (Guillaume 1967: 714–15). Muhammad, in turn, consulted the men of the Quraysh, who approved the adoption, and he declared: 'Bear witness that Zayd is my son and heir, as I am his heir. May the soul of his father thus rejoice!' (Ibn Hisham, 1858, II: 54). Zayd reciprocated through faith. Many sources say that he was the second man to enter Islam, after Muhammad's father's brother's son and son-in-law, 'Ali ibn Abi Talib. Some speak of Abu Bakr, the first caliph, as the first convert. Yet, 'others say that the first man to believe and follow the Prophet was Zayd ibn Haritha, his *mawla*' (Tabari 1988, VI: 86).

The emotional intensity of the relationship between Zayd and Muhammad is expressed in many details of the Prophet's biography. Muhammad's pagan detractors insulted him as *al-abtar*: 'he is but a man amputated, without progeny'[12] (Ibn Hisham 1990, I: 356). Although Muhammad had two sons by Khadija, both died before weaning. Of all the women Muhammad married after Khadija's death, only his captive wife, Mariya the Copt, gave him a son, named Ibrahim in memory of Abraham the patriarch (see Conte 2000b). For the sonless Prophet, it is understandable that Zayd ibn Haritha was viewed, for a time, as Zayd ibn Muhammad. When, after fleeing Mecca, Muhammad 'instituted brotherhood between his fellow emigrants and the helpers (of Medina), Hamza, the Lion of God and the Lion of his apostle and his (paternal) uncle, became the brother of Zayd ibn Haritha the apostle's freedman. To him, Hamza gave his last testament on the day of Uhud when battle was imminent in case he should meet his death' (Guillaume 1967: 234). Tabari (quoted by Madelung 1997: 213) reports:

> Whenever matters got tough and the battle cry was sounded, [Muhammad] used to put the people of his house *(ahl al-bayt)* in the front rank and protected his Companions from the heat of the lances and the sword. Thus 'Ubayda was killed at Badr, Hamza on the day of Uhud, Ja'far [ibn Abi Talib] and Zayd on the day of Mu'ta'. Did the Prophet thus count Zayd his fallen 'son' among the 'people of his house', a mention 'quite incompatible with 'later Shi'ite argumentation', hastens to add Madelung (1997: 213, n. 5)?

Watt, in turn, goes as far as to suggest 'that, had ... Zayd been alive at the time of the Prophet's death, he might have succeeded without difficulty (although Qur'an 33, 40 had expressly denied that Muhammad was a father in relation to Zayd)' (ibid.: 5, n. 17). Indeed, in the cultural context of the time, *tabanni* might still have appeared to many followers of Muhammad a closer tie than that obtaining between uncle and nephew, between the Prophet and 'Ali.

Muhammad's affection for Zayd lived on in his fondness for Usama ibn Zayd, born of an Abyssinian captive mother. When the Prophet died, Usama was by all accounts present, and, with Shuqran, 'undertook to wash his body' (Madelung 1997: 27). Claims to a special portion of the Prophet's estate by his Banu Hashim kinsmen notwithstanding, 'only Muhammad's wives, [his father's brother] al-'Abbas, the two grandsons of the Prophet and Usama ... were granted larger shares than they otherwise deserved' (ibid.: 64). Caliph Abu Bakr, 'in order to comply with the Prophet's wishes ... immediately ordered [a] planned campaign towards the Syrian border area to go ahead [and] insisted on retaining Usama ... as the commander despite the unpopularity of this choice because of Usama's youth and lack of experience' (ibid.: 43).

In recalling these circumstances gleaned in standard sources (all compiled long after the Prophet's death), my purpose is not engage in conjecture on the lives of one Zayd or Usama, and much less on their possible relevance for the succession to Muhammad. However, when considered together, as constitutive elements of an implicit, subsidiary narrative in the wider and diversely interpreted history of the birth of Islam, these biographical particulars do suggest that even the canonical abolition of full adoption does not preclude intense paternal or filial sentiment between Muslims who are not of 'one blood'. Moreover, such attachment may significantly affect the status and prerogatives of agnatically defined corporations large and small, of the Banu Hashim. Equally, the literary themes here cited sketch out an array of emotional bonds and social devices, that Arab custom, while respecting Qur'anic injunctions, has fostered through the centuries. The strength and ostentation of Arab patrilineal ideology notwithstanding, these practices show that agnation is not a rule of descent, rather the result of ongoing negotiation.

One might subsume under the Arab notion of 'adoption' a wide range of socially accepted forms of recognition of filiation or legitimation, liable to compensate the absence of life and, more specifically, of male offspring. Adoption can precede or succeed, establish, reinforce, indeed recreate agnatic bonds. The corresponding public procedures are conducted by men, but nonetheless strongly dependent on female mediation. Often, they can only fully be understood in relation to affinity. Hence, to specify the scope of adoption, different modes of assimilation based on the recognition of quasi-filiation may be briefly described:

H. Granqvist relates the moving case of a man of Hebron whose first wives had begotten only daughters. A subsequent spouse, however, bore him a boy. Fifteen years later, the son was killed just a few days before his marriage, run over by a lorry that had come to deliver goods for his wedding feast. The driver belonged to a weak clan, and, fearing vengeance, sought refuge with the police. It was agreed between the parties that 330 Jordanian dinars would be paid in compensation to the father. As the remittance ceremony came to its conclusion, the aged father called the driver and said: 'O, my son! I did not have the chance to have a son in this world (to bear my name after me). I lost my only son by the way of fate and destiny. Now thou art my son. My son's ransom is thine' (Granqvist 1965: 128–29). And he handed him the *diya*. One could here speak of 'blood-compensation by adoption', analogous to 'blood-compensation by marriage', consisting in the granting of a spouse by the responsible to the injured party in a homicide case (Granqvist 1931–35, I: 140). In one instance, the recognition of filiation precludes vengeance through the restitution of life, in the other, affinity opens the road to birth.

Adoption by manumission deletes the bond of servitude through the social and legal recognition of biological paternity *(istilhaq)*. The pre-Islamic Arabs, reports Abu al-Faraj al-Isfahani, considered their sons by slave mothers as slaves, and would only manumit them if they proved valorous (1935: 237, Thorbecke 1868: 2–3). The most renowned example of a 'bastard's' quest for legitimacy in Arabic literature is no doubt the *Sirat 'Antara*. 'Antara was the son of the noble Shaddad and the Abyssinian slave Zabiba. Having emerged victorious from countless contests and having outwitted those (his mother included) who deployed stratagems of deceit to hinder his ascension to full recognition, 'Antara, *in fine*, is not only received into the *nasab* of his father, but is granted the hand of his beloved 'Abla, the daughter of his father's brother. The exemplary pattern here given, idealized though it is, offers keys for understanding filiation today in those contexts where servitude still obtains. *Istilhaq* may even be granted by a master to the child of two slave parents, as in the case Peters (1990: 212) recorded among the Bedouin of Cyrenaica: 'X was the son of a slave wife; his genitor was a slave, but his mother's master reared him, freed him and he is now given as his son in the [master's] genealogy.'

Adoption may equally stem from the recognition by a man of a 'son by proxy'. Ibn Manzur (n.d.: s.v. BDH), among others, describes the pre-Islamic custom known as *nikah al-istibdha'*, whereby a man desirous of obtaining offspring of nobler stock than his own requires his wife to cohabit with another and then takes as his own her child by the substitute genitor (see also al-Tarmanini 1989: 20–3).[13] This practice is proscribed by Islam as fornication *(zina)*; however, the pater/genitor distinction it is based on is differently interpreted by the major schools of legal thought (see Linant de Bellefonds 1965, II: 109–10). This is reflected in the universally accepted maxim *al-walad li-l-firash*, that attributes 'the boy to [the master or owner of] the bed' (i.e., the wife or concubine), whoever the genitor may be. 'And to the fornicator the stone!' Indeed, the incapacity to produce offspring, if a husband is convinced of it, may lead him to delegate a kinsman to serve his wife for procreative purposes: he has legal authority, as husband, to do so and to require his wife to submit, for the only alternative, if he is not to die without "issue", is to "take" a son from his brother and fulfil the obligations towards this boy required of a pater ... Granting the acceptance of paternity, whatever the circumstances of conception, a male child, *ipso facto*, accedes to membership of a corporation ... (Peters 1990: 193–4).

Rights of procreation, while legitimated by marriage, are thus vested in a core of close agnates and ensure that their named corporation perpetuates itself. Yet recourse to procreation by proxy is but seldom required since Islamic law, through the method known as *iqrar* (acknowledgement, admission), allows the childless to establish a relation of filiation *(banuwwa)* with a child, boy or girl, of unknown descent *(majhul al-nasab)* (al-Tarmanini 1989: 199).

The three examples chosen stress the very social nature of paternity and filiation, as elaborated in the Arab tradition. None contravenes the Qur'anic precept that forbids the attribution of a new patronymic and the status of heir to a man not 'born of the loins'. Quite to the contrary, all three procedures reinforce paternal and agnatic prerogatives, as defined in Islamic law. This is so, albeit indirectly, in the exceptional Jordanian case reported by Granqvist: here a son is indeed 'transferred' from a biological to a social father, but this is a just compensation meant to restore a man's progeny, unduly cancelled by manslaughter. It settles a debt of honour opposing two groups of agnates, a social requirement that overrides the individual genitor-son relationship. In turn, the paradigmatic story of 'Antara draws our attention to a complementary aspect of legitimation, namely the interplay between filiation and affinity. The importance of marriage in reinforcing the tie of adoption was already inferred by the curtailed union of Zayd and Zaynab. Indeed, the recognition of paternity is often but a legal moment that initiates a long-term, inter-generational process of assimilation, summed up in the Tunisian expression *dakhlu bi-l-nsawin*, 'they entered through women' (Bédoucha 1994: 195).

Agnatic Illusion 2

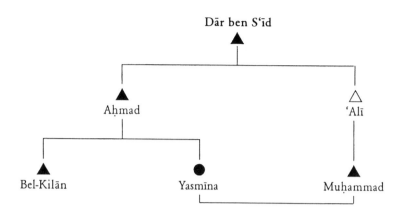

G. Bédoucha (1994: 194–5) depicts 'adoption through marriage' in her account of al-Mansura, an oasis of the Tunisian Sahara: The Dar ben S'id here form a weak group, arrived long ago from Algeria. Their genealogy mentions that S'id had two sons, Ahmad and Ali. Yet, on closer examination, it appears that Ahmad was S'id's only son. Whence Ali? At this juncture, the diminished lineage, although still well endowed with water rights, was facing extinction. Ahmad, as sole heir, feared that his estate would be divided between his only son, Bel-Kilan, and his only daughter, Yasmina. If she then married a 'stranger', her share would be lost to Dar ben S'id and the lineage reduced to Bel-Kilan. So, her father married her to one Muhammad, son of Ali. Ali was declared son of S'id, which made him 'brother' of Ahmad. Muhammad, while keeping the name of his father, was instituted 'grandson' of S'id and brother's son of Ahmad. Thereupon, Ahmad duly divided his estate, *inter vivos*, among his son Bel-Kilan, while his son-in-law and adoptive nephew in effect received the share of his wife Yasmina. Muhammad was thus poised to perpetuate, biologically and economically, the lineage of S'id and Ahmad. Through this oblique assimilation, he relinquished the right to found a lineage of his own, yet gained spouse, wealth and 'agnates'. This case is doubtless only just acceptable in terms of strict legal propriety, but who would contest that genealogy must sometimes be 'accommodated' so that the perpetuity of the patrilineage, principle above all principles, may prevail?[14]

Here, marriage gives substance to admittedly fictive *nasab* (agnation). Inversely, elective kinship may modify the nature of *sihr* (affinity). In this regard, special reference must be made to the practice of *badal*, a term which, in the current sense, means 'exchange' or 'substitute'. It consists of one man giving the hand of a female ward to another man, who in turn allows the former to marry one of his female wards. Yet another misapprehension that arises in the discussion of Arab kinship is that 'Islam' disapproves of *badal*.[15] But is *badal* forbidden? Imam Malik (d. 179/795), true to the *sunna*, condemns *shighar* (and not *badal*), a 'pre-Islamic' custom, whereby a man 'marries his daughter to another so that the latter will give him his daughter in marriage, without there being any payment of bridewealth *(mahr)* between them' (Malik n.d.: 535). Of course, the conclusion of any marriage, compensated through immediate reciprocity or not, is reprehensible if bridewealth is not paid or at least promised. *Badal* is hence not prohibited *per se*, but only when used as a subterfuge to forgo in effect the payment of dowry, prescribed in the Qur'an. With this easily circumvented proviso, *badal* contravenes no legal norm or social code. What, then, are its structural implications?

When two unrelated men permute sisters, the children born of the marriages thus concluded are both paternal and maternal cross cousins. These, in turn, are perfectly permissible but not the most welcome marriage partners, for their chain of relationship always involves a female link. No prohibition deriving from consanguinity *(nasab)* impedes such unions, but they are not fully consistent with the Arab representation of agnation, according to which marriage should ideally be concluded between cousins whose bond is traceable through males only. On the contrary, when two unrelated men exchange daughters, the offspring of these unions stand to their respective mothers in a relation of children of agnatic half sisters (Ag ō ZS/D). As such, they are considered forbidden partners. Malik's choice of terms is therefore anthropologically very perceptive: he disapproves of the permutation of daughters and not that of sisters. *Badal*, however, is also practised among marriageable kin (Ibn Manzur n.d.: s.v. Sh-Gh-R, Peters 1990: 239–40) and reinforces pre-existing agnatic links.

Agnatic Illusion 3

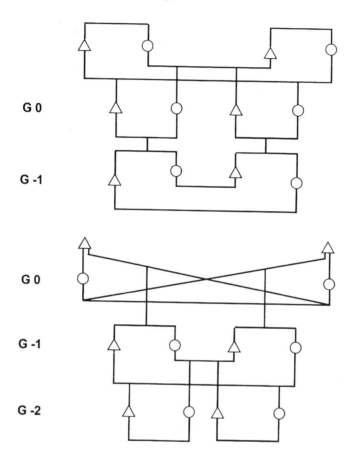

G 0

G -1

G 0

G -1

G -2

With the exception of effectively shunned daughter exchange, *badal* is thus permissible and frequent, if not valued in Arab discourse on kinship (see Granqvist 1931–35, I: 109–19, cf. Tapper 1990: 141–56 and *passim*). Although diverging from a stated cultural preference, it would allow, if practised exclusively, cross-cousin marriages from generation to generation *without* the adjunction of new elements (see Copet-Rougier 1994: 457). By facilitating the integration of outside women into the male-focused residential group, it can compensate imbalances in the locally available number of marriageable men and women. In subsequent generations, it helps solve the 'dilemma' posed by the non-reproducibility of so-called 'Arab marriage'. Far from being contradictory, marriages between patrilateral cousins *(awlad al-'amm)*, on the one hand, and strangers *(ghara'ib)*, on the other, emerge as the poles of a continuum that *badal*, in its diverse modalities, articulates. Although *badal*, taken alone, indeed 'keeps failing to encompass difference' (Dresch 1998: 124), it may be combined with pacts of brotherhood or the merging of lineages through collective adoption, transforming cross- into parallel cousins, and strangers into 'ideal' partners. I would, therefore, suggest that the key specificity of 'Arab marriage' lies not in the much extolled union of paternal brothers' children, but rather in the very adaptability the wide range of possible combinations just described offers.

Cousins and Brothers Elect

The Bani Isad of the Euphrates Delta

Salim's well-known study of the sedentary, agro-pastoral Bani Isad of the Euphrates delta is, I believe, of special relevance in understanding the structural continuity between the voluntary association of individuals through elective kinship and the fusion of families into or with larger groups. Moreover, it elucidates the redefinition of boundaries between tribes (*qaba'il* or *asha'ir*) through the complementary processes of lineage segmentation and aggregation (1956–57, 1962). The Iraqi author looks beyond 'official' agnatic representations to embrace the field of cognatic kinship. Salim writes:

> The members of each lineage *(fakhidh)* are related to each other and to the founding ancestor of the lineage by patrilineal descent *(al-nasab al-abawi)*. However, higher kinship *(al-nisba al-'aliya)*[16] established through marriage exchanges inside the lineage (lineage endogamy), implies a differentiation between agnatic affiliation (*intisab,* agnation) and affiliation on the father's side and on the mother's side conjointly, a differentiation which is not

consonant with the constitution of the lineage on an agnatic basis (Salim 1956: 115–16).

The distinction here suggested by the author between *nasab*, or agnatic descent, and *nisba*, cognatic kinship, in turn supposes an opposition between intra-lineage marriage and unions which entail the assimilation of an external spouse in virtue of the principle of *jiwar*:

> When agnatic descent prevails, without there being marriages between the men and the young women of the lineage, the entire lineage will come to be divided into two distinct categories: outside wives on the one hand and, on the other, the remaining members of the lineage who are agnatically related. When the men of the lineage do marry young women of the group, the lineage members born of these unions are related both through their fathers and through their maternal uncles who are at the same time their paternal uncles. Under these conditions, kinship becomes cognatic (cognation) without there being a contradiction with the general principle on which *nasab* is based, namely patrilineal descent (ibid.: 116, n. 1).

In the society described by Salim, affiliation of isolated individuals to the *hamoula* (clan) is mainly conceived of in terms of marriage. Notwithstanding, the incorporation of non-kin may proceed through adoption *(tabanni)*. This rarely applies to individuals. Indeed, Salim found that only three persons among the 242 inhabitants of the locality studied, Chibayish, had been adopted. 'Recourse is made to adoption when an orphan is without a family *(bayt)* or because both parents hope to perform a good work of which they will reap the fruits later through the respect they will gain within the community. Childless couples will also adopt, but they are very few in number … ' (ibid.: 76). Islamic precepts are respected in that the adopted child may not inherit from its foster parents, unless of course the bequest takes the form of an *ante mortem* donation (Chelhod 1971, Jaussen 1948: 23, 116). This type of adoption, *iqrar*, concerns only the orphan child and not the adult asylum seeker. Yet the latter is not excluded from the ongoing process of affiliation, which proceeds through another mode of incorporation known as *kitba*. This written, publicly negotiated and proclaimed pact *(mithaq)* combines various aspects of the covenants of brotherhood *(mu'akhat)*, neighbourly protection *(jiwar)* or political alliance *(hilf, muhalafa)*, all three in existence from the remote past.

According to Salim, *kitba* signifies 'the assimilation *(indimaj)* of one or several persons, of a sub-lineage or even of a full lineage into a lineage or clan through adoption *(tabanni)* after the drafting and signature of a specific document'. The corollary of this process is *fasl*, the segmentation affecting the lineage of those who 'break off'. Salim adds that:

> at the time when tribal wars were commonplace … many weak segments of other tribes sought refuge with the powerful tribe of the Bani Isad in order to live under their protection, to assemble under their banner and to incorporate themselves by way of adoption … It is not easy to distinguish clearly those who entered the tribe … through adoption and those who belonged to it from the beginning. In spite of this, it is notorious that many lineages and clans are foreign (*ghariba*) … In recent years, and particularly since 1934, there has been a broad movement of adoptions between lineages and their segments (ibid.: 138).

Salim maintains that he who 'enters', the *dakhil*, is the 'complete equal' of his protector, 'a part of him'. This, however, is not to deny the status implications of assimilation, for *kitba* is an asymmetrical process that tends to enhance the political and economic standing of the host groups among the Bani Isad. 'Absolutely no lineage' of the dominant Ahl al-shaykh, observes Salim, 'has been adopted by another clan' (ibid.). Severance generally results from disputes concerning land use and the division of inheritance. *Kitba* thus tends to attract the less fortunate or dispossessed into the orbit of those best endowed with land. When a readjustment of allegiances concerns Bani Isad segments alone, the parties involved 'act with great care and special deference towards all the members of the tribe' in order not to offend or generate excessive rancour (ibid.). A lack of tact could threaten the cohesion of the *hamoula* (clan) or indeed of the *'ashira* (tribe), and thereby, ultimately, the dominant position of the Ahl al-shaykh. The hierarchical ranking of formally homologous agnatic units is thus a central trait of social organization, and it is in this non-egalitarian perspective that collective adoption must be interpreted.

The 1944 *kitba* that Salim documented is but one episode in a process of recurrent adjustment of lineage composition and ranking within the *hamoula*. In this case, the Albu Mas'ud, affiliated to the clan of the Haddadiyyin or 'blacksmiths', at once entered into a pact with two lineages of the dominant Ahl al-shaykh clan. The hierarchical nature of this compact is manifest in the very names of the parties: the 'Shaykh's people' welcome into their midst the 'smiths'. It is not the chiefly clan in its entirety that subscribes to the arrangement, but only two lineages of this group. Yet, these act as if they were but one. Each maintains its name and genealogical identity, but joins forces with the other, establishing, as it were, a pact within a pact: 'the two lineages are tightly affiliated to one another and behave as one lineage in important matters such as adoption'.[17] The enhanced status the *kitba* guarantees to the adopted group operates in turn to consolidate the prior rapprochement between the adopting groups and reinforces their joint prestige within the clan. The analogies with the classical *jiwar* or *hilf* agreements are here only too apparent.

In the contract Salim reproduces, one reads that 'we, the men of the [Bani Isad] clans *(hamoulat)* of al-Hajj Sawwad and of the clans of Albu Zdiyu, had [our] names inscribed and have entered into a relationship of brothers' sons *(dakhalna anfusana bi-l-'ammati)* with the men of the *hamoulat* of Albu Mas'ud.' It is further declared:

'We shall pay our shares of blood compensation to the extent that this will be incumbent upon us or upon them, and may God turn us away from black [abominable] crimes, the responsibility of which shall rest with him who commits them! And this apart, we are brothers *(ikhwan)*' (ibid.: 140). Of special interest in the wording chosen is the distinction established between two different degrees of purportedly agnatic proximity. The man to man relations established between the members of the groups contracting alliance, dubbed classificatory *banu-l-'amm* for a decisive initial instant, are forthwith reformulated in terms of brotherhood. All occurs as if the signatories agree to pass, in a fictive legal moment, from the closest degree of proximity possible between persons who are only kin in word to a bond that unites their destinies with regard to blood obligations and establishes a community of honour. The passing of this threshold both denotes and minimizes the new alliance's hierarchical character. Thus is enunciated, in the optative mood, a situation of quasi-equality, nonetheless attenuated by an implicit right of seniority, among the newly united 'siblings'.

The eventuality of a shared *nasab* is written into the pact, but will only become effective through intermarriage. *Badal* can considerably accelerate this unification, establishing an organic link between collective adoption and the brotherhood through which it is implemented, and developing effective descent from fictive collaterality. The adopted group accedes to the status of agnates of the adopters as a collectivity. This group will take on the group name of its hosts and conceivably, with time, people will come to forget (or omit to recall) that they in no way descend from the forefather thus invoked.

One could object that the discriminating criterion of 'true' adoption, rather than the collective use of an ancestral patronymic or group name, is the adopted man's right to inherit as an individual from his adoptive father. This, of course, is proscribed in law and custom. Hence collective adoption does not establish person-to-person ties liable to modify patterns of inheritance within any of the partner groups. The agreement only specifies a common responsibility in penal issues involving the group as a whole, to the exclusion of dishonourable crimes committed by individual parties to the contract. However, to brush aside on these grounds the pact as a simple, if courteously formulated, metaphor of clientship would be quite misleading. Indeed, the children to be born of the marriages that ensue between elective brothers will be kin to those who are adopted as well as to those who adopt. They will be members of one and the same *'asaba*, of an agnatically focused community of heirs including not only those explicitly designated as parties to the pact but equally of their next of kin. In the space of a single generation, this procedure can widen the range of heirs. Equally, it can modify access to land. At the subsequent generation, unions between the grandchildren of signatories will be considered 'noble' in the paternal as well as maternal lines, *mu'imm wa mukhwil*. One thus sets the stage for unions that come very close to the ideal of marriage between full equals, notwithstanding residual differences of status and wealth. In other words, the ties that patrilateral parallel cousin marriages cause to weaken when the offspring of brothers' children in turn intermarry may be selectively consolidated by the recognition of so-called fictive kinship. Whatever the form chosen, this is indeed unavoidable if the myth of agnation is to be maintained. Where, however, do the social boundaries begin beyond which agnation may no longer obtain?

Christians and Muslims of Nazareth in Ottoman Palestine

The 1850s were years of hardship in Palestine: 1854 saw drought, 1855 an epidemic of smallpox. The inhabitants of Nazareth, in particular, suffered numerous assaults and aggressions, which the Ottoman *wali* of *Sayda* (Governor of Sydon) was not in a position to check. Hence, the townspeople undertook to act on their own, formulating their resolve in an idiom of kinship (*qaraba*) at once broader and more restrictive than that founded on genealogical relatedness.

In 1857, only 1,500 of Nazareth's 5,890 inhabitants were Muslims. The largest Christian community was constituted by the Greek Orthodox (2,500 members), whose relations with the Roman and Greek Catholics (750 and 550 members, respectively), the Maronites (370) and the newly established Protestant congregation (220) were not devoid of antagonism (Mansur quoted by Steppat 1974: 241–42).[18] In their statutory relations with the imperial authorities, these communities acted as three confessional factions *(tawa'if)*: the Muslims, the Orthodox and, lastly, a composite *ta'ifa*, aggregating the *latin*, the *kathulik* and the *brutistant*. In the face of external danger, the representatives of these parties attempted to quell discord in and among themselves, and entered into a relationship of mutual protection designated as *'umumiyya*. Correspondingly, they concluded a 'pact of agnatic cousinship' or *muʿamma*, a term derived from the root *ʿamm* and akin in its pattern of derivation to the classical *muʾakhah*, or 'covenant of brotherhood'. The agreement was formalized in a contract *(ʿahd)*:

Praise unto God and blessings and peace upon the Messenger of God!

1. Since the wind [or spirit] of our time has died out and its lamps are extinguished, and evil has been intensified, and despair reinforced, whereas the unjust have spread and the depravity of the corrupters has become universal … extending through the administration and taking hold therein, the inhabitants of Nazareth and of its district are forced at their own behest to decide upon a way to protect their means of existence.

2. Thus they have resolved to become agnatic cousins among themselves, by a pact of patrilateral cousinhood, as well as a single community of agnates[19] in order to repel those who commit aggression against them: thieves, highway robbers and scoundrels who rebel against the High [Ottoman] Empire. [This shall be done] in such a way that anyone who commits aggression against them or envisages evil doing in the manner mentioned may be repelled, first through something better [than that they seek to do] and, if he is not thereby deterred, he shall be killed and the blood money *(diya)* [due for his victim] apportioned to all those named in this document.

3. [The latter] have truly become as children of fathers' brothers and founded a community of agnates in deterring those who would assault them and in raising compensation for anyone whom they kill together for having demanded compensation from them without legal ground; for he who commits an assault is an illegal attacker, and no compensation is legally requisite for illegal attackers. [When mandatory,] compensation is raised among all adult males of Nazareth and surroundings.

4. When a person bound by the pact of cousinhood is killed and compensation received for him, one third goes to his private heirs and two thirds to the community of patrilateral cousins.

5. The preceding dispositions are applicable to those who have suffered aggression. If one of the members of the community of cousinhood kills people who have not attacked the community … then the

compensation must be raised by the killer personally in order that he be dissuaded from his felony.[20]

This pact is thus mainly a defensive treaty among neighbours acting as a vengeance group in the face of external menace. It does not safeguard those who kill an outsider without the prior sanction of the 'community of cousins', but does condone preventive measures against potential aggressors. The language of kinship here serves to validate these obligations of mutual support while in effect circumventing the notions of consanguinity and affinity in all but word. For the elective cousins of Nazareth, the *muta'ammun*, belong to different religious communities whose members do not, as a rule, intermarry. Denominational endogamy deprives the 'contract of cousinhood' of any relevance with regard to the relations of kinship. Steppat accurately describes it as a *contrat social*, an agreement that preserves the socio-religious identity of the parties and aims to strengthen peaceful co-existence within the boundaries of the local community. This is achieved by stating the jural equality of all agnatic/confessional corporations, whatever their relative demographic importance.

The pact's restricted scope does not imply, however, that the key expressions used in the document ('cousinhood', 'community of agnates') reflect lax rhetoric: they assert the pre-eminence of neighbourship *(jiwar)* over consanguinity *(nasab)* and affinity *(sihr)*. The *qaraba* thus founded rests upon a common interest in preserving territory and social space; without this security the balance between communities, indeed their identities, cannot be maintained. The Palestinian term *mu'amma* must thus be read differently from the related yet distinct Bedouin expression *ban'amma*. In Nazareth, 'cousinhood' without common faith signifies solidarity without *connubium*. The recognition of 'cousinhood' among the Bedouin, as in Chibaysh, implies recognizing intermarriage as a potential prelude to brotherhood, and a fusion of ancestors as conceivable. Still, it appears that even in Nazareth the establishment of co-responsibility regarding blood-debt demands recourse to the metaphor of agnation. The stronger, overarching language of kinship is culturally required to reinforce the weaker, more restricted tie of neighbourly solidarity.

Seen in this light, the Nazareth contract presents an interesting analogy to the confederation treaties established by Muhammad at Yathrib [Medina]. These 'had as a special feature that the *din*, i.e., religion/law of the tribes who formed it, differed from that of their Jewish client tribes' (Serjeant 1978: 4). The recognition of relatedness without affinity, of blood-debt without common ancestry, establishes one of the most extensive forms of *qaraba* obtaining in the Near East. The 19th century Lebanese *'ammiyya* system provides a modern example of attempts to organise local society on an interdenominational basis (see Harik 1968). But where, in recent years, has the absence of such agreements proved more devastating than in Lebanon? Even today intermarriage between communities presupposes conversion or apostasy, and this implies, for one partner at least, a severance of kinship. The absence of civil marriage in the Near East, and not only in Lebanon, perpetuates forms of community endogamy which no form of elective kinship can transcend. Yet, the common language of agnation can be a factor of peace.

Asymmetry, Parity and the Agnatic Illusion

In spheres where a single faith prevails, the ultimate limitation imposed upon the establishment of elective kinship derives from the parties' assessments of their compatibility in terms of rank and status. Constraints affecting acceptable degrees of genealogical accommodation or the proper use of patronymics intervene only at a later stage, and may reflect persistent inequality between 'hosts' and 'newcomers' (Bédoucha 1994: 196–99). At the 'aristocratic' pole of the social scale, certain tribes of pre-Islamic Arabia were described as 'ardent coals': these men were so convinced of their excellence that they could not conceive accepting any form of confederation (Lane 1863–93: s.v. JMR). Certain Arabs were reputed to be too proud of their paternal and maternal ancestry to admit that an outsider could be their equal (Goldziher 1889: 131). In cases where exorbitant rhetoric reflected traits of social practice, the range of marriage options beyond the kindred must have been singularly restricted. Even then, the early Arabian covenant of brotherhood described by Smith (1885: 50–51, 1914: 314–18) and Wellhausen (1884: 124, 127–29) offered an elegant and dignified way for equals of different descent to satisfy the desire to marry 'among one's own' while at once extending the circle of affinity. A 'collateral' relation could be instituted between the wards of potential spouses through a fiction of consanguinity. Exogamy could thus easily be cloaked in the mantle of common ancestry or formal equality.

Yet elective kinship is often enacted between parties, be they individuals or groups, divided by an asymmetry of status. A classical saying indirectly stresses this by recalling that 'the relation of clientship is a [form of] kinship *(luhma)*, just as kinship by agnatic descent *(nasab)*.' The compass of tolerable differentiation is, however, bounded by the imperative of 'honour preserved'. Disparity must not attain a degree of intensity such that it would be debasing for the initially 'higher' party to engage the 'entering' party in a relation other than of durable subordination. Inversely, the acceptance of sanctuary is not compatible with condescending patronage, for this would disgrace the 'host' as well as the 'protected neighbour'. Often, asymmetry concerns only he who changes affiliation and his protector, whereas their respective groups of origin remain formal equals. A fine line must be tread that discounts manifest discrepancies of condition as circumstantial and attributable to passing adversity. Channels thus remain open that lead to the realization of a parity in brotherhood, itself often founded on adoption.

In a patrilineal and patriarchal context fraught with hierarchy, elective kinship is one of the few social techniques that may be summoned to redefine spheres of propinquity while preserving the illusion that agnation prevails over all other forms of relatedness. In the idiom of genealogy, status by descent is timeless and intangible: once a son of Quraysh, always a son of Quraysh, whatever misfortune may beset he who inherits noble descent. Hence, to acquire a lineal status admittedly not one's own requires, beyond the reciprocal consent of the associates, a certain assiduity in persuading outsiders of the connection's validity. And this wager is not made lightly. As Dresch rightly points out, 'men will only change tribe as a result of duress' for soliciting the support of others against one's own implies a severance of kinship and loss of vital resources such as access to land and water' (1989: 108). A man not destitute through loss of herd and kin, or fleeing in the face of impending vengeance, only requests re-affiliation when persuaded that his legitimate claim to equality among his own is not respected. If established, elective affinities, as Bédoucha (1994: 190–91) shows, are paradoxical in that they appear to challenge agnation, descent and pedigree: they rest on selective, ever revocable omissions of memory. Fragile, they are disputed by the ill intentioned wielding 'long tongues'. Elective ancestors declared to be common ('We have been separated, but our forebear is one, *jiddna wahid*') thus 'dwell' on or beyond the pale of documented ascent, in an ancestral limbo of sorts, where disputes over ancestry cease to threaten an otherwise established (yet precarious) order in the present. New ties of solidarity may then be contracted.

A. Jaussen relates that 'among the *Ghanamat* [of Transjordan] one Harrawi came to the sheikh and said: "Give me a woman and I will be of the tribe by name and by blood *(samawi wa damawi)*." He today counts among the most prominent members of the tribe' (1908: 116). In this apparently unexceptional 'success story', the genealogical assimilation of the adopted outsider implies formal ascription to an alien *nasab*, as distinct from a line of filiation; it entails not only the sharing of blood-debt but enjoins, sooner or later, uxorilocal marriage. Thus, among the Bedouin of Cyrenaica, when the *laff*, i.e., 'the attached' or 'connected', who do not own natural resources, 'have resided with their freeborn hosts for several years and one of them has married one of the host's daughters, they are grafted to the genealogy at the point of tertiary segmentation, that is, where ambiguity occurs in the genealogy ... [This] permits manipulation to include new lines' (Peters 1990: 99). Inversely, among the ... al-Murrah of Arabia, adoption 'often results from marriages between lineages and generally reflects a man's lack of camels' (Cole 1975: 88). In Yemen, having stated his 'request of brotherhood' *(talib al-mukhwa)*, a refugee or fugitive at first becomes a *naqil*, literally one 'relocated', without recognized *nasab* or residence, dependent upon an individual male guarantor. The passage to kinship, however, results from a collective act, a decision by the assembly of heads of households: only when they have approved the adoption, can the meat of the 'slaughter-beast of brotherhood', *'aqirat al-mukhwa*, be shared among all parties in a ritual of incorporation.[21] The *naqil* then becomes *mu'akh* and accedes to land rights (Dostal 1985: 209–10); this 'makes him not only a "brother" (one who shares the ancestral name), but a 'neighbour' *(jar)*, and thus one who shares the ancestral territory' (Dresch 1989: 81). In any case, the stranger must initially enter into a debt-relationship implying access to means of (re)production. He thus accepts the relative humiliation of clientship, but, as an in-marrying husband, may soon be treated as an agnate, and not as a uterine kinsman subject to a regime of protection *(jiwar)*. Adoption through marriage and the conferring of lineage membership constitute together the full tie of elective kinship, preceding the emergence of possible consanguinal relationships at the next generation.

These examples suggest a symmetry between the aversion toward hypogamous marriage by women and that of men to affiliate themselves, as individuals or groups, to a lineage of lower status than their own. The latter would imply a 'feminization' of sorts. Likewise, the gender hierarchy underlying the notion of *kafa'a*, the requisite of parity between spouses, renders almost inconceivable the adoption of an adult woman, for the loss of a female ward would greatly shame her agnates and question their manliness. Indeed, 'a woman will only be admitted as a protected neighbour if her family (i.e., her agnates) grants its authorization' (Wellhausen 1889: 72). Considerations of *kafa'a*, a malleable notion indeed, may even be opposed to the otherwise acceptable union of a woman, perceived as placing her agnates in a situation of unwanted debt or dependence *vis-à-vis* another person or group. Conversely, male hypogamy is 'standard' practice. Male hypergamy, however, is not unknown: as just mentioned, assimilation may ensure the social ascension of an in-marrying man whose status in an alien group, while at first subject to doubt, is seen as reinforcing the position of close agnates in the longer term. When parity of status tends to prevail between the lineages of a man requesting haven and that of his future wife, differences in rank and wealth between the future spouses can easily be veiled by the fiction of agnatic kinship which adoption *(intisab)* creates. In general, once the principle of elective kinship is accepted by all parties, the margins of variation regarding tolerable discrepancies of status and means become an object of negotiation to be examined practically rather than dogmatically. All know, moreover, that unforeseeable events such as a feud may render the agreed parity criteria of yesterday suddenly obsolete. Hence, within the realm of free tribes, the definition of female hypogamy tends, within admittedly well-protected bounds, to be dealt with as a matter of appreciation, always implying an element of risk.

At the lowest echelon of social stratification, however, elective kinship offers no option of upward social mobility to the ostracized. One of the so-called 'pariah' tribes of Arabia, the Sulayb studied by Henninger (1939), were alternatively called the 'dogs of the desert' and the 'tribe of asses'. Donkey raisers, the Sulayb were also hunters and smiths. Their relations with Bedouin camel herders excluded marriage and hence the institution of kinship. Only the annual payment of tribute ensured the preservation of their persons and meagre assets. This subordination excluded them from the field of warfare and hence of honour. Born according to certain traditions of the incestuous relation between an Arab and his mother, an absolute denial of agnation, they are banished from the tribal order, inferior by birth, and condemned to endogamy. Their name is an insult. This is an extreme illustration of the fact that 'agnation, if taken to mean the consanguinous relation of males of common patrilineal origin, cannot mean the same thing for clients as it does for nobles; its two forms are embedded in wholly different matrixes' (Peters 1990: 55).

Elective kinship may only emerge where intermarriage is accepted and possible. Still, the former does not necessarily imply the latter. While 'true adoption' is generally sealed through marriage, the conclusion of an alliance *(hilf)*, or its reinforcement through brotherhood *(ikha', mu'akhah)*, does not per se modify patterns of marriage within or among the units involved. Shifts of allegiance simply redefine the social field in which equality is recognized and the shedding of blood (in principle) banned. Transformations of boundaries – symbolic, genealogical and spatial – are thus enacted by 'deactivating' (and hence recognizing) the distinct origins of 'brothers': 'No difference of ancestry shall divide them,' states the 1980 Yemeni agreement recorded by Dresch (1989: 331). But pacts make no specific mention of marriage: it may well 'flow' from alliance and parity, but fostering affinity is never a stated goal.

The interplay between political and matrimonial alliance is neither ethnographically nor historically simple to decipher. In principle, when individuals connect groups by becoming 'brothers', they instantly open the way for 'father's brother's daughter' marriages among their children. Yet, when one examines a long-established political identity, that of a Yemeni tribe for example, instances of elective kinship that might once have favoured intermarriage among groups that today jointly claim its heritage are by definition forgotten or unspoken. Inversely, when an ethnographer is lucky enough to witness or document a recent pact of brotherhood, the duration of fieldwork is rarely adequate to ascertain its further matrimonial implications. And when the articulation of elective kinship and marriage is observed (e.g., Bédoucha 1994), time is scarce to assess the wider or durable impact given unions may have on the realignment of the sections involved. Synchronic comparison of individual and collective pacts does suffice to show, however, that these modes of elective kinship present structural analogies, and are part of a single complex. Individual pacts may have collective consequences, and vice versa, but there is never an inevitable causal relation between the two. Their effects on affinity are ever negotiable, ever fragile. This very room for manoeuvre is indeed an integral aspect of Arab social organization. Wherever formal equality prevails, wherever men seek to extend or re-establish it, elective bonds may accommodate the boundaries of patrilineality in the face of conflict. The element of choice in Arab kinship is thus essential to sustain the illusion of agnation.

From Elective Kinship to Essentialism?

Interest in the 'chosen' aspects of Arab kinship, initially sustained by the 'Orientalist' precursors of anthropology, was subsequently tempered by a rather exclusive debate on lineage theory, segmentarity and preferential marriage. It is now re-emerging at a point in time when relations between tribal and state organizations, as well as Arab conceptions of identity, are undergoing profound alteration (Bonte, Conte & Dresch, eds. 2001). What role does extended (let alone elective) kinship today play in societies where urbanization has, in the space of a generation or two, often reduced pastoral or rural populations to minority status? In certain (rare) cases, the increased role of parliaments may affect the conjoint exercise of kinship and power, modifying the ways in which descent-focused entities may coalesce regionally and nationally, support potentates or seek support from kin in state service. One counter-reaction to this has been the emergence of new forms of hereditary transmission of power, indeed of incipient 'republican dynasties'.

In this shifting civil and political context, the illusion of agnation proves, however, deep-rooted. It is notably reflected in what A. Shryock (1997) terms 'genealogical nationalism', a language of identity some deploy to confiscate authenticity of descent in favour of a given stock of Arabs, such as Jordanian Bedouin, all under the aegis of the 'national family'. Parallels may possibly be

43

found to such endeavours in the genealogical literature of old but, in the present setting, a new element seems to intervene, namely explicit essentialism. In its extreme contemporary forms, genealogical absolutism recalls rhetoric of 'blood and soil'. Situations in which local Arab populations co-exist for economic reasons with large groups of aliens, some Muslim, some not, but most of subordinate status, has profoundly affected the meaning of 'neighbourship' or *jiwar*. New frontiers of matrimonial exclusion crystallize, as 'genealogical consultants' cater to the craving for authenticity of those whose well-being and marriage strategies require comforting 'purity of descent'. Should one not distinguish the *asliyyun*, the 'rooted', from the *ghara'ib*, the 'strangers', the employers from the employed? Here, the banal expression *'aylaqat al-dam*, 'blood relations', acquires new shades of meaning.

At once, rapid changes in patterns of procreation and fertility rates hint at profound transformations in gender relations. Staunch reactions are noted, opposing changes in personal status laws. As in many non-Arab countries, doctors of the faith and of medicine express grave misgivings as they assess the ethical implications of new reproductive technologies (Jam'iiyya 1995). These, if misused, can easily cancel legitimate paternity while splitting motherhood between a giver of genes and a bearer-nurse (Conte 2000: 296–304). Further, could not the creation of milk-banks (as opposed to long-established blood-banks) induce 'confusion of lines of descent', *ikhtilat al-ansab* (al-Najjar 1986)? These are some of the menaces seen as threatening *nasab* in the modern world. Moreover, the development of state welfare institutions, the slow adjustment of civil codes, religious convictions and clerical resistance notwithstanding, can facilitate adoption through *iqrar* and fosterage, especially in the urban environment (al-Azhary Sonbol 1995). The care of the 'child found' *(laqit)* will, in all likelihood, acquire new significance. Yet, in an increasingly 'post-tribal' time, can 'genealogical nationalism' suffice to bar the transformation of gender relations? While the illusion of agnation will doubtless endure under revised auspices, the notion of 'brotherhood', as here considered, might slowly fade into the realm of genealogical oblivion.

Notes

1. See, for example, Bonte 2000; Bonte (ed.) 1994: passim; and Dresch 1998, pp.121–5.
2. See, for example, Abu-Lughod 1993, al-Torki 1980; Conte 2000; Inhorn 1994; Musallam 1983: passim; Peters 1990: passim; Tapper 1990.
3. Cf. Ibn Manzur, n. d.: s.v. *(sub verbo)* DMM, KHLT, and MHJ.
4. Cf. Muslim, *Sahih kitab al-nikah*, and Giladi 1999: passim.
5. Cf. Smith 1914 [1889]: pp. 314–18, 479–81.
6. Noble descent is indeed expressed through the metaphor of the vein (*'irq*, plur., *'uruq*). The basic meaning of *'irq* is, however, 'root'. Goldziher nonetheless translates *'irq* as 'blood' (1889, I: pp. 41–2). Yet, when it is said of someone *'irqhu zakhir*, this indicates that his 'root', his ascendants, are noble (cf. Kazmirski 1860, I: p. 981). To translate this term as 'of noble blood' is to forget that the term *'irq* means 'milk still in the udder'.
7. Eg., Cole 1975: p.84 and Wellhausen 1893: pp. 480–81. The word *khal* (mother's brother) is used by extension, in the plural *(akhwal)* to designate one's maternal relatives. In modern usage, it can be applied to neighbours with whom one has or could develop ties of affinity and uterine kinship. Yet, the term is not applicable to a social or residential unit also including one's agnates.
8. *la nasaba fi l-islam, la hilfa fi l-islam.*
9. Concerning this incident, related by Bukhari 1864, III: p. 417 and Ibn Sa'd 1928, VIII: pp. 73, 19, see Smith 1885: pp. 44–5, Wellhausen 1893: p. 441, n. 3, Celhod 1965: p. 44. Comp. Watt 1962: pp. 328–29.
10. Madelung (1997: 4, n. 8) refers to 'Caetani's view [that] Muhammad was not in fact a Hashimite or even a Qurayshite, but rather an orphan of unknown origin who had been taken into the family of Abu Talib b. 'Abd al-Muttalib.' See Caetani 1905–26, I: pp. 58–75 and passim.
11. 'Hypergamy' designates marriages with a person of lesser social standing; 'uxorilocality' is a union in which the husband takes up residence with his wife.
12. *huwa rajulun abtarun, la 'aqiba lahu.*
13. I thank Hosham Dawood for drawing this work to my attention.
14. 'When any group is threatened with extinction [...] there is a definite tendency for the lineage rump to fuse with a collateral lineage (and in so doing fuse their resources with those of the adopting lineage), or for the numerically more powerful group to take it over by force' (Peters 1990: 93).
15. Unfortunately, *badal* is often translated in the anthropological literature by 'exchange marriage', even though this formulation may convey Lévi-Straussian connotations concerning prescriptive rules that are inapplicable in the Arab context (comp. Bonte 2000, Conte 2000b, Lévi-Strauss 2000).
16. The English terms here given in parentheses also appear in the Arabic text.
17. Salim (1956: 139) writes: *yantasabani ba'dhahuma intisaban wathiqan.*
18. I am grateful to Professor Fritz Steppat who, aware of my interest in elective kinship, was kind enough to give me his 1974 article (itself based on Mansur 1924), from which the data presented in this section are drawn.
19. *wafaqa ra'yahumu al-hazima an yakunu muta'aminaa ma'a ba'dhihim 'ahdan 'umumiyyatan wa muta'assibina 'asabatan wahidatan.*

20. The Arabic original of this text (accompanied by a German translation) is reproduced in Steppat.
21. Bulls are also slaughtered and shared in rituals of re-incorporation, through which a tribe retrieves a man who has fled, thus 'lifting the blood with the blood' and cancelling severance (Dresch 1989: 109–10).

References

Abu-Lughod, L., *Writing Women's Worlds. Bedouin Stories*, Berkeley, Los Angeles, Oxford: University of California Press, 1993.

Altorki, S., 'Milk-Kinship in Arab Society: An Unexplored Problem in the Ethnography of Marriage', *Ethnology*, 19, 1980, pp. 233–44.

Bédoucha, G., 'Le cercle des proches: la consanguinité et ses détours (Tunisie, Yémen)', in P. Bonte, (ed.), *Epouser au plus proche. Inceste, prohibitions et stratégies matrimoniales autour de la Méditerranée*. Paris: Editions de l'EHESS, 1994, pp. 189–219.

Bonte, P., 'Manière de dire ou manière de faire: Peut-on parler d'un mariage 'arabe'?', in P. Bonte, (ed.), *Epouser au plus proche. Inceste, prohibitions et stratégies matrimoniales autour de la Méditerranée*. Paris: Editions de l'EHESS, 1994, pp. 371–98.

—— 2000. 'L'échange est-il universel?', *L'Homme*, 154–55: pp. 39–66.

—— (ed.), *Epouser au plus proche. Inceste, prohibitions et stratégies matrimoniales autour de la Méditerranée*, Paris: Editions de l'EHESS, 1994.

Bonte, P. et E. Conte, 'Introduction – La tribu arabe: approches anthropologiques et orientalistes', in P. Bonte, E. Conte, C. Hamès et A. W. Ould Cheikh, *al-Ansab. La Quête des origines. Anthropologie historique de la société tribale arabe*. Paris: Editions de la Maison des Sciences de l'Homme, 1991, pp. 3–48.

Bonte, P., E. Conte et P. Dresch, (eds), *Emirs et présidents. Figures de la parenté et du politique dans le monde arabe*, Paris: CNRS-Editions, 2001.

al-Bukhari, Abu 'Abd Allah Muhammad ibn Isma'il (d. 256/870), *Kitab al-jami' al-salih*, al-Qahira, Matba'at Dar ihya' al-kitab al'arabiyya, 4 vol, n.d.

—— 1864 *Kitab al-jami' al-sahih*, Tome III, Krehl ed., Leiden: E. J. Brill.

Caetani, L., *Annali dell'Islam*, Milano, U. Hoepli, 1905–26.

Chelhod, J., 'Le mariage avec la cousine parallèle dans le système arabe', *L'Homme*, V (3–4) 1965, pp. 113–73.

—— *Le Droit dans la société bédouine. Recherches ethnologiques sur le orf ou droit coutumier*, Paris: Marcel Rivière, 1971.

Cole, D. P., *Nomads of the Nomads. The al-Murrah Bedouin of the Empty Quarter*, Arlington Heights (Illinois): Harlan Davidson, 1975.

Conte, E., 'Le pacte, la Parenté et le Prophète: Réflexions sur la proximité parentale dans la tradition arabe', in F. Héritier-Augé et E. Copet-Rougier (eds), *Les Complexités de l'alliance, IV: Economie, politique et fondements symboliques*, Paris: Editions des Archives contemporaines ('Ordres sociaux'), 1994, pp. 143–85.

—— 'Choisir ses parents dans la société arabe: la situation à l'avènement de l'islam', in P. Bonte, (ed.), *Epouser au plus proche. Inceste, prohibitions et stratégies matrimoniales autour de la Méditerranée*. Paris: Editions de l'EHESS, 1994, pp. 165–87.

—— 'Enigmes persanes, traditions arabes. Les interdictions matrimoniales dérivées de l'allaitement selon l'ayatollah Khomeyni', in J.L. Jammard, E. Terray, M. Xanthakou, eds., *En subtances*, Paris: Fayard, 2000, pp. 157–81.

—— 'Filiations prophétiques. Réflexions sur la personne de Muhammad', in. P. Bonte, E. Conte et P. Dresch, *Emirs et présidents. Figures de la parenté et du politique dans le monde arabe*, Paris: CNRS-Editions, 2000, pp. 55–78.

Copet-Rougier, E., 'Le mariage 'arabe'. Une approche théorique', in P. Bonte, (ed.), *Epouser au plus proche. Inceste, prohibitions et stratégies matrimoniales autour de la Méditerranée*. Paris: Editions de l'EHESS, 1994, pp. 371–98.

Dostal, W., *Egalität und Klassengesellschaft in Südarabien. Anthropologische Untersuchungen zur sozialen Evolution*, Horn-Wien: Verlag Ferdinand Berger & Söhne, 1985.

Dresch, P., *Tribes, Government, and History in Yemen*. Oxford: Clarendon Press, 1989.

—— 'Mutual Deception: Totality, Exchange and Islam in the Middle East', in W. James et N.J. Allen, eds., *Marcel Mauss. A Centenary Tribute*. New York-Oxford: Berghahn Books, 1998, 111–33.

Giladi, A., *Infants, Parents and Wet Nurses. Medieval Islamic Views on Breastfeeding and Their Social Implications*, Leiden-Boston-Köln: Brill, 1999.

Guillaume, A., *The Life of Muhammad. A Translation of Ishaq's Sirat Rasul Allah*. Karachi: Oxford University Press, 1967.

Goldziher, I., *Muhammedanische Studien*. Halle an der Salle, M. Niemeyer, 2 vol. 1889.

—— 'Die Fiktion der Blutsverwandtschaft bei orientalischen Völkern', *Globus*, LXIII, 1893.

Granqvist, H., *Marriage Conditions in a Palestinian Village*. Helsingfors: Societas Scientiarum Fennica, 2 vol., 1931–35.

—— *Muslim Death and Burial*. Helsingfors, Societas Scientiarum Fennica, 1965.

Harik, I. F., *Politics and Change in a Traditional Society: Lebanon 1711–1845*. Princeton: Princeton University Press, 1968.

Henninger, J., 'Pariastämme in Arabien', in *Festschrift zum 50jährigen Bestandsjubiläum des Missionhauses St. Gabriel*, Sankt Gabrieler Studien, VIII: 501–35. Wien-Mödling, Missionsdruckerei St. Gabriel, 1939.

Héritier, F., *Les deux sœurs et leur mère. Anthropologie de l'inceste*. Paris: Editions Odile Jacob, 1994.

Ibn Hisham, 'Abd al Malik ibn Ayyub al-Himyari (d. 213/834), *Sirat al-nabawiyya*, Cairo: Dar al-Manar, 2 vols, 1990/1410.

Ibn Manzur, Muhammad (d. 711/1311), *Lisan al-'arab*, Cairo: Dar al-ma'arif, n.d.

Ibn Sa'd, Abu 'Abd Allah (d. 230/845), *Kitab al-tabaqat al-kabir (fi l-nisa')*, Leiden: Brill, VIII, 1928/1231.

Ibn Taymiyya, Taqiyy al-Din Ahmad (d. 728/1328), *Ahkam al-zawaj*, Beirut: Dar al-Kutub al-'Ilmiyya, 1988.

Inhorn, M. C., *Quest for Conception. Gender, Infertility, and Egyptian Medical Traditions*. Philadelphia: University of Pennsylvania Press, 1994.

al-Isfahani, Abu-Faraj (d. 356/967), *Kitab al-aghani*, Matba'at Dar al-Kutub al-Misriyya, Cairo, 8 vols, 1935.

Jam'iyyat al-'ulum al-tibiyya, *Qadaya tibbiyya mu'asira fi dhaw' al-shari'ah a al-islamiyya*. Amman, Dar al-bashir, 1995/1415.

Jaussen, A., *Coutumes des Arabes au pays de Moab*. Paris: Lecoffre, 1908.

Kazimirski, A. de B., *Dictionnaire arabe-français*. Paris: Maisonneuve, 2 vol., 1860.

Klapisch-Zuber, C., *L'Ombre des ancêtres. Essai sur l'imaginaire médiéval de la parenté*. Paris: Fayard, 2000.

Lane, E. W., *An Arabic-English Lexicon*, London and Edinburgh: Williams and Norgate, 1863–93.

Lévi-Strauss, C., 'Après la richesse et la diversité des articles ... ', *L'Homme*, 154–55, pp. 713–20, 2000.

Linant de Bellefonds, Y., *Traité de droit comparé musulman comparé*, Tome II : *Le mariage. La dissolution du mariage*, Paris-La Haye, Mouton, 1965.

Madelung, W., *The Succession to Muhammad. A Study of the Early Caliphate*, Cambridge: Cambridge University Press, 1997.

Malik ben Anas (d. 179/795), *al-Muwatta'*, Cairo, Matba'at dar ihya' al-kutub al-'arabiyya.

Morgan, L. H., *Systems of Consanguinity and Affinity of the Human Family*, Washington DC, Smithsonian Institution, 1871.

Musallam, B. F., *Sex and Society in Islam. Birth Control Before the Nineteenth Century*. Cambridge: Cambridge University Press, 1983.

Muslim, Abu al Husayn (Muslim) ibn al-Hajjaj (d. 1261/875), *Sahih Muslim [al-Jami' al-sahih]*, Cairo, Matba'at Dar Ihya' al-Kutub al-'Arabiyya, n.d.

al-Najjar, 'Abd Allah Mabruk, '*Mawqif al-islam min bunuk laban al-umahat*', in A. Giladi, *Infants, Parents and Wet Nurses. Medieval Islamic Views on Breastfeeding and their Social Implications*, Leiden-Boston-Köln: Brill, 1999, pp. 143–57. [reproduced from *Majallat al-azhar*, 1986, 59: 447–55.]

Peters, E. L. (edited by J. Goody & E. Marx), *The Bedouin of Cyrenaica. Studies in Personal and Corporate Power*. Cambridge: Cambridge University Press, 1990.

Proksch, O., *Über die Blutrache bei den vorislamischen Arabern und Mohammeds Stellung zu ihr*. Leipzig: B. G. Teubner, 1899.

Salim, S. M., *al-Chibayish: dirasat anthropolojiyya li-qarya fi ahwar al-'iraq*, Baghdad: Rabita, 2 vols (I: 1956; II: 1957).

—— *Marsh Dwellers of the Euphrates Delta*. London: Althone Press, 1962. [Abridged English translation of the former.]

Said, E., *Orientalism*, New York: Pantheon Books, 1978.

Serjeant, R. B., 'The *Sunnah Jami'ahi* Pacts with the Yathrib Jews, and the *tahrim* of Yathrib: Analysis and Translation of the Documents Comprised in the so-called 'Constitution of Median'', *Bulletin of the School of Oriental and African Studies*, XLI, I: 1–42, 1978.

Shryock, A., *Nationalism and the Genealogical Imagination. Oral History and Textual Authority in Tribal Jordan*. Berkeley–Los Angeles–London: University of California Press, 1997.

Smith, W. R., *Marriage in Early Arabia*. Cambridge: Cambridge University Press, 1885.

—— *Lectures on the Religion of the Semites*. Cambridge: Cambridge University Press, 1914 [1st ed.: 1889].

Steppat, F., 'Ein "Contrat social" in einer palestinensischen Stadt, 1854', *Die Welt des Islams*, XV (1–4), 1974, pp. 233–46.

Tabari, Abu Ja'far Muhammad ibn Jarir (d. 310/923), *The History of al-Tabari (Tarikh al rusul wa l-muluk)*. New York: State University of New York Press, Vol VI, 1988.

Tapper, N., *Bartered Brides. Politics, Gender and Marriage in an Afghan Tribal Society*, Cambridge: Cambridge University Press, 1990.

Tarmanini, 'Abd al-Islam, *al-Zawaj 'ind al-'arab fi l-jahiliyya wa l-islam*. Aleppo: Dar al-qalam al-'arabi, 1989 [1st ed.: 1984].

Thorbecke, H., '*Antarah, des vorislamischen Dichters Leben*. Heidelberg: F. Bassermann,1868.

Watt, W. M., *Muhammad at Mecca*, Oxford: Clarendon Press, 1953.

—— *Muhammad at Medina*, Oxford: Clarendon Press, 1962.

Wellhausen, J., *Reste arabischen Heidentums*. Berlin & Leipzig: W. de Gruyter, 1884.

——'Die Ehe bei den Arabern', *Nachrichten der Königlichen Gesellschaft der Wissenschaften und der Goerg-Augusts-Universität zu Göttingen*, Nr. 11, 1893, pp. 431–81.

—— *Ein Gemeinwesen ohne Obrigkeit.* Rede zur Feier des Geburtstages Seiner Majestät des Kaisers und Königs am 27. Januar 1900 im Namen des Georg-Augusts-Universität, Göttingen, Dieterisch'sche Universitäts-Buchdruckerei, 1900.

Wilken, G. A., *Het Matriarchaat bij de Oude Arabieren*, Amsterdam: J. H. de Bussy, 1884.

TWO

Ibn Khaldun and Contemporary Anthropology: Cycles and Factional Alliances of Tribe and State in the Maghreb

Pierre Bonte

In the mid-14th century, drawing on his study of the societies of the Maghreb, Ibn Khaldun offered the first coherent theory of the relations between tribes and states – a theory that would become well known to subsequent scholars in the West. It is not my purpose here to reconsider their discussions of the contribution of Ibn Khaldun to modern social science. Rather, the focus will be on showing how his theory is located in his epoch – and yet offers an important perspective on the representations and mental categories organizing contemporary tribes and states.

Four Key Aspects of the Khaldunian Theory

One

Let us begin by examining the place that the key concepts of *'asabiya* (solidarity) and *nasab* (origin) occupy in Ibn Khaldun's work. The notion of *nasab* is bound up with the idea of sharing a common male ancestor, although Ibn Khaldun himself does not emphasize this masculine dimension, as we shall see later. However, *nasab* defines the cohesion of groups that share not only genealogy but also 'solidarities' (*'asabiyat*). There is a quasi-Aristotelian relationship between *nasab* as a primary principle and *'asabiya* as its concrete realization.

> I.134 We have demonstrated that the fruit of the line of descent and, equally, its utility, lies in *'asabiya*, particularly because of the feelings of social pride and mutual defence. (French translation by Hamès, 1987.)

> I.154 Attack and defence are organized through *'asabiya* because it touches the springs of group susceptibility (*nu'ra*): defence of family honour (*tadhamur*) and the spirit of sacrifice unto death between the members of the tribe (*ibid.*).

While it is tempting to assimilate *'asabiya* to the notion of corporate group, traditionally associated with unilinear filiation in segmentary lineage theory, for Ibn Khaldun *'asabiya* is fundamentally linked to power and competition.

Two

The preceding quotations throw light on a second aspect of Ibn Khaldun's theory that I wish to emphasize. In a kind of first stage of civilization (*'umran*) according to Ibn Khaldun (who associated it with the pastoral and nomadic way of life of the Bedouins), the *'asabiyat*, solidarity groups, militate to attain the first, highest rank in the tribe. The key point is that this regrouping could not have been accomplished without strong competition between groups and the monopolization of power by one of these groups, the one that held the chieftainship (*riyasa*). In a long and very important passage, Ibn Khaldun connects, always from an Aristotelian angle, this process of competition with the impossibility of reducing group identity to the sort of equilibrium and proportion associated with the system of lineage segments based on the rules of complementary opposition: on the contrary, what is implied is hierarchy.

> I.326 The tribal spirit is composite and results from the mixing of several clans, one of which is stronger than the others. This is the origin of social organization (*ijtima'*) and superiority over men and dynasties. The key to success is the fact that the clan that dominates the whole tribe tallies with the 'temperament' (*mizaj*) which is in the process of gestation. The temperament results from the mixing of the elements. As we have seen, no mixing can take place if the elements are in equal proportion. One of these elements must be superior

relative to the others in order to achieve mixing. In the same way, one of the clans must be stronger in order to unify the others and fuse them in a single corporate spirit (*'asabiya*).[1]

Three

The notion of *'asabiya* is relative: it is not related exclusively to the solidarities of a common *nasab* but also to the hierarchical solidarities that flow from the localization of power in one group. This is the third fundamental aspect of Ibn Khaldun's theory. Tribal spirit and competition among *'asabiyat* converge in the (state) localization of political power (*mulk*) and the establishment of an *'asabiya al-kubra* – a superior *'asabiya* – englobing and incarnated in the dynastic state (*dawla*). The formation of the Maghreb dynasties was, in Ibn Khaldun's view, the manifestation of a historical law whose concrete realizations he examined in Books II and III of *Kitab al-'ibar*.

Four

Finally, the fourth notable aspect of Ibn Khaldun's analysis is the notion of the dynastic 'cycle' – the necessity of periodic collapses (*fasad*) of ruling dynasties according to historical laws. Ibn Khaldun offered various explanations for such collapses. They could result from the exercise of power across generations, with the gradual decay of ancestral virtues. He also invokes the greater competitiveness of the Bedouin nomadic *'asabiya* which allowed them to mobilize, at the periphery of the state, new tribal and supra-tribal solidarities and thus to oppose the successive dynasties weakened by time, the luxury of the settled life and power.

   Such is, albeit in summary form, the way in which Ibn Khaldun's work has been received and read in contemporary social science, justifying his title as precursor of modern anthropology, history and sociology. But does this now almost canonical reading exhaust everything that can be drawn from his monumental work? The modern aspects of Ibn Khaldun's work is one thing (Lacoste, 1966), and the aim of Ibn Khaldun, himself caught up in the political struggle of that period, in studying the societies of his own epoch, is another. As anthropologists, whether working in the field of contemporary societies or historical ones, we must take into consideration the aim of the author.

Aspects of *Nasab*: Differentiation, Variability, Competition and Hierarchy

The *Muqaddima* is the 'prolegomenon' to a global project, which has 'disappeared' in most scholarly Western commentaries on Ibn Khaldun's work. The other books of *Kitab al-'ibar* are regarded simply as documentary sources of information about the events of the period rather than as integral parts of a work. Instead, we should take the work as a whole, beginning with the idea that *Kitab al-'ibar* is in fact a pretty standard attempt at a *tarikh* ('history') of the period and earlier times, intended to explain the diversity of tribes, peoples and political formations in the Muslim world and in particular the Maghreb. Its aim simply is not to found a historical approach as we conceive it based on the definition of historical facts. It is meant (Cheddadi, 1986) to establish the very criterion of the 'true' (valid, authentic i.e. *sahih*) and the 'false' (corrupted, *fasid*) as they relate to 'origins' (*nasab*). This is the project shared by Ibn Khaldun and many authors of *tarikh* in medieval times. The true originality of Ibn Khaldun lies elsewhere, in the 'methodological revolution' by which he attempts to establish the criteria of the true, the authentic, drawing on a kind of internal support (*batin*) by gauging facts in the light of their coherence with the 'principles' of human nature which, in turn, are strongly linked, as we have already seen, to the notions of *nasab* and *'asabiya*. The content of these notions, as Ibn Khaldun presents them, is particularly important for modern anthropologists.

This importance is apparent to me in the light of my Sahara experience (Bonte, 1998), in a world which is not so different from the world described by Ibn Khaldun. To illustrate this continuity, six centuries later, a traditional Mauritanian scholar, Mukhtar uld Hamidun, who, incidentally, had contributed to the field of Western studies of Mauritania under colonialism, devoted himself to writing a history (unfinished) of Western Sahara, *Hayat Muritaniya* (Mauritanian Life). It is in many ways comparable to Ibn Khaldun's project. Here one finds the same distinction between the true and the false, the same will to elaborate a 'total', if not universal, history of *nasab*. The perpetuation of the same project, after a lapse of six centuries, underlines the native dimension of Ibn Khaldun's work.

Of these native representations and categories, *nasab* is the most important. As a search for 'origins', it does not appear to me to be rooted in any modern concept of the historical. Even though their generational dimensions and the chronological concerns of the authors of *tarikh* inscribe it in a certain temporality, this is a kind of 'historicity' whose role is essentially to illustrate the deeds and gestures of the ancestors. In fact *nasab* is above all a principle of classification. It has various features:

Nasab as Classification

First, *nasab* presents itself as a linear and ascendant reading of genealogy, as Arab genealogists witness – masculine ancestral chains (or 'linkages') reaching back to one founding individual (male), situated at a variable generational distance, depending on the distance that the genealogy wants to establish between an individual and his collaterals. The degree of proximity corresponds to the desired effects of identity and difference sought by the classification. So, the latter may correspond to the 'segmentary' structure of the tribe, marking the fractions or lineages, which make up the tribe (Bonte, 1991a): the *nasab* thus classes the corresponding groups, establishing their difference and their identities.

Alternatively, the classification may be deployed in long generational chains, such as the Sharifian succession in which belonging to the house (*bayt*) of the Prophet Muhammad underlies the identity of the *bayt* but also creates internal differences, depending on whether one is descended from Hasan or Husayn, thus interweaving with religious differentiation. Or, drawing on the post-Hegira[2] re-elaboration of Arab genealogy, classifications can distinguish the descendants of Adnan and Qahtan, i.e. the Arabs of the north and the Arabs of the south. They can also refer to the mythical scriptural ancestors, Adam, Ham, Shem, and so on.

This classification by *nasab* is thus essentially a principle for distinguishing between 'species' or peoples: a genealogy of the human world (*ansab al-'alam*) which Ibn Khaldun expounds at length in the *Muqaddima*. The desired effects are always the same: to separate what is identical from what is different, in other words, to perform the act of classification as such.

We must note, however, that Ibn Khaldun was highly suspicious of certain claims:
1. the capacity to trace *nasab* back to distant times (with the notable exception of the line of the Prophet) and
2. the capacity to explain the differences between 'peoples' and 'nations' solely by reference to these different lines of descent. Hence he presents an alternative explanation inspired by the ancient Greek theory of climate, emphasising the influence of territory and milieu. This can be seen as an aspect of modernity in Ibn Khaldun's theorizing.

Variability of Nasab

The second notable feature, taking us back again to the issue of the 'historicity' implied in *nasab*, is its variability. There is some misunderstanding (not to mention ethnocentric bias) on this point among modern anthropologists due to their dependence on the 'genealogical method',[3] its imagery of branching trees reifying the 'facts' of unilinear filiation. When confronted with the variability of generational chains, they invoke the genealogical manipulations which 'make good' the constant restructuring of relations between segmentary groups. Coming closer to reality, they sometimes speak of 'generative genealogy', but all the while preserving the structural determination of the facts of filiation as beyond questioning – hence the distinction between, on the one hand, distant genealogical chains which may be manipulated and, on the other hand, the 'corporate' character of more proximate genealogies.

To return to the anthropologist's favourite image, should we see the formal organization of *nasab* as a botanic metaphor (genealogical tree), a *ramified bifare cyme*, as in the model of the segmentary lineage (a regular binary bifurcation) or, rather, the *compound corymbose* (a chaotic ramification), more resonant of the hierarchical character of relationships between groups. Perhaps it is better to return to Ibn Khaldun.

> I. 128–129 *Nasab* is a matter of imagination, not a reality. Its utility resides in the fact that the social links and sentiments of affiliation that it creates appear as natural (*tabiʿa*) in the *mentality*. (trans. by Hamès, 1987)

> I. 1.84 *Nasab*, even though it depends upon the order of nature, is nevertheless an illusion (*wahm*). (trans. by Hamès, 1987)

Nasab is a social relation, the result of a consensus (*mutaʿaraf*), even if this relation has a natural foundation. But 'nature' is also a matter of the imagination; it is a way of speaking, first and foremost, of social relations as such. Ibn Khaldun repeatedly insists that a common *nasab* and consequent integration into the *ʿasabiya* does not arise only from kinship filiation but also from the integration of external elements: strangers who marry into the tribe, clients, freed slaves etc.[4]

> I. 135 Dependents (*al-mawali*) and associates (*al-mustanaʿun*) mix their *nasab* with the *ʿasabiya* in which they integrate completely as their 'own' *ʿasabiya* and as a result they form part of the of the organization of this *ʿasabiya* and participate in its *nasab*. (Hamès 1987)

Is this then a matter of a metaphorical and hence 'illusory' treatment of agnatic filiation? Ibn Khaldun poses the issue in a far more complex way in terms that have been badly misunderstood by Western commentators. What is the 'nature' of the relations established by *nasab*? Will it turn out to be agnatic filiation? In fact, when Ibn Khaldun evokes not the principle, *nasab*, but the nature of the feelings of 'familial social pride' and 'mutual defence' which animate the principle of *nasab* and warrant putting the *'asabiya* into motion, 'concretizing' it, he does make reference to the importance of 'kinship links' (*silat al-arham*). The term corresponds to the Qur'anic term *rahim* (womb) (pl. *arham*), which V. Monteil (1967–68 I: 256–257) very improperly translates as 'matrilineage'. Rather, it corresponds to the notion of cognatic kinship but with the feminine dimension of this kinship underlined, a usage which, as E. Conte (1994b) has shown, can be found elsewhere in the vocabulary of the Qur'an.

To resolve the apparent contradiction between agnatic and cognatic aspects of kinship, I propose the hypothesis that I have also developed elsewhere (Bonte 1994a), that the notions of *nasab* and *'asabiya* correspond to a masculine reading, founding exclusively masculine solidarities, of the notion of cognatic kinship relations and the related 'natural' sentiments – to use Ibn Khaldun's expression – that accompany them. This structural opposition, echoed by Ibn Khaldun, is based on a strict distinction in Arab social theory between the masculine and feminine principles.

Nasab, Competition and Hierarchy

A new anthropological reading of Ibn Khaldun's works underlines this third feature of *nasab* as related to the competition between *'asabiyat* which I mentioned earlier. It is the masculine reading of the social order in general, and kinship organization in particular, which explains the opposition between *nasab* and the competition of *'asabiya*. We are in the heart of the Arab system of kinship and alliance. The distinction between the masculine and feminine is structurally determinant. The alliance/marriage system is based on the opposition between marriage prescribed by kinship and status proximity, of which Arab marriage between patrilateral parallel cousins is the cultural norm on one side, and marriage with distant partners on the other (Bonte, 1994a). The field of competition between males is circumscribed by these marital policies. On the one hand, men 'share' rights over women. The 'right of the cousin'[5] is one particular aspect of this social control of men over women, as are, more generally, agnatic rights and the institution of the *wali*, or tutor.[6] On the other hand, men can take the risk of marrying distant partners, a risk because such marriages imply transformations of rank and status (Bonte, 1994b). But the two practices have the same basis: the management of the symbolic and matrimonial capital of women. This is generally explained in terms of honour, and honour representations emphasize the competitive aspect of social relationships. By contrast to the *complementary* opposition rules, which organize segmentary lineage societies, I thus identify in Arab tribe society *competitive* opposition rules, which organize social relations. These two models of social organization are radically different. The role of filiation is structurally determinant in the segmentary lineage system,[7] but not in the Arabic one. The function of marriage/alliance is not determinant in the first system where, in Nuer society for example, the rule of exogamy and the circulation of cattle between kinship groups manage the marriage practices without modifications of the lineage structure. In the second model, the role of marriage/alliance is determinant. It organizes the kinship group and their hierarchical relationships on the basis of opening or closing the groups involved in marriages. To marry far or near is the principal element of competition between groups; another aspect is the manipulation of violence (Bonte, 1998).

It is true that the masculine definition of solidarities (*'asabiyat*) implies some egalitarian view of these solidarities and their extension to a part of society along the line of genealogy: the tribe is fictitiously a group of patrilateral relatives (*awlad 'amm*). But men are equals because they share common rights over women and not by virtue of genealogical position. Genealogy does not have the same function in Arab representations and Nuer society!

In Arab representations, genealogy is a classification which establishes hierarchy, first in Louis Dumont's sense of this term, a principle by which the elements of a whole are ranked in relation to this whole (Louis Dumont, p. 104), but secondly, along quite different lines, hierarchical social relations. In Saharan societies, for example, tribes are organized in different 'orders':

- *hasan* denotes 'Arab' warriors, founders of the emirates.
- *zawaya* denote administrators of the sacred and of Muslim affairs.
- *znaga* are 'Berbers', tributaries, pastoralists and farmers.

Maghreb and Sahara

Genealogy appears to play an important role in these distinctions. In fact, it is a political ideology related to the historical transformation of Berber-cognatic society into an Arab-agnatic one, between the 14th and 16th centuries. The family of one emirate[8] founded by a Berber-*lamtuna* family is now considered *'Arab*, a term referring to status and honour more than to genealogical considerations.

In other places, the Maghreb for example, egalitarian representations seem to take precedence over hierarchical ones. Gellner (1969) thinks that this 'egalitarianism' is a specific feature of these Maghreban tribal societies, which is characteristic of the model of segmentary lineage societies. On the contrary, I think that this egalitarianism is not structural, but a conjunctural feature. Other authors, criticizing Gellner, have underlined the intense competition of the *'asabiyat,* solidarity groups, in these Maghreban societies and the rank differences, which are the result of this competition: the role the manipulation of violence plays is particularly noted by Hammoudi (1974) and Jamous (1981). In fact, in this competitive opposition model, social relations are based on the challenge, expressed generally in terms of honour, to affirm difference, particularly of rank and status. They are also based on the development of matrimonial and political strategies, in short on a genealogical competition, which affects individuals and groups, in particular agnatically related individuals and groups. As a result, the agnatic solidarities of the *'asabiyat* are, as Ibn Khaldun correctly saw, the locus of competition inducing progressive re-elaborations of identities and differences across centuries.

Ibn Khaldun not only expresses native representations but also attempts to produce explanatory categories to expound them. The notion of cycle can thus be seen as a translation of these competitive opposition rules. Regularly, new lines establish their power at the local level, enlarge their alliances, create new solidarities at tribal and regional levels (these *'asabiyat al-kubra,* i. e. superior *'asabiyat,* of which Ibn Khaldun speaks) and take over the central power, the *makhzan*[9] in the Maghreban terms, founding new dynasties. This is, in fact, the framework of Maghreb history for the last 10 centuries.

This analysis, however, leaves one important problem unresolved: the perennial nature of the *makhzan,* the State, in spite of territorial and historic changes. Gellner's theory offers one solution to this problem. The constitution of the central state is submitted to the same rules of equilibrium of power as between the segmentary egalitarian groups of the tribe. These rules define power as a power of conciliation, of arbitration. The same principle explains the nature of the central state, according to M. Morsy (1984), and the local functions of power of the Saints of the Atlas that Gellner studied (1969).

However, examination of the Saharan political situation raises questions about Gellner's analysis. The Moorish emirates are not based on arbitration, but clearly on social hierarchy. They organize and centralize status differences between tribes, and they contribute to fix these status differences in a system of order analogous to that of the Greek *polis* or the Roman *urbs,* legitimated here by genealogical differences. Between these orders relations of protection are established. So *znaga,* tributaries, formerly Berbers, do not carry arms and depend on 'Arab' warriors for protection: symbolically, tribute is called *hurma,* a term that underlines the differences of honour capital between the two groups. *Znaga* are also collectively called *lahma,* a term formed from an Arabic root which gives also *luhma*, cognatic kinship. As in the matrimonial alliance policies, *znaga* are also wife-givers, but without reciprocity: they are in a way feminized and protected as a man protects his family.

In the Moorish emirates, by contrast to the Maghreb, there is no territorial and political contradiction between *makhzan* (the state) and the *sayba* (dissidence, or chaos). Dissidence, which often results in the exile of individuals or tribes in these nomadic societies, is more clearly here a structural feature of power. The permanence of the emirates over two or three centuries is thus in apparent contradiction with the relative instability of political life, particularly at the time of strong conflicts for the emir's succession (Bonte, 1982)

State and Tribes

In the light of this comparison between the Maghreb and the Sahara, we can re-examine the fourth aspect of Ibn Khaldun's analysis of dynastic cycles regarding relations between state and tribes. The egalitarian aspect of the Maghreban tribes is, principally, the consequence, illusory in part, of the stabilization of power inside the *makhzan*, the state. Competition and resulting conflicts are transferred to the periphery of the state and determine the opposition between the *makhzan* and *sayba*. This opposition and the egalitarian aspects of the tribe express the state's capacity to manipulate the tribal structure, particularly conflicts and violent relations inside the tribes and between them. The genealogical ideology of *shurafa'*, the *qayd* system, [10] creating intermediaries between state and tribe, and the general allegiance (*bay'a*) of men and tribes to the sovereign, are also important elements of the political system.

But in fact, to take on an aspect of perenniality, the state must also integrate some dimensions and values of *nasab* and *'asabiya*. The rituals of power, although generally ignored by anthropologists (with some exceptions, such as Combs-Schilling, 1989 and, recently, Tozy, 1999), express this demand. In Morocco, the Sharifian dynasties, Sa'dians and 'Alawites, have progressively elaborated a series of rituals related to familial and tribal values. The solemn commemoration of the Prophet's birthday, the Mawlid, emphasizes the *nasab* of the Sharifian Dynasty. During the 'Eid al-Kabir, the sovereign appears as the first sacrificer of the Kingdom, giving the signal for sacrifices in all the kingdom-households. He is thus the first of the family-heads, repeating the sacrifices of his ancestors, Muhammad and Ibrahim. Even more notable is the marriage ritual: during the ceremony, the groom is called the Sultan and is treated as the sovereign. This marriage ritual expresses the symbolic competition between ruler and ruled, the fact that the man who participates in power through allegiance (*bay'a*) is also a sovereign in his family. The transformation of marriage rituals in contemporary Morocco, parallel to the constitutional evolution of the monarchy, expresses the transition from the masculine relationship of the *bay'a* to the gender-undifferentiated relationship of the 'subject'. This transformation has been approved by King Hassan II on the occasion of his daughters' marriages, which were very unusually transmitted by television inside the king's palace. The central feature – the ceremony of the feminine ritual of seven dresses – and the reduced role of the groom, underlines a kind of feminization of the ritual and of the king's subjects (Azizi, 1998).

In spite of this kind of patrimonalization of the state, Ibn Khaldun's notion of dynastic cycle remains relevant in the Moroccan case. The last attempt to create a new dynasty was the peripheral Saharan movement of Shaykh al-Hiba ibn Shaykh Ma' al-'Aynayn, 'the Blue Sultan of the French', in the 1920s. The weakening of the 'Alawite dynasty due to French colonization, and the loss of the religious legitimacy resulting from this foreign invasion, was the beginning of this movement: Shaykh al-Hiba proclaimed himself as Sultan in Marrakesh but his dynastic claim was victoriously opposed by the colonial troops. But is this still, even today, relevant? The fact that, during the independence struggle, the *Glawi*, a *qayd*, regional notable, attempted to assemble the mountain tribes of the Atlas, suggests that it is still a conceivable claim. I think it is difficult to pre-judge the present succession of Hassan II, a charismatic sovereign in spite of constitutional transformation. The situation of states and the difficult familial succession of kings and presidents in the Middle East illustrates the same situation and illustrates Ibn Khaldun's analysis – as does the history of the Arab Muslim dynasties. The notion of the *dawla*, which emerges during the Umawid/'Abbasid periods initially has the meaning of 'taking turns' or 'my turn', before it becomes the term designating the State.

The absence of rules of succession is a general feature of the Arab-Muslim dynasties. Elsewhere I have discussed the same phenomenon in the Moorish emirates (Bonte, 1982). Power is localized in an agnatic line but internal struggles between the sons and brothers of the deceased emir are constant and murderous. Upon the death of emir Ahmad 'Ayda in 1861, six of his sons and one of his brothers were killed. It was finally his grandson, Ahmad uld Mhamed, who succeeded him 10 years after the emir's death. In the Khaldunian terminology, the Moors call this period 'the time of weakness of Ahl 'Uthman' (the name of the dynastic line). There is no rule of succession because competition is stronger among the agnates than among other relatives, who are excluded from the emiral *nasab*. But it is in fact in the field of cognatic kinship, expanded to political alliances, that these conflicts of succession are finally regulated.

Ibn Khaldun's Present-day Validity

It is perhaps time to break with the apologetic exegesis of Ibn Khaldun's quasi-anthropological expression of social representations of his epoch, for it is only *partially* valid to understand current tribal and political order. In the light of my field data from the Moorish experience, specifically the Adrar emirate in the north of present-day Mauritania, I disagree with him on two points.

Religion and Dynastic State

First, Ibn Khaldun gives particular and quasi-exclusive importance to the religious dimension of state power. From his point of view, religious values are essential for the establishment and perenniality of the dynastic state. It was probably the result of his personal knowledge of Maghreb history, with the notable exception of the Marinid dynasty (Hamès, 1991). The example of Moorish emirates underlines that the religious dimension is not an absolute historical regularity in Muslim state power. Not only is the origin of the emirate dynasties localized in the warrior-*hassan* order but, in particular, it is the result of conflict between *hassan* political ambitions and the attempts by the *zawaya*, the French 'marabouts', to build a theocratic, Mahdist-inspired state in the south of Mauritania and in Senegal during the second half of the 17th century.[11] The *zawaya*, administrators of the sacred and of Muslim culture, remained opposed to the political power of *hassan* which they characterized as *sayba*, i.e. dissidence or anarchy, and not as *makhzan*, i.e. Muslim state. They particularly condemned unjust taxes levied on Muslims, i.e. tributes justified by protection, and the fact that the rights to collect tribute were transferred exclusively between men, excluding women, contrary to Muslim law – a transfer which is consistent with the exclusively masculine capacity to give protection.

Agnatic Ideology

The other point on which I disagree with Ibn Khaldun's analysis is the importance that he concedes to the agnatic ideology of *nasab* and *'asabiya*, neglecting, probably for political reasons, the function of matrimonial alliance. He properly establishes the 'natural' character of *silat al-arham*, cognatic kinship, but forgets, or unconsciously masks, the social and political characters of these cognatic relationships.

I use first the term 'alliance' in the precise anthropological sense of matrimonial alliance. I have discussed the role of matrimonial alliance in gender-structured Arabic society elsewhere (Bonte, 1991b; 1994 a; 1994b); what follows is a summary of my earlier publications. The 'Arab marriage' between parallel patrilateral cousins, children of brothers, is only one form of marital policy in these societies. It is a normative form of marriage between close relatives that corresponds to the ideal of equality and quasi-identity of husband and wife, and which expresses the masculine agnatic ideology. But there are also other forms of matrimonial practices. They reintroduce feminine values and the hierarchical effects of these values, arising in particular from the rule prohibiting feminine hypogamy (marriage with a social inferior). In assuming the 'risk' of distant marriage from the point of view of consanguinity or status, people affirm their differences and open the field of competition. These differences, as I have already indicated, are conceived as the management of the human and matrimonial capital of the solidarity group also conceived in terms of honour: the sexual integrity of women and the physical integrity of the men of the group. These values are directly related to the tribal conception of power in the Moorish emirate.

The organization of Moorish emirate society makes obvious the continuity between marital policies, their hierarchical effects and the political order. Women circulate between orders hierarchically, but without reciprocity (Bonte, 1991b): the wife-givers are of a lower level. Within the orders, the balance of reciprocal circulation of women signifies at once the equal ranks of the different groups. The *qisma* alliance, implying the sharing of matrimonial access to women, of war-booty and of blood payments, creates new solidarities and enlarges the range of the alliance. In this context, wife-givers can become husband-takers, reinforcing the demographic and military potential of the tribe: such is the case of Awlad Qaylan, which I have studied in *al-Ansab* (Bonte, 1991b).

Generally, there is a strong continuity between marital policies and political alliances. I use the term 'factions' to refer to unstable alliances established to pursue political objectives. In Moorish emirates, the localization of the political title (*amir*) in the emiral line and strong tribal stratification define the nature and objective of factionalism (Bonte, 1997). It is a large system of alliance and clientship, which is related to the exercise of emiral power. This system is manipulated in part by emirs as a result of the redistribution of the *bayt al-mal*, mainly tribute and taxes. It is at the moment of succession that the system is particularly active and unstable: the alliances are progressively re-organized around two claimants, and if the result is an equilibrium, the conflict is strong and long, as in the case of the succession of Ahmad 'Ayda. But factional conflicts continue during the emir's reign, resulting in a structural situation of dissidence and exile (*zowga*), which is an expression of political competition in this nomadic and pastoral society. The core of these factional alliances is the matrilateral and affinal network of each claimant; networks enlarged by the network of similar relationships of the military leader of factions and their warrior clients (Bonte, 1997).

This dual opposition – *makhzan* versus *sayba*, emiral power versus dissidence – is, I would argue, a general feature of the political order in these tribal societies. Anthropologists have not correctly identified this feature. The only exception is Chelhod (1965), who puts it improperly in terms of the 'dualist organization' of the Bedouins. Chelhod studies these dual alliance systems in different points in the Middle East, including sometimes not only tribes, but also peasants and town dwellers. We can also evoke the Maghreban *leff* and *soff* [12] systems (Montagne, 1930). This old system of dual alliances, transcending genealogies and tribes, declined and almost disappeared during the French colonization. They were particularly developed in the *sayba* zone (the Moroccan Sus, the Rif, Kabylie), founding a political order, managing tribal competition and stabilizing the social order outside the immediate intervention of the *makhzan*.

The study of the political organization of the emirate reveals another general feature of the political order: the gender structuration of social representations and practices. In Moorish emirates, the *hella*, the emiral camp, is a true nomadic capital, including more than 100 tents, where climatic and pastoral conditions are favourable. The *hella* includes the leaders of the faction supporting the emir, clients, blacksmiths, poets and musicians, and also the mares, which belong exclusively to the emiral line. Like all nomadic camps, the *hella* is the symbol and the practical focus of masculine authority. To constitute a distinct *hella* was a manifestation of dissidence and a veritable declaration of war against the present emir. To constitute a separate *hella* in honour of one of his sons was the sign of the emir's choice of his successor, although in practice, this often was not respected.

Conversely, the tent is a symbol of feminine values, but it also has an important role in political representations and practices. This appears in several levirate marriages [13] in the emiral line on the occasion of difficult successions. The wife-mother in favour of the son/nephew thus settles the conflict for succession between the agnatic uncle – the *levir* – and his nephew. The symbolic occupation of the emiral tent by the brother or the son recalls the importance of the feminine dimension of emiral power: it is men who circulate between the tents of their mothers and wives. The tent is also a sanctuary and a symbol of protection. In other representations, women play another important political roles, for example, it is only women who beat war drums, another major symbol of emiral power.

In conclusion, I have argued that reading Ibn Khaldun's works as a reflection both of and on the social categories of the tribal and political society of his epoch is not only fascinating in its own right but provides valuable insights for the anthropologist who seeks to analyse more recent similar societies. Nonetheless, a key element is missing from this work: the role of matrimonial alliance and gender representations. Partly unconsciously, it has been the hidden dimension of the social organization from the point of view of the masculine ideology – and perhaps consciously as well, given the danger of exposing the ultimate motive of the masculine exercise of power. The *Kitab al-'Ibar* being completed, Ibn Khaldun, an experienced political man, left Tunis immediately and took refuge in Cairo.

Notes

1. This quotation from Ibn Khaldun is translated by V. Monteil, *Ibn Khaldun*, 1967–68.
2. At the time of Umawid and 'Abbasid dynasties particularly, see for example the works of al-Qutayba.
3. That is to say, the analysis of kinship terms in the exclusive field of consanguinity (and affinity), defined by genealogical (filiative) relationships, as Lewis Henri Morgan, the founder of anthropological kinship theory, first propounded.
4. I examine a similar situation in contemporary Moorish society (Bonte, 1991a); see also Conte, 1994a.
5. To marry his patrilateral parallel cousin.
6. Particularly in the Malekite school of law.
7. As is described by E. E. Evans-Pritchard in the Nuer Case and used by E. Gellner to analyse the Maghreban Berber-tribe system.
8. The Tagant emirate was founded at the end of the 18th century, after the Arabic emirates.
9. The 'state' in Maghreban terminology.
10. *Qayds* are tribal notables invested with this title by the *Makhzan* to regulate the relations between tribes and state.
11. This political-religious movement is the first of a succession of *jihad*-revolutions in West Africa, particularly in pulaar-speaking populations.
12. The *leff* is a formal system of alliance, carrying on from generation to generation and subject to regular adjustments, which establishes across a large territory of the Maghreb an alternative local social organization. These do not follow genealogical tribal affiliations, but cut across them, opposing, in the very heart of the tribe, a fraction, a line of descent, even a family, to kin groups in the agnatic line, thus inscribing them in this new dual system whose outcome is a certain local political equilibrium transcending tribal values. The *soff*, on the other hand, is another form of inter-tribal alliance implicating families and personal relationships and no descent groups and tribes as such.
13. Marriage between a man and the wife of his deceased brother.

References

Azizi, S., 'Cérémonies de mariage en changement dans le Grand-Agadir (Sous, Maroc)', *Thèse de doctorat d'ethnologie et anthropologie sociale*, Paris: EHESS, 1998.

Bonte, P., 'Tribus, factions, Etat, les conflits de succession dans l'émirat de l'Adrar', *Cahiers d'Etudes Africaines*, Vol XXII, Nos. 3–4, 1982, pp 489–516.

——'Ramages maures', *Journal des Africanistes*, Vol. 55 , Nos. 1–2, 1985, pp. 39–52.

——'Egalité et hiérarchie dans une tribu maure, les Awlad Qaylan de l'Adrar mauritanien' in P. Bonte, E. Conte, C. Hamès et Abdel Wedoud ould Cheikh, *al-Ansab, La quête des origins, Anthropologie historique de la société tribale arabe*, Paris: Editions de la Maison des Sciences de l'Homme, 1991a, pp. 145–99.

——'Alliance et rang dans la société maure. Les fonctions du mariage arabe', in F. Héritier-Augé et E. Copet-Rougier (ed.), *Les complexités de l'alliance II. Les systémes complexes d'alliance matrimoniale*, Paris: Editions des archives contemporaines, 1991b, pp. 29–60.

——*Epouser au plus proche, Inceste, prohibitions et stratégies matrimoniales autour de la Méditerranée*, Paris: EHESS, 1994a.

——'Les risques de l'alliance. Solidarités masculines et valeurs féminines dans la société maure' in F. Héritier et E. Copet-Rougier (ed), *Les complexités de l'alliance IV. Economie, politique et fondements symboliques*, Paris: Editions des archives contemporaines, 1994b, pp. 107–42.

——'La constitution de l'émirat de l'Adrar. Essai sur les formations politiques tribales', *Maghreb Review*, Vol 22, Nos. 1–2, 1997, pp. 40–54.

——'L'émirat de l'Adrar. Histoire et anthropologie d'une société tribale du Sahara occidental', *Thèse de doctorat d'Etat*, Paris, l'EHESS, 1998.

Chelhod, J., 'Les structures dualistes de la société bédouine', *L'Homme*, Vol. 9, 1965, pp. 89–112.

Combs-Schilling, M. E., *Sacred Performance: Islam, Sexuality and Sacrifice*, New York: Columbia University Press, 1989.

Conte, E., 'Entrer dans le rang: Perceptions arabes des origines', in P. Bonte, E. Conte, C. Hamès et Abdel Wedoud ould Cheikh, *al-Ansab. La quête des origines. Anthropologie historique de la société tribale arabe*, Paris, Editions de la Maison des Sciences de l'Homme, 1994a, pp. 55–99.

——'Le pacte, la parenté et le Prophète. Réflexions sur la proximité parentale dans la tradition arabe' in F. Héritier et E. Copet-Rougier (eds.), *Les complexités de l'alliance IV. Economie, politique et fondements symboliques*, Paris: Editions des Archives contemporaines, 1994b, pp. 143–85.

Dumont, Louis, *Homo Hierarchicus*, Palladin, 1970.

Gellner, E., *The Saints of the Atlas*, Chicago: Chicago University Press, 1969.

Hamès, C., 'La filiation généalogique (*nasab*) dans la société d'Ibn Khaldun', *L'Homme*, Vol. 102, 1987, pp. 99–118.

——'De la chefferie tribale à la dynastie étatique: généalogie et pouvoir à l'époque almohado-hafside (XII°–XIV° siècles)', in P. Bonte, E. Conte, C. Hamès et Abdel Wedoud ould Cheikh, *al-Ansab, La quête des origines. Anthropologie historique de la société tribale arabe*, Paris: Editions de la Maison des Sciences de l'Homme, 1991, pp. 101–137.

Hammoudi, A., 'Segmentarité, stratification sociale, pouvoir politique et sainteté', *Hespéris-Talmuda*, Vol XV, 1974, pp. 156–60.

Ibn Khaldun, *Discours sur l'histoire universelle*, translated by V. Monteil, Paris: Sindbad, 3 vols, 1967–68.

——*Peuples et nations du monde*, Extracts from the *'Ibar*, translated from the Arabic and introduced by A. Cheddadi, Paris: Sindbad, 1986.

Jamous, R., *Honneur et baraka. Les structures sociales traditionnelles dans le Rif*, Cambridge and Paris: Cambridge University Press et Editions de la Maison des Sciences de l'Homme, 1981.

Lacoste, Y., *Ibn Khaldoun, naissance de l'histoire. Passé du Tiers-Monde*, Paris: Maspéro, 1966.

Montagne, R., *Les Berbères et le Makhzen dans le sud du Maroc*, Paris: Alcan, 1930.

Morsy, M., *North Africa: 1800–1900*, London: Longman, 1984.

Tozy, M., *Monarchie et Islam politique au Maroc*, Paris: Presses de la Fondation Nationale des Sciences Politiques, 1999.

PART TWO

Totalitarianism and Tribalism: The Ba'th Regime and Tribes

Sheikhs and Ideologues: Deconstruction and Reconstruction of Tribes under Patrimonial Totalitarianism in Iraq, 1968–1998

Faleh A. Jabar

The reconstruction and manipulation of tribes and tribalism have become prominent features in recent Middle Eastern politics, notably in Jordan and Iraq.

This chapter studies the reconstruction of tribes in Iraq under the Ba'th totalitarian regime. This reconstruction has, mistakenly, been taken either as one undifferentiated process, or as a novel phenomenon relevant to the 1990s.[1] Our argument here is against this kind of reductionist approach. Such conceptions confuse various processes of different and contradictory nature, or overlook the fact that the tribal factor has been politically and socially in operation for a longer span of time, even before the advent of Ba'th to power in 1968. Reconstruction/deconstruction of tribes took various forms. Two major patterns have developed under the Ba'th; one may be termed as etatist tribalism and the other as social tribalism. In the transition from one to the other, a third, minor, pattern of military and ideological tribalism has also developed. These various patterns have their roots in cultural tribalism, the urban social space where migrant segments of disintegrating tribes and clans have persisted.

Tribal Domains

Etatist tribalism is a process in which tribal lineages, symbolic and fictive primordial systems and cultures are integrated into the state so as to enhance the political power of a certain fragile and vulnerable state elite. In this process the elite enhances itself as the determining force controlling the state in and for itself, in its capacity as a regulative agency. Thus, etatist tribalism is focused on the state itself, relating the state to itself by itself. It is also exclusive in nature, in the sense that it is focused on certain Arab, Sunni clans and groups related to the elite itself. The process stems from a deep crisis of the Iraqi state system, which lacked the adequate legitimizing, participatory, inclusive and integrative mechanisms necessary for stable governance and nation building. Etatist tribalism went through various phases from 1968 on and reached its peak in the late 1980s and early 1990s. Together with other factors, it contributed to the enhancement of a patrimonial totalitarian state.

Social tribalism, by contrast, signifies a new turn in the development of the totalitarian system in which this regime lost much of its potency to govern a growing, restless mass urban society. Contrary to the etatist pattern, social tribalism stems partly from the resilience of cultural tribalism, and partly is manipulated or designed to strengthen state versus society. It involves a legalized devolution of power by the state to reviving and/or reconstructing tribal or kin segments on a local level, denoting the de facto withdrawal of the state from such 'normal' areas as judicial functions, tax collection, enforcement of law and order. This spread or devolvement of state authority to extraneous social centres of power is anchored in a new hierarchical power structure with reconstructing tribal and clannish groups acting as an extension of the state itself. Contrary to etatist tribalism, this pattern was, broadly, spread across the communal and ethnic divide.

The transition from etatist to social tribalism was marked by a third minor pattern of military-ideological tribalism, in which Shi'ite and Kurdish tribal groups were, spontaneously or otherwise, mobilized to meet an external threat during the Iraq-Iran war, 1980–88. In those years, additional combat manpower was needed as much as were cultural markers: the former to stem the human waves of Iranian soldiers, the latter to override any potential communal uniformity among Shi'ites on both sides of the ethnic divide. But this was a minor, temporary pattern, confined to some Kurdish and Shi'ite tribes.

To discuss these aspects of social and political processes, we should first dwell on the meaning of the tribe, or the mutation of tribes and tribalism in the Iraqi context. Second, we shall examine the context and structure of etatist tribalism. Third, we shall analyse the context, nature and tensions inherent in social tribalism. Lastly, some mediocre generalizations on state-tribe and society-tribe correlations will be discussed.

Tribes and Powers: Mutation Beyond Recognition

The tribe is perhaps the oldest, most enduring and controversial social entity in the Middle East. From the rise of literate, centralizing polities in the agrarian epoch, down to the era of industrialism and nation-states, the tribe has sustained incessant change, acting in and reacting to a changing political, military, economic and at times even topographical environment. The extent of this change has been so great and so diverse that it has defied any meaningful and applicable generalization as to what the tribe has come to be. Hence the term 'tribe', and with it a host of other terms such as tribalism, *badu* (nomads), *hadhar* (urbans), *fakhd* (sub-clan), *hamoula*, *sheikh* and *dira*, may well denote various patterns of organization, actors, leadership patterns, economic functions and socio-political structures. One indication of the dilemma is the controversy as to the definition of the term 'tribe', or the controversy over whether or not the mode of political development of the tribe was cyclical or lineal, from the simple to the complex,[2] or the debate on the difference between tribes and tribalism.[3]

Ibn Khaldun

We need to turn to the 13th-century sociologist Ibn Khaldun and his theory. In the Khaldunian tradition we may derive a classical concept of the tribe as a self-contained social organization based on lineage and imbued with autonomy, having social, economic, political, military and cultural functions. This classical category was the *differentia specifica* of the agrarian epoch, or the pre-industrial age. In this era, the Khaldunian dichotomy of pastoralism and agriculturism presents two antagonistic and complementary modes of existence: one revolving around nomads organized in tribes, the other on sacred empires anchored in central city-states. A dynamic equilibrium existed between the two wherein nomadic warriors, united by *'asabiya* (solidarity), would conquer centres of civilization and assume power for a period, but then disintegrate within the walls of the city. He saw this confrontation between *hadhara* (civilization) and *badawa* (nomadism), as the essence of human existence.[4] To him, tribes had their meaning only in contradistinction to the city, or city-state. These two poles lived in an uneasy tension, a dynamic symbiosis known as the Khaldunian cycle. Briefly, this Khaldunian cycle runs as follows: tribes had superiority over the city in military terms. By dint of weak division of labour, all male adults are de facto warriors. They are fearless because they are free of government, and their very means of subsistence, based on camel or horse breeding, are the very instruments of their mobile force backed by a vast manpower. By dint of their *'asabiya* and religious fervour, they form a formidable force and invade and seize the city.[5]

The moment the city is seized, it sets in motion counter-mechanisms to absorb and dissolve the tribe, which has already mutated into an *'asabiya*-bound ruling military aristocracy: by dint of superior wealth and ramified division of labour, the city changes the nature of nomadic invaders, ignites rivalries among them over the political power and distribution of wealth and causes continuous fission and schisms in their ranks. In three generations, the city urbanizes the tribe, which loses its cohesion and succumbs to final decay. And since this decay of mechanical solidarity is irreparable, a new and intact tribal group steps in to set the scene for a new cycle of conquest-decay.[6]

Ibn Khaldun considered this an eternal regularity. His observations did apply more or less to vast areas in the region. But, paradoxically, Ibn Khaldun exempted historical Iraq (Mesopotamia) from his theory.

In his words, Iraq was the land of *'ulooj* (peasants or settled agricultural communities) and *dahma* (city dwellers) guarded by strong Persian and Roman (and later Arab) legions and castles. A host of historical changes turned this world upside down. The Mongol invasion in 1258 destroyed the centre of the empire in Baghdad. By intent or neglect, the Mongols, themselves nomads, caused the destruction of the developed irrigation system, and topographical change led to desertification. The collapse of the empire weakened the political central authority, and desertification weakened settled agricultural communities. Finally, the incessant migration of and invasions by nomads from Arabia, Anatolia and Persia, turned the historical territories of Iraq into a Khaldunian land. This process is known in the sociological literate as *al-Mad al-Badawi*, (the Bedouin tide).[7]

Thus the Khaldunian cycle extended its validity to Iraq at least from the 13th century onward.

Inner Structure and Hierarchies

Before the advent of modernization under the reign of the Ottoman governor Medhet Pasha (1869–72), tribes retained much of their inherited solid inner structures. Each strong tribe was a miniature mobile state, with its patriarchal headship usually held by a warrior household; its own military force; its customary law, which was preserved by the *'arfa* (literally, 'the knowledgeable', actually tribal jurists or adjudicators); its non-literate culture; its territoriality in the form of *dira* (tribal pastures) or, later, arable lands; and its mode of subsistence economy, i.e. pastoralism, commerce and conquest. Exacting tribute (protection money) was as important for their livelihood as animal breeding, or the spoils of war. Their existence, however, was as fragile any life

73

could be on account of inter-tribal wars, government campaigns and the mercy of nature.

The *qabila* (tribe) is usually the larger unit, whose affiliated clans claim to have a common lineage or descent. As these clans live apart, the unity of the tribe (or of tribal confederations, for that matter) is very loose and informal in military or political terms. Only external hazards lend them a *raison d'être*.

The *'ashira* (clan) is the second level of organization. It has this unity of purpose, thanks to the unifying role played by the sheikh (or his house) and to the territorial proximity of the various sub-clans (*fakhdh* or *afkhadh*) of which it is composed. The *afkhad* are the third level, the basic units in productive terms: they organize pastures, own sources of water and have a strong sense of territoriality. The *fakhdh* is formed, in turn, from smaller patrilineal groups, extended families called the *hamoula*, which lead a real common life and constitute the real kinship group; but each *hamoula* is again divided into small households, or *bait*. As some anthropological studies have shown, the first two (the tribe and the clan) were political and military units, while the last three were economic, camping and housing units. Leadership was reserved to the outstanding *hamoula* of the strongest *fakhdh* in each clan, while the strongest clan provided the headship of the tribe. In the case of a pan-tribal confederation emerging, the strongest tribe held the *sheikh al-mashayikh* position.[8]

A system of hierarchy developed among tribes relative to their varying numerical size and military prowess. The hierarchical stratification is marked by or embedded in differences in modes of subsistence, with the *ahl al-ibl* (camel breeding tribes) at the top, the *shawiya* (sheep breeder) just below, the *Harratha* or *filalih* (tillers or peasants) down lower, and the *mi'dan* (marsh dwellers who raise buffalo) at the bottom of the scale. The camel breeders had superior mobility and superior fighting techniques and abilities. They regarded non-camel tribes and clans with disdain.[9] In a word, they were the masters and viewed themselves as such. When sedentary agriculture prevailed, another hierarchy developed placing rice planters at the helm, with *khudhairi* (vegetable growers) and manual artisans at the bottom. Intermarriage was prohibited or abhorred.[10]

Such profession-linked hierarchies differed from one country to another, and each case had its own peculiar arrangements.

Tribal confederations of tens of thousands of warriors emerged under the Mameluke phase of Ottoman rule. In that Hobbesian world of the war of all against all, weaker tribes sought security through alliances with larger entities.[11]

Some tribes developed political structures and turned into emirates (principalities) with an organized (partly standing) military power, others had strong sheikhs.[12] Titles like Sheikh, Agha, Emir and Imam, for example, denoted the absence or development of different modes of embryonic political structures.

In the period under consideration, a precarious and bloody equilibrium between tribes and cities existed. Beyond a handful of cities, some solid, some fragile, tribes ruled supreme in their domains or even beyond them. Nine tenths of Iraq's territories were controlled by various formidable tribal confederations who controlled communication systems and trade routes.[13] The strength of tribes may be understood from the population census figures in the late 19th and early 20th centuries, in the three *wilayats* (governorates) of Iraq.[14] Cities accounted for only 9 per cent of the population. The numerical superiority of the nomadic, semi-settled and sedentary tribes, it should be remembered, were augmented by the fact that adult tribesmen were generally armed, whereas urban centres had for their protection only quarter-based armed gangs, or thinly manned Ottoman garrisons. In both cases, city walls were a symbol of both vulnerability and security.[15]

Mutation

Under the 'terrible' Ottomans, as Gellner puts it,[16] the Khaldunian cycle came to a halt. This was largely due to the existence of a relatively stable central power, but, more importantly, the Ottomans entered the era of gunpowder, which in relative terms tilted the power relations between the city and the tribes. However, the actual process of decay began during the reign of Medhet Pasha.

Two forces, the modern central state and the market economy, triggered processes which changed the tribe beyond recognition. These processes were initiated by the Ottomans in the 1870s, but continued vigorously under the British Mandate and the monarchy they installed (1921–58).

A general view of this process runs as follows:

During the Mameluke period ending in 1831, larger tribal confederations were developed and encouraged. As a political device, it was easier to deal with fewer centres of power, in order to keep security, sustain a reasonable level of trade and protect small city-states from recurrent tribal incursions. The tribes were not vassals *vis-à-vis* the Mamelukes, but were equals among equals. When the Ottoman Sublime Porte brought about the demise of the Mamelukes, this policy was reversed.[17] A ramified system of central administration was introduced, backed by fast and reliable communication and transportation systems (telegraph lines, steamboats and, later on, railways). In the framework of the *Tanzimat*, land tenure was re-organized.[18] Tribes were encouraged to embrace sedentary agriculture, or settle in newly created mercantile towns, as was the case with Suq al-Sheyukh, or Nassiriya, established respectively by Sheikh Thuwaini and the Sa'doon house (*bayt*) of the Muntafiq confederation in the 19th century.[19] By adopting sedentary agriculture, larger confederations lost their sense as military alliances and dissolved as a result of fierce competition over land and water.

Warrior chieftains (sheikhs and *aghas*) were turned into tax farmers. It was the camel-breeding chieftains who could now impose their will on the weaker tribes, the sheep-breeders and land tillers, turning them into semi-serf peasants, thus mutating the military hierarchy into a social and economic hegemony. Hitherto, *ahl al-Ibl* imposed their tribute on weaker tribes and exacted them directly. Under the Ottomans, however, the tribute was transformed into tax farming. The change was not purely economical but rather political. It denoted a political shift in power relations, whereby tribes recognized central power, and collected the tax on its behalf. This created mutual interdependence and transformed the nature of tribal chieftains from independent warriors into tax collectors or state vassals, better still agents. A further development was the introduction of forms of possession and/or ownership of communal land.

Whenever this new economic-military power was imposed on alien, weak and lower (or debased by tribal norms) tribes, the lines of tribal division in the 20th century developed into antagonistic social divide of the landed and landless. Wherever the new landlord-peasant relationship was imposed by the strongest on the weaker sub-clans of the same tribe, the patriarchal unity of the tribe collapsed, yet common lineage and culture relatively cushioned the new social divide.[20]

In both cases, the newly transformed sheikh-landlord introduced a military force independent of the tribe, the *zilim* (armed men) or *hoshiya* (deterrence force) to enforce his will. These changes were institutionalized and constitutionalized[21] in the Land Settlement Law and Law For the Rights and Duties of Cultivators enacted in 1933. This was further consolidated by the exclusion of Iraq's countryside from the jurisdiction of national laws and judiciary system. Down to 1958, the Law of Tribal Disputes reigned.

Parallel to this line of development, the state, developing its bureaucracy, military and educational system, gradually took away the various, military, economic, judicial powers of the tribe: from registration of land to ownership rights, water distribution, law enforcement and monopoly of means of violence, the state imposed its supremacy.

The pattern of tribal leadership sustained constant change. Powerful *ahl al-Ibl* tribal sheikhs developed into landowners, and weak tribesmen into peasants. The sheikh emerged into either a powerful absentee landlord, or into a small or medium land owner who could barely cope with economic change, i.e. the decline of agriculture and the concomitant migration of peasants.[22] His allies, the *sayyid* or Sufi notables, who represented the authority of the sacred inside the tribe, lost their status with the advance of learning.[23] The decay was completed by the agrarian reform which destroyed the power base of sheikhly landlords and their vassals, the *sirkals* (village stewards).

Thus did the 19th-century tribes and tribal confederations disappear altogether as a self-contained social organization. In their stead, the *dira* and the *hamoula* retained part of their vitality as economic and residential units. These communities might still hold their tribal name, although the name could not any more denote what the tribe is or was. The *hamoula* and *dira* signify, in fact, the basic socio-economic unit in the structure of the 'classical' tribe. But the new 'agrarian *hamoula*' is linked to the 'market' rather than to subsistence economy, and has various patterns of organization: the hamoula may claim common lineage with specific tribal name, or may be formed of heterogeneous segments linked by common residence and intermarriage. They may also develop informal patterns of social authority in which some former and weakened sheikh or *sirkal* may play a part.

All in all, these communities were based on either lineage or intermarriage, common residence or a combination of any two of these, coupled with collective economic interests and mutual social support. These village collectivities provided individuals and families with social, economic and cultural safety nets. They also preserved their cultural traits and organized interaction with urban influences. Yet, they did not escape erosion. Perhaps the American anthropologist Robert Fernea grasped this reality when he depicted the cultural duality of the peasant villages:

> As a fledgling cultural anthropologist, I lived and conducted research from 1956 until 1958 in a tribal settlement on the edge of the small town of the Daghara, on a bifurcation of the Euphrates near the provincial capital of Diwaniyyah. My view of life in southern Iraq is based on a fairly good knowledge of a small community, whose lives were caught up in two very different but interesting ways of coping with the struggles of daily existence. One way was through government bureaucracies, to which they were obliged to go for certifications of birth and death, registration of land, identity cards, medical care, irrigation water, to enroll their children in school, to lodge complaints and receive punishment. The other part of their lives centred around the shared understandings of tribal knowledge and practices-identities ascribed by genealogical descent, hierarchies which were constantly contested, preoccupations of peacemaking and revenge, obligations to each other based on marriages and common blood. These two different ways of thinking and acting, the ways of the state versus those

of the tribe, involved the same people in very different discourses of power and knowledge. The struggle between these two ways of organizing and thinking about the world was still part of everyday Iraqi life in the 1950s.[24]

The *dira* or *hamoula* spirit dwells in rural areas, but gradually creeps into adjacent towns and larger cities, retaining much of its vitality among migrant communities. Dozens of Iraqi towns and cities emerged only in the 19th century, as was the case with Umara, Kut, Nasiriya, Diwaniya, Falloja, Ramadi and scores of other provincial centres. At the beginning they were tribal residences, which later became urban centres proper, yet the process of detribalization in them has apparently been very slow.

Among urban tribal migrants, some former tribal notables and elders still occupy a leading role as centres of social authority. At times they are assisted and supported by other status groups such as *sayyids* (nobles from the 'Alid lineage) or even *mullahs* (clerics). Tribal ethos or culture, rather than tribal organization, persists in these spaces and keeps them bound together. This may be reasonably termed cultural tribalism, where migrant elements retain their tribal name, value system, lifestyle and above all solidarity commitments: blood money, material and moral support in life and death, exchange of women, i.e. intermarriages as contracts among equals, and so on. One particular example may serve to illustrate this phenomenon:

The peasant migrants in Baghdad, who fled from the feudal sheikhs of Umara and Kut in the 1950s, were settled in the eastern suburbs of Baghdad during General Qassim's era (1958–63). Their suburb, Madinat al-Thawra (The Revolution City) was divided into parallel avenues cut across by minor streets and alleys. Each avenue or street was numbered in an order similar to New York. In a matter of one year, these numbers were displaced by tribal names, usually of the *hamoula*. Taxi and mini-bus drivers, as well as civil servants, had to then learn the new names.[25] The ethos underlying cultural tribalism is preserved by the short duration of detachment from the tribal domain, as well as by the impact of urban life itself. Social alienation from urban life with its fragmenting division of labour, commercialized economy, alien lifestyle and hostile environment, are but some factors which strengthen cultural tribalism. At times the expectation of benefits on the part of the migrants – joining the family business or using tribal connections to gain government employment, and so on – strengthen solidarity ties.

Cultural tribalism is mainly, but not exclusively, an urban phenomenon distinct from, but complementary to, rural *hamoula* community. The former feeds constantly on the latter, and is found in large cities like Baghdad among the migrant neighbourhoods and quarters; it is also manifest in provincial towns. Cultural tribalism is so resilient and flexible that it may live in peaceful symbiosis with the most advanced of ideologies and social movements, without losing most of its major traits, detribalization notwithstanding.

In the 1950s and 1960s, cultural tribalism was integrated into communist-led modern trade unionism, in as much as they could integrate into the Islamist Najaf-led mosques and religious ceremonies and rituals. Thus one could observe the second generation of migrant peasants pay their union fees as well as their contributions to tribal blood money, or the *Khums* (fifth), the Islamic tax paid out to *mujtahids* (jurisprudents).[26]

It is in this space of cultural tribalism that the reconstruction of tribes under the Ba'th regime was triggered by the advent of the new political system and the social change it furthered.

We shall now examine how and why cultural tribalism worked under the Ba'th regime to reach its present, upsurging level. We should remember that etatist tribalism emerged first, followed by social tribalism, with ideological and military tribalism in between.

Etatist Tribalism

The General Context

As has been noted, etatist tribalism is a process which stems from the crisis of the Iraqi state, both as a political system and as a national entity; but it could only thrive if and when cultural tribalism preserved much of its vitality.

Among the main features of this state is its detachment (in relative terms) from society in terms of military relations (by dint of the British colonial support in 1921–1950) or power relations emanating from social wealth (due to oil rentierism from 1954, and more strongly from the early 1970s). This feature was strengthened by the fact that the state could destroy or reduce classes of capital and property, and control the bulk of social wealth, ultimately eliminating the separation of the economic from the political sphere. This unleashed authoritarian tendencies which annulled the embryonic institutional division of powers and with it the nascent mechanisms of representation and participation of the political machine in a multi-ethnic, multi-religious society. As this state was in search of a nation it initiated, under monarchy, nation-building and participatory mechanisms through traditional status groups, but overlooked the new, modern and burgeoning middle and working classes. When the radical regimes toppled the monarchy, they reversed this process: while representation and consolidation of the middle class were improved, national integration of ethnic and religious groups was disturbed (thus far beyond repair), triggering instability. Worse still was the dismantling of the institutional structures for nation building, such as the parliament and the upper house.[27]

With institutional violence the only mechanism left for assuming or sharing power, the organizers of legitimate means of violence, the military, assumed supremacy. This class had sundry political leanings and divisive social tendencies, a fact further aggravated by the sombre ideological politics pursued along communist, social pan-Arab nationalist or purely Arabist or Iraqi nationalist lines. A full-fledged conspiratorial atmosphere overwhelmed the power struggle at the helm among the middle class, mostly by provincial, high-ranking officers. The elite which ruled during the revolutionary era (1958–68) discovered the validity of the ex-prime minister Nuri Said's warning to one of their conspiring lot, 'If you assume power, God forbid, you will cut at each other's throats.'[28]

A sort of Hobbesian logic prevailed, the war of all against all, which created a need for peace, but unlike the Hobbesian conclusion, no 'covenant' (contract) among the warring factions was ever attempted in order to reinstall institutional and constitutional structures of power. Instead, new sources for bonding the state elite to face rival contenders were sought out. The successive sources or forms of cohesion were seen as inadequate. General Qassim (1958–63) relied on military discipline and radio-mass politics (like Nasser of Egypt and Mosaddeq of Iran); the 1963 short-lived Ba'th regime tried the single-party model embedded in partisan discipline; lastly the 'Arif brothers (1963–1968) combined military discipline with clan and kinship allegiance, *jumailat*. These arrangements for state-elite cohesion proved weak, at times disastrous. Four successful, and a dozen would-be, *coup d'états* shook the nation during this period. This proved beyond any doubt that the modern disciplinary regimes in the military, bureaucracy or party organizations were vulnerable. The engineers of the second Ba'th takeover in July 1968 were well aware of this dilemma and determined to remedy it.

This new elite had four decisive features:

1. As they descended from provincial, semi-Bedouin small towns and villages, where primordial solidarities are the strongest, they were in a position to comprehend tribalism and exploit it;

2. The civilian part of this group was all too aware of the powerful role of the military and was concerned about the disruptive and sundry nature of the latter.

3. They were also leaders of mass politics who appreciated modern organization.

4. The group was also aware of its own segmentary and thin nature[29] given the complex structure of Iraqi society, and the fact that the Ba'th membership was only 150 or so; some say estimates vary between 300–400.[30]

This is why the elite lived in constant fear of losing power and was thirsty for reliable sources of cohesion. One indication of this horror is Saddam Hussein's statement: 'We cannot allow some three or four officers riding tanks to come and take power again.'[31] The Report for the Eighth Party Congress authored by Saddam and Tariq Aziz, was dense with derogatory remarks about 'the military aristocracy' and 'Arif's 'tribalism'.[32]

Within this context, the Ba'th party leadership tried to mould an enduring model, geared for secured survivability. This drive produced a totalitarian model, with a patrimonial character, combining populist modern mass politics, state-rentierism and primordial solidarity networks or, in plain terms, the single party, single clan systems fused into one and based on rentierism. This mix imparted on the Iraqi state, as a system of governance, a novel and formidable character, radically different from the traditional-liberal monarchy (1921–58) or the modern-populist authoritarian military regimes (1958–68).

The Kinship System and Its Development

The problem facing the Ba'th state elite was how to control the state as a control system in the face of menacing internal or external challenges. Two parallel processes were initiated: one was expanding the means of mass mobilization and control through the party, which grew massively from a few hundred to tens of thousands to reach some 1,800,000 in less than eight years;[33] the other was to mobilize and integrate clan and family networks into the institutions of coercion and violence: the military and security services. Clannish recruitment crusades were carved out through three bodies. The first was the military bureau of the party in charge of selecting cadets and indoctrinating and organizing party members in the military. The bureau was invariably presided over by Beijats or their close allies: Bakr, Saddam and Doori took direct charge of this bureau. For a brief period in early 1970s, Taha Yasin Ramadhan led this bureau but was soon removed when his Mosulite liaisons increased the number of his city mates and next of kin in the military academy.[34] The second was the *Maktab al-'ilaqat al-'amma* (Bureau of Public Relations) which was, in fact, the national security bureau in charge of all security services, presided over by Saddam Hussein in person. The third is

Lajnat al-'Asha'ir, the Committee of Tribes. The Regional Command and the RCC established this body in the early 1970s. Upon the initiative of Saddam Hussein and under his direction, this committee was to work among tribal groups in the Sunni triangle, presumably to protect the porous Iraq-Syria borders at a time of fierce inter-fighting between the Syrian and Iraqi Ba'th wings. The western desert adjacent to the Syrian border was, in fact, the route through which the trafficking of militants, weapons and print hardware necessary for clandestine activities took place. Hussein himself trod this path in his flight from Baghdad in 1959, after he had taken part in the attempt on the life of General Qassim. Combining these three bodies in his control, Hussein could literally 'shop' elements from the various poor *hamoula*, extended families and clans in the Sunni triangle. The Beijats were given preference in sensitive security organs, such as the 'protection units' providing the bodyguards of high officials or the security services, the Presidential (Republican) Guards, the Defence ministry, Baghdad Garrison and the Air Force.[35]

Primordial networks extended the narrow base of the state elite, provided it with sizable manpower to control state machinery, and helped bring relative stability to structures of power. But most importantly, tribal solidarities were sources of cohesion, loyalty, disciplinary regime and providers of trust with life in a conspiratorial atmosphere fraught with the uncertainty of power struggles. This mode of loyalty, obedience and trust of life is generated by the mobilization of cultural values: group solidarity, obedience of elders and the cherishing of lineage. But the nature of this traditional relationship is modified, by dint of service-money relations, into a bureaucratic/clientele system. Paradoxically, by this process, which I termed etatist tribalism, the state, in fact, detaches tribal elements from their original primordial habitat, thereby deconstructing cultural tribalism and reconstructing it into its own body. Primordial networks are integrated into the bureaucratic web of the party, the administration and the military, reinforcing the modern disciplinary regimes based wholly on economic rewards, political interests or ideological catalysts. The patron figures, before this segment, are the great patriarch, the leader of the party and the head of the state.

Etatist tribalism, at least in its first phase, sucks tribal solidarities into its own body, and thrives on them in a parasitic manner, without destroying them altogether. On the other hand, as the elements drawn from tribal cultural spaces grow richer and more powerful within the new web of the state, they assume higher positions in their own clan. The clan in turn uses them as conduits for economic and political power. The various clan groups gain handsome government contracts and make their upward mobility, joining the ranks of the nouveau-riche classes. The upper class of millionaires, which consisted of some 23 in 1958 and fewer than 100 in 1968, grew to 800 in 1982 and around 3,000 by the end of the Iraq-Iran war. Preliminary research in this area seems to suggest that the Beijats and their allies joined this upper class of *muqawiloon* (contractors).[36] So, while the state was manipulating the various clans, the clans involved were reciprocating. The social and economic power amassed by the various households through tribal connections would enable these households to reassert themselves the moment the state was weakened.

Ibn Khaldun vis-à-vis Durkheim, or the Tribe versus the Party

Modern mass politics and tribal networks aimed to integrate modern and traditional primordial relations. From both sets of relations cohesive forces were extracted to produce a solid, almost monolithic mix. Indeed they created a powerful, cohesive space at the centre of the state, but, on the other hand, they also collided, generating fission.

The clash between the two modern/organic and traditional/mechanical solidarities stems from a host of sources.

Durkheimian organic solidarities are based on fluid specialization and division of labour. They are achievement-oriented, have money-service relations content backed by moral and material rewards (upward mobility, promotions, benefits, salaries, recognition, fame, decorations) or a system of punishment (reprehension, censure, discharge, loss of benefits). It represents a universally inclusive system of law and contract. This system produces its own impersonal discipline (chain of command), cohesion (team work, *esprit de corps*) or submission (of lower to higher ranks). While the organic logic permeates society, it is manifested in societal institutions and modern organizations, from private enterprises to political parties to trade unions and government departments.

Khaldunian mechanical solidarity, by contrast, operates within segmentary tribal groups (or even kinship groups); it is characterized by similarity rather than differentiation, and is based on personal bonds, backed by traditional norms and values. Kinship bonds are predetermined for members of the group; even when these bonds are seemingly prone to mobility through intermarriage (alliances), the exchange of women is almost invariably an exchange of equals which shuns male members of the lower, i.e. non-equal, groups (females are the exception in certain cases). Egalitarianism notwithstanding, such primordial relations are structured in a hierarchy which is, like its counterpart in modern organization, productive of discipline, cohesion and submission. Yet the Khaldunian logic is unstable, as we shall see.[37]

These two logics lead a peaceful symbiosis at times, but in the long run are set for a headlong clash. Thus under the Ba'th regime, the two systems were bound to enter into the uneasy relations which developed into antagonism.

Interestingly, the rise of kin in state and party during the early years was explained and justified in modern partisan idiom: militant spirit, loyalty to the 'revolution', dedication to the cause, implementation of party directives, and sacrifices for its sake.[38]

During the first four years of Ba'th rule, no sign was evident of any opposition to the vast inclusion of tribal kinsmen into the various bodies and departments. In fact, it was welcomed as a means of promoting the party and strengthening its ranks.

As early as 1970, H. Batatu had already observed, 'their role [the Takritis] continues to be so critical that it would not be going too far to say that the Takritis rule through the Ba'th party, rather than the Ba'th party through the Takritis.'[39]

The clash, however, was inevitable and erupted during the first decade of the Ba'th rule. Two episodes, in 1973 and 1979, serve to illustrate this rebellion against the primordial kinship system from within the party: The first is the failed coup organized by the ex-director general of the security service and RC member, Nazim Gizar, in July 1973; the second case involved 26 RC and RCC members in the so-called June 1979 'conspiracy' against Saddam, led by RC members Muhammad 'Ayish and Adnan Hussein. In both cases, the initiative came from non-Beijat figures, in fact non-tribal, middle-class, mostly Shi'ite, old-party apparatchiks. Among the many catalysts behind their opposition was dissatisfaction at the overgrowth of the power of the Beijat, including Saddam Hussein, Bakr, Adnan Tulfah and Hammad Shihab, among others. For those who opposed it, the exploitation of clan networks had shifted power relations and created almost undisputable centres of power which eclipsed them in particular and party leadership in general; in a word, they challenged this shift of power simply in self-defence. They did not defend the modern system in and of itself; rather they sought practical power sharing, which involved cohabitation with formidable, monopolistic tribal groups.

In the 1979 episode, party opposition tried to deploy part of the Beijat, President Bakr in this instance, against another part, Saddam and his half-brothers, to strike a more balanced power sharing arrangement. That is why the group reacted against Bakr's resignation and did not favour Saddam Hussein's presidency.[40] The success of the Beijat and their tribal allies proved the validity of the Khaldunian wisdom: headship is assumed by tribal group solidarities, *al-riyasa fi ahl al-'asabiya*.[41]

The Beijat: Internal Schisms

So far, only the cohesive and binding aspects of the Khaldunian *'asabiya* have been examined. Like all forms of social association, mechanical Khaldunian solidarities are not in the least monolithic. In fact they are prone to the fiercest, Macbethian bursts, breaks and ruptures. Power struggles, conflicting marriage alliances and sundry economic and social interests plague primordial, clannish groups and rip them apart.

The Beijat leading clan buried its supremacy beneath a thick layer of modernist ideological barrage, through vast distribution of rewards, through clientele networks or by harsh punishment. In 1976, the RCC prohibited the use of tribal titles. In the early 1980s, by contrast, when the modernist, non-tribal segments of the party acquiesced, the president divided his party 'militants' into two categories: *ahl al-khibra* (experts, i.e. technocrats, bureaucrats and other categories), and *ahl al-thiqa* (trustees),[42] denoting all his tribal entourage, in particular the Beijat clan and the Majid *hamoula* on top of it. By the end of the Gulf War, the Majids' advance to the highest echelons of the state proceeded in broad daylight and no effort was made to conceal it. An internal party circular put the Khaldunian axiom bluntly: it said towns in Iraq were either urban, agrarian or Bedouin in their nature and ethos, and that 'leadership emerged only from within the Bedouin centres'. Since the term 'Bedouin' has at its centre the purity of Arab lineage, it could well fit in the pan-Arab nationalist ideology of the party, rather than contradicting it on ideological grounds.[43]

The Beijat are a clan, and clans, just like their higher units, the tribes, are loose social organizations whereas the *afkhadh* (sub-clans) or better still the *hamoula* (lineages or extended families) are the most effective units. Rivalries and power struggles within the state in particular, set households against each other. To understand the significance of the three episodes of inter-Beijat struggle, it is necessary to briefly introduce the major households of this clan.

According to records of tribal *nasab* (lineage), Albu Nasir is the original tribe, which ruled at one point in Aleppo, Syria, and established emirates during various points of its history. This tribe, according to modern records, allegedly descends from the house of prophet Muhammad.[44] According to earlier accounts by British intelligence, the Beijat clan is a mixed group with no common lineage, which has descended from various segments of the Dulaim tribe in the Anbar (previously Dulaim) province. The clan inhabited Takrit, Ouja, Beiji and Shirgat on the upper Tigris valley, and spread even wider to Ana and Heet to the west, on the upper Euphrates valley. When Batatu examined their ascendency under Ba'th rule in 1968–72, he mistakenly described them as Takritis. In fact, Takritis were only a minor segment of larger tribal groups. According to Figure 1 the mixture of tribes in Takrit is divided into three distinct sections:

1. Albu Nasir (a tribe in its own right).
2. The Takritis, who include four clans and one section of the so-called 'original or historical Takritis', the descendants of the founders of Takrit in Roman times when it was a castle/garrison overlooking the Tigris river, known as Tigridis.[45]
3. The Hadithiyoon, who descend from the Dulaim.

Albu Nasir is now the fictive tribe, formed from five clans as shown in Figure 2. The Beijat clan is presumably the leading segment of the whole tribe. While little is known of the other four clans of the Albu Nasirs, the Beijat has been the focus of academic attention.[46] A ramified tree of the Beijat was presented by Baram, which is very useful in many aspects, but has two problems. One, it mixes the clan level (Beijat) with the tribe level (Albu Nasir), in terms of the unit as a whole or the generations involved. Two, the generations are presented as parallel lines of offspring unstructured in households, *hamoula* (also called *finda*, i.e. breast, in the Beijat jargon) although it is the *hamoula* or *finda* configuration that is the basis of organization. These remarks do not in the least alter the fact that the lineage sketch Baram presents is of paramount importance, in fact the first of its kind, which may help scrutinize the clan structure.

The division of the Beijat clan into *afkhadh* and households that we are presenting here relies on Amiri's book, based in turn on the security service archives and direct access to the Beijat elders through Watban al-Hasan, then minister of the interior. One problem with this sketch is that the households may have overlapped with *afkhadh* or sub-clans. We will, nevertheless, take them as households. The Beijat is formed of 10 households as shown in Figure 3. The traditional leadership in the first half of this century was held by the Nida family from Albu 'Imar (house no.1). The power shifted to Albu Bakr, when Ahmad Hassan al-Bakr assumed the presidency of the republic in 1968. With his demise, the power shifted to three households: Albu-Ghafour, from which the Majids descend; Albu Musallat, the branch of which Tulfah and his son Adnan Tulfah come; and Albu Khattab, the section from which Saddam's half-brothers descend.

We have discussed the clash between the Khaldunian logic of the clan and the Durkheimian logic of the modern social organization. Now we examine the inner Khaldunian logic. The first aspect of this logic is cohesive solidarity (*'asabiya*) and leadership (*riyasa*). This logic, as we know it in theory and practice, is of dual nature. It is not a stable logic, but also divisive and sundry in motion. In the old framework, the moment the *mulk* (power and wealth) is seized, a fracturing process is unleashed, and within three generations the *'asabiya* withers away. Now, this Khaldunian logic operates in a modern oil-rentier state with accelerating and mutating factors. A series of schisms and rifts erupt in a chain fission process.

The first split came with the purge of the Takritis proper, composed of small but powerful military and civilian figures such as the ex-defence minister Hardan Abdul Ghaffar al-Takriti who was ousted in 1970 and assassinated in Kuwait in 1971, and Salah Omar al-Ali, the ex-RCC member who was discharged of his leading post and transferred in 1970 to a minor diplomatic post abroad (in the USA). Lastly, Murtadha al-Hadithi, the ex-oil minister, was killed with one of his kin under torture in 1976. The Takritis proper, as stressed, were and still are secondary allies.

The second and major episode in the drama of the Beijat cleavages is the forced resignation of President Ahmad Hassan al-Bakr in June 1979.

Both these episodes, however, implied generational, military-civilian, factional inter-struggle, in which kinship and party networks were instrumental. In these two cases, both the party and the clan were used against each other.

The third rift was epitomized by the flight, (followed by the pardon, return and assassination) on 7 August 1995 of Saddam Hussein's two sons-in-law, Marshal Hussain Kamel and Saddam Kamel, their brothers, sister and father.

In this case it was the clan against itself in pure form. In fact, the struggle erupted on two tracks, within the Majid extended family and between al-Majid and Albu Khattab.

In the post-Bakr period, President Saddam Hussein relied heavily on three distinct groups to control the security and intelligence services: his half-brothers Barzan, Sab'awi and Watban (Albu Khattab). The second group was from al-Majid proper: Ali Hassan al-Majid, Hussain Kamel al-Majid and his brother, Saddam Kamel al-Majid. Ali al-Majid took charge of the Northern Branch of the party (and the army), the military bureau of the party, the defence ministry until his fall from favour in 1996. Hussain Kamel was in charge of the *Jihaz al-Khas*, the ministry of military industries, oil ministry and defence ministry before his fall. His brother, Saddam Kamel al-Majid headed the Jihaz al-Khas.

The third group comprised the two rising sons, Uday and Qusay.

Frictions flared up between the Majids, on the one hand, and the al-Mussallat and Albu Khattab, on the other hand. The president's paternal cousins removed the Mussallat from the defence area (the mysterious helicopter crash which claimed the life of the ex-defence minister Adnan Khairallah Tulfah in 1989 was seen an indication of this shift), and the

Khattabs from the the security and intelligence (through the gradual removal of the three brothers, Barzan, Sab'wai and Watban al-Hassan). The rising sons, Uday and Qusay, bluntly or indirectly relegated both the half-brothers and the Majid cousins to secondary positions or to oblivion.[47]

These antagonisms had some of their roots in marriage alliances, which took on the aura of political sex. The president has three daughters and two sons. Their marriages involved a re-distribution of political power in which all households would try to vie against each other for predominance, power and wealth, or to preserve their supremacy through such marriage strategies. For his daughters, the president opted for the agnatic pattern. Rana and Raghad were given to Hussain and Saddam Kamel, much to the dismay of other groups, particularly the Albu Khattab (his half-brothers), who felt threatened. When Hussain Kamel's younger brother proposed for the third and youngest daughter of the president, even the other families of the Majid reacted fiercely against it as an abnormal concentration of power in the hands of three brothers.

For his sons, the president adopted a pattern of far alliances with the Albu Mun'im (the Rasheeds) and the Dooris.

The bloody demise of the Kamels created bitter rifts in the narrow household, which have prompted a rearrangement of power distribution through marriage alliance to include Albu Sultan, the twin household of the Majids, who share a common lineage, Albu Ghafour. From Albu Sultan come the new bridegroom of the third and youngest daughter of the president, and his elder brother, the commander of the Republican Guard.

The next potential rift may involve the two brothers, Uday and Qusay. The pattern of heirs in the Middle East is either horizontal, inclusive of brothers and cousins, or vertical, involving sons. The two may overlap and cause tensions, as was the case recently in Jordan. Potential tensions on similar lines may well flare up in Iraq, triggering a collision between Albu Majid and Albu Sultan.

In a wider context, the households of the Beijat or other clans which sustained moral, material or physical loss are sources of latent schisms and challenge.

Social Tribalism: New Phase, New Challenges

The Nature and Context of Social Tribalism

Etatist tribalism, as we have seen, is a segmentary, exclusive phenomenon focused on controlling the state as such. It was instrumental in controlling the state rather than society. For that matter it was complemented by clientele distribution of oil wealth and the party mass politics to generate consent and organize controlled participation, while security undertook coercion, in order to govern society. This combination continued until well into the Iraq-Iran war, but began to falter under the effects of two devastating wars and sanctions. When the economic power of the state dwindled and party structures collapsed, social tribalism emerged as a generalized, strengthened and revitalized form of cultural tribalism, as we have discussed earlier.

This mode of tribalism was not invented but rather detected by the state, which soon recognized it and did its best to manipulate it. Etatist tribalism relates the state to itself; social tribalism pertains to the relation of state to society.

If social tribalism, which has spread across the gamut of social spaces in Iraq in the last decade or so, is the result of the social generalization and state recognition of cultural tribalism, it is necessary to examine the sources of this mutation. Why, how and when has cultural tribalism not only sustained its vitality, but rather increased it?

Under the Ba'th patrimonial-totalitarian regime, the single party system hegemonized, destroyed and absorbed all nascent civil society structures and institutions, such as unions, professional associations, an independent press, chambers of commerce and industrial leagues. As individuals or groups in modern societies face the state by means of institutions (courts of law, the media, pressure groups, unions and the like), the vacuum created by the omnipotent and omnipresent state hegemony activated the role of cultural tribalism (with *hamoula* kinship networks at their core) as defensive shields, conduits of clientele links and safety nets.

The uncertainties implied in the commercialized environment under these circumstances also increase the need for tribal spaces as sources of social security. This need grows stronger the weaker the state welfare benefits become.

Counter to these factors was the tendency to weaken and displace the traditional patterns of community leadership, like *sayyids*, tribal notables or sheikhs in rural settings, by the party apparatchiks and government administration, who assumed the roles hitherto traditionally assumed by community notables of the tribal domains even in ceremonial rituals like the Shi'ite 'Ashura assemblies in Muharram.

This state and party penetration disturbed the tribal hierarchy in various areas. A party cadre from lower clans (*khudhairi* for example, or marsh dwellers) would rule over tribal segments from a higher status. This penetration, however, did not reduce the growing functions of cultural tribalism mentioned earlier; it only temporarily modified leadership patterns.

During the Iraq-Iran war, the situation changed. Party members, recruited *en masse* into the war machine, spread thinly in these tribal spaces. As economic hardships, social pressures and the effects of the war increased, taking a harder toll on the rural areas and rural migrants, cultural tribalism grew stronger. Gradually, even old leadership patterns regained their previous forms.

During the war, a cultural trend consolidated this line of development. Media propagated the most popular forms of tribal war poetry, from the *husa* to the *abuthiya* and *darmi*. Targeting the soldiers, the bulk of whom were from tribal areas and spaces, the Propaganda Department in the Ministry of Defence under General Jabbar Muhsin, and government media in general, focused on tribal concepts of manly valour, military prowess, courage, revenge and honour.[48]

The strongest turn came with the second Gulf War. The state lost much of its potency in economic, military and security terms. Deprived of revenues, the state withdrew from social services; the salaried middle and lower urban and rural classes were hit hard by hyperinflation and the newly introduced heavy taxation. Uncontrolled commercial activity increased together with poverty.

The state, as an instrument of control and governance, sustained heavy damage. While Iraqi society had grown massively into a mass urban one which needed a more sophisticated mechanisms of control and management, adverse trends were set in motion weakening control agencies: the army was downsized to less than a third of its pre-war level, the party disintegrated, and the security services suffered heavy losses during and after the March 1991 uprisings. A deep vacuum ensued.[49]

In this context, cultural tribalism emerged full-fledged to fill the gaps left by a totalitarian regime. In this process, new hierarchies of autonomous social authority developed from cultural tribalism. This observation of course applies only to rural and provincial urban settings among Shi'ite and Sunni Arabs, but more strongly among Shi'is, where the state is weakest.

Beginnings of a Discovery

Social tribalism as defined earlier had a life of its own, and it was detected rather than invented by the state. The detection began in a spontaneous manner during the fierce battles with Iran on the fronts of Basrah and Umara in the mid-1980s. Arab tribes in the Qurna districts and the marshes spontaneously resisted Iranian forces during the years 1982–85. This event never escaped the watchful eyes of the Ba'th regime, and it soon moved to better mobilize what looked like military tribalism. Such military tribalism was a tradition in the Kurdish region where the government hires the services of the Herki, Zibari and Surji tribes to combat the nationalist peshmergeh [Kurdish partisans]. The mercenary force, known in the nationalist Kurdish jargon as the *jash* (donkeys), ran into 150–200,000 part-time warriors, named the Salahudin Forces, after the Fatimid leader who was of Kurdish descent. These units were deployed as border guards, a mercenary force to assist the army on the war front against Iran. This pattern of purchase of military services has been political folklore for successive Iraqi governments since the breakout of conflict with the Kurdish nationalist movement in the early 1960s.

Arab Shi'ite military tribalism, by contrast, displayed new elements: it was of an Iraqi nationalist character, and it was spontaneous.

As the Salahudin Forces were under Ali Hasan al-Majid in his capacity as the secretary of the Northern District of the Party, the Shi'ite tribes and clans of the south were acting locally on their own. Upon an initiative from above, Rokan Ghafour al-Majid, the president's nephew and *aide de camp*, was put in charge, as a liaison officer who had direct access to the president himself.[50]

Arab Shi'ite tribes were thus approached, mobilized, recruited and armed as a national defence force on the battle grounds of Basrah, Umara, Kut and the marshes. While in the case of the Kurds military prowess was sought in the first place, the ideological factor was of paramount importance in the case of Arab Shi'ite tribes. The cultural/ethnic divergence of Arab Shi'ism from Persian Shi'ism was important. Shi'ism in Iran, it should be stressed, has been an integral part of Persian and later Iranian nationalism. In its Sufist, Persian garb, it differs culturally from the nature of rural Shi'ism in Iraq, which has a tribal character.[51] The Arab-Persian ethnic rivalry or antagonism has marked even the existence of the clerical class in Najaf.[52] The ethnic divide was strongly felt among the Arab marsh tribes. It is these traits that were pragmatically appraised in order to stem any possible communal Shi'ite unity with the Iranians, as conceived by the regime. In many party circulars of this period, tribes were praised for their cultural values stressing valour, manhood, courage and military prowess.[53] Tribes were also hailed as the authentic depository of pure, unadulterated Arabism, an old theme in Ba'th ideological arsenal from the time of the Syrian Ba'th theoretician Zaki Arsuzi.[54] Themes of Arabism among these tribes were elevated to an ideal feature and easily incorporated into the modernist ideological system of Ba'th ethnic nationalism.

The phase of 'military' tribalism seemed contingent on an external threat which soon waned, but it reacted favourably on the burgeoning 'cultural tribalism' we have described in the previous section. As the war and the 1991 uprising revealed the decline of the party and the resurgence of local authority structures, the Ba'th regime changed course and sought alliance with the rising force.

State Recognition and Alliance with Social Tribalism

For the first time in Iraq's modern history, a major delegate of tribal chieftains was received at the presidential palace on 29 March 1991, shortly after both the defeat of Iraq in the second Gulf War and the demise of the uprisings, which erupted thereafter.[55] From that moment on, delegate after another, representing tribal groups came to vow loyalty (*bay'a*), an Islamic oath of allegiance for rulers, or to vow a covenant (*'ahd*), a word of tribal honour, to support and obey the ruler. Each delegate hoisted aloft its tribal banner (*bayraq*) and gave it away at the palace as a sign of total obedience. In the words of one observer:

> Tribal banners (*bayariq*, plural of *bayraq*) were lowered and thrown at the feet of the President of the Republic. The *bayraq* bore the symbol of each tribe and was an expression of their autonomy as if they were a mini-state. But giving away the *bayraq* was akin to presenting their diplomatic credentials to another, although higher, state.[56]

The symbolic action in this ceremony is important and merits examination. It has many elements to it. The *husa* (chanting war couplets), and the lowering of the *'iqal* (male headware), are basic symbols.

The *husa*, or war chanting, is a tribal tradition usually undertaken by the *hamoula*, which expresses small group solidarity within a larger unit, the clan. It functions as a marker of this group from the rest of the clan and assigns to this group a feat, or a daring deed. Yet, loyalty to the clan is preserved. The *husa*, in this case, is directed from a lower or smaller to a higher or larger group. Sheikhs are usually the objects of veneration in such *husa*. In the case of the *husa* at the Presidential Palace, the sheikhs and their entourage performed it. This performance symbolizes a hierarchy in which the sheikhs place themselves at a lower position by elevating the president to the highest post of *sheikh al-mashayikh*, the chief of chieftains.

Another aspect of this symbolic performance is the lowering of the *'iqal*. This tribal headware is a thick, black cord woven in the shape of two rings and fixed over the head-covering *kafiyya*, kerchief. When this headwear is forcibly removed, one's honour is tainted, and blood has to be shed to remove shame (*ghasl al-'ar*). But if the *'iqal* is removed voluntarily, the actor is signifying he (for it is always a male) accepts the challenge to defy humiliation. Again, blood should be spilled to cleanse honour. This is the traditional representation inherent in both acts. At the Presidential Palace, however, the sheikhs and their entourages willingly and without any challenge to their honour, lowered their *'iqals*. By this act, they signified their readiness to shed their honour before the president and for his sake, and that by this performance they gain rather than lose greater honour. Through this idiom they intimated that his presence is a source of honour that far exceeds the minor loss they willingly accepted. This loss/gain is a mutual honour-preserving bond, forged in public, not before the tribal community, but before cameras and videotapes, i.e. the watching eyes of a nationwide audience. In short: it is their word of honour to give total allegiance.

In some motives, this symbolic action creates a fictive, common lineage, unifying their honour with his, and their banners with his. This recognition of the president as the supreme sheikh creates a fictitious egalitarian space, a covenant of tribal equals, and a unity of honour and purpose.

On the other hand, this symbolic action exhibits a fictive and real hierarchy of power. It establishes and justifies the procedural arrangement according to which the tribal sheikh serves the state as an extension of the central power, drawing from the latter his meaning and reality.

In one of his early meetings, the president apologized for the past agrarian reforms, which destroyed the power base of the landlord-sheikh.[57] Two of the three land reforms, it should be mentioned, were implemented under the Ba'th regime in 1970 and 1971. Redistribution of land to compensate them was initiated.

From 1992, Iraqi newspapers reflected the rehabilitation of the tribes in various ways. In place of the usual telegrams of support conveyed by modern organizations and associations like students, workers or other unions and societies, tribal sheikhs were given prominence.

This episode indicates a change of direction from reliance on modern party forms of mobilization and control to recognition of a new-old social actor: the sheikh and his tribesmen. It also reveals a change of power hierarchies in society and an inclination on the part of the state to exploit it to make good for its own weakness versus its own society.

Structures, Spaces and Patterns of Leadership and Social Functions

Reconstruction of clans, sub-clans and tribal extended families took many forms, assumed a definite structure and produced a multitude of leadership patterns. These aspects merit some consideration.

In a number of random cases studied,[58] tribal households and groups had sufficient elements to reconstruct their old configurations. The existence of a recognized tribal leading house and the spatial proximity of the old clan or tribe members were the decisive factors behind the effective organization of an authentic tribal group. But these factors differed from one place to another.

In some cases, the initiative came from non-leading families, which manufactured an entity in order to gain power and wealth. Where the initiative was weak, the government enthused prominent members to take the initiative with full official backing. In other cases, appointment by the government was the decisive factor.

As some examples from Heet (Anbar province) and Khalis (Diyala) and Baghdad[59] suggest, tribal names were either in use or selected at random from the old clan, tribe, or sometimes the *hamoula*. There are cases in which the tribal name was a fake with no actual lineage or alliance bearing.

In all these cases of recruitment, tribal groups were either authentic or manufactured. By authentic we mean that, by dint of various factors, a certain clan or sub-clan has kept its leading core, even if deprived of real power, or kept a degree of mutual assistance and social liaisons. The authentic mode is abundant in rural settings and small villages, but it is also observable in provincial towns and, to a lesser extent, some neighbourhoods in large cities like Baghdad.

Yet in the majority of cases, disintegration of actual tribes and clans had reached such a point that any real reconstruction was too difficult to achieve. Migration, diverging economic and social interests and change of lifestyles and value systems almost wiped out the old cultural-spatial markers of the clan or the tribe. In a nominal fashion, some families have retained old tribal names and symbols. The new opportunities offered to recognize and empower tribal chieftains encouraged nominal tribal figures to contrive a local gathering, often made from heterogeneous elements, give it the old tribal name they have and put it in the service of both the group itself and a government keen on expanding its shrinking social and power base.

While powerful and authentic tribal chieftains are held in high esteem, the public disdains manufactured or fake ones. A degrading term has been coined to mock at these false tribal creatures: they are called 'chieftains made in Taiwan'.[60] To grasp the full meaning of this derision, it should be mentioned that Japanese cars and electronics are imported to the wealthy in Iraq. Lower classes have to contend with cheaper licensed products made in Taiwan. 'Taiwan sheikhs' are thus fake *dramatis personae*, imitations or second-hand copies of lower value.

Fake or authentic, the reconstructed and empowered tribes have little in common with the old tribe. The new entity is predominantly based in the city. It relies no more on agriculture; it has no transparent or territorially marked community. The leaders are, in most cases, middle-class educated figures, professionals, civil servants and the like. Instead of the *mudhif*, the traditional guesthouse, as a focal point of tribal social life, the new chieftains rent a modern apartment, focusing the tribal centre of power in a tribally heterogeneous space where the borders of solidarity groups are blurred and become problematic.

The new tribe maintains law and order locally, deals with and settles disputes among members, between them and the members of other clans or between them and the public at large.[61] Thus it becomes a collectivity in its own right. Disputes range from commercial to criminal offences, including the settlement of blood money. A group of clans in Baghdad, for example, negotiated an agreed list of financial penalties for various offences as follows:

> A number of clans agreed to the levels of tribal compensations as follows: for physical assault with the bare hand ID 75,000, for an assault with a wooden club causing no bleeding ID 100,000–150,000; for an assault with a sharp instrument which involves no loss of leg or limb, ID 200,000–300,000. If death is caused, the blood money runs into millions depending on the victim's gender, age or work ... The signatories on this agreement are four tribes: Daraji, Ka 'bi, Miahi and 'Ubudi. Possible other tribes may join in.[62]

With the corruption of law enforcement agencies and laws of court, powerful and influential tribes are approached to settle disputes or provide protection. These services bring revenues. With compensations, tributes, penalties, taxes and other sources, an independent financial base is generated to sustain and expand their influence.

Functional Differentiation

In May 1996, a decisive measure was taken to meticulously organize state-tribe relations. Hitherto, tribal units were either linked to the Ministry of the Interior, or were to have direct access to the Presidential Palace through Rokan Ghafour as a liaison and coordination centre.[63] A draft plan proposed a package defining the duties and rights of tribes *vis-à-vis* the state in the following manner:

1. A High Council of Tribal Chiefs (HCTC) is to be created. It is to have direct access to the president.
2. The sheikhs have the duty of: (a) absolute allegiance to the president; (b) ensuring security and stability in their designated districts (some 50 sheikhdoms were nominated); (c) judicial powers to settle disputes; (d) financial powers to exact taxes and penalties on behalf of the government.
3. In return for their duties, the sheikhs will receive: (a) light arms and ammunition, electronic communication devices, vehicles and other logistics, from the government; (b) tracts of land (if previously confiscated

in agrarian reforms); (c) special government rations; (d) diplomatic passports and (e) exemption from military service.[64]

In addition to policing, law enforcement, judicial and financial jurisdiction, other national security tasks were also entrusted to certain tribes. This was observed in November and December 1998 during the Iraq-US showdown. Tribal armed units in civilian clothes and tribal headwear were deployed in strategic points in Baghdad and other cities to assist special security forces in carrying out contingency plans. Such actions were previously the duty of paramilitary troopers, the Popular Army (party militia). From the available data, it seems that there are three patterns of tribe-state liaisons, the first via the Ministry of the Interior, the second via the Presidential Palace (Rokan) and the third via the National Security Bureau (Qusay).[65]

It is not clear whether or not all tribes are connected through these three channels, or whether these forms of connection imply a functional division of tribal duties, in the sense that some tribes are entrusted with national security tasks, others with law enforcement and order, and others with local administration. This possible division of labour may have to do with the differentiation of tribes according to their degree of loyalty, thus setting Sunni tribes in key positions.

Whatever the nature of the arrangement, it involves a de facto devolving of central power to local, autonomous authority. It is a new local power sharing based on a new hierarchy of social authority at the grassroots level, because previous mechanisms were either eliminated or are too weak to function.

Areas of Tension

Alliances with the new tribes may have strengthened the state, but the new reality is too complex to develop one-sidedly. It is, in fact, fraught with actual and potential destabilizing tendencies. Tensions permeate the relations between tribalized and non-tribal segments of society, or relations between tribes, or within tribes themselves. These tensions also strain the relations between state and tribes in general and impact on institutions in particular. At least four major areas of conflict have so far been observed.

Tribalized versus Detribalized

The first and most acute area of social tension is between tribalized and detribalized or non-tribal segments of Iraqi society. Before 1958, the rural customary law was legalized in the rural domain, not outside it. The Tribal

Dispute Act had the same force as the state laws and statutes, which were in force in the city. The legal duality was separated spatially, in the way the Weberian city was separated from feudal domains by physical lines.

Reconstructed tribes now are a rural, provincial and urban phenomenon. The *mudhif*, as mentioned earlier, had been the centre of tribal power and social interaction in the old days, and has now been reinstalled in city apartments. This is in itself a paradox, a contradiction in definition, for the word *mudhif* always carries with it a rural flavour. Tribes started to impose their customary law and code within the urban environment, recreating the old duality which now cuts, in varying degrees of course, throughout urban social life, disturbing the lives of urban neighbourhoods of mixed tribal/non-tribal composition. This extension of the customary law has reached such an extent that it has led to chaos and insecurity among detribalized segments.

Tribal gangs are another manifestation of this tension with the non-tribal segments. Some tribal groups were themselves engaged in looting and hijacking. One of the many examples is that segments from the Dulaim terrorize passengers on the Baghdad-Amman route. Cars and buses have to travel in convoys in broad daylight to avoid raids by tribal gangsters. The official press and informants, depicting a gloomy picture of lawlessness, have also reported recurring incidents of this nature. This may reveal to what extent reconstructed and empowered tribes constitute an uncontrollable structure both by their own chieftains and the government.[66]

The rate of violent crime so rapidly increased that it became a source of embarrassment both to law enforcement agencies and empowered tribes. As a result, non-tribal segments have been driven either to invent tribes of their own, seek protection from solid tribes or couch their opposition in ideological idiom. Hence the many protests from the party against retribalization in general, an expression that implies social rather than ideological cleavage.[67]

How far Iraqi society has been detribalized is difficult to gauge or determine in measured accuracy. A tiny example may, however, serve to give one insight. The al-Shabanah clan from the Daghara, a village south of Diwaniya, numbered some 3,000 in the late 1950s. A telegram sent by the same tribe to Saddam in the mid-1990s bore the signature of the sheikh of the tribe along with 300 male adult signatories.[68] We do not know whether or not there were other 'male adult groups' of this tribe who did not contribute to the telegram. No information is also available to figure out how many nuclear family units those 300 represented, or the average number of dependants any male would represent. Yet, we have no details about the tribal population increase between 1958 and 1995, approximately four decades. Omitting increases on both sides, the ratio is 1:30. We may assume, for the al-Shabanah clan, that detribalization has been a continuous line of development. We may also assume that the majority of the al-Shabanah has been detribalized in spatial terms, i.e. shifting from rural/agricultural to urban/commercial existence. Field research in this area is still lacking. We have so far only two papers. And the evidence is to a great extent still anecdotal. Iraqi press and informants reveal only part of the tip of the huge iceberg. The reality is that that Iraqi society has been going through such deep structural changes that the results of these might be so far reaching as to surpass even the best of any sociological or anthropological imagination.

Tensions Within Inter-tribal Realms

In terms of status, power, size, patronage, wealth and location, tribes and clans are, as a rule, uneven. Some are small, medium or large, rural, partly urban or urban, provincial or central, based on landlordism or businesses running into billions, with powerful footholds in the army, bureaucracy or party or without such connections, some with anti-government records, and so on and so forth.

Like the old hierarchy of the classical tribes, the new tribal creatures form a hierarchy in which rivalries never wane and alliances shift constantly. Since members of these configurations cannot act as monads, individual conflicts assume a tribal dimension and vice versa. A precarious equilibrium exists but is fragile, vulnerable and exposed to the fiercest of antagonisms. Common external threat provides a cohesive glue, but partial or differentiated threats are divisive agents. This has political significance when applied to the top, ruling clans and confederations. But it has a social significance when applied to minor and low tribes. The latter may enter into incessant local wars or seek out accommodation. Alliances and mutually binding agreements are reached. Some tribal segments in Baghdad, for example, forged cooperation based on a system of rewards and retribution independently from the state, and thus solved the frictions arising from the uneven spread of power among them. In this process, the enhanced autonomous social power these primordial entities enjoy is reminiscent of what civil society usually has in advanced nations. Their segmentary nature notwithstanding, they may develop or operate along the line the spontaneous *hay'at hussayniyya* did under the Shah of Iran in the late 1960s and early 1970s. If and when the segmentary nature of these entities is removed, their legacy of self-administration might reinforce the drive of Iraqi society towards autonomy, provided that the power of social wealth is kept detached from the realm of the political.

Tribe Versus State

Another area of tension is between the tribe and the state. The duality of social authority and the penal code has been conducive to clashes between the state agencies and tribal power. As tribes have become active almost everywhere, chaos has assumed a universal character and threatened the very functioning of state agencies and party organization. Those functionaries who have no tribal affiliation or whose power rests solely on the bureaucracy have voiced alarm. Clashes reached such a proportion that tribes have now begun to file legal or tribal suits against state and party functionaries demanding tribal compensation or even blood money.[69] There have been recurrent incidents where police, security officers, judges and civil servants who were dealing with various cases were threatened or assassinated by tribal groups as an act of revenge. In other cases, such officials were formally suited by tribal chieftains for alleged injury on one of their members, even when the latter was wanted for being deserters, suspects or culprits. In March 1997, the RCC was prompted to issue Resolution no. 24, prohibiting tribes from challenging, suiting or taking any action against state functionaries, if and when the latter had caused any injury or damage while performing their duty. The text reads as follows: 'Any person who advances tribal demands against he who has committed an act upon orders from higher authority or to enforce the law, shall be imprisoned for a period no less than three years.'[70]

The official press explained the resolution was taken to 'contain some negative effects of confusing state power and the role of the tribes.'[71]

Reciprocal Institutional Tensions and Schisms

The fusion of state and tribe has produced a circular reflexivity of tribal and institutional conflict. This overlap was the natural result of the interaction of the effects of etatist and social tribalism. Groups and individuals, who were de-linked from their tribal habitat in the first phase of what we termed etatist tribalism, were re-linked to these tribal spaces when social tribalism peaked.

Linkage created an intricate and precarious overlap in which any tribal conflict would create a potential institutional conflict and vice versa, and any institutional clash might be conducive to tribal repercussions. This applies strongly to the ruling tribal groups, but could well apply even to secondary groups. Several incidents support such an assumption. The case of Brigadier General Mazloom al-Dulaimi, a member of the strong Albu Nimr clan (Dulaim) serves as a good example. His execution triggered massive demonstrations and protests in his hometown, Ramadi, while some of his kin reportedly staged a military insurrection in the Abu Ghraib military base in the aftermath of which the defence minister, Ali Hasan al-Majid, was sacked.[72] Other examples vary in scale and intensity but still epitomize the same problem, such as the defections of Hamid Juboori, or the al-Majid brothers, as both incidents had strong tribal repercussions.[73]

Conclusions

Three forms of tribalism are posited: etatist, military and social. By etatist tribalism, a fragile, thin and shaky state elite tried to integrate tribal networks to consolidate its own control over state machinery as a national system. This form acted as a complementary instrument of management and control to overcome a chronically divided state elite, bereft of institutional legitimacy, mechanisms of representation, power sharing or crisis management. Paradoxically, this pattern of tribalism developed under conditions of the supremacy of state over society. No less ironic is that this pattern severed individuals from their tribal habitat and absorbed tribal vitality into the state, rendering tribes themselves weaker in terms of internal cohesion and group solidarity but stronger in terms of wealth and access to power.

Social retribalization, by contrast, has been the effect of two major causes; one is the social vacuum stemming from the destruction or absorption of civil society institutions; the other is the decline of state itself, both as a provider of security and of social services. Tribes were active long before they were rediscovered by the state as a revitalized social actor. This pattern of retribalization involved, on the part of the tribes, a de facto reorganization of social power hierarchies, but on the part of the state it involves devolution of central power to actual, fictitious or engineered tribal networks and groups at a moment of sharply manifested weakness of the state as a whole.

Retribalization, however, has produced conflicting results: it involved a clash between the state and the tribes; a clash between tribalized and detribalized sections of society; a clash among tribes themselves; lastly, tribal rivalries and competition triggered inter-institutional clashes within the state, in as much as state institutional rivalries reacted on the tribes themselves. The end result is contradictory and may evolve along a Frankenstein-like line.

The reconstruction of tribes under Ba'th patrimonial totalitarianism has been mistakenly viewed as stemming only from deliberate state policies if not, in fact, mere state creations. Within this conceptual framework, retribalization appears simply as one undifferentiated process. This approach is reductionist par excellence. However rich some aspects of this concept might have been, they lack three points. One, there is no clear conceptual or actual distinction between tribe and tribalism, or between the different forms of tribalism, say, differentiating etatist tribalism from military tribalism or the latter from social tribalism, which have contradicting functions and unique structures. Thus all forms of tribalism and retribalization are uncritically mixed up together under one rubric. Two, there is no clear concept of what the tribe is in late 20th-century Iraq after almost a century and a half of continuous decomposition of tribes as we have known them to have been in late 19th and early 20th centuries. Three, the tribe itself is presented as a passive actor by attributing all power arrangements and activity to the state itself, thus obfuscating the fact that tribes have a life of their own no matter how dependent on the state they might have been or would be.[74]

Appendices

Table 1
Bedouin Rural and Urban Population, 1867–1905

Year	Province	Bedouin Pop. in 1,000s	% of Total	Rural Pop. in 1,000s	% of Total	Urban Pop. in 1,000s	% of Total	Total
1867	Mosul	70	26	140	52	55	22	265
	Baghdad	115	23	170	39	206	41	491
	Basrah	260	50	215	41	49	9	524
	Total	445	35	525	41	310	24	1280
1890	Mosul	93	23	223	55	85	22	40
	Baghdad	65	13	340	59	270	28	675
	Basrah	275	37	400	53	75	10	750
	Total	433	25	963	50	430	25	1826
1905	Mosul	153	28	254	47	133	25	540
	Baghdad	70	7	468	78	317	15	855
	Basrah	170	19	602	72	83	9	855
	Total	393	17	1324	59	533	24	2250

Source: Muhamad Hasan, *Economic Development in Iraq* (in Arabic), Beirut, 1960, Part I, p. 53.

Figure 1
Takrit Tribe and Clans

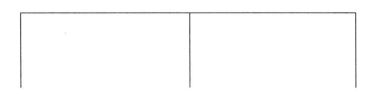

Hadithiyoon
Migrants from Rawa, Ana and
Haditha, towns and villages
inhabited by various groups
from the Dulaim Tribe.

Takritis proper
a. Migrant clans, such as
1. Owaysat
2. Shiaysha
3. Albu Khishman
4. Albu Bazzun
b. Original Takritis
   (non-tribal)

Albu Nasir
A tribe of six clans, with the
• Beijat Clan on top of them.

Source: T. Amiri, V.I., pp. 204–5.

Figure 2
Clans of the Albu Nasir Tribe

I. The Beijat (or Beikat) Ten sub-clans	II. Albu Fayadh Eleven sub-clans	III. Albu Ihmayyid Seven sub-clans	IV. Al-Lutayfat Eight sub-clans	V. Albu Qara Ahmad ?	VI. Al-Ja'afrah Three sub-clans

Figure 3

The Beijat (Beikat) Clans Division into Afkhadhs (Thighs) i.e. Sub-Clans, and/or Extended Families
with Prominent State and Party Figures

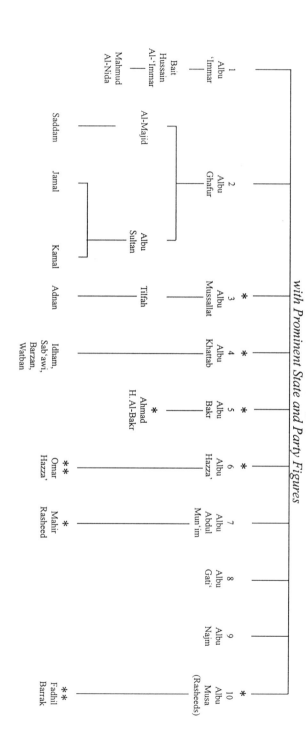

* Sub-clans with asterisk: removed from power or have been curtailed.
1. Albu 'Immar had assumed the leading role until the early 1960s.
2. Albu Ghafur has the leading role now.
5. Albu Bakr assumed leadership after 1968 and lost it completely in 1975.
** Persons executed or assassinated.

Figure 4
The Male Composition of the Albu Ghafur Sub-Clan

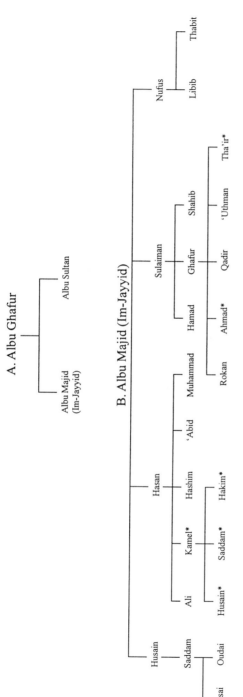

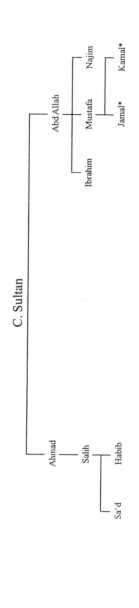

* Individuals with asterisk killed in the Hussain Kamel episode.

* Individuals with asterisk: most influential from 1998 onwards.

Notes

1. See Baram, Amatzia, 'Neo-Tribalism in Iraq: Saddam Hussein's Tribal Politics 1991–96', *International Middle East Studies*, 29, 1997, pp. 1–31. For Baram, the state is the sole and final actor in the process of retribalization, while the tribe seems passive. The anthropological researcher Hosham Dawood, by contrast, explores the socio-cultural historical dynamics of the tribe. See, Dawood, Hosham, *al-Hawiya al-Shuyu'iya, al-'Ashira wal Sultat* (Communist Identity, Tribe and Powers), *al-Nahj* Quarterly, no. 53, 1997, p. 34 and passim; Dawood, Hicham, *al-'Ashira, al-Aqarib wal Dawla fi ba'dh Buldan al-Sharq al-Awsat* (Tribe, Kinship and State in Some Middle-Eastern Countries), unpublished paper, 1995. In my comparative study on Ibn Khaldun and Ali al-Wardi, I tried to synthesize socio-economic-cultural-military and political dynamics in the process of detribalization. See my essay *Sosyolojiyat al-Badawah bayn 'Ali al-Wardi wa Ibn Khaldun* (Sociology of Nomadism Between Ali al-Wardi and Ibn Khaldun), Nusus annual review, no.1, 1994, pp. 5–18.

2. Tapper, Richard, 'Tribe and State Formation in the Middle East', in Khoury, Philip, S., and Kostiner, Joseph (eds), *Tribes and State Formation in the Middle East*, I.B. Tauris, London, 1991, pp. 50–51; al-Rasheed, Madhawi, *Politics in an Arabian Oasis*, Arabic edition, I.B. Tauris, London, 1991, pp. 24–8. Consult also Pierre Bonte and Ken Brown in this volume.

3. al-Naqib, Khaldun, *Sira' al-Qabaliyya wal Dimuqratiya, Halat al-Kuwait* (The Struggle between Tribe and Democracy: The Kuwaiti Case) Dar al Saqi, Beirut, 1996, pp. 17–19. Needless to say, the definition of tribes and tribalism is a long disputed issue among anthropologists. The segmentary lineage theory, for example, is widely contested and debated. The conceptualization of the tribe on the basis of 'structure' is one strand, defining it in terms of 'strategies' in another. Another dispute relates to the significance of lineage, or the ideology of kinship, whether it is real, fictive or a combination of the two. See Kenneth Brown, Pierre Bonte and Edouard Conte in this volume.

4. Gellner, Ernest, *Muslim Society*, Cambridge University Press, Cambridge, 1981, 1989, p. 86–9; Ibn Khaldun, *al-Muqaddima*, Cairo, n. d., p. 110, pp. 150–3, p. 154.

5. Wardi, Ali, *Mantiq Ibn Khaldun* (The Logic of Ibn Khaldun), Qum, al-Maktabah al-Haydariya, 1997 (Baghdad, 1962); also, *al-Muqaddima*, ibid., p. 136 and p. 143–4.

6. Gellner, op. cit., p. 88; *al-Muqaddima*, p. 131, 150, 152 and 262.

7. Wardi, Ali, *Lamahat Ijtima'iyya min Tarikh al-'Iraq al-Hadith* (Social Aspects of Modern Iraq History), al-Ma'araf Press, Baghdad, 1961, Volume I, p. 298; Wardi, Ali, *Dirasa fi Tabi'at al-Mujtama' al-'Iraqi* (A Study of Iraqi Society), Qum, al-Sharif al-radhiy, 1981, p. 13, 117–8.

8. Rasheed, op. cit., p. 29–31; Vassiliev, A., *The History of Saudi Arabia*, Arabic edition, tr. by Khairi al-Dhamin, Moscow, Progress Publishers, 1986, pp. 36–70.

9. Batatu, Hanna, *The Old Social Classes*, Princeton, Princeton University Press, 1978 and 1982, p. 68; Pierre Bonte, op. cit.

10. Vassiliev, op. cit., pp. 62–4; Wardi, 1981, op. cit., pp. 59–62.

11. Marr, Phebe, *The Modern History of Iraq*, Boulder, West view Press, 1985, p. 19–20. Longrigg, Stephen Helmsley, 'Iraq, 1900 to 1950', *A Political, Social and Economic History*, (1953) 1956, London, Oxford University Press, p. 22–6; Batatu, ibid., pp. 66–7.

12. Bonte, Pierre, op. cit.; Rasheed, op. cit., p. 61–5; Batatu, 1982, p. 69.

13. Wardi, 1981, p. 122–3; Longrigg, op. cit., p. 54 and passim.

14. According to Wardi, 1981, p. 119, Bedouin formed 76 per cent of the population in the late 19th century.

15. Consult Table 1 on Iraq's population, and Batatu's map on the location of major tribes in Iraq.

16. Gellner, op. cit., p. 73.

17. Marr, op. cit., p. 22.

18. Kazimi, Nasir Said, *al-Hizb al-Shuyo'i wal Mas'ala al-Zirai'ya fil 'Iraq*, (The Communist Party and The Agrarian Question in Iraq, The Centre of Social Studies in the Arab World,) Beirut, pp. 45–9.

19. Karmali, *Lughat al-'Arab*, July 1912–June 1913, collected by Jamil al-Juburi, Ministry of Information, Baghdad, 1975, p. 245 and 295; Hasani Abdul Razzaq, *al-'Iraq Qadiman wa Hadithan* (Iraq: Past and Present) 'Irfan Press, Sydon, 1948, pp. 138–9 and p. 142.

20. Among the students of Iraqi rural areas, there is a general agreement on that land ownership triggered various modes of tribal disintegration and peasant-landlord configurations, see, Batatu, 1982, op. cit., pp. 68–72, 79; Longrigg, op. cit., pp. 213–14, Kazimi, op. cit., pp. 93–5, and others. Sluglett, Marion-Farouk and Sluglett, Peter, *Iraq Since 1958, From Revolution to Dictatorship*, I.B. Tauris, London, 1990, pp. 30–35.

21. For an assessment of Sir Ernest Dowsen's report, see, Batatu, 1982, op. cit., p. 116 and passim; Kazimi, op. cit., p. 107 and passim, Longrigg, p. 214.

22. Kazimi, ibid., pp. 107–15.

23. Wardi, 1981, pp. 246–7; Salim, Shakir Mustafa, (1970) *al-Cibayish, Dirasa anthropologiya liqarya 'Iraqiya* (An Anthropological Study of an Iraqi Village) Baghdad, Ani Press, 2nd print, p. 125 and passim, and Naqash, Yitzhak, 1994, *The Shi'is of Iraq*, Princeton, Princeton University Press, p. 46 and passim.

24. Fernea, Robert A., 'State and Tribe in Southern Iraq: The Struggle for Hegemony before the 1958 Revolution', in Fernea Robert and Louis, Roger W., (eds.), *The Iraqi Revolution of 1958, Old Social Classes Revisited*, 1991, I.B Tauris, London, p. 144–5. See also Fernea's, *The Shaykh and the Effendi, Changing Patterns of Authority Among the El Shabana of Southern Iraq*, Harvard University Press, Cambridge, 1970, p. 118 and passim. Batatu, Hanna, 'Iraq's Shi'a, Their Political Role and the Process of their Integration into Society', in Stowasser, Barbara (ed.), *The Islamic Impulse*, Croom Helm, 1987, p. 209; Zubaida, Sami, 'Community, Class and Minorities in Iraqi Politics', in Fernea and Louis, (eds.), 1991, pp. 199–201.

25. This is based on my personal observation and experience.

26. Interviews with tribal actors from mid and upper Euphrates.

27. Batatu, op. cit., 1982, p. 807.

28. Another version of this text is offered: 'If ever your plot succeed a merciless factional struggle will oppose all of you until death.' Hopwood, Derek et al, *Iraq, Power and Society*, 1993, published for St. Antony's College, Oxford, Ithaca Press, p. 24.

29. Jabar, Faleh, 'The State, Society, Clan, Party and Army in Iraq: A Totalitarian State in the Twilight of Totalitarianism', in *From Storm to Thunder, Unfinished Showdown Between Iraq and the US*, Institute of Developing Studies, Tokyo, 1998, pp. 8–9.

30. Interview, Salah Omar Ali.

31. al-Khalil, Samir, *Republic of Fear*, University of California Press, 1989, pp. 26–7.

32. Report of the 8th Congress of the Ba'th Party, Baghdad, January 1974, pp. 134–6.

33. Jabar, op. cit., p. 16.

34. Jazairi, Z., *Husain Kamel wa Qisat al-'aila-aldawla* (Husain Kamel and the Episode of the Family-State), *Thaqafa Jadida monthly review*, no. 269, April–May 1996, pp. 6–18.

35. Batatu, 1981, p. 109.

36. Chaudry, Kiren, 'On the Way to Market', *MERIP*, 170, pp. 12–16.

37. On the Khaldunian Logic see Wardi, Mantiq, 1962, introduction, and Wardi, 1981, pp. 20–5; Gellner, op. cit., p. 20, 88 and passim. For the Durkheimian logic see, Durkheim, Emile, *Division of Labour in Society*, Macmillan, 1984; Lukes, Stenen, *Emile Durkheim*, Penguin, 1973, pp. 144–5, 147, 148, 152–5.

38. In a satirical essay, Jazairi described how Barzan, Saddam's half-brother, was presented as the 'youngest' participant in the 'revolution', while Uday, as an infant, carried leaflets underneath his clothes! See, *Thaqafa Jadida* review, no. 6, 1993, p. 51 and passim.

39. Batatu, 1981, p. 1088.

40. For more details see Slugletts, op. cit., pp. 160–4 and 205–213.

41. Ibn Khaldun, *al-Muqadima*, ibid., pp. 119–20.

42. Interviews, Salah Omar Ali and Hamid al-Juboori. See also my article 'Le régime irakien dechiré par les luttes de clans', *Le Monde Diplomatique*, May 1997, pp. 63–5.

43. Interviews with Ba'th party cadres.

44. al-'Amiri, Thamir Abdul-Hasan, *Mawsu'at al-'Asha'ir al-'Iraqiya* (Encyclopedia of Iraq Tribes), Baghdad, Dar al-Shu'oon al-thaqafiya al-'amma, 1992, volume I, p. 204 and passim.

45. See, Hasani, 1948, op. cit., p. 91; *al-'Asha'ir wal Siyasa* (Tribes and Politics), British confidential reports on Iraqi tribes, translated by Dr. Abdul Jalil Tahir, Iran, Qum, 1413, p. 39 and passim; Yunis, al-Shaykh Ibrahim al-Samara'i, *al-'Asha'ir al-'Iraqiya* (Iraqi Tribes), Baghdad, al-Sharq al-Jadid, 1989.

46. For the study of Albu Nasir, see, Dawood, Hocham, 'Tribalism and Powers in Iraq, The Case of Albu Nasir', unpublished paper; Idem, 'Tribe, Kinship and State in Some Middle Eastern Countries', Paris, 1993, unpublished paper. On Saddam's tribal policies, see, Baram, Amazia, 'Neo-Tribalism in Iraq: Saddam Hussein's Tribal Politics 1991–96', *International Journal of Middle Eastern Studies*, 29, (1997), pp. 1–31. Baram also presents the first clan tree of the Beijat and of the Majids, which merit recognition, see, Baram, Amatzia, *Building Toward Crisis, Saddam Husayn's Strategy*

for Survival, Policy Paper no. 7, The Washington Institute for Near-Eastern Policy, 1998, pp. 14 and 22–23.

47. Jabar, Faleh, 'Le régime irakien dechiré par les luttes de clans', *Le Monde Diplomatique*, Mai 1997, pp. 63–5; Jazairi, Z., op. cit., 1996, pp. 6–18; and Jazairi, op. cit., 1993, p. 51 and passim.

48. Interviews with the Folkloric poet Dr. Hashim 'Iqabi.

49. Hazelton, Fran (ed.), *Iraq Since the Gulf War, Prospects for Democracy*, London, ZED, 1994, pp. 97–117.

50. Interview with Abbas Janabi, Uday's former private secretary.

51. This cultural difference had been the focus of Wardi's attention in his *Lamahat* (1961) and *Dirasa* (1982). His line of argument has been pursued by later scholars, such as Abdul Halim Ruhaimi's *Tarikh al-Haraka al-Islamiyta fil 'Iraq, 1900–1924* (The History of Islamic Movements in Iraq), Beirut, al-Dar al-'Alamiya, 1985, chapter one, pp. 79–114; and Nakash's *The Shi'a of Iraq*, op. cit., chapter five, pp. 141–162. To this very day, Iraqi Shi'ite scholars, writers and activists emphasize the 'Arabist' and 'Bedouin' nature of Shi'ism in Iraq in contradistinction to the Persian nature of Sufism in Iran.

52. Nakash, ibid., and Ruhaimi, ibid.

53. Interviews with Ba'th party cadres.

54. On Arsuzi see George Tarabishi's, *Mathbahat al-Turath* (Destroying Heritage), London, Saqi Books, 1992.

55. Iraq TV coverage and Baram, 1997, *IJMES*, p. 11 and note 60.

56. Interviews with Iraqi tribal figures, Jordan, 1996.

57. Hazelton, op. cit., p. 115; *al-Hayat daily*, London, 30 July 1991.

58. Interviews and letters from Iraqi tribal members residing in Europe, Jordan, Saudi Arabia and Iraq Kurdistan.

59. Interviews and letters, ibid.

60. Interviews and letters, ibid.

61. Interviews and letters, ibid.

62. *Nabdh al-Shabab*, newspaper, Baghdad, 6 April 1998.

63. Based on interviews with and letters from tribal members residing in Europe, Jordan, Saudi Arabia and Iraq Kurdistan.

64. *al-Sharq al-Awsat daily*, London, 14 May 1996.

65. Interviews with eyewitness informants from Baghdad.

66. Interviews with Iraqi tribal figures, Jordan.

67. Baram, *IJMES*, op. cit.

68. *al-Hayat*, London, 6 April 1998.

69. *al-Sharq al-Awsat*, London, 30 March 1997.

70. Iraqi News Agency, 29 March 1997.

71. Ibid.

72. *al-Wasat weekly*, London, 26 June 1995.

73. Interviews.

74. Baram in *IJMES*, op. cit. Note 46; and Dawood, op. cit.

The 'State-ization' of the Tribe and the Tribalization of the State: the Case of Iraq

Hosham Dawood

Any person who advances tribal demands against he who has committed an act on orders from higher authority, or in order to enforce the law, shall be imprisoned for a period of no less than three years. The resolution shall take the force of law as from its publication in the official gazette.

The Revolutionary Command Council (RCC)
Resolution No 24, *INA*, 10 March 1997, Baghdad

The daily newspaper *al-Jumhuriyya* welcomed this RCC resolution, and explained it was taken in order to:

contain some negative effects of confusing state power and the role of the tribes and to put an end to any factor that may emerge to hinder the functioning of state apparatuses or weaken its powers to serve the public interests. Tribes, the State maintained, were only specific social layers whose significance could only be achieved to the extent the tribes are incorporated into the state itself ... the state recognized the role of the tribes in defending Iraq; but while it conceived tribes as part and parcel of the social fabric, it believed that tribes were incapable of providing leadership for the nation because of the nature of their organization and their culture.[1]

In examining the formation of Saddam Hussein's political power and, more widely, the Ba'thist State in Iraq since 1968, this chapter does not seek to present a 'balance sheet' of anthropological research on the region. Rather, by a series of re-engagements with anthropological sources, the aim is to develop some key themes, arising both from my own work and that of other Middle East researchers. These themes concern the tribe and the current retribalization of a part of Iraqi society (Iraq, however, being hardly unique in this phenomenon); and the over-arching question why are people today inclined, constrained or even encouraged to regroup themselves into large domestic units, such as tribes (real or fictive)?

The Place of Iraqi Society in the Social Sciences

Iraqi Studies: A Brief Survey

From the perspective of these opening propositions, what, then, is the current state of social science research on Iraqi society? The least one can say is that it presents a very strange and paradoxical situation: here is a society that is notoriously among the most 'media-tized' in the world (particularly since the Gulf War of 1991), yet, which remains enigmatic and largely misunderstood. Very little of the available work (of which certain examples will be given here) truly deserves the name 'social science'.[2] This situation can be explained in terms of certain key failings.

The first failing I would see as a direct – and, putting it mildly, 'odd' – consequence of the Gulf War. The quantity of political literature produced about Iraq is huge yet strikingly limited in its claims to knowledge.[3] On the one hand, there are apologetics: the appeal to Iraq's romantic or Bonapartist past, already a rich source of motifs of loyalty for the Iraqi political authorities; these translate, in turn, into favours and privileges granted to researchers in the 'Orientalist' tradition,[4] primarily European and North American archaeologists – in contrast to the blatant refusal of access to the same territory when it comes to other anthropologists, sociologists and political scientists.[5] On the other hand, there is the exaltation of the 'Civilizing Mission' of the New (read: 'Western') World Order. This partly explains why social anthropology today – even after refining and de(ethno)centring its theoretical and methodological apparatus – is treated as suspect and tainted with colonialism in the eyes of many African and Asian societies. Of course, the task of 'decentring' anthropology in relation to 'the West, its native home' remains always incomplete.[6] Even today, most Arab-Muslim societies perceive contemporary social anthropology (unjustly) as nothing more than a colonial science. Nonetheless, the paucity of anthropological research on the Middle East cannot be explained solely by such ideological-political accusations, nor their equivalent at the level of the petty administrative and police interference that ethnologists – as those not 'belonging' to the country – have to deal with. Other causes must be sought. The most significant are, undoubtedly, to be found in the cultural density of Iraqi society: a population that has been in a process of continual mixing since the Neolithic, a Muslim society for more than 1,000 years, yet constantly mutating and, at the same time, historically continuous with other still more ancient inhabitants, a complex tangle of societies bearing the weight of history, rapid urbanization (and other factors of change).[7]

A second weakness lies in the area of social science techniques: the problem of making comparisons when terms and categories are neither standard nor simple: 'tribe' and 'tribalism'; 'house'; 'domestic unit'; 'kindred'; 'kinship' and so-called 'Arab marriage'; 'power' and the like.[8]

The third deficiency is the lack of any large-scale data on the distribution of the social phenomena being studied. Obviously, no map will be without its blank spots but, even so, the sum of credible available information is very weak.[9]

The fourth problem is rather more difficult to pin down: it concerns the nature of the explanation that we can aspire to. More specifically, how can we explain the reappearance of a social phenomenon? Are there devolutionary, like evolutionary, phenomena? If irreversible phenomena and processes exist, are there then also some aspects of reality that are reversible?[10] This issue has been raised by Edmund Leach, Maurice Godelier, Jonathan Friedman and others, when faced with two forms of organization of power in the same society. They asked, therefore, whether one of these forms of power could have evolved from the other.[11]

Contemporary Iraqi Society: Some Landmarks

The major socio-political and economic changes that took place very rapidly between 1920 and 1958 should not obscure the fact that Iraqi society was composed of elements that had never before been closely associated with an independent state.[12]

Then, as now, the population (about 22 million inhabitants in 1997) was divided into diverse but overlapping categories, corresponding to social and ethnic origin, religious denomination, occupation and regional and tribal affiliation.

Today, at the beginning of the third millennium, the situation seems far removed from those times. Largely under the influence of Middle East 'experts', a highly simplistic image of Iraqi society[13] has appeared: on the one side, the 'Sunni Arabs' supporting the 'Sunni' regime of Saddam Hussein, on the other 'the Shi'ites', somehow 'not quite real Arabs' (a sort of Iranian fifth column) in hot opposition, with the Kurds located somewhere else entirely. It is undeniable that a revival of Islamic sentiment, the Iranian revolution, the Iraq–Iran war and the Cold War worked together to create a resurgence and reaffirmation of religious sensibilities.[14] But, in fact, what has been the most decisive of all these factors (at least on the political level) is the persistence and renewal of a type of factional allegiance and spirit of solidarity (*'asabiya*) among members of the same tribe, at the heart of the domestic group or coming from a common region and so on.[15] The question to ask, therefore, is whether the persistence of these types of attachments serves to consolidate the political 'revival' of Islam or, on the contrary, weaken it. From there, which of these denominational groups, Shi'ism or Sunnism, adapts best to tribal structures?[16]

We have indicated above that contemporary Iraqi society is divided along many lines: ethnic, religious, denominational, social (social class and also other socio-professional groupings) and between urban and rural. In fact, the disappearance of the nomadic world and the reduction of society to two poles are phenomena of very recent origin. For it is not very long since Iraqi society, like all Arab societies, was divided into three interdependent yet strongly antagonistic groups: nomads, agriculturalists and town-dwellers. Rapid and massive evolution has meant that, in a very short time (several decades), nomads, who in the 19th century still represented about 35 per cent of the total population, and then 4 per cent by 1957, now constitute less than 1per cent. Despite this rapid decline, the Bedouin tribal model has profoundly influenced the rural population and also the newly-settled populations of small – and medium-sized – towns in the western and southern regions and the Mesopotamian plain, both in its social organization and in its way of thinking. This character and tribal structure distinguishes the rural Arab Iraqi world very strongly from other peasantries of the Middle East, in Egypt, Syria and even Kurdistan. Generally speaking, the tribes of the West and mid-

Euphrates, in direct contact with the desert, have maintained (or re-created) some of their traditions far more than those of the East, mixed as they have long been with settled populations (of course, there are always exceptions: the grand tribal confederation of Beni Lam, for example). It is fascinating to observe how the symbolism employed by Saddam Hussein imitates, almost to the point of caricature, the Bedouin model of western Iraq (dress, having a little herd of camel, keeping a link with the desert and so on) to such an extent that he displays total scorn for the peasants of the East and the South of Iraq (the pejorative employed is the word 'M'adan'). A second important effect of the decline of the nomadic world, here at the level of basic social morphology, is the rapid transformation in social relations and former structures undertaken in order to undermine the opposition between town and country.

More fundamentally and arbitrarily limiting our analysis here to internal factors (acknowledging that there are many exterior causes as well), factional allegiance and the spirit of *'asabiya* solidarity types of allegiance, now functioning on a new base, have been reinforced at two historical moments and for two contradictory reasons: the first moment – and here disputing Bertrand Badie's thesis concerning the state and new phenomena in international relations[17] – in Iraq it is the universalist state in all its power (initially through the 1970s and 1980s) which was the prime mover of maintaining, subordinating and then propelling certain forms of tribal and clan structures. For it was the absence of individual power in the face of an arbitrary State, and the lack of any intermediary social bodies (without which there is simply the pure universalist Hobbesian State; alternatively the State functioning according to the Weberian model) that drove men and women to turn to infra-ethnic and infra-state levels, both to protect themselves or, conversely, to seek political and social promotion within this same State. The central Iraqi power itself consolidated this through its frequent appeals to kinship relations and tribal elements as a way of managing politics. The second reason (and the second historical moment) was precisely the weakness of the Iraqi 'sovereign' State, specifically its incapacity (particularly since the 1990s) to assure the security of the population and territoriality of the country. Here, it was the State's inability to lead that induced individuals to return to their infra-state layers. Thus what Bertrand Badie calls 'empty social spaces' [*espaces sociaux vides*], that is, social spaces that escape the authority of the State,[18] are nothing more or less, in my opinion, than a devolved form of power in the national and new world context. In the Iraqi situation, recourse to such layers signifies a reinforced engagement with a tribe, region or particular house. In this, the central Iraqi power (through yesterday's strength or today's 'weakness') has contributed just as much to the reproduction and promotion of heterogeneity as to its disappearance.[19]

What Is an Iraqi Tribe?

This is a double question: what is the nature of tribal organization in Iraq and, second, what are the conditions of their reactivation today? It is remarkable how much attention the contemporary international press pays to tribal phenomena and their place in the organization of Iraqi society (obviously subordinate to the State but nonetheless real). Some even advance the hypothesis that the reactivation and manipulation of the tribal factor constitutes one of Saddam Hussein's secret weapons of political survival. For an anthropologist, these types of interrogation have a theoretical as well as a practical bearing, opening on to a discussion of the concepts of tribal organization, clan, lineage, house [*maison*], kindred [*parentèle*] and analysis of their real or fictive implications for Iraqi political and social life.[20]

Let us begin by examining certain terms relating to tribal organization that are in current usage in the Arab regions of Iraq. It is always difficult to present a terminological analysis of Arab tribal nomenclature, which varies historically and geographically. Consider a few examples: *sha'b* – 'small tribe' [*peuplade*] (i.e. springing from a distant common origin, for example the Qahtan origin of the Arabs of Southern Arabia, Adnan for those of the North); *qabila* – generic term designating a tribe or confederation of tribes; *'imara* – sub-tribal structure (a rarely-used term which, in former times, metaphorically evoked parts of the body, the *sadr* – chest – and *'unuq* – neck – and then, subsequently, *'imara* came to mean 'flourishing'); *'ashira* – sub-tribe or tribe (for the Turks and Kurds *'ashira* means clan); *batn* – clan (this term, according to the ancient Hebrew, is derived from the word for stomach, but for other groups, Hebrew or Arab, *batn* also means 'womb' (that is why in Robertson Smith's evolutionist vision *batn* means a matrilineal clan preceding the era of patrilineality);[21] *fakhith* – for the Arab tribes of the Northwest of Iraq this means patrilineal clan (in Arabic, literally, 'thigh') while, for the southern tribes of Iraq as for the tribes of other Arab societies, *fakhith* refers to a lineage; *fasila* – a large house (*maison* or extended family) but also, according to the metaphorical language of the body, *fasila* is the lower part of the leg; *firqa*[22] – lineage, *hamoula* – household [*maisonnée*] or lineage for the tribes of the North-West, but 'clan' for the tribes of the South; *bayt* – (*maison* or house); *mashaykh* – chiefdom. In Iraq only *'ashira, fakhith, hamoula* and *bayt* remain in current use, along with various other terms of which some are specific to this region : *albu, fenda, al-gurmeh*.

These terms *'ashira, fakhidh, albu, fenda, hamoula, bayt* describe the fundamental relations constituting Iraqi social tribal organization, as much among the urban as the rural population. They each denote a particular order of relations allowing each individual to situate himself in the social system. On this basis, how should one think of continuity in relation to earlier tribal organization? How are we to situate this evolution in relation to the opposition/complementarity between state power and tribal power? In which particular ways does contemporary tribal organization differ from earlier forms?

In local cultural usage, the term *'ashira* (tribe) signifies an ensemble of individuals and groups speaking the same language and dialect, split into multiple sub-groups: many *fakhidh*s,[23] many *hamoula*s,[24] many *bayt*s and in each *bayt* many *'aila*s (families) of variable number and size, which define themselves by their common patrilineal descent, more often claimed than literally true. The appropriation of a territory claimed by the tribe as its own (whether through inheritance, conquest, by right of customary use or received from central power) and which it is prepared to defend by force, constitutes another fundamental element of this reality. In fact, what is called *'ashira* is a socio-political entity which exercises a large or limited sovereignty over a determined territory. In depicting the diversity of tribal structures, one notices how relations of kinship and consanguinity, real or fictive, are made primary in explaining rights, loyalties and obligations between persons and groups. Certain tribes collect sometimes thousands of people around a sheikh (one man) who regulates the tribe's internal relations and represents the tribe as a whole and its interests in relation to other groups and the central power.[25] The structural novelty that characterizes the contemporary Iraqi tribe is its dependence on the State to reproduce itself, and hence a relative loss in its larger political and territorial sovereignty. It is clear that contemporary tribal phenomena clearly cannot be understood in isolation from Iraqi central State power.

Apart from this reconfiguring of the political field of the tribe through its new dependence on the State, what are the other major differences between former and contemporary Iraqi tribal structures? In the period prior to British colonization, most of the tribes were in the process of regrouping themselves into grand tribal confederations (*'ashai'r*) under a *sheikh al-mashayikh* as supreme leader (a sort of chiefdom). In theory, the sheikh of each tribe did not enjoy hereditary power: rather, through exercising his leadership capacity and his political ability to maintain the unity of his group as a whole, playing the role of arbiter within the tribe or the confederation, he would show his appropriateness, whether by the suppleness of his manoeuvres or his ability to gain the consent of the tribal members to the use of force in order to maintain order within the tribe or gain prestige in the outside world. Hence the members of a tribe are associated with the sheikh's control of the territory and its resources. Nonetheless, transmission of the title of sheikh from father to son is not absolutely prohibited, provided that the new sheikh lives up to the expectations of status and can defend himself against possible rivals. If not, a man of the same house, or even another, is entitled to cut him off from his claim and take over the title. Thus, from early on, and contrary to the arguments of certain segmentarist discourses, [26] the presumption of the title to power has long favoured the emergence of a particular house, that of the sheikh, and operated against other claimants – a reality that goes against the 'egalitarian' image which in principle may seem to reign within the tribal structure.

This 'non-egalitarianism' has been reinforced by the socio-economic transformations which Iraq has undergone from the end of the 19th and throughout the 20th century. The classical *'ashira* (of the Bedouin type, or functioning according to a Bedouin ideology) has undergone profound alterations since the Ottoman reforms of the 19th century. The Sublime Porte introduced the requirement to register land (*tapo*) by those who had worked it for a period of 10 years. These use-rights entailed exemption from state taxation, with the State retaining the right to repossess non-exploited land. This reform gave birth to a regime of peasant private property and profoundly modified the social and political relations at the heart of the tribe and its relations with the outside world. Under the British Mandate, the English repealed the Ottoman laws and introduced more radical measures, including many that politically favoured the power of the sheikhs. Sheikhs were no longer elected but compelled recognition on the basis of their wealth and trans-local political alliance.

Consequently, the links of solidarity among tribe members weakened entirely without disappearing, and a massive rural exodus to the cities threw tribal members on the connections of their *hamoula* and their house. This segmentation was encouraged and accelerated by the agrarian reforms of 1958 and 1970, conferring private property according to the principle of redistributing land to peasants and offering them various technical aid and resources, thus making the peasantry more autonomous as a group. In this short period in which the settled population sought to 'de-tribalize' the country, new forms of political cohesion appeared, totally or partly based on lineage solidarities. This tendency also marked the urban social fabric structured by houses. Part of local political power (particularly in the countryside) thus passed from the tribe and the sheikhdoms to the State. The development of the State brought in its wake the disappearance of tribal organizations to the extent that the tribe is a political entity requiring certain autonomy of decision-making in order to continue to exist. On the local level, village communities survived or developed with certain forms (at the level of internal solidarity) more or less similar to classic tribal organization – but with the difference that the village communities exercised local control without imposing political power over a larger region or neighbouring communities of the same type.

Thus, generally speaking, the appearance and development of the post-colonial State saw the tribes continuing to exist, integrating themselves more or less easily within the State order which, often by violence, became a pluri-ethnic and pluri-tribal State. In very recent Iraqi history, one can point to certain groups being arbitrarily transformed into 'tribes' in the successive censuses as the State seeks to control the population, or encouraged (by pragmatism or fear) to put themselves under the protection of a long-established tribe.

Of course, there are other factors explaining this expanded use of tribal affiliation: in our field work in Iraqi Kurdistan (in northern Iraq) we have established that, since the beginning of the 1990s, the consequences of wars, deportation, repression, immigration and the loss in land value of vast tracts (under other circumstances: industrialization, globalization etc.), have all invariably have favoured the re-emergence of tribes and other types of particularism, and also of new tribes (we have called attention to this same phenomenon in the case of the reappearance of tribes in the regions of Bahdinan). However, it is interesting to observe how these factors have produced a double and contradictory effect. On the one hand, they have undermined the bases of influence of the old tribal groupings by liberating individuals from links with their groups of origin but, on the other hand, they have brought about new social realities over which the old tribes had not yet extended their control. The distribution and attribution of these social and symbolic material 'surpluses' have become the 'broth' of the culture that nourishes the new tribalism in its claim to participate directly in the political and economic mechanisms of the country. Hence the question: will these types of tribal identity – whether invented, dumped or reactivated – survive in a society whose social relations are completely disarticulated and deformed?

To pose the issue this way is not to subscribe to the idea that all tribal reality, or tribalism, is simply an invention of colonialism (yesterday) or the post-colonial State (today). Despite the modern current that has recharged tribal phenomena, this 'institution' is inscribed within a history of the *longue durée,* within a complex system of ethnic, religious, religious denominational, social and politico-military relations. Certain tribes living today in Iraq have an active history going back several centuries! Also, tribes and local groups are not totally devoted to the permanent quest for political power: the relations between the majority of members of the large and important tribes are generally limited to the sphere of everyday social life. In retrospect, at the level of the sheikhs and the important houses the links of filiation, descent and alliance have taken a quite different form. Undoubtedly, their mobilization and their proximity to the central power could confer various advantages on the rest of the tribe and increase the success of members' claims to benefit from the distribution of land, arms, economic means and honorific positions, or assuring access (for them or their children) to certain politico-symbolic positions, for example entry to the regime's elite paramilitary forces (the Special Presidential Guard, the Republican Guard), the military-industrial complex. Such practices in turn exert a reciprocal pressure of subordination on tribe members and a sense of having an asymmetrical debt towards the sheikhs and, across them, to the central power. [27]

In these conditions, the relations between the various tribes close to State power may develop relatively peacefully or, on the contrary, be accompanied by violent conflicts. In most cases, the struggles occur mainly between the old established groups and new groupings seeking a political role. In the absence of any strong competition between these groupings, the new tribes have no chance of gaining tangible power. Even if successful, the position of any new tribe tends to be unstable and fragile in the long term. Nor has the force of the old groupings been diminished by the loss of various high-level posts in the State. For example, most of the tribes in the Sunni Triangle in Northwestern Iraq who participated in or supported the central power in Iraq before the rise of the Ba'th Party in 1968 are still very much present on the political, military and national scene. This explains why the appearance of any new tribe close to the governing group can result in very serious social and political conflicts. But equally, the reduction, just as much as the enlargement, of the number of tribes involved in decision-making can unsettle the politico-social equilibrium.

Tribalism and Power

Let us now examine the articulations that operate between powers (central and local political power, military, religious) and the contemporary tribal structure, focusing on the case of
Albu Nasir, the tribe of Saddam Hussein, and most of those persons who have occupied the key positions in the Iraqi State since 1968.

1. Above all else, the effectiveness of any group that aspires to a political role is determined by its size and political importance. This explains why tribes as large as Dulaim, Jubur, Ubayd or Shammar have maintained important

positions and their closeness to power despite the change of regimes. When it comes to the tribes at the heart of the State then it may be a matter of as many as dozens or hundreds of active members. Saddam Hussein's tribe (Albu Nasir) suffered a major handicap at the start, knowing that its tribe, its own house (even its nuclear family) was not of a size sufficient to 'furnish' a cadre of active members. That is why the tribal orbit grew to include distant relations (*parents*), friends from the same region, favourites and old companions on the road to political power. [28] But, very quickly, the tribe's numerical 'weakness' was transformed into a force of quasi-total monopolization of the key posts in the hands of the descendants of the Albu Nasir – to such an extent that, over the years, Saddam Hussein has succeeded in building a complex power structure in which the tribe, the house and kindred have been and remain his first circle of protection. Even early on, it was due to his distant cousin Ahmed Hassan al-Bakr (from the same tribe but a different house; Albu Musallat is the house of Saddam's mother and Albu Khattab the house of his four half-brothers), the first president of the Ba'thist Republic after the 1968 coup d'état, that Saddam Hussein became the second most important person in the regime. It was thus in his cousin's shadow that Saddam Hussein put together the power that allowed him to succeed in 1979.

Saddam Hussein's father being dead, it was with the help of his mother's house (in particular his maternal uncle, Khairallah Tulfah) that Saddam Hussein also found the capacity to advance himself. In 1963, he married his matrilateral cross cousin (Sajida Khairallah Tulfah). She gave him five children, two sons and three daughters. Naturally, cross-cousins and half-brothers very soon occupied important posts. His brother-in-law and matrilateral cross-cousin, Adnan Khairallah Tulfah, passed rapidly from the rank of colonel to a post of Minister of Defence, and would become one of the few military members of the RCC, the supreme organ of power in Iraq. Three of his half-brothers from the second marriage of his mother, with one of his cousins, Ibrahim Hassan (of the house of Albu Khattab) have since 1974 occupied positions of responsibility, notably in the domain of security. This overburdening weight of maternal cross-cousins and half-brothers has been counterbalanced since the second half of the 1980s by the massive entry of patrilateral cousins (notably of the lineage Albu Abdel Ghafour and the house of al-Majid). The most celebrated of these was Ali Hassan al-Majid, member of the regional command of the Ba'th Party, who was for a time Minister of Defence, responsible for the military and security aspects of part of the North of the country (the Kurdish region) and today the southern region (mainly Shi'ite). It did not take long for the two branches, maternal and paternal, to begin contesting the division of power. For, as distant as the tribal and family links may be, and despite the image given by this 'collective' participation, definitive decisions are taken in a supremely authoritarian and brutal character, which contrasts with the familiar 'collectivism' of the Middle East. Saddam Hussein thus did not hesitate in the mid-1980s to temporarily cut off his three half-brothers when they protested against the marriage of his two daughters to his patrilateral cousins, the famous Hussain Kamel al-Majid and his brother Saddam Kamel al-Majid, who were both assassinated by men from their own tribe.

The second circle of power is formed around the Takritis, already numerous in the army under the British on the eve of the First World War, when they knew how to help each other out. They were very well represented in the security services. At its height, the phenomenon was such that Saddam Hussein, from the end of the 1970s, made a decree prohibiting the use of the name of the region after a person's surname. From 1973 he stopped calling himself Saddam al-Takriti and used Hussein, his father's name. The third circle of Saddam Hussein's power, formed far more recently, involves the tribes of the Sunni triangle, the Dulaimis, the Juburis, the 'Ubaidis, the 'Azzawis. All the same, he has kept close to himself, and in particular at the heart of the RCC and in regional command of the Ba'th Party, long-standing faithfuls from whom he has, for various reasons, nothing to fear.

2. The effectiveness of the tribe depends equally on its own internal relations. The most acute problem on any tribe's agenda today is the relation between its constitutive kindred base (*l'armature parentèle*), patrilateral cousins (close and distant), the members of the same house and the members 'recruited' though marriage.[29] The latter (those not of Albu Nasir origin) are given the inferior status of 'outsiders' by contrast to the 'principal' and pure relations (*parents*).Yet this probably does not have much effect on the degree of political sympathy: material and political interests are often more important in conditioning the preferences of non-blood relations. That is why pure relations are often given the place of personal servants of the chief and his guard, which allows them to exercise an informal supplementary influence over the leader.

Any modification of the rank, status and function of members of the tribe linked to the consolidation of the genealogical kernel and its generational renewal can represent a serious threat to those in the first generation. It has been at least 15 or 20 years since the political appearance of the tribe and if the conflicts at the heart of the group are not settled, it can not sustain further blows. This became very clear at the end of the 1970s with the political and then physical liquidation of the former president (distant cousin and descendant of the lineage of Albu Musallat) and his entourage by the house of Saddam (from the house of Albu Ghafour). The second renewal (again violent) was in the 1990s when the subtle equilibrium which had been established between the three major groups was broken: the first group comprises the patrilateral cousins who had become sons-in-law (descendants of Albu Ghafour [Consult figures on Albu Nasir and its sub-clans and houses in the previous chapter]); the second consists of the half-brothers who were linked to the house of Albu Khattab (by blood/filiation and marriage); the third consists of the direct kindred of Saddam who, in fact, function as the core active group (his two sons and in particular his eldest, Uday). After 30 years of strategic alliances and marriages, conflicts and physical elimination, the conclusion one can draw is that it is not the members of the Albu Nasir tribe, with all its clans and houses, who unite members around the central power. Today, it is the kindred who stand at the forefront, even when the tribal ethic (surviving or revived) holds it together internally. But the weakening of the tribe and the house to the benefit of kindred, in turn, reduces its cohesive force and the absolute hegemony of persons belonging to the kernel of kindred (*parentèle*), and hence bears finally on the competence of the group. For kindred cannot substitute either for political or juridical or social structures or for kinship and tribal organization.

3. Another very important condition contributing to the political success of a tribe is the personality of its chief. In the old large tribes, the faults of the chief could be partly compensated for by the competence of his close entourage; in the new tribes which have a major political role it is simply not possible to confer the leading role on a weak personality (except in certain African countries or in the Arab-Persian Gulf, for example, where the weak personality of the chief is consolidated by support of 'foreign bayonets'). Access to such a position by an outsider is thus always fleeting.[30]

The moment of succession of a new chief is linked to all sorts of ill-omened consequences, whether the tribe is old or new. If, for the old groups, the form of transmission of power was relatively elaborate, the majority of the new ones disintegrate with the loss of their leaders. This is what happened, for example, with the clans of Idi Amin or J. B. Bokassa. By contrast, the record of 'longevity' of the clans of West Africa (M. Keita, Sekou Touré) whose origins go back to the Middle Ages, or the Sharifian, noble, line of Hassan II in Morocco and the descendants of the dynasty of Ibn Saud in Arabia, attest to their active political role since the 17th century.

But equally, within the tribe, the vulnerability of both old and new factions at the moment of chiefly succession also comes from the fact that, willingly or not, the chief may have to crush their families for the sake of the 'bigger picture'. The departure of the chief creates a particular void which cannot be filled except at the price of sharp confrontations and 'settling of accounts'. The cohesion of factions within a tribe is sorely tested when important political successes are at issue. At the time of the succession of a chief of a faction to the supreme post in the State, the style and the character of his relations with his near entourage changes considerably.

Typical pretexts for violating tribal or factional unity at this stage are discord between kindred and contempt for certain rules and basic tribal traditions.

4. Another feature necessary to the political prosperity of the tribe is a feminine element in the chief's entourage. Even in societies where the cultural tradition ascribes mothers and wives a very secondary role, the positions of spouses or even mothers of the chief are always important. Sajida Khairallah Tulfah, the wife of the Iraqi President Saddam Hussein (his matrilineal cross-cousin) and Sabha Tulfah (his mother) have clearly helped his political career. The wife and the mother of the chief exercise an influence over the daily mood; they are in touch with the secret code of confidential political business. Sustaining rigorous respect for certain traditions, and hence the affirmation of internal unity, also depend very much upon the *savoir faire* and mode of communication of the lady of the *Rayis*. She gives the appropriate tone to relations between women and seeks to manage family conflicts. It is precisely these kind of moves that Saddam Hussein employed, at first without success, in the episode of the flight of Hussein Kamal, his cousin and son-in-law, to Jordan but eventually achieving an internal settlement with a group of secessionists in 1996.

In other cultures and societies, strategies of matrimonial alliance have played an important role in political success, notably B. Aquino in the Philippines, Z. Bhutto in Pakistan and others across the world, thanks to the kinship links of their wives or mothers. This is because strategies of this type create conditions particularly favourable to rapid expansion of the role of these groups. Polygamy especially makes it possible to form, in a very brief time, the genealogical kernel of a tribe and associated substructures of birth, and guarantees an introduction to a different level of the social hierarchy. In one generation, the group can be in a position to constitute a ramified system of links as much at the heart of the social elite as with their client groups of inferior social strata. Having taken this initial step, the new political clans quickly become almost indistinguishable from the classic tribes, whose positions are so difficult to breach from the outside.

Here again, in the case of Saddam Hussein and the Albu Nasir tribe, this factor was absent: instead, we find much recourse to alliance strategies of a 'lower' form (so-called 'Arab marriage').

It is true that the role played by women in this type of male-dominated tribal society remains very polyvalent and deeply misunderstood. On the one hand, local tradition ordinarily grants even mothers and wives of chiefs secondary roles. Nonetheless, at the higher levels of political power, these roles become very important.

On the other hand, and still following the logic of the tribe, we can find among the group associated with Saddam Hussein much recourse to alliance strategies of a 'lower' form (so-called 'Arab marriage'). This may also be explained by the negative role very often imputed to women from the point of view of group development. For if the matrimonial links of the chief become excessively numerous and wide-ranging, feminine favouritism may obscure the internal rules of the game within the tribe and thus reduce its capacity to act as a unified group. This fear of group dislocation is well illustrated by the events of 1989 when Samira Shabandar, the ex-wife of the Director General of Iraqi Airways (and an outsider to the Albu Nasir tribe) unsettled the position of the entire Albu Musallat and Albu Khattab lineages, and especially the house of Tulfah and precipitated the physical elimination of the Minister of Defence, Adan Khairallah Tulfah (matrilateral cross-cousin and brother-in-law of Saddam Hussein).

5. The stability and the unity of many tribes is reinforced by various types of cult, the public glorification of the chief being one of the most widespread forms of exercising ideological influence over the members of the concrete group and the social environment. Such cults serve to isolate and, ideally, to distinguish the tribal community spiritually and politically from the rest of the population thereby affirming the *'asabiya,* solidarity based on the links of kinship as the supreme value in life. Although often aided by other specific religious practices (for example, confraternities) to secure a monopoly of influence over the members of the group, the aspiration of the tribal hierarchy may be realized by other routes. Thus in the Bahdinan region (Iraqi Kurdistan), whose religious traditions are solidly attached to

the *Naqshabandi* Sufi order, this is in turn largely legitimated and ensconced within an absolutization of political authority from the Barazani chiefdom and the centralization of decision-making on all questions large and small that confront the members. The exercise of these spiritual-political legitimations creates another ideological effect, affirming among the members of the group not only the differences that distinguish them from others, but also their superiority. For example, the 'illusory' belief held by various Shi'ite houses and groups, of having a direct genealogical link with the honoured ancestors (the Prophet, Ali, and so on) articulates the political group's objectively combative mood.

6. Lastly, the viability of tribes, clans, involved in the political game grows tangibly with the enlargement of their activity outside the initial sphere of their principal occupation. This involves guided migration by members of the group, but equally the activation of links with adjacent kin and or compatriots of a different division. The new ecological niche creates possibilities highly favourable to quantitative evolution of tribal/clan structures. The groups that leave the peripheral ethnic regions for the capital undergo particularly noticeable transformations. Positions of responsibility, foreign travel and access to the centralized system of distribution of material goods by one member of the tribe offer openings for social betterment (although unequal) for all of the substructures. A further consequence of migration is the appearance of a network of ramified groups, arising from the permutations of the leader, who, if this involves physical relocation to other regions, will 'acquire' in each new area a clientele with which his followers will maintain contact. This is why the relation of forces of the governing elite concentrated in the capital cities is determined not only through formal nomenclature but also by tribal links maintained in the periphery.

All these characteristics of the political groups (tribe, large house or regional group) are not speculative abstractions. They serve as key indices to the viability of tribal groupings in the short and middle term. Both constructive and destructive elements will periodically surge up in the course of the evolution of tribal groups.

Translated from the French by Beverley Brown

Appendix

Table 1: The Iraqi Regime: Distribution of Power According to Group Affiliation

Name	Position	Kindred of Saddam Hussein	Direct frequent access to S. H.	Albu Nasir tribe	Of Takrit origin	Command Council of the Revolution	Ba'th Regional Command	Military Post	Special Grade	Army	Intelligence Service	Republican Guard	Other Important Tribe	Iraqi Arab Ethnic Group	Iraqi Kurdish Ethnic Group	Other Iraqi Ethnic Group	Sunni Religious Group	Shi'ite Religious Group	Christian Religious Group	Total
Qusay Saddam Hussein	Joint Chief of the Army	+	+	+	+			+	+	+	+	+		+			+			11
Uday Saddam Hussein	Deputy	+	+	+	+									+			+			6
Ali Hassan al-Majid	Governor of the Southern Province	+		+	+	+	+			+	+	+		+			+			9
'Abed Hemoud	Special Secretary to Saddam Hussein	+	+	+	+				+	+	+	+		+			+			10
Sultan Hashim	Minister of Defence			+	+							+		+			+			5
Barzan Ibrahim al-Hassan	Half-brother	+		+	+									+			+			5
Watban Ibrahim al-Hassan	Half-brother	+		+	+									+			+			5
Sab'awi Ibrahim al-Hassan	Half-brother	+		+	+									+			+			5

Name	Position	Kindred of Saddam Hussein	Direct frequent access to S. H.	Albu Nasir tribe	Of Takrit origin	Command Council of the Revolution	Ba'th Regional Command	Military Post	Special Grade	Army	Intelligence Service	Republican Guard	Other Important Tribe	Iraqi Arab Ethnic Group	Iraqi Kurdish Ethnic Group	Other Iraqi Ethnic Group	Sunni Religious Group	Shi'ite Religious Group	Christian Religious Group	Total
Arshad Yassin	Son-in-law	+		+	+									+			+			5
Mohammad al-Zubaidi	Governor of Mid-Euphrates					+	+						+	+				+		5
S'adum Hammadi	Vice Prime Minister													+				+		2
Izzet al-Duri al-Samara'i	Vice President		+			+	+						+	+			+			6
Mohammad Sa'id al-Shataf	Minister of Foreign Affairs													+				+		2
Tariq Aziz Hana	Vice Prime Minister					+	+									+			+	4
Taha Yassin Ramadhan	Vice Prime Minister					+	+	+		+			+	+			+			7
Latif Nesayif Jasim	Minister					+	+						+	+			+			5
Mohammed Zimam al-Sa'doun	Minister of the Interior					+	+	+			+		+	+			+			7
'Amir Mohammad Rashid al-Ubaidi	Minister of Petroleum												+	+			+			3
Taha Mohyi al-Din Ma'rouf	Vice President														+		+			2

Name	Position	Kindred of Saddam Hussein	Direct frequent access to S. H.	Albu Nasir tribe	Of Takrit origin	Command Council of the Revolution	Ba'th Regional Command	Military Post	Special Grade	Army	Intelligence Service	Republican Guard	Other Important Tribe	Iraqi Arab Ethnic Group	Iraqi Kurdish Ethnic Group	Other Iraqi Ethnic Group	Sunni Religious Group	Shi'ite Religious Group	Christian Religious Group	Total
Madhat Omid	Minister of Health														+		+			2
Fahad al-Shagrah	Minister of Education					+							+	+			+			4
Munther al-Shawi	Minister of Justice				+								+	+			+			4

This chart attempts to classify in an empirical way by order of importance and power the principal members of the Iraqi 'nomenklatura'. The categories are obviously a little arbitrary but they are the ones that appear important in the eyes of Saddam Hussein and to those who interpret everyday observable practice of the exercise of power and influence on public life. Despite its limitations, the results can be experimentally verified; its purpose is simply to demonstrate that the real hierarchy of power does not map onto the institutional power of the State, or the Ba'th Party or the Army but, rather, is organized around belonging to kindred, house or tribe (Albu Nasir) plus the supplementary emergence of new solidarities (belonging to a religion, region, district or particular army structure).

Notes

1. On 25 March 1997, the RCC issued Resolution No 24, prohibiting tribes from challenging, suing or taking any legal action against state functionaries who caused any injury in the course of performing their duties. The Iraqi newspapers reported this as indicating that the RCC had prohibited any use of the well known tribal courts to seek 'tribal settlement' (*Fasl 'Ashairi* – this includes compensation and other penalties). *Fasl 'Ashairi* had become a widespread phenomenon in recent years, a fact which led the domestic press to launch a campaign to put an end to it. *(al-Hayat* newspaper, London, 26 March 1997.)

2. It has been repeatedly shown that, when it comes to Iraq, some western researchers are often reduced to relying on reports with hidden purposes or ends dictated by the politico-military and financed by the intelligence services of certain regional or world powers.

3. Publicly, Saddam Hussein identifies himself with many figures drawn from Mesopotamian or Islamic or modern Arab/Third World history. For example, he sometimes presents himself as descended from the neo-Babylonian king, Nebuchadnezzar; in other circumstances as direct descendant of the Bani Hashim house, which is the house of the Prophet Muhammad and his cousin and son-in-law, Ali, even going so far as to rebaptise his natal village (al-'Ouje near the town of Takrit) as Um al-Qura (the name used by Arabs in the time of the Prophet for the town of Mecca). He has had the words Allah Akbar (God is Great) inscribed on the Iraqi flag. Saddam Hussein has also given himself the name Al Mansur Bi-Allah (honorific title of the Caliph conquering Andalusian Umawide – Mohammad Ibn Abi 'Amir, called 'the victorious' or, more precisely, 'the one to whom Allah gave victory'.) On top of that and following the Muslim theological texts which recognize the 99 names of God (Allah), the official Iraqi media displays attribute 99 names to Saddam Hussein! Hundreds of books, colloquia, articles, films etc. by Iraqi, Arab and European authors have been devoted to legitimating this enterprise. Here I mention only one of them, very little known either to the public or specialists (for political reasons and reasons specific to Saddam Hussein's own family, the publication was very quickly banned and withdrawn from Iraqi libraries): al-Sayid Ahmad al-Rijebi al-Hussayni, *al-Noujoum al-zawahir, Fi shajarat al-sayid al-amir Nasir,* Baghdad: Dar al-Houriya lil-tiba'a, 1980.

4. It is both very sad and totally symptomatic to mention here the connivance, not to say political complicity, that the great French historian and orientalist, Jacques Berque, has given to Saddam Hussein's political system.

5. Well before the Gulf War and the Iraq–US hostilities since 1990, most Arab writers and intellectuals (particularly from Egypt and the Maghreb) have openly and without any critical reserve, defended the humanly indefensible official Iraqi politics, thus confirming a flagrantly schizophrenic politics. From memory, I cite here only certain names, known in the West for their struggle for liberation from European cultural tutelage: the Tunisian historian Hisham Ja'it and the Moroccan thinker, Mohammed 'Abid al-Jabiri.

6. See Maurice Godelier, 'Is social anthropology indissolubly linked to the West, its birthplace?', *International Social Science Journal*, No. 143, 1995, pp. 141–59.

7. Jean-Pierre Dignard and Carmaine Bernand, 'De Tehran à Tehuantepec: L'ethnologie au crible des aires culturelles', *L'anthropologie sociale: état des lieux*, Paris: Le Navarin livres de poche, 1986, pp. 54–77.

8. Although the work which has recently appeared by the historian Pierre-Jean Luizard, one of the rare French specialists on the Shi'ite population of Iraq, is undoubtedly important, he suffers from a certain imprecision, approximation and overarching conceptual confusion, particularly when it comes to such important social structures and relations as those between: house, family, chiefdom, kinship and even the tribe (*la maison; la famille, la chefferie, la parenté, et même la tribu*)! Nor are these simply generic confusions shared by all contemporary researchers on Arab-Islamic societies. For example, two very instructive and critical studies are about to be published on kinship and so-called 'Arab marriage'. The first is by Pierre Bonte, in which he re-interrogates the universal bearing of Claude Lévi-Strauss's theories of exchange and its limitations in respect to the 'Arab-Islamic world'. He emphasizes that 'Arab marriage', based on the union of the 'agnatic' lineage, is not based on exchange and reciprocity but above all on a system of division between men of the same lineage. Edouard Conte implicitly but crucially puts in issue the anthropological approach of Françoise Héritier concerning matrimonial prohibitions and the logic of transmission of bodily substances and its implications from the perspective of Arabic and Persian traditions. See Pierre-Jean Luizard, *La formation de l'Irak contemporaine*, Paris: Editions du CNRS, 1991, especially Chapter C, pp 62–80; Pierre Bonte, 'L'échange, est-il universel? *L'Homme, Revue franaise d'anthropologie*, No. 154–155, 2000, pp. 39–66; Edouard Conte, 'Enigmes persanes, traditions arabes, les interdictions matrimoniales dérivées de l'Allaitement selon l'Ayatollah Khomeyni', Jean-Luc Jamard, Emmanuel Terray and Margarita Xanthakou (eds), *En substances: textes pour Françoise Héritier*, Paris: Fayard, 2000, pp 155–81; Françoise Héritier, 'Identité de substance et parenté de lait dans le monde arabe' in Pierre Bonte (ed), *Epouser au plus prôche*, Paris: Editions de l'EHESS, 1994, pp. 149–64; also by Françoise Héritier and on the same theme, *Les deux soeurs et leur mère*, Paris: Editions Odile Jacob, 1994, especially Chapter 2: 'Que disent la sagesse grècque, la Bible et le Coran', pp. 55–87.

9. Among the factual studies of tribes in Iraq that I would consider valuable at least in part (some are a little dated) are: Amin al-Hassan, *al-hala al-ijtimaiyya li'al-'asha'ir al-'iraqiyya* (The social situation of Iraqi tribes), Baghdad, 1929; Abbas al-'Azzawi, *'Asha'ir al-'Iraq* (The Tribes of Iraq) Bagdad, 1937, 3 volumes); Shakir Moustafa Salim, *Ech-Chibayish: An anthropological study of a Marsh village in Iraq*, University of London: PhD, 1955 (two versions of this thesis have appeared in Arabic in Baghdad, one in 1956 and the other in 1970); Ali al-Wardi, *Lamahat ijtima'iyya min tarikh al-Iraq al-hadith* (Social Aspects of the Modern Histories of Iraq), Bagdad, 1972, 6 volumes; 'Abd al-Jalil al-Tahir, *al-'Asha'ir al-'iraqiyya* (The Tribes of Iraq) Bagdad, 1972; and in recent years, following the instructions of the Iraqi authorities, in particular, the Minister of the Interior and the Office of Tribal Affairs, an encyclopaedia has been published by one Thamer 'Abd al-Hassan al-'Amiri, *Mawsou'at al-'asha'ir al-'iraqiyya* (Encyclopaedia of Iraqi Tribes), Bagdad: 1992–95, 9 volumes.

10. See Maurice Godelier, 'Afterword: Transformations and lines of evolution' in Maurice Godelier, Thomas R. Thrautman and Franklin E. Tjon Sie Fat, *Transformations of Kinship*, Washington and London: Smithsonian Institution Press, 1998, pp 386–413.

11. Edmund Leach, 'Virgin Birth', The Henry Meyers Lecture, Proceedings of the Royal Anthropological Institute, 1996, pp. 39–49; Maurice Godelier, 'Afterword ... ', op. cit, no. 19; Jonathan Friedman and M. J. Rowlands (eds) *The Evolution of Social Systems*, Liverpool: Duckworth, 1977, pp. 201–76; Jonathan Friedman, 'System, Structure and Contradiction in the Evolution of 'Asiatic' Social Formations', *Social Studies in Oceania and Southeast Asia*.

12. Hanna Batatu, *The Old Social Classes and Revolutionary Movements of Iraq*, Princeton, Princeton University Press, 1978, especially Chapter 6 'The Sheikhs, Aghas and Peasants', pp 63–152; Ali al-Wardi, *Dirasa fi Tabi'at al-mujtama' al-'iraqi* (A Study on the Nature of Iraqi Society), Baghdad, 1965, especially Chapters 3 and 6. Hanna Batatu, op. cit., no. 23, especially pp. 53–361 and 465–82. To add to the work of Hanna Batatu, and with a critical perspective, see Robert A. Fernea and Louis W. Roger (ed.), *The Old Social Classes Revisited*, London & New York: I. B. Tauris, 1991. For a detailed approach to the origins and first years of the modern Iraqi State, see Peter Sluglett, *Britain in Iraq, 1914–1932*, London: Ithaca Press, 1976.

13. Marion Farouk-Sluglett and Peter Sluglett, 'L'Irak et le Nouvel Ordre Mondiale', *La pensée*, No. 285, 1992, pp. 7–28.

14. Equally, it could be that large fractions of the Sunni population who, under other circumstances, would not have supported Saddam Hussein, have been led to do so by the fear of a fundamentalist Shi'ite regime. At the same time, outside the holy cities of Karbala and Najaf, many 'secular' Shi'ites probably share these fears and support the regime for similar reasons.

15. For a very interesting account of how a society constructs its political universe (taking the case of Morocco), thinks its relation to power and follows a mechanism of allegiance, see Mohamed Tozy, *Monarchie et Islam, politique au Maroc*, Paris: Presses des Sciences Politiques, 1999. The work of the Moroccan anthropologist, Abdella Hammoudi, (even though the information on the Arab societies of Maghreb is out of date) remains very useful. See his *'Master and Disciple: The cultural foundations of Moroccan authoritarianism'*, Chicago and London: University of Chicago Press, 1997.

16. Islam, from the start and as a universal religion, has faced this contradiction. Thus it seems that the reaffirmation of these forms of *'asabiya* go together with the promotion of forms of life and a system of values that are deeply anchored in an Arabic-Islamic consciousness, particularly in the countryside. But it is also true that Shi'ite institutions in Iraq (as instances of the supra-tribal supra-ethnic-national) adapt themselves with more difficulty to tribal realities: see various seminars given by the great Ayatollah Mohammad Sadiq al-Sadr (several years before his assassination in 1999 by the Iraqi powers that be). These seminars were collected and printed in a pamphlet which was banned and then secretly distributed. It is titled: *al-Fiqh al-'ashairi (Tribal Jurisprudence)*.

17. Bertrand Badie, *L'Etat importé, l'occidentalisation de l'ordre politique*, Paris: Fayard, 1992, pp. 249–52; see also his 'Ruptures et innovations dans l'approche sociologique

des relations internationales', in Revue des mondes musulmans et de la Méditerranée (*RMMM)*, Vol 68–69, No. 2–3, 1993, pp. 65–74.

18. Bertrand Badie, *La fin des territoires, essai sur le désordre international et sur l'utilitié sociale du respect*, Paris: Fayard, 1995, and also his *Un monde sans souveraineté, les Etats entre ruse et responsabilité*, Paris: Fayard, 1999, especially Chapter 4, 'Les souverainetés déchues'.

19. I think that it is profoundly wrong to reduce Saddam Hussein's political power base solely to the tribal dimension, especially since the tribal group, house (*maison*) and kindred (*parentèle*) occupy a determinate place within the State. Already, the organization of the political system involves a combination of three overlapping levels (see Appendix 1): a religious denominational-political level; a second, tribal-regionalist level (to which we have devoted the second part of this study); the third level is the politico-institutional order which has not been the object of any deep analysis in the present essay. However, these levels do not present themselves neatly separated in reality. For example, the politico-institutional power is articulated around eight centres: (i) the RCC, which is officially the most important Iraqi political institution; (ii) The Special Presidential Guard (around 14,000) in charge of Saddam Hussein's security and placed under the command of the president's own direct kindred (his younger son Qusay); (iii) the Republican Guard, a hand-picked military unit of about 35 men usually commanded by members of the Albu Nasir tribe (Saddam Hussein's tribe) or by someone from the town of Takrit; (iv) the militias, which are composed of two organizations, the first being far more important or the regime, Saddam Hussein's *Fedayin* or Commandos, about 60,000 men, the other organization being the Popular Army 'al-Jaysh al Sha'bi', also about 60,000 men, a sort of Party militia. The Commandos were set up by Uday, the elder son of the president, in 1994. They are in charge of (among other things) the security for all those with powerful positions. In the wake of an attempted assassination in 1996, with serious injuries inflicted on Uday, this militia is today commanded by the younger son, Qusay, whose elevation now seems to have been confirmed:he was named responsible for the new inter-army *Umm al-ma'arik* (mother of all battles) and Joint Supreme Chief of the armies (joint with his father). As for the Popular Army, it is entrusted to an old comrade of Saddam, Taha Yassine al-Jazrawi (originally from Mosul), who is part of the core group around Saddam Hussein; (v) the fifth decision-making centre is Intelligence and Security Services; (vi) the sixth is the regional command of the Ba'th Party; (vii) the seventh is the Army; and (viii) the last is the Government.Of course, all these centres are not of equal importance.For example, belonging to the RCC and under the direction of the Ba'th Party would not totally guarantee having the ear of Saddam Hussein.But to be direct kindred or from the same house or tribe and in the Special Presidential Guard would assure a very important position in the hierarchy of the regime. See, Faleh A Jabbar, 'The State, Society, Clan and Army in Iraq: A totalitarian state in the twilight of totalitarianism' in Faleh A Jabbar, Ahmed Shikara and Keiko Sakai, *From Storm to Thunder: the unfinished showdown between Iraq and the US*, Tokyo: Institute of Developing Economies, 1968, pp. 1–27.

20. On nomadic culture in Iraq and the Maghreb countries, see Ali al-Wardi, *Lamaha*t, op cit; Mas'oud Zahir, *al-Mashreq al-'arabi al-mu'asir, min al-badawa ila ad-dawla al-*

haditha (The Contemporary Arab Maghreb: From nomadism to modern state), Beirut: Ma'had al-inma' al-'arabi, 1986 (especially Chapter 2), pp. 203–39.

21. Robertson W. Smith, *Kinship and Marriage in Early Arabia*, Boston: Beacon Books, 1966 (1903), p 38.

22. Daniel Marin Varisco, 'Metaphors and Sacred History: The genealogy of Muhammad and the Arab tribe', *Anthropological Quarterly*, Volume 68, No. 3, 1996, pp. 139–56.

23. The term *fakhith* is in general usage by Iraqis to designate patrilineal kinship groups arising from the application of a principle of unilinear descent in which the kinship links extend over four to five generations. A *fakhith* is thus a set of men and women who consider themselves related (*awlad 'am*) by their patrilineal descent from a common ancestor. But, in reality there is an equivocation around this term: the use of the word *fakhith* has long been very polyvalent, depending on the region, as was already remarked by Abbas al-'Azzawi, op. cit., no. 18, Vol. 1, pp. 52–54 – since the 1930s. According to him, other words exist to designate such structures: *bdida*, plural: *bedayid* or *fenda*, plural: *fened*. Thamer 'Abdul-Hassan al-'Ameri, in his *Encyclopaedia of Iraqi Tribes* – op cit, no. 19, Vol. 1, p. 30, established an equivalence between the term *fakhith* and clan, such that the word *fenda* became, in this classification, the equivalent of lineage (the term used among the southern Iraqi tribes). Linguistically speaking, the term *fakhith* signifies 'thigh', as was indicated above, while *fenda* is the meaty part, the flesh without the bone. Each *fakhith* has its chief and often its own name and a specific territorial seat generally corresponding to a single village or even a part of a village.

24. The word *hamoula* means 'carry away' in Arabic. The root *h m l* evokes the mutual aid that men of the same *hamoula* are supposed to bring to each other. This word, which does not belong to Iraqi Arab society, is used as much in the countryside as among town-dwellers without reflecting the same social structure. There is no consensus among anthropologists about the *hamoula*. For example, Shakir Moustafa Salim, in his thesis, *Ech-Chibayish* (op. cit. no. 18, pp. 128–33), used the word *hamoula* to designate a patrilinileal clan. According to him, it is made up of several lineages and can be referred to not only as a domestic unit but also as a political unit encompassing many *fakhith*, due to its socio-political and numerical importance. By contrast, neither Abbas al-'Azzawi nor Thamer 'Abdul-Hassan al-'Ameri have actually sought to analyse the *hamoula* in their respective works. Then again, anthropologists working among the Palestinian village populations have for a long time observed that the *hamoula*, while an important agnatic group, nevertheless does not constitute an agnatic lineage. According to them, the village groups sharing the same patronymic are often wrongly treated as being Bedouin *hamoula*, with the segments of a unilinear structure of filiation and direct genealogical links. Thus, the *hamoula* is a group articulated in an agnatic idiom and composed of a variable number of patrilineal units invoking a common ancestor, real or fictive, which the genealogy can trace back – the patrilateral line – for five or six generations. It is virilocal (patrilocal), that is, on marrying, the wife goes to live in the house of the father of their conjoint, or in a neighbourhood of the *hamoula*, or in the hearth (*dar-home*) of their husband. The size of the *hamoula* can be very variable. There are small *hamoula* that number dozens or hundreds of individuals and large *hamoula* that can go up to many thousands. The number and the dimension which make up a *hamoula* is an important factor determining its power. This factor combines with its political force

(access to local and national power), and material wealth. If a large *hamoula* is poor and has not succeeded in weaving relations with other larger *hamoulas* in the local, regional and national ladder, it cannot secure its power and social prestige either in the village or in the urban milieux nor, consequently, in the area of the central political power. See Scott Atran, 'Hamoula organisation and Masha'a tenure in Palestine', *Man* (N.S.), Vol. 21, 1986, pp. 271–295; Antoun, A., *Arab Village* (Bloomington, Indiana: Indiana University Press, 1972); Rosenfeld, H., 'Social and economic factors in explanations of the increased rate of patrilineal endogamy in the Arab village in Israel' in Bristiany, J. (ed.), *Mediterranean Family Structures* (Cambridge: Cambridge University Press, 1976) ; Mohammad Murad, '*al-nitham al-qarabi wa 'asabiyat al-sulta fi al-Mashrek al-'arabi al-mu'asir*' (Le système parental et l'Assabiya du pouvoir dans le Machrek arabe contemporain), *al-Fikr al-Arabi*, No. 77, 1994, pp. 169–200; Shakir Moustafa Salim, *Ibid*, pp. 128–33.

25. In the case of Iraq, the relations that link tribes to the central power pass principally through three channels: the Bureau of Tribal Affairs, directed personally by Saddam Hussein and his younger son, Qusay; the Minister of the Interior through various politico-security representatives; and the Ba'th Party, through various security services, the paramilitary militia and the Army.

26. On segmentarist discourses and analysis, see in particular, Middleton, J. and Tait, D., *Tribes without Ruler*, London, Routledge, 1952; Gellner, E., *The Saints of Atlas*, Chicago, Chicago University Press, 1969; Hart, D., 'Dadda Atta and his Forty Grandsons: the Socio-Political Organization of the Ait Atta of Southern Morocco.' MENAS, Cambridge, 1981; Akbar, S., and Hart, D., (eds.) *Islam in Tribal Societies. From the Atlas to Indus.* London, Routledge, 1984. For more information about the segmentarist theory, see Kenneth Brown's contribution in this volume.

27. Following and elaborating on this logic of the creation of asymmetric debt, *hiba*, Saddam Hussein has presented himself for a number of years as *Sheikh al-Mashayikh*, i.e. the sheikh of all sheiks, a title used in the great sheikhdoms of the past. This new title suggested to various rich tribes and houses, to build, in the suburbs of Baghdad and in other towns, various *Maudhif* 'guest-house' in the name of *Sheikh al-Mashayikh*, i.e. Saddam Hussein.

28. In 1968 the Ba'th Party had very few active members and did not have a credible political base among the population from which to draw officers prepared to manage the affairs of State. That is why, after the coup d'état of 1968, the majority of powerful men came from the same tribe (Albu Nasir), the same town (Takrit), the same region (the Sunni Triangle in the Northwest), the same religious denomination (Sunni Islam) and the same ethnic background (Arab). See Marion Farouk-Sluglett and Peter Sluglett, 'From Gang to Elite: The Iraqi Ba'th Party's Consolidation of Power, 1968–1975', paper presented to the International Political Science Association, Paris, 15–20 July 1985.

29. The term *parentèle*, 'kindred' in English, has for several decades provoked much debate among anthropologists, especially the British. According to John Freeman, kindred (which one could translate in Arabic as *Ahl*), means all the known cognates of a given individual and who have common kin. Thus, for a start, kindred is generally constituted by the (living) consanguines of 'Ego': the paternal and maternal parents and descendants. However, it is not limited only to consanguines, of the sort that often surround the matrimonial kinship links of Ego. The members of a

kindred group are not necessarily bound to each other but they are all bonded (*apparenté*). Ego has a poetnatial set of relations which varies according to the society and the stakes. He has kindred who can be called upon for help (*parentèles d'entraide*), kindred by heritage (*parentèles d'hèritage*), ritual kindred (*parentèles de rituel*), political kindred (*parentèles politiques*). This flexibility opens up a vast array of individual strategies. One approaches a particular kin member in certain circumstances or, in a different situation, kin by marriage, neighbours, or friends who amplify the kindred network. From the internal point of view of kindred, an individual can be seen as possessing a set of potential relations. It is important to understand how he makes use of them, since the repertoire of choices available within the kindred group often determines the entire physiognomy of local groups. Once a person has brought his kindred into play, he is committed to maximizing the possible strategies. These strategies depend upon the density of the kindred group. Such strategies are extremely important in any society (such as Iraq) with a system that does not differentiate filiation and descent to the extent that they are reduced to a unlinear (patrilineal) system. The kindred group of Ego always already depends upon the strategies chosen by his ascendants (and the choices of those before) and the way in which he himself has made connections to the web of solidarity. With the exception of full brothers who share exactly the same kindred up to the moment of marriage, each individual establishes his own kindred, which can alter with circumstances and life moments. Kindred is thus essentially 'kin potential' (*un potential de relations*) which may be lost if not maintained or taken up (especially so with distant kin). In short, kindred is a set of open and practical relations around Ego, permitting him (if there are no constraints or particular limits) to opt for open and fluid affiliations yet, even so, without the power to constitute a group of the form of a house. For a useful summary of this debate, see Francis Zimermann, *Enquète sur la parenté*, Paris: Presses de l'Université de France, 1993, pp. 140–44. See also Meyer Fortes, 'Descent, affiliation and affinity', *Man*, Vol. 59, 1959, pp. 208–212; Maurice Freeman, 'On the Concept of Kindred', *Journal of the Royal Anthropological Institute*, Vol. 91, 1961, pp. 192–220; Peter R. Goethals, 'Personal Kindred and Community: An Indonesian example', Paper presented at the 58th Annual Meeting of the American Anthropological Association, Washington DC, 1958; Mitchell, E. William, 'Theoretical problems in the concept of "kindred"', Paper presented at the 58th Annual Meeting of American Anthropological Association, Mexico City, Mexico, 1959.

30. The most delicate question for a tribe or a clan with a role politically situated at the helm of the State is to assure the passing of power within the interior of the group and thus to establish a succession without interior disturbances. The cases of Syria, Jordan and Morocco, to cite few examples, show that one can direct affairs in such a way as to establish a seeming 'tradition' giving direct/immediate kindred (filiation) primacy over full-blood brothers, cross-cousins, and their descendants. This is not necessarily easily done: in Syria, Rifat al-Assad's refusal to allow power to pass from his late brother (Hafiz al-Assad) to the latter's son (Bashar); in Jordan with the dismissal of Crown Prince Hassan in favour of the sons of King Hussein and the sons of King Abdullah II; and in Iraq the preparations for the passing of power have multiplied in the last few months with the constitution of the Board of Guardians and the public return of the half-brothers of Saddam in the service of the two sons.

FIVE

Tribalization as a Tool of State Control in Iraq: Observations on the Army, the Cabinets and the National Assembly

Keiko Sakai

The resurgence of tribes and tribalism in Iraq is the outcome of a multitude of factors, cardinal among which are power structures. This is our starting point.

Under the Ba'th single party rule in Iraq, an authoritarian and totalitarian hegemonic structure has permeated social and political spaces since 1968. Through the control of all social and political organizations and by demolishing other rival political groups, the state established its supremacy over society by dominating and perfecting instruments of coercion, the military, intelligence and security organizations, while controlling autonomous social associations and centres of authority and power.[1] Organizations like trade unions, student unions, women's unions and professional unions, were reconstructed and incorporated into state-party structures of power. The thrust of this hegemonic drive, however, was directed against both modern associations and traditional social and economic centres of power and authority. The basic principle was to subsume society under an unchallenged, omnipresent, omnipotent state control. Accordingly, not only rival trade unions or associations but also traditional structures and authorities, like *ulema*, religious schools, religious endowments, tribal sheikhs and other local notables, were hegemonized.

Paradoxical as it may seem, the Ba'th regime weakened autonomous societal structures on the one hand, but on the other hand it accelerated the atomization of individuals and their detachment from the web of family, guild or the tribe, a condition sin qua non of an autonomous modern civil society.[2]

In the eighties, however, the Ba'th party changed course relative to traditional value systems and structures. This change may have been the outcome of the shift from a system of control based on party hierarchy to another based on the one-person control by Saddam Hussein. After the mid-eighties, Saddam carried the networks of his power base beyond the party apparatus, using traditional social ties. Creating or reviving traditional social relations, he put himself at the center of these patronage and loyalty networks as an 'absolute authority' both in the realm of the modern and the traditional. This 'revival of the old traditional loyalty' led, for example, to the emergence of the notion of 'Iraq as a reborn Babylon' or 'Saddam as the reincarnation of Nebuchadnezzar.'[3]

For Saddam Hussein the manipulation of traditional social networks and identities has been an instrument of expanding his own power base and mobilizing the broader masses with minimal risk to his own authority.

The resurgence of tribalism under Saddam's regime was first evident in the resurgence of literature on tribes in the mid-1980s. Much earlier, the publication of such books as 'Abbas al-'Azzawi's well-known classical volumes, *Iraqi Tribes*,[4] originally published in the mid 1950s, was banned under the Ba'th. The party tried to restrain such research works on tribes, claiming that tribes were a 'traditional' pre-modern social factor, and a 'shameful' aspect for 'revolutionary' development.

Among the early indications of the rebirth of tribal values was the publication of Dr. Yusuf al-Shaykh Ibrahim al-Samarrai's work on Iraqi tribes in the northern parts of Iraq in 1985,[5] and then his more general work in two volumes entitled *Iraqi Tribes* in 1989.[6] His works were followed by those of other scholars, and in 1990, two volumes on Iraqi tribes in upper and middle Tigris and upper Euphrates areas were published.[7] In 1992 al-Mashhadani published a book on his tribe, and al-Maliki published one on the tribes in the Maysan provinces.[8] Most of these works depend on 'Azzawi's research, but one of the most noteworthy things which they added, was information on Saddam's clan, Albu Nasir, which is claimed to be of *sayyid*, noble, lineage. Undoubtedly, this boom of publications on tribes in the latter half of the 1980s is a kind of 'rewriting' of family history.

This shift was a preparatory step to further encourage the revival of tribal identity. This is evident from the fact that tribalism and tribal networks re-emerged on the surface of Iraq's political scene in the late 1980s and 1990s. But the question is whether the regime's policy accelerated the resurgence of existing tribalism, or whether it created a novel tribal identity, different from the one which had existed before the advent of modernization. Another key question concerns the possible divergence between the regime's intent in using tribal groups, and the latter's political aspirations. In other words: has the renewed tribal value system been totally controlled by the state, or has it preserved (or come to possess) any autonomy from state control? These and other questions require an examination of several aspects, above all: the changes in Iraq's tribal society, the deployment of tribal and other networks for mobilisation and recruitment, in the army, the cabinets and the National Assembly.

Tribal Factors in Modern Iraqi Political History

Early Tribal Society

Pre-modern Iraq (or, better still, Mesopotamia and the Arabian Peninsula) has had a long history of lacking a strong central government. Parallel to this was the presence of powerful tribal groups such as the Muntafiq, Shammar, Dulaim, and Khaza'il confederations during the Ottoman era. Some of these enjoyed autonomy as *Imara* or principalities, similar to those in other Gulf areas. Centralization started in the last period of the Ottoman era, after Medhet Pasha's reforms in the 1870s. The land reforms introduced by the Ottomans provided tribal sheikhs the right to usufructuary possession of the land, and many of them became large landholders. This changed the position of the sheikhs in their tribal society, as their relation with their tribesmen was transformed into a relation of landholders and peasants, and they ceased to be military and political leaders in their community. As a result of the Ottoman military campaigns against strong tribal confederations and the policy to conciliate them by offering them administrative posts, tribal leaders became more and more subordinate to the central authority, and lost their integral power over their kinsmen.

Some tribes, however, resisted state administration. This was evident during the First World War, under the British Mandate, or under the newly installed monarchy. These intransigent tribal groups were active in opposing the centralization by the new regime, especially the introduction of the conscription system in the modern army in the 1930s.[9] The major forces in the anti-British resistance that developed in 1920 were tribes in the Middle Euphrates and Shi'ite *ulema* and *sayyid*, in addition to the Shammar tribal confederation in the north, known as Shammar Jarba, which supported Prince Faisal's independence movement for the Arab Kingdom.[10] The former tribes made use of their military supremacy over the newly born national Army until they were subsumed in late 1930s. Otherwise, most tribal leaders were embraced by the new regime as a part of an aristocratic feudal class of the monarchy. Many of the tribal leaders in the south became absentee landholders and joined the circle of the political elite, became members of the parliament, the upper house and the council of ministers. British policy toward tribal sheikhs was to incorporate them in the regime and separate them from other anti-government or revolutionary forces. When the time came for the revolutionary era after 1958, most of them were purged from their high government posts and lost their land and privileges.

Tribalism in the Army

Although the traditional tribal system was much weakened both by the centralization that occured during the late period of Ottoman rule and by the monarchy, informal and emotional ties between tribesmen remained in modern organizations.

In the Army, which expanded rapidly in order to sustain the integrity of the newly built nation-state, cadets were recruited mainly through the personal networks of high government officials in the 1930s. The Army itself was established around a core of ex-Ottoman officers. In particular, this group was composed of the so-called 'Sharifian Officers,' who supported King Faisal in his efforts to build the Arab Kingdom in Syria, and who were almost completely Sunni Arab. High-ranking posts in the Army were dominated by Sunnis (both Arab and Kurd), and under these Sunni officers and high government officials, large numbers of impoverished inhabitants from Sunni areas flowed into the Army.

The best-known example is the case of the Takriti tribal segment in the Army. Inhabitants of Takrit had made a living in the region's traditional manufacturing industry, which was the production of *kalak* (rafts for river transportation and trade). However, the industry declined in the late 19th century as river navigation system was modernized. A large number of youths from this small town flowed into Baghdad searching for employment. Mawlud Mukhlis, one of the most important Sharifian officers and politicians of the monarchy, who had close ties with King Faisal and Nuri al-Sa'id, introduced them into the Army. Mukhlis was born in Mosul but his father was originally from Takrit, as was his wife, and he had kinship relation with Ahmad Hasan al-Bakr, the first president under the Ba'th regime in 1968.[11]

Recruiting through kinship and local networks is also evident in the case of other local groups. Two ex-Sharifian officers, who held cabinet posts under the monarchy, were from al-Jumaylat clan of the Upper Euphrates, and they encouraged their tribesmen to enrol in the Army. Also members from different segments of Rawa, a small Sunni town on the upper Euphrates, were able to find in high ranking positions in the Army and the government, ex-Sharifian patrons like Ibrahim al-Rawi, Commander of the Fourth Division, Jamil al-Rawi, Minister of Communication, and Rashid al-Khawjah, Minister of Defence. Residents of the Upper Euphrates had already suffered the same decline of their local industry, and like the Takritis, they migrated to the capital, as did, and constituted the great majority of junior and medium ranking officers in the Army in the final years of the monarchy.

Thus, the composition of the Army under the monarchy reflected the tribal and local networks of ex-Sharifian officers who dominated the political scene until the 1958 revolution. The presence of such groups of common local/tribal backgrounds in the Army, however, led to the consolidation of informal personal networks within the military, which were external to the institutional chain and command structure. Parallel to the politicization of the Army and its involvement in politics beyond the thirties, military figures relied to a great extent on their local/tribal networks in the question of whether to seize power or to stabilize control of the government. The 'Arif Brothers' regime (1963–68) relied heavily on members of their tribe, al-Jumaylat, such as Sa'id Sulaybi, Commander of Republican Forces, Ibrahim al-Dawod or Abdul Razzaq al-Nayif, chief of Military Intelligence. More obviously, the first Ba'th regime in 1963 leaned on Army officers from Takrit through the local networks of Ahmad Hassan al-Bakr and others. Each clannish faction in the military, however, sustained ups and downs with the change of hands, and shared their fortune, or misfortune, with their patrons at the helm.

Even among the same local group, tribal conflicts occurred, as in the case of the al-Beijat (also-Begat) and al-Shiyaisha sub-clans in Takrit. The former is the sub-clan of Ahmad Hassan al-Bakr, and the latter is the local group of Hardan Takriti, Minister of Defence in the second Ba'th regime of 1986, and Tahir Yahya, a Ba'th sympathizer in the early 1960s. Tahir Yahya was overthrown together with his mentor, Abdul Rahman 'Arif in July 1968, whereas Hardan Takriti, who was the first defence minister of the second Ba'th regime, was sacked and later assassinated in 1971 at the hands of the rising young leader, Saddam Hussein, a member of the Beijat clan.

Thus the mechanisms of tribal and local networks started to affect the political scene through the Army in its modern context. The regime's continued dependence on tribal/local networks is the result of its lack of legitimacy, absence of effective methods of mass mobilization and of any political support beyond the clanish groups in the military.

The New Policy Under the Ba'th Regime

In its initial stages, Saddam Hussein's Ba'th regime pursued a dual policy. On the one hand, he tried to minimize the direct influence of the Army, and sought to 'Ba'thize' it, i.e. to subsume it under the control of the civilian organs of the party. As he had had no military career and his political rivals were mainly high officers with close relations to Ahmad Hassan al-Bakr, Saddam Hussein made use of the rivalry between civilian and military factions of the party, and moved to undermine the power base of the latter. Takriti officers dominated the supreme organizations in both the state and the party before Saddam Hussein was elevated to the post of Vice Secretary General. After his ascendance, however, he selectively elevated non-military, non-Takriti party cadres (such as Tariq 'Aziz, Sa'dun Shaker, Hasan 'Ali, Na'im Haddad) to top civilian posts, leaving them no room to rely on power sources other than their personal loyalty to him. In addition, he banned the usage of *laqab* (tribal title) or *nisba* (lineage title), in the name of revolutionary policy, and advocated the eradication of aristocratic factors such as 'nobility of origin' based on tribes, status groups or notable families. Thus, on the surface of the regime, he opened the government and party posts to those who had not been part of the rivalries between the major tribal/local groups based in the Army.

On the other hand, Saddam Hussein did his best to deploy and recruit members of his own clan and extended family to coercive agencies, such as the security and intelligence services and the military. 'Adnan Khairallah, his maternal cousin and brother-in-law, Barzan Ibrahim, his half brother, and 'Ali Hasan al-Majid, his paternal cousin, started their careers in the mid-1970s as Minister of Defence, Head of Intelligence and Head of the Security Office respectively. With the exception of 'Adnan Khairalla, they remained quite far from the official scene of party politics, and remained 'wire pullers' until the mid-1980s. Their advancement was based on their personal relationship with Saddam Hussein.

The Cabinets' Composition Under the Ba'th Regime (until 1990)

While the mainstay of power was the RCC and the agencies of organized violence, the government, an administrative and executive branch of less importance, was yet another arena of contest, patronage and tribal networking. The appointment of cabinet ministers was more of a tool for widening political participation, a means to curb the power of the military, and, in a sense, a showcase for the facade of an even distribution of power among the different segments of society, such as the Shi'is, Kurds, Christians, or various Ba'thi regional or clannish groups.

To follow the shifts of Saddam Hussein's policy in this respect, it is necessary to analyse the composition of the cabinets in terms of segments and groups (see Table 1).

Table 1: Ministerial composition under the Ba'th party

	President Bakr		President Hussein		
	Stage 1 7/68–4/74	Stage 2 6/74–6/79	Stage 1 7/79–6/82	Stage 2 7/82–12/86	Stage 3 1/87–90
Total number of ministers	48 (100)	60 (100)	39 (100)	38 (100)	41 (100)
Ethnic/sectarian					
Arab/Sunni	25 (52.1)	28 (46.7)	18 (46.2)	20 (52.6)	22 (53.7)
Arab/Shi'i	7 (14.6)	11 (18.3)	7 (17.9)	8 (21.1)	8 (19.5)
Kurd	7 (14.6)	8 (13.3)	8 (20.5)	7 (18.4)	6 (14.6)
Christian	- (-)	1 (1.7)	1 (2.6)	2 (5.3)	1 (2.4)
Occupational Background					
Served in Previous Regime	18 (37.5)	9 (15.0)	3 (7.7)	2 (5.3)	1 (2.4)
Party worker	19 (39.6)	31 (51.7)	21 (53.8)	16 (42.1)	15 (36.6)
Technocrat	9 (18.8)	19 (31.7)	13 (33.3)	13 (34.2)	18 (43.9)
Local career	- (-)	7 (11.7)	4 (10.3)	6 (15.8)	6 (14.6)
Origin of birth					
Middle Tigris	9 (18.8)	8 (13.4)	5 (12.8)	7 (18.4)	9 (21.9)

	President Bakr		President Hussein		
	Stage 1 7/68–4/74	Stage 2 6/74–6/79	Stage 1 7/79–6/82	Stage 2 7/82–12/86	Stage 3 1/87–90
(Takrit)	6 (12.5)	4 (6.7)	3 (7.7)	4 (10.5)	6 (14.6)
(Samarra)	3 (6.3)	4 (6.7)	2 (5.1)	3 (7.9)	3 (7.3)
Upper Euphrates	5 (10.5)	10 (16.6)	6 (15.4)	4 (10.5)	3 (7.3)
('Ana)	3 (6.3)	5 (8.3)	2 (5.1)	- (-)	- (-)
Other Upper Euphrates	2 (4.2)	5 (8.3)	4 (10.3)	4 (10.5)	3 (7.3)
Mosul	3 (6.3)	3 (5.0)	4 (10.3)	8 (21.1)	7 (17.1)
Followers of Saddam					
	- (-)	6 (10.0)	6 (15.4)	7 (18.4)	12 (17.1)

Sources: *al-Thawra*, 1968-1989; *al-Waqa'i al-'iraqiya*, 1968-89

As mentioned before, in the early years, the military Takritis dominated the state and party power setup, and Saddam was still relatively weak, and unable to push his protégés forward to the cabinet. But after purging powerful Takriti and military rivals, he was able to expand the ranks of the higher leading body in the party (the Regional Leadership – RL) on the one hand, and also amend the provisional constitution in order to allow for all members of the RL (mainly civilian and hand-picked by Saddam Hussein) to be included in the supreme national decision-making body (i.e. the Revolutionary Command Council). By this process, he achieved several aims: First, the formal control of the party over government agencies; second, appointing his followers in important posts under the guise of enhancing the party's control of the state; and finally, weakening both the Takriti faction and high-ranking Ba'thi officers.

Another feature of this policy was appointing Shi'ite and Kurdish ministers in minor posts. After the Gulf War and the subsequent popular uprisings, characterized by broad Shi'ite participation, Saddam appointed a well-known Shi'ite party member, Sa'dun Hammadi, as Prime Minister, just as Nuri al-Sa'id had done in the late forties. If cabinet appointments are showcases to conceal the real nature of power, what is the significance of our examining the composition of cabinets beyond the balanced proportions of sectarian/ethnic representation?

First, in the process of establishing his absolute power base, Saddam Hussein used the Cabinet to play off the major local groups in the Sunni triangle, in order to conceal his inclination to particular local/tribal groups. This was different from the policy of Bakr, who had not hesitated to promote tribal kinsmen openly to ministerial posts. Because of this, the percentage of Takriti ministers in the first Bakr phase (1968–74) was high (12.5 per cent) compared to other local Sunni groups. But in his second phase (1974–79), before Saddam assumed the presidency, the percentage of Takritis in general dropped to less than 8 per cent. It rose again under Saddam Hussein (1987–90) to 14.6 per cent. Thus, we can clearly say that Takriti predominance existed in the Cabinet only in the early 1970s and the late 1980s.

Looking at the proportion of other local groups from the Sunni triangle, we may notice that there is a certain balance between local, clannish groups from the Upper Tigris (mainly from Mosul), the Middle Tigris (mainly from Takrit, Samarra and Dur) and the Upper Euphrates (from 'Ana, Rawa, Ramadi, and others). In the second phase of Bakr's rule and the first phase of Saddam's, the percentage of those from the Upper Euphrates exceeded those of other groups. This could be due to the fact that the Ba'th party relied on local groups from Upper Euphrates when it succeeded in its coup against the 'Arif regime, which had depended mainly upon those very groups. But after 1982, especially after the resignation of Sa'dun Ghaydan, the percentage of Upper Euphrates dropped remarkably. In their stead, the groups from the Mosul and Upper Tigris area increased their weight. It is worth mentioning that the share of representation of tribes from the Middle Tigris has never been the largest among the Sunni Triangle groups, except during the first phase of Bakr's rule and the third phase of Saddam's.[12]

Given that certain local/tribal groups had some form of political access through influential politicized military officers since 1958, ministerial composition shows a kind of appeasement of potential rivals, offering them a chance to participate in the government. It was necessary for the regime to preserve a kind of local coalition among Sunni groups, maintaining certain numbers of Takritis and playing off the other two rival local groups, the Upper Euphrates and Upper Tigris, against each other. Such considerations are also reflected in the recruitment of the top political elite. The nominal post of Vice Secretary General of the Party was given to Izzat Ibrahim, from the small town of al-Dur neighbouring Takrit and Samarra towns. Samarra, incidentally, produced many political rivals who challenged the Takritis. Taha Yasin Ramadhan, from Mosul, was given some of the most important posts in the council of ministers. Sa'dun Ghaydan, from the Upper Euphrates, used to act as a representative for his local group until 1982, but after his dismissal few from this group were promoted. Instead, some tribal members from the

Upper Euphrates found higher posts in the Army, such as the Commander of Republican Guard during the late 1980s.

Another characteristic is the gradual decline of professional party workers after 1982. Instead we may see during this period a rise in the share of technocrats and those with careers in local administration. This tendency for less participation by party members can also be seen in the change in composition of the National Assembly.

Another feature of cabinet composition is that Saddam was inclined to appoint his old colleagues and followers individually, people who served him before and after he assumed the presidency. Examples include Muhammad Salih, the Minister of Trade, Omar Mukhaylif, the Minister of Finance (in the mid-1980s), and Ahmad Husayn, Prime Minister after the Gulf War (1991).

This corresponds to Saddam's policy of nepotism, which has been quite obvious since the third phase of his rule (1987–90). The share of Takritis in the cabinet rose in that period, but this tendency differs in nature from that in the first phase of Bakr's rule. In the early 1970s, the ascendance of Takritis in the government and party was a reflection of their predominance in the Army and in the 1968 coup; whereas their predominance in the late 1980s was the direct result of the ascendance of Saddam's family members, who were acting from behind the political scene. This was the end of the two-faced policy of maintaining power by overt Party control and covert security and intelligence forces. Thus, the political actors in the latter field (security) emerged openly on the centre stage.

The National Assembly (al-Majlis al-Watani) 1984 to 1989

Although the National Assembly is constitutionally a legislative organ, the RCC is actually the highest legislative-executive body. From its advent to power in 1968 until the rise of Saddam Hussein to presidency in 1980, the Ba'th rejected 'parliamentary democracy' as being a 'bourgeois fallacy'. When the assembly was established in 1980 and elections were held (after a 22-year gap), all opposition groups were disenfranchised by a host of regulatory acts and procedures, either for being 'separatists' (i.e., Kurds and some Shi'i's), 'collaborators with the enemy,'(this involves all strands) or 'persons who do not believe in the 1968 revolution' (liberals, communists and Arab nationalists from outside the Ba'th). The 'leading party', the official single party system, strictly controlled nomination, campaigning and other aspects of the ballot process.

The revival of the National Assembly in 1980 was part of Saddam Hussein's plan to secure popular legitimacy after the resignation of President Bakr and the execution of some 22 leading members of the party. But, in 1988, the status of the National Assembly had, in a way, altered. It was empowered to recall ministers and scrutinize the cabinet, thus acting as a counterbalance to the latter. It was also allowed to pass resolutions, which the party elite might seem reluctant to approve, and hence turned into a counterbalance to the old party cliques.

In addition, the 1989 election was hailed as a 'harbinger' for further 'democratization' in the period after the Iraq-Iran War. The Assembly was to ratify a new constitution which, according to the master plan announced at the end of July 1990, included measures for 'democratization' such as the abolishment of the RCC, the introduction of a new presidential election system, approval of a limited multi-party system and so on.[13] In this way, the Assembly was carefully opened to those whom the present political system could not accommodate, although apparent opposition groups were still excluded from the process.

With a strong censorship system, strict information control and party direct supervision of the process (the Observation Committee by 'Izzat Ibrahim), the result could not have been free from the regime's will. Yet, the social and political characteristics of the candidates reflect the regime's attempt to broaden its base, and indicates what new segments of society it tried to harness and which segments were being curbed.

The National Assembly 1980–1984

The Assembly members elected in 1980 were described as 'people who are central in the Ba'th apparatus, holding middle and more often, upper-middle ranks ... between 35 and 42 years of age ... the majority [of them] joined [the party] ... during the period of the struggle against Qasim,' and 'the percentage of those possessing a post-high school education is significantly high,' and most obtained jobs 'in the party and government service' or as 'teachers in elementary and high schools.' As for the process of promotion of candidates in the Baghdad constituency, the majority 'were born in the provinces and their first steps were made in the party hierarchy in their respective provinces.'[14] This is a pattern similar to that of the party members who assumed ministerial posts up to the early 1980s.

In the 1984 elections, the general picture of the candidates was generally the same.[15] More than 40 per cent of the candidates were affiliated to the party (including party supporters), and more than half of them were in responsible positions at various levels of the party organization. Of the candidates, 9.4 per cent were professional party workers, and 6.6 per cent were government officials (see Table 2). The most prevalent occupational background of the candidates was educational (27.3 per cent of the candidates); nearly half of the candidates held diplomas above university level. This kind of preference for intellectuals has been common in Iraq since the foundation of the Assembly, and reflects the government's tendency, since the mid seventies, to recruit non-politically oriented technocrats to fill ministerial posts. Another continuity from the 1980 election can be seen in the high percentage of ex-members of the Assembly, and also ex-members of the legislative council of the Kurdish Autonomous Region (Kurdish Assembly – 10 per cent).

Table 2: share of candidates and probability of election according to social background in the 1989 election

(probability = Ca/C/Ea/E ; Ca = candidate with characteristics (a); C = total numbers of candidates; Ea = winners with characteristics (a); E = total winners)

Social background	Share of candidates		Probability	
	1984	1989	1984	1989
Party career				
party member	40.6	27.0	1.8	1.5
(party cadre)	24.3	7.3	2.7	2.5
Occupation				
party organization	9.4	3.5	2.6	2.8
government	6.6	2.0	1.4	0.8
social sector	9.9	2.4	0.8	0.8
local administration	5.7	2.3	1.3	1.4
education	27.3	23.9	1.1	1.4
legal	6.8	6.7	0.8	1.2
medical	3.0	2.5	0.7	1.6
engineering	1.9	2.3	0.4	0.5
private sector	2.7	4.1	0.0	0.6
agriculture	8.4	10.0	0.9	1.0
defense	5.6	11.8	0.5	0.7
Social contribution				
popular activities	11.0	4.2	1.8	1.8
intellectual activities	17.6	15.3	1.0	1.0

Social background	Share of candidates		Probability	
	1984	*1989*	*1984*	*1989*
local activities	17.7	11.3	0.6	1.1
ex-member of National Assembly	9.9	4.3	2.5	2.1
Academic career				
higher than university	44.9	37.8	1.1	1.4
without official education	3.3	5.5	0.5	0.7
Other factors				
laqab/nisba holders	6.5	50.6	1.4	1.1

Sources: *al-Thawra*, 3–13 Oct. 1984; *al-Jumhuriya*, 13-21, March 1989

A General View of the 1989 Election

In the 1989 elections, by contrast, there was a sharp fall in the number of the candidates from the party (27 per cent of the total candidates). Most candidates were of low status in the party, without any responsibility or even full membership in the organization. The share of professional party workers decreased as well, to one third of that in 1984. Candidates who claimed to be active in semi-party organizations such as the Women's Union, Farmers' Union, or occupational associations (teachers, lawyers, and so on) also decreased, compared to their higher percentage in 1984. (The total rate fell from 28.6 per cent in 1984 to 19.5 per cent in 1989.) The percentage of the candidates who had been members of the Assembly dropped to half of the previous level. As for the preference for a higher academic career, it also went down slightly. Instead, there was an increase in the rate of candidates with no official educational background other than participation in the party's anti-illiteracy campaign, which had been promoted by the regime in the late seventies. Parallel to the decline of the rate of candidates with occupations in the government or social sectors (one third or one fourth of that of 1984), the share of the candidates from the private sector rose.

Thus the composition of the field of candidates in the 1989 election greatly diverged from what had been typical in 1980 and 1984, when it had been similar to that of ministers and the party elite. This change shows the tendency to transform the Assembly from a political body subject to the party and state apparatus into an organization autonomous from them, which Saddam then tried to use to bypass the party structure.

Emergence of Tribal Identity in the 1989 Election

A close analysis of the characteristics of the 1989 election

Changes in the composition of the field of candidates also reflect changes in the political attitude of the people who were willing to join the regime. In a way, the increase in the number of candidates with certain social characteristics means the rise of the political awareness of that group and their recognition that their views will be accepted by the present system. Conversely, groups in decline realize that their social characteristics are no longer required by the regime. The decline in the number of party members reveals that candidates noticed the ineffectiveness of promoting themselves as party functionaries, and instead searched for other ways of promoting or identifying themselves. In other words, in the eyes of the candidates the National Assembly, which used to be subservient to the party/state hierarchy, became more open to those who were considered to be less suitable for the existing hierarchy.

The increase of professionals (engineering, agriculture, and private business) reflects the regime's policy of encouraging the private sector at the expense of the public and what is officially called 'socialist' sectors, which was introduced in the mid-1980s.[16] The increase of candidates with military careers reflects the policy of propitiating the military and people engaged in national defence against Iran. These newly emerging groups held lower ranks in the party or were non-party individuals.

Lastly and most significantly, there was a tremendous increase in users of tribal *laqab* or *nisba* among the candidates. As mentioned above, the official usage of *laqab* or *nisba* was prohibited in the early 1970s. And there was almost no use of *laqab* or *nisba* in the 1984 elections. Without official clearance, however, some ministers or party members started to use *laqab* or *nisba* in the mid-1980s, a practice which spread rapidly. In the 1989 elections, more than half of the candidates used their *laqab* or *nisba* officially, showing their tribal background and origin. *Laqab* or *nisba* was related either to tribe, clan or place of origin. This means that people with political awareness started to stress their tribal or local background, believing it would be an effective way to join the regime.

Who Uses Laqab?

Although there seems to be no specifically large tribal or local concentrations of candidates for the National Assembly in 1989, some major *laqab/nisba* holders among them can be identified. According to Table 3, the biggest group of *laqab* holders are from the Juburi tribe. Of the 18 major groups in the table, which have tribal or notable tribal-family backgrounds, only the Takritis and Duris are regional groups. These major groups exist in more than one province and hold a strong influence in large areas. Other than the major ones, most tribal groups are minor in scale, and are influential only in their local provinces. In other words, their authority or nobility of origin is not recognized nationwide, but limited to their home area.

Table 3: Major Laqab *Holders in the 1989 Election*

	Number of candidates (probability)	Province where he stood for election	Social background
Al-Juburi	27 (0.7)	Nivewa/ Salahadin/ Tamin/ Najaf / Baghdad	Zubayd confederation
al-Dulaymi confederation	15 (1.1)	Baghdad/ Babil/ Diyala	Zubayd confederation
al-Janabi	11 (0.3)	Babil/ Baghdad/ Diyala Qadisiya	Zubayd confederation
al-Mashhadani	11 (1.4)	Baghdad/ Salahadin/ Ninewa	Sayyid
al-Shammari	11 (1.0)	Wasit/ Babil/ Diyala/ Najaf/ Qadisiya/ Anbar	Shammar confederation
al-Nua'imi	9 (1.7)	Baghdad/ Ninewa/ Tamin Wasit	Sayyid
al-Takriti	9 (1.7)	Baghdad/ Salahadin/ Tamin/ Ninewa/ Duhok	local group
al-Burwari	8 (0.5)	Duhok	Kurd
al-Barzanchi	8 (0.5)	Sulaymaniya/ Arbil/ Ninewa/ Baghdad	Kurd, Sayyid
al-Ta'y	7 (0.7)	Arbil/ Duhok/Tamin/ Babil/ Ninewa/ Diyala	original tribe of Shammar
al-Bayati	6 (1.3)	Tamin/ Salahadin/ Babil Diyala/ Ninewa Baghdad/ Tamin	Rabi'a confederation or Turkoman

	Number of candidates (probability)	Province where he stood for election	Social background
al-Duri	6 (-)	Sulaymaniya/ Diyala	local group
al-Jaf	6 (0.6)	Basra/ Wasit	Kurd
al-Saʿdun	6 (1.3)		Muntafiq
		Baghdad/ Babil/ Diyala	confederation
al-ʿUbaidi	6 (2.5)	Ninewa	Zubayd confederation
		Diyala/ Wasit/ Baghdad	old notable family
al-ʿAzzawi	6 (1.3)	Tamin/ Baghdad	Zubayd confederation
al-Hamdani	6 (-)	Babil/ Najaf	
al-Maʿmuri	5 (0.8)		Zubayd confederation?

Sources: same as Table 2

Remarkably, these potentially influential tribal groups listed in Table 3 are Sunnis, who reside in the northern and western parts of Iraq. Historical facts show that tribal formation in Iraq is not only concentrated in the Sunni or northern/western area, but rather is stronger in the southern and Kurdish areas. Yet, there are no tribal groups from the southern part of Iraq which have nationwide influence among the candidates of the National Assembly in 1989. The only exception is al-Saʿdun, who are the Sunni *sheikh* family of the Muntafiq confederation. This leading family symbolizes the historical role of Sunni sheikhly-landlord control over Shiʿite peasant-tribesmen in the south since the Ottoman era.

Examining the proportion of the *laqab/nisba* holders among the candidates sorted by province (Table 4), it is rather higher in the Upper Tigris area,but lower in the eastern parts such as Karbala and deep south in the Marsh area (the provinces of Dhi Qar, Muthanna, and Maysan), as well as in Kurdistan. These areas have been hotbeds, so to speak, for anti-government activities for decades; and the political aspirations on part of the *laqab/nisba* holders in these regions, even within the framework of the present regime, are not encouraged; rather, political participation is suppressed. This might be the result of the fact that the share of party members among the candidates from these areas (i.e. the provinces of Wasit, Maysan, and Muthanna) is still high.

It may thus be concluded that the relative presence of major tribal groups in the political field does not accurately and evenly reflect Iraq's social conditions and tribal structures, rather it indicates the regime's political attitude towards and dependency on certain tribal groups in the Sunni Triangle.

The reason why the major tribal groups from the Sunni Triangle were the only ones allowed to raise their political awareness, has to do with the influence of tribal/local coalition-like characteristics of Saddam's regime in the late 1970s and early 1980s. Al-Jubur, the biggest tribal group among the candidates, reside mainly in the provinces of Ninewa, Salah al-din and other Sunni Upper and Middle Tigris areas, except for considerable numbers who reside in Babil province, most of whom are Shi'is. The second biggest group is from the Dulaim tribe, who reside mainly in the Upper Euphrates area. The three biggest *laqab/nisba* holding groups (al-Jubur, al-Dulaim, al-Janabi) are all from the Zubayd tribal confederation, in addition to other major groups like al-'Ubayd and al-'Azza. The integration of this coalition has not been as tight as that of Shammar or Muntafiq, however. The fifth biggest group is Shammar, which used to control a wider area in the northern and western parts of Iraq, as well as the eastern part of Syria and some parts of Jordan and Saudi Arabia.

What is important here is that these groups participated in the Army under the Ba'th regime, especially in the Republican Guard in the mid-1980s, when the expansion of the Army was necessary for the protracted war against Iran. One of the leaders of al-Jubur noted that the regime started to recruit members of the major tribes such as al-Jubur and al-Dulaimi from 1982–3, mainly from the towns of Takrit, Beiji, and Sharqat.[17] Some members of these tribes were appointed to ministerial posts in the eighties (e.g., Information Minister Latif Jassim, from al-Dulaim, Minister of State for Foreign Affairs Hamid Alwan, from al-Jubur).

The balance between local groups from the Sunni areas, which was observed in the formation of cabinets, may also be one of the factors which stimulated the political awareness of these tribal groups in the Assembly. While they were recruited as parts of a supportive body for the regime – not in formal political positions in the party or government, but rather as operatives in coercive organizations such as the Republican Guard, security forces and Saddam's corps of private bodyguards – they, in turn were tools to their kin who endeavoured to gain access to the regime in the realm of official politics, benefiting from the policy of maintaining balance among influential localities. Under such circumstances, it might have been only natural for them to have greater expectations to take part in the official representation system. They may have not felt any need to cast away their group identity, as they saw ministers were representatives of their local groups in a coalition-like regime. Actually, these groups were the first to use their own *laqab* in the general elections, as the share of *laqab*-holders in the candidates was already high in the provinces of Anbar and Salah al-din (that is, in the Upper Euphrates and

Middle Tigris) in the 1984 election, before it became evident in other tribes or local groups (see Table 4).

Table 4: Share and Probability of Laqab/Nisba Holders among the Candidates, 1989

Provinces	Share of the candidates %		Probability	
	1984	1989	1984	1989
Duhuk	0.0	73.0	0.0	1.1
Arbil	10.0	28.1	0.9	0.6
Sulaymaniya	0.0	24.4	0.0	0.6
Ninewa	3.7	57.1	2.3	1.1
Tamin	0.0	59.0	0.0	0.6
Diyala	4.5	59.7	3.4	1.0
Salahadin	21.7	62.5	1.7	1.0
Anbar	21.3	31.1	1.4	1.2
Baghdad	1.9	54.3	0.8	1.3
Babil	12.1	56.9	0.0	1.2
Karbala	9.1	42.3	2.2	1.0
Najaf	0.0	57.1	0.0	1.2
Qadisiya	37.5	64.0	1.8	1.0
Wasit	0.0	76.2	0.0	1.1
Maysan	8.7	40.0	1.4	0.6
Dhi Qar	19.4	28.6	0.8	0.8
Muthanna	0.0	36.4	0.0	1.1
Basra	0.0	50.9	0.0	1.4
Average	6.5	50.6	1.4	1.1

Sources: same as Table 2

The Relation Between Tribal Groups and Local Groups

The revival of tribalism in Iraqi politics featured tribal groups and local groups as equal political actors. Local groups, based on common residence and intermarriage, and tribal groups, based on common lineage and united by the principle of *'asabiya*, are intrinsically different in nature. In the Upper Euphrates area, most of the population is related to the al-Dulaim tribe in one way or another; to some extent, the situation is similar in the Middle Tigris area. By contrast, the population in the Upper Tigris area, such as Mosulites and other urban inhabitants, cannot be easily attributed to specific tribal groups. It is often the case that tribal differences undermine the integrity of local groups (e.g., Shiyaisha vs. al-Beijat in Takrit) and local differences cause divisions in the same tribal group (e.g., al-Rawi and al-'Ani in Dulaim. The Rawi legitimize their tribal supremacy by proving their origin as *sayyid*, while al-'Ani are proud of their historical position).[18]

Nevertheless, tribal and local groups function according to the same political dynamics. One remarkable aspect of this tendency is that the *tha'r* custom between tribal groups is not only confined to those with a shared tribal origin but includes local groups as well. This has a political significance which, as we shall see later, brought about bloody confrontations among various tribal groups in the army.[19] In anticipation, we may refer to the May 1995 insurrection by some Dulaim junior officers to avenge the execution of one of their high-ranking officers.[20] Thus the perception that the ruling elite is some kind of Takriti local group motivates other tribal segments to seek *tha'r*, revenge.

The Regime's Preference for Rising Groups

If the composition of candidates shows the political awareness of potential supporters of the regime, it by no means reveals the regime's preference for these groups. Assuming that the results of elections largely reflect the regime's will, each social group's probability of success in elections shows to what extent the regime considers the candidates to be truly suitable as supporters. Here 'probability' means the chance that a candidate with certain social characteristics can be elected more easily than other candidates.[21]

In both the 1984 and 1989 elections, the 'probability' for party members was quite high compared to others, although this decreased a little in 1989. This signifies that the regime still needs party members more than other social groups. On the other hand, although there is a considerable rise in the numbers of candidates who are *laqab/nisba* holders, their 'probability' has not increased; in fact it has diminished. As for government officials and former Assembly members, their 'probability' has decreased, as has their share of candidates. It is clear that while their political ambitions to play a role diminished, the regime no longer holds them important for representation in the Assembly. As for party functionaries, their political activism is dwindling, although the regime still depends on them. As for the *laqab/nisba* holders, their political ambition in the Assembly is increasing, but it is still not fully welcomed by the regime.

The social groups that have raised their 'probability' are intellectuals, such as those in educational, legal and medical occupations as well as those belonging to professional associations, and those who work in the private sector and in certain local activities. The increasing propensity for professionals – that is, the regime's preference for non-politically oriented intellectuals in the state apparatus – can be seen continuously since the elections and ministerial composition of the 1980s.

Candidates from the private sector and local activities are less associated with the existing hierarchy, and not affiliated with any organizations, which may potentially threaten the party. It is true that those who are engaged in local activities, such as popular committees and popular mobilization campaigns, are in a way under the supervision of the party, but their appeal rests rather on their local, traditional prestige in treating customary issues and connecting the lives of ordinary people to political authority.[22] The characteristic of their activities is that their range is limited to a small area. Thus the regime may find it safe to penetrate local society through these groups instead of using party branches, but without stimulating them to expand their activities nationwide.

Let us now examine the successful candidates who are *laqab/nisba* holders. Interestingly, the *laqab* and *nisba* holders who enjoy a higher 'probability' of election are members of certain clans, namely al-'Ubayd (a notable clan with leading families based in Baghdad since the Ottoman period), Takriti, and Nu'aimy (a notable family of *sayyid* based in Mosul, Huwayja, and Baghdad). There is no common denominator between these groups other than they are all Sunnis. The probability for the biggest groups – al-Jubur, al-Janabi or Shammar – is not high.

It is hard to generalize about what type of *laqab/nisba* holders are most likely to be selected by the regime. The only exception is the Takritis. It may be deduced, however, that the rise of political aspiration of certain *laqab* and *nisba* holders does not match the regime's interest in them. Inspired by the regime's informal coalition-like system drawn from Sunni local groups, certain tribal sections which have quite a long history of autonomy and integrity in the northwestern area have increased their self-consciousness of their tribal origin. But the regime is rather cautious in allowing these tribes, such as the Jubur and Shammar, open political representation. Since tribes with high political aspirations are mainly those known for their recent participation in the Army and other coercive organizations, it is natural that Saddam fears the full-scale activation of tribal/local solidarity, which may develop autonomous tendencies and result in arousing the Army against his regime.

Another sign of caution in the regime's handling of rising tribes is the ideological practice of retribalization and ranking tribes. One example is the identification of Saddam's *'ashira* (Albu Nasir) as *sayyid*, noble lineage. This differentiation of rank is anchored in religious and communal nobility. Its significance is self-evident when we remember that the historical role of the *sayyid* was to mediate tribal conflicts.

In addition to religious values, Arabism as a basic Ba'thi ideology is also deployed to differentiate tribal groups in a hierarchy. In Mashhadani's work on his tribe (see Note 8), the author says:

> Respect for *nisba* of Arab tribes became ... a responsibility cast on the shoulders of the leaders of the movement of Arab thought in order to defend Arabness, its origin and its presence against the attacks from *shu'ubiya.*

Shu'ubiya is the notorious term used by Ba'thists for some of the Shi'ite people to deny their Arabness and define them as being of Persian origin, which the regime takes to mean 'agent of Iran, enemy of Iraq.' So while tribal identity is incorporated into the Ba'th Arabist ideology, it is also aimed at excluding the Shi'is, whose Arab and Iraqi identity is repeatedly denied.

Developments After the Gulf War

The difference between political aspirations and the regime's preferences has caused recent conflicts. During the 1989 elections, the difference between tribal political aspirations and the regime's preference was not so apparent. But after the Gulf War in 1991, its reliance on tribal value systems became more obvious and open. Saddam Hussein announced his acceptance of 'nobility of origin,' which he had rejected 20 years ago. On the occasion of the Prophet's birthday in 1991 he reiterated that:

> No one should be allowed to emerge in the ... leadership in the Ba'th party if ... [he does not] come from a good origin ... [a good] family background.' He even described Ba'th party itself as 'the tribe of all tribes.'[23]

In the last elections to the National Assembly in March 1996, the previous tendency to increase tribal candidates with *laqab/nisba* gained more momentum. The number of candidates from Jubur, for example, rose from 27 in 1989 to 31 in 1996; that of Dulaim from 15 to 26; of Shammar from 11 to 15; of Nua'imi from nine to 13; of 'Ubaidi from six to 17; of 'Azzawi from six to 15. There is also a change, interestingly enough, in the number of candidates from Takrit: this dropped significantly from nine to five, and their probability decreased from 1.7 to 1.3 (two winners out of four candidates). In addition, the Samarrai, historical rivals of the Takritis, appeared with four successful candidates.[24]

The regime's acceleration of the resurgence of tribalism, however, apparently proved to be a double-edged sword. Seeking mobilization of the populace through pro-government tribal groups, the regime has found more and more tribal groups who claim a relatively larger share of power, operating beyond the regime's control. The ascendance of certain tribes in the political field has resulted in armed conflicts between tribal groups with political aspirations and existing privileged groups.

In 1992 conflicts erupted between segments of the Jubur and Takriti in the Army, stemming from the former's involvement in planning a coup attempt on the eve of the Gulf War. This was followed by the successive arrests and executions of Jubur officers, until Hamid Alwan, a Jubur ex-minister of state for Foreign Affairs, defected from Iraq in 1993. This event may have caused the regime to lose support from certain parts of that tribe. Then segments from the Dulaim followed suit, challenging the regime. This reached a peak when one of their kinsmen, General Mazlum al-Dulaimi, was executed, and an anti-government demonstration erupted in 1995. Other major tribes and local groups in Upper Euphrates like al-Jumailat, al-'Anis, al-Rawis, and al-Kubaysis, sympathized with the Dulaim in this show of defiance.[25] Other tribal groups mentioned in Table 3 are no exception. The 'Ubaidi, for example, were involved in the above-mentioned coup attempt with the Jubur in 1990 and they had to endure subsequent purges.

All these conflicts first took the form of tribal rivalries between Takritis, on the one hand, and other tribal groups, on the other. These stemmed from a quest on part of the latter for more political representation and a larger share of economic and social benefits under the present regime, but, under the obtaining circumstances, they developed into a kind of opposition movement against the regime. At present, one of the influential personalities from the Jubur, Mash'an al-Juburi, who claims that he is from its *sheikh* family, is active in the opposition movement in exile. Conflicts and purges also erupt within other local groups: al-Duri, long-time associates of the Takriti-led coalition, suffered a loss of trust by the regime in 1994, as some of their lot were expelled from high posts in the Security service and the party.[26]

Thus, it seems that Saddam's family and kinship networks have lost some supportive segments, especially in the Army and security forces. These cracks in tribal and local coalitions, together with the inability of the regime to control the rising political aspirations of tribal groups, triggered schisms within the ruling family itself, contributing to the defection of Hussain Kamel, the president's son-in law and the third man in the regime, in August 1995, and his subsequent elimination upon his return in February 1996.

Recognizing that re-tribalization policies have gone beyond the desired limits, Saddam Hussein tried to gear formal institutional control, by promoting 'democratization.' He carried out a presidential referendum in 1996, achieving an overwhelming 'victory', and consolidated his new legitimacy through popular mandate rather than party hierarchy. In March 1996, a prolonged election of the National Assembly was accomplished. In that election several 'parties' were allowed to join; the regime invited some Kurdish figures, ex-Communists, and ex-Arab Nationalists to participate in order to give the appearance of political 'pluralism'. But these efforts to build a democratic image simply signalled the return to the old dual pattern of control. The attempt to assassinate Uday at the end of 1996 and the forced return of Barzan Takriti from Geneva in 1998 may be signs of the continuing power struggle within the ruling family. The frequent meetings among Saddam's family and the rumoured house arrest of his major family members in 1996 showed that his retribalization policy had backfired.

Conclusion

The policy of encouraging tribal solidarity was promoted in a very cautious way in the eighties, but after the Gulf War it spread beyond the Sunni tribes to Shi'ite and Kurdish areas, which are far less controllable. The security forces cannot easily arrest tribal members who do not obey the central authority any more, and tribal chiefs are approached.[27] In general, they now, under international economic sanctions possess greater power in local economies.

Facing growing tribal power, the regime is trying to adapt the traditional policy against tribe; i.e., playing intra-tribal factions – generally *sheikh* family factions – off against each other within the various tribes. Offering military and financial support to certain factions in a tribe, the regime interferes in the selection of the paramount *sheikh*.[28] The regime's discrimination among tribal groups and its preference for smaller tribal groups outside the mainstream shows its intent to undermine the unity of large tribal bodies. Confronting recent challenges from some large tribes like the Dulaim and the Jubur, the regime tried to reorganize these tribal groups, and appoint *sheikhs* from pro-government clans. It also tried to reconfirm the loyalty of various tribal groups and started to publish a nationwide 'list of loyal tribes' who have given a *bay'a* oath to Saddam.[29]

Retribalization does not only affect tribal groups inside the country, but also opposition forces abroad.

Among the political figures who defected from Iraq after the Gulf War, for example, several political groups have emerged which base their identities on their tribe and nobility of origin. They are mostly from Shi'ite tribal groups, who raised their political aspiration in a different way from that of the Sunni, i.e. through the opposition movement. In line with their reassessment of their role in constitutional liberalism before the 1958 revolution, some groups seem to have developed a patriotic consciousness based on their tribal authority. Such a development is facilitated by their recognition that their homeland in the south has been essentially abandoned even by opposition groups and international forces, as well as by the regime. Some believe that only tribal society can be a source of opposition in Iraq, and be much more effective than the existing ideological political forces.[30]

Notes

1. Regarding the party's dominance over the state and its control of violent apparatus, see Falih Abdul Jabbar, *al-Dawla, al-mujtama' al-madani wal-tahawwul al-dimuqrati fil-'Iraq*, Cairo, Ibn Khaldun Centre, 1995.

2. Isam Khafaji, 'War as a Vehicle for the Rise and Demise of a State-Controlled Society: the case of Ba'thist Iraq', *Amsterdam Middle East Papers*, No. 4, December 1995, Research Center for International Political Economy and Foreign Policy Analysis, University of Amsterdam, p. 28.

3. See Amatzia Baram, *Culture, History and Ideology in the Formation of Ba'thist Iraq, 1969-89*, New York, St. Martin's Press, 1991.

4. 'Abbas al-'Azzawi, *'Asha'ir al-'iraqi*, Baghdad, Sharikat al-tijara wal-tiba'a al-mahduda, 1956.

5. Yusuf al-Shaykh Ibrahim al-Samarra'i, *al-Qaba'il wal-buyutat wal-a'lam fi shamal al-'iraq*, Baghdad, Matba'at al-umma, 1985. From the same author, *al-Qaba'il wal-buyutat al-hashimiya fil-'iraq*, Matba'a al-umma, 1986.

6. Yusuf al-Shaykh Ibrahim al-Samarra'i, *al-Qaba'il al-'iraqiya*, Baghdad, Maktabat al-sharq al-jadid, 1989.

7. Khashi'a al-Mu'adaidi, *A'ala al-rafidayn*, Baghdad, Dar al-shu'un al-thaqafiya, 1990. From the same author, *A'la al-furat*, Baghdad, Dar al-shu'un al-thaqafiya, 1986.

8. Muhammad Jasim al-Mashhadani, 'Ashira al-Mushahada, Jami'a al-Mustansiriya, Baghdad, 1992, 'Aqil 'Abd al-Husayn al-Maliki, *Maysan wa 'asha'irha*, Matba'at al-Jahiz, Baghdad, 1992.

9. Mohammad A. Tarbush, *The Role of the Military in Politics: a case study of Iraq to 1941*, London, Kegan Paul International, 1982.

10. Keiko Sakai, 'Social Networks and State Formation in Iraq', Sakai (ed.), *Social Identity and National Formation in the Arab World* [in Japanese], Tokyo, Institute of Developing Economies, 1993.

11. For the origin of the ascendance of Takritis in the Army, see Hanna Batatu, *The Old Social Classes and the Revolutionary Movements of Iraq*, New Jersey, Princeton University Press, 1978, pp. 1088–89. Also the background on al-Jumayli and al-Rawi in the Army is based on his analysis. op. cit., p. 1034, pp. 322–23.

12. Keiko Sakai, 'From One-party Rule to One-person Rule in Iraq: Transformation in its Ministerial Composition', Manabu Shimizu (ed.), *Crisis in Arab Socialism and its Perspective* [in Japanese], Tokyo, Institute of Developing Economies, 1992.

13. According to the government announcement on 29 July, 1990.

14. Amatzia Baram, 'The June 1980 Elections to the National Assembly in Iraq: An experiment in controlled democracy', *Orient*, September, 1981.

15. Classification of the candidates in the 1984 and 1989 elections was done by the author according to data derived from the candidates' self-introductions published in the Iraqi newspapers before each election. Newspapers referred to are as follows; *al-Thawra*, October 3–13, 1984, *al-Jumhuriya*, March 13–21, 1989. See Keiko Sakai,

'From Party Elite to Local Elite', *Azia Keizai* [in Japanese], Vol. 36, No. 4, 1995.

16. The agricultural sector has become part of the private sector rather than the public as a result of the government's privatization drive during the middle 1980s. Thus the significance of the rise of farmers and agricultural engineers is completely different than it would have been in the days when the regime emphasized farmers' protection under a socialist policy.

17. Interview with Mash'an al-Juburi, *The Independent*, 20 August 1995.

18. For details of the origin of al-Rawi, see al-Mu'adidi, op. cit.

19. For details of tribal characteristics in the conflict between al-Juburi and Takriti, see *al-Sharq al-Awsat*, 25 September 1992/ *al-Hayat*, 13 March, 1993.

20. For details, see a*l-Sharq al-Awsat*, 17 June, 1995.

21. 'Probability' can be calculated as follows: let Ca = candidate with characteristics (a); C = total numbers of candidates; Ea = winners with characteristics (a); and E = total number of winners. Then probability can be given as $Ca/C/Ea/E$. If it is greater than 1, it means a candidate with characteristics (a) can be more easily elected than others.

22. People's Committees (*majlis al-sha'b*) are set up on the level of local administrative units, with membership determined on the basis of nomination. The Committees seem to be under the supervision of the Popular Organization Bureau in RCC, but compared to other professional and popular organizations (such as the Women's Union and Trade Union), the chain of command is not clear and the party's involvement seems weak.

23. As for these developments after the Gulf War, see Amatzia Baram, 'Neo-Tribalism in Iraq 1991–1996', *International Journal of Middle Eastern Studies* 29, February 1997, pp. 1–31.

24. According to *al-Jumhuriya*, 23 and 26 March 1996.

25. For detail, see *al-Wasat*, 11 June 1995.

26. See *al-Hayat*, 21 May 1994.

27. According to the author's interview with a member of *sheikh* family of the south of Iraq in 1997.

28. In October 1992, for example, large scale *tha'r* occured in the Wasit province as a result of a huge flow of arms from the government to certain pro-regime tribes there. *FBIS, Middle East and North Africa*, 21 October 1992.

29. According to the announcement of Iraqi News Agency, 12 May 1993, and *Babil*, 30 Jan. 1994. It claimed that Saddam received the oath from parts of the Shammari tribal confederation during that campaign. This kind of campaign was still continuing in 1998, when Saddam gained the oath from the clans of various provinces such as Najaf, Anbar, Dhi Qar and Ninewa. *Al-'Iraq*, 27 August 1998.

30. According to the author's 1996 interview with Sami al-Ma'jown, one of the leaders of the opposition organization Islah party, in London, which is composed of tribal figures.

PART THREE

Kurdish Tribes and States: Tribalism, Ethnicity and Nationalism

SIX

Kurds, States and Tribes

Martin van Bruinessen

Historically, Kurdish society has mostly existed at the periphery of, and functioned as a buffer between, two or more neighbouring states. From around 1500 until the First World War, these states were the Ottoman Empire in the west and Safavid, later Qajar, Iran in the east (with Russia and the British Empire gradually encroaching upon the region from the north and south, respectively). In the aftermath of World War I, Kurdistan was divided among four of the modern would-be nation states succeeding these empires, and became a peripheral and often mistrusted region for each of these states. All these states, whether empire or nation-state, have exercised various forms of indirect rule over Kurdistan, which have had a profound impact on the social and political organization of Kurdish society. The specific tribal formations that existed in Kurdish society during various historical periods were, in many respects, the products of the interaction of these states with Kurdish society.

Continuity and Variability

A comparison of the names of the Kurdish tribes mentioned in various sources over the past four centuries shows that, while some tribes simply disappeared and new ones kept emerging, many of the larger tribes showed a remarkable continuity over time.[1] The size and the degree of complexity of these tribes fluctuated considerably over time, so it cannot be assumed that, for example, the Milli or the Jaf tribe of 1950 resembled in important respects the tribes of the same names in 1850 or 1999.[2]

The tribes of which more or less reliable descriptions exist (at one period or another) vary widely in size and complexity of organization.[3] Some are, or were until recently, pastoral nomads; others combine settled agriculture with transhumance and animal husbandry; others again consist of settled peasant farmers. Today large parts of many tribes are urbanized without having completely given up tribal values and tribal organization – which in certain urban contexts may even be an advantage. In the view of the older urban classes, notably so in Istanbul or Ankara, the massive immigration of Kurds into those cities during the past decades has had the effect of steering local as well as state-level politics into 'tribal' directions, meaning patronage of family, tribe or regional affiliations.

Some of the tribes – especially the smaller ones – approximate real descent groups, although there are commonly some hangers-on whose genealogical relationship to the core lineages is dubious or who are recognized as unrelated but loyal members. In the larger tribes, the aspect of political affiliation and loyalty to a common chieftain or chiefly lineage is more clearly present, although kinship ideology is important. The Kurds do not share the fascination with their genealogies for which Arab tribesmen are famous, so even in large Kurdish tribes the belief in common descent of all members can establish itself within a few generations after a tribe first emerged as a political coalition.

Most of the large tribes have a hierarchical structure, with a leading lineage, a number of commoner clans/lineages, client lineages and subject non-tribal peasantry. Some of these tribes explicitly recognize the heterogeneity of their component parts (for which reason some authors would call them confederacies). Thus the large Milli (in a wide area between Urfa and Mardin) in the 19th century included Arab and Kurdish sub-tribes, including in the latter Yezidi as well as Sunni Muslim groups. Similarly the Heverkan of the Tur 'Abdin included Yezidi as well as Sunni Kurdish sections and Christian client lineages.

Although the autonomous dynamism of Kurdish society should not be underestimated – inter-tribal conflicts and coalitions have had profound impacts on tribal structure – the degree of complexity and internal stratification of the tribes seems to have depended primarily on two external factors: the available resource base and the extent of state interference in the region.

Indirect Rule and Tribal Structure

This correlation is nicely illustrated by the history of the Kurdish emirates (chiefdoms that were confederacies of named, and in many cases still identifiable tribes), led by hereditary dynasties that were formally recognized by the (Ottoman, Safavid or Qajar) state. These emirates are first mentioned in the *Sharafnama*, completed in 1597 by the Kurdish ruler of Bitlis, Sharaf Khan. Although Sharaf Khan attributed a venerable age to most of the emirates, none of his accounts is concrete before the Qaraqoyunlu period, and his account emphasizes the differences in the treatment of the Kurdish dynasties at the hands of the Qaraqoyunlu, Akkoyunlu, Safavids and Ottomans. The structure of the emirates is reminiscent of that of the Turkoman empires, the tribes being organized into a left and a right wing, kept in balance by the ruler. Each of the tribes had a hereditary chieftain (in some cases two competing ruling families alternating as leaders), whose sons or other close relatives had to live at the court of the emir as a means of keeping the tribes in check.

It has been suggested (by X. de Planhol) that Kurdish mountain nomadism, as it was known in Ottoman times, first emerged as a cultural synthesis of the Turkomans' long-distance horizontal nomadism and the originally short-distance vertical transhumance of the Kurds. We know that nomadic Kurdish-Turkish tribal confederacies existed into Ottoman times (the Boz Ulus being the most important of them).[4] It is not impossible that at least a number of the Kurdish emirates also emerged from the Turkoman-Kurdish encounter. At any rate, the emirates became more or less stabilized and consolidated upon their incorporation into the Ottoman Empire, which granted formal autonomy and backed up the authority of the emirs with the potential sanction of state power. In the course of their interaction with the Ottoman state, the courts of the Kurdish emirates became more and more like smaller models of the Ottoman court.[5]

Each of the emirates was made a separate Ottoman administrative unit, and most or all of the administration was delegated to the emirs. Some emirates paid a lump sum in taxes, others not even that. The only obligation that all the emirates had towards the central Ottoman state was to perform military service during campaigns in the region. Not surprisingly, we find the autonomous emirates located in the most geographically peripheral areas, where revenue collection would be very costly anyway. Productive agricultural regions near urban centres were administered directly through centrally appointed governors and other agents (Bitlis is the only one of the major emirates that commanded an important strategic position on a major trade route and had a very large community of craftsmen and merchants.)

Large nomadic tribes had a status similar to the smaller emirates: a large degree of autonomy, and delegation of all tasks of revenue collection to the chieftain, who paid the state a lump sum or nothing at all.[6] Neither the emirates nor the large nomadic tribes were creations of the Ottoman state in a literal sense; they existed when the first fiscal surveys were made. However, their recognition and delegation of powers to them by the Ottoman centre fixated the state of affairs in the Kurdish periphery and solidified them as political units.

It should be noted that Safavid policy towards the tribes was different from that of the Ottomans. Whereas the latter consolidated those tribal formations which they found willing to collaborate with them, the Safavids attempted – in many cases successfully – to forge new large tribal units out of many disparate smaller groups of heterogeneous origins. In the case of the Kurds, the most spectacular case of such tribe formation by the state is that of the Chamishkazaklu, allegedly numbering some 40,000 households originating from Anatolia and Caucasia, whom Shah 'Abbas had settled in northern Khurasan around the year 1600 to guard Iran's frontier against Uzbek incursions. They were held together by a centrally appointed *ilkhani*; later they split up into three large *ilkhanis*, each under a centrally appointed, but henceforth hereditary, *ilkhani*.[7]

Some emirates responded to the weakening of the Ottoman centre in the 18th and early 19th centuries by expanding the territories under their control and usurping revenues previously accruing to the treasury. However, the military reforms and efforts at centralization carried out under the sultans Mahmud II (1808–39) and Abdulmajid (1839–61) heralded the end of the last autonomous emirates. The emirs were replaced by centrally appointed governors, but these governors lacked the traditional legitimacy needed to keep the notables and chieftains of their districts in check; consequently, they were forced to leave the latter a large degree of autonomy. Thus it was that individual tribes or confederacies, which had previously been part of the emirates, became the most important social and political units. Chieftains everywhere made efforts to extend their power and influence at each other's expense. Missionaries and other travellers in the region in the mid-19th century repeated local people's claims that security had seriously decreased since the abolishment of the emirates and that there were unceasing feuds. The segmentary nature of Kurdish social organization was then more in evidence than it had been under the emirates.

During each new drive for administrative reform and centralization, representatives of the central government penetrated further into the region. Each new generation of centrally appointed officials had to find a point of accommodation with the tribal environment and ended up practising some form of indirect rule, albeit at ever lower levels of administration. The tribal entities that we see articulating themselves in each consecutive phase of administrative centralization became correspondingly smaller, less complicated and more genealogically homogeneous: emirates gave way to tribal confederacies, confederacies to large tribes, large tribes to smaller ones.[8]

Segmentary Alliance and Opposition versus Alliance with Strangers

The well-known anthropological model of segmentary alliance and opposition corresponds well with the map of social reality that many Kurdish tribesmen have in their heads. The feud was my informants' favourite example by which to illustrate what a tribe is and how it functions. It is perhaps not an accident that the cases of feuds that proceeded more or less according to the ideal rule concerned relatively small and genealogically homogeneous tribes and involved the killing of common tribes people rather than chieftains.

The 'purest' case of a tribal feud that I came across in my fieldwork took place in Uludere, a small town near the Turkish-Iraqi border consisting of a number of wards that were each inhabited by a different lineage of the same tribe. The feud had been triggered by an elopement, in the course of which a man was accidentally killed. The feud had been continued for several years, mobilizing two entire lineages against each other.

In the case of conflicts between or within leading families, however, the segmentary is only one of the organizing principles of the pattern of alliances that develops. Chieftains, as tribal ideology has it, reach and maintain their position due to a combination of descent, character ('manliness', i.e. generosity and courage) and consensus among the members of the tribe. In practice, however, their position is based on political skills and the support of outside allies. One of the major functions of a chieftain is to constitute a bridge between the tribe and the outside world, in which other tribes and the state (or states) are the most important actors. The recognition of a chieftain by the state – which in the case of the emirates took the form of sumptuous robes of investiture and beautifully calligraphed deeds of confirmation, and now at the lowest level of collusion with the regional gendarmerie commander – is the best possible prop of his position.

In the not uncommon case of a conflict within the leading family of a tribe, for instance between two rival contenders for paramount chieftainship, the conflict will tend to spill far beyond the two groups of closest relatives involved and may split the entire tribe. It is usual for both rivals to attempt to enlist the support of the most powerful external forces, i.e. neighbouring tribes and especially a powerful state in the region. Kurdistan differs from many other peripheral regions in that there has always been more than one nearby state with which a chieftain could ally himself.

Thus we find that around 1600 the large Mukri Confederacy divided into two violently opposed factions, because two closely related candidates for leadership allied themselves with the Safavids and the Ottomans respectively. In one particular battle, one part of the tribe fought on the Ottoman and another part on the Safavid side. We have no precise information as to how the tribe was split, but since the rivals were close relatives it can hardly have been according to a neat segmentary pattern.[9]

The proximity of Kurdistan to more than one state has also had the effect of enabling Kurdish chieftains to play one state off against another, or at least to seek protection from one against the other. The *Sharafnama* contains several examples of Kurdish princely houses alternating between sultan and shah as their royal sponsor. The author of this work, Sharaf Khan, spent a considerable part of his life in Safavid service himself before returning to Bitlis and being honoured by the Ottomans.

More recently, British political officers in southern Kurdistan in the wake of the First World War observed that in many of the larger tribes, there was one chieftain who was 'loyal' (i.e. willing to co-operate with the British authorities) and in favour of law and order. However, in the same tribe there were also one or more rival chieftains, usually close relatives, who were 'rebellious'.[10] A chieftain's 'rebellion' was often provoked by a conflict within the leading family of his tribe (or a conflict with a neighbouring tribe) rather than by disaffection with the government of the day.

Since the early 1960s, Kurdish nationalists have waged a guerrilla struggle against the central government, in which both sides mobilized Kurdish tribes against the other in a complicated pattern of alliances and oppositions. In several large tribes, some leading members were actively involved in the Kurdish movement (which was a state-like actor) whereas others co-operated with the government and even led sections of their tribes as pro-state militias.

The same phenomenon can also be observed in Turkey in the 1980s and the 1990s, when the PKK fought a violent armed struggle against the central government and its Kurdish 'collaborators'. Many leading Kurdish families had a few members in government service and others active in the PKK.[11]

The most striking example is that of the Bucak tribe, a leading family which has long been split in pro-government and Kurdish nationalist factions. In 1965, Fayik Bucak was one of the founders of the KDP of Turkey. He was assassinated in obscure circumstances, probably in a tribal feud; his children have since become prominent in the Kurdish movement, one of them, Serhat, closely associating himself with the PKK. Another branch of the family, led by Mehmet Celal Bucak and his successor Sedat Edip Bucak, has co-operated closely with the state. The PKK targeted Mehmet Celal Bucak in its first symbolic attack on a Kurdish 'collaborator' in 1979, which led to an extended feud between this branch of the Bucaks and the PKK. Sedat Edip Bucak has led a large 'village guard' militia force, established in the context of the war against the PKK but used by him primarily to establish his domination over neighbouring tribes. In the past two decades, members of the Bucak tribe have been killed fighting on both sides.[12]

The apparent split of tribes, or their leading families, into pro- and anti-government factions is not always the reflection of a serious conflict dividing the family. In some cases it appears to be the consequence of a deliberate decision not to put all one's eggs into one basket – a time-honoured strategy of elite families everywhere.

Tribal Militias

The impact of the state on tribal society has been particularly pervasive in periods when it organized tribal militias. The prototype of a Kurdish tribal militia was the Hamidiye regiments established under Sultan Abdulhamid II in 1891, allegedly on the model of the Russian Cossacks. Both the Ottomans and the Safavids had made extensive military use of their tribal subjects before, moving them over large distances to recently conquered or threatened parts of their empires in order to consolidate them. The Hamidiye were different, however, both in organization and in function. Existing Sunni Kurdish tribes (as well as a single Karapapakh tribe and a few Arab tribes) were made into irregular cavalry regiments commanded by their own tribal chieftains. A regiment numbered between 500 and 1150 men; some large tribes constituted more than one regiment (the Milli, for instance, raised four regiments). By the end of the decade, there were altogether 55 regiments.[13]

The Hamidiye regiments remained outside the command structure of the regular army, but all regimental commanders were placed under the authority of the commander of the 4th Army Corps in Erzincan, Zeki Pasha. The ostensible duty of the Hamidiye was to guard the frontier against foreign (i.e. Russian) incursions and to keep the Armenian population of the Empire's eastern provinces in check. For the sultan they represented a parallel system of control of the East, independent of the regular bureaucracy and army, which he did not fully trust. The Hamidiye enjoyed a high degree of legal immunity – neither the civilian administration nor even the regular military hierarchy had any authority over them, and no court had the competence to adjudicate crimes committed by members of the Hamidiye – and the regiments turned into virtually independent chiefdoms. Their commanders could not only consolidate control of their own tribes but also expand it at the expense of neighbouring tribes that did not constitute Hamidiye regiments. The establishment of the Hamidiye entailed the creation of new tribes, but also strengthened some of the existing tribes economically and politically at the expense of their neighbours, and made them internally more hierarchical. It also sowed the seeds of tribal conflicts that would surface decades later.[14]

The Hamidiye regiments were disbanded by the Young Turk regime that deposed Sultan Abdulhamid in 1909, but within a few years they were revived under another name. Kurdish tribal regiments took part in World War I and disappeared, along with the Ottoman Empire itself, after the war. The British in Iraq briefly experimented with a tribal police force but soon enough gave up when they discovered that the deployment of these levies was exacerbating tribal conflicts rather than making the British occupation palatable to Kurdish society at large.

A new type of tribal militia, mobilized to fight Kurdish nationalist guerrillas with their own methods, first emerged in Iraq in the 1960s. Even before the first armed clashes between Kurdish nationalists and Iraqi army troops broke out in 1961, the relations between the Barzanis and neighbouring tribes, especially their traditional rivals the Zibari, Bradost and Lolan, had been rapidly deteriorating and occasional fighting had occurred.[15] The return of 850 Barzani warriors from Soviet exile had changed the local balance of power and was experienced as a serious threat by these neighbouring tribes. The Barzanis believed that the central government was inciting the other tribes against them in order to keep the Kurds divided. Be that as it may, once Mulla Barzani and the KDP were openly at war with the central government, the latter actively supported the tribes that were hostile to the Barzanis and used them as its proxies in the guerrilla struggle.

Initially, both the Barzanis and their Kurdish opponents fought the war as a 'traditional' tribal war; neither side had any sort of formal military organization. From 1963 on, the government attempted to impose some form of order on the tribal forces, integrating them into the army command structure as irregular cavalry regiments (al-Fursan). The number of tribes who were mobilized as Fursan gradually expanded over the years.[16] Although the tribes were happy to accept the arms and pay that the government gave them, their participation in the conflict continued to depend more on the dynamics of their own relations with the Barzanis (and with other Kurds who had allied themselves with the Barzanis) than on policy decisions by the central government. The tribes who joined the Fursan (nicknamed *jash*, or 'donkey foal' by the nationalists) were not at all times hostile to the nationalist movement and its tribal allies; in fact, the nationalists claimed that they secretly received some of their arms and ammunition from 'jash' tribes. There are also reports of tribes switching allegiances more than once, depending on the perceived fortunes of the government and the Kurdish movement.

The Kurdish war thus provided the occasion for very considerable government subsidies to tribes (or rather, to tribal chieftains) and gave these tribes a new relevance as forms of social and political organization. There are no concrete descriptions of how incorporation into the Fursan affected any single tribe, but the general effect was one of consolidation of these tribes and of the leadership of those chieftains with whom the government dealt. These militia regiments were dealt with collectively; all arms, money and commands were communicated through the chieftain. This had the effect of reinforcing the chieftains' control over their tribes, strengthening the hierarchical and centrifugal rather than the egalitarian, segmentary aspects of tribal organization.

Initially, it was existing tribes that were made into Fursan regiments, but later similar units were formed that were not properly tribes (in the sense of named socio-political formations with an ideology of common descent) and that were commanded by influential personalities other than tribal chieftains. In the late 1970s and early 1980s, peasant followers of one particular religious leader, a sheikh of the Qadiriyya Sufi order, also made up a Fursan regiment that acted more or less as a tribe although they were by no means a descent group.

During the Iran-Iraq war (1980–88), a considerable part of the Kurdish population was incorporated into the militias; this was considered a substitute for military service and therefore permitted young men to stay away from the front. The militia commanders (named *mustashar* or 'counsellor') received arms and salaries for all their men, often even in excess of the real number of warriors under their command, and were allowed a measure of autonomy. Under these conditions the tribes, or more precisely their chieftains, became more powerful than they had long been. Significantly, it was, in most places, the *mustashar* who in the wake of Operation Desert Storm expelled Iraqi troops from Kuwait and started the great Kurdish uprising of March 1991. The Kurdish nationalist parties had, out of fear of reprisals against the civilian population, kept a low profile during the occupation of Kuwait and appeared to have been surprised by the uprising. Even after the parties succeeded in regaining leadership they saw themselves forced to share power with the former *mustashar*, and this remained so throughout the 1990s. Engaged in a permanent rivalry with each other, the two leading parties had little choice but to conclude alliances with as many of the *mustashar* as possible. This enabled the latter to bring a large share of the economic resources of the region under their control and to continue ruling as warlords over their own districts. One foreign observer described the Kurdish parties in the mid-1990s as 'tribal confederacies', which perhaps is an exaggeration, but shows an appreciation of the prominent role that the large tribes have come to play in Iraqi Kurdistan.[17] The tribes commanded by these warlords appear to have become less egalitarian, and seem to be held together by strong clientelist links rather than by kinship.

In Turkey, the authorities responded to the guerrilla offensive unleashed by the PKK in 1984 by establishing a similar Kurdish militia, the 'village guards' (*köy koruculari*). The first recruits to the 'village guards' belonged to tribes of the districts north of the Iraqi-Turkish border, the region where the PKK had carried out its first military actions. One of these tribes was the semi-nomadic Jirkan, whose chieftain Tahir Adiyaman had for years been an outlaw after he had killed a number of soldiers. He had been pardoned on the condition that he prevent PKK fighters from passing through his tribe's territory. Several of the first *korucu* units were well-known smuggler tribes, who knew better than anyone else how and where the border could be crossed. Thus they continued smuggling with impunity because of the military services they rendered to the state.[18]

The 'village guard' system was gradually expanded. Wherever there had been PKK activities, villagers were persuaded, sometimes coerced, to accept arms and become *korucu*. The numbers increased steadily; by the end of the 1990s there were officially some 65,000-70,000 of them. Some chieftains, in fact, maintained a private armed force that far exceeded the official number.[19]

Initially, 'village guards' were only expected to deny PKK guerrilla fighters access to or passage through their own districts. They were given arms, a monthly salary, and a bounty for every 'terrorist' killed. In the following years they were also expected to take part in military campaigns against the PKK. The *korucu* units were commanded by their own chieftains (who received the arms and pay for their men, which greatly strengthened their positions) and were loosely integrated into the command structure of the gendarmerie, the part of the armed forces that polices the countryside. Civilian authorities had no jurisdiction over them, and they were not placed under the district gendarmerie commander but under officers at higher levels. Predictably, this gave them immunity to exercise violence for their own ends, oppressing, looting, raping and killing their neighbours. In response, these neighbours had to draw together and reassert their tribal solidarity. One of the striking effects of the establishment of the 'village guards' is what one could call the re-tribalization of large parts of Turkish Kurdistan.

Another Prop of the Tribe: The Electoral Process

The re-tribalization of Kurdish society in Turkey is not only due to the 'village guard' system; the process began well before this system was put in place. Tribal organization acquired a new function when, in the wake of the Second World War, Turkey became a multi-party democracy with free elections. Since Turkey opted for a district system, in which each province elected a number of deputies to parliament, it became imperative for the competing political parties to have strong grassroots representation. Each party sought local workers and candidates who could be expected to mobilize numerous votes. In the Kurdish-inhabited provinces – most notably in Hakkari, the most 'tribal' province – the big parties' candidates were often either tribal chieftains themselves or men put forward by tribal chieftains as their representatives.

Affiliation with a political party was highly profitable for tribal chieftains for a number of reasons. When their party was in power, it could reward its loyal supporters in various ways, most conspicuously in the form of infrastructural investments and government contracts. Elected deputies, even for opposition parties, were the best advocates for local interests. In fact, a large share of these deputies' time was spent receiving people from their constituencies who requested various services. The political parties therefore found many tribal chieftains quite eager to join them, irrespective of their party political programmes.

Chieftains who were in conflict or rivalry with one another would, obviously, join different parties. Competition between political parties thus became intertwined with tribal conflicts and rivalries. Elections became occasions for the redistribution of important resources (in the form of government patronage) at the provincial and local levels. No tribe was large enough to send a deputy to parliament by itself; to do so, it had to forge a coalition with other tribes and/or interest groups. The electoral process thus came to shape important aspects of the mode of operation of tribes.

This was most visible in Hakkari, the smallest province and the one most dominated by tribes. For a long time only the two major parties contested the elections for Hakkari's single seat. The leading two tribes affiliated themselves with either of them, and the other tribes followed, depending on their conflicts or alliances with the first two. Thus a checkerboard pattern emerged, in which only minor shifts occurred over time as a result of new conflicts that forced one tribal group out of its own coalition into the opposing camp. Because Hakkari had long had only one seat, the stakes in the elections were high, as a result of which the tension between competing tribes increased significantly in periods preceding new elections. Tribal solidarities were strengthened (or, to put it less benevolently, strict control was exercised so that all members of the tribe expressed this solidarity at the ballot booths) and the boundaries between tribes were sharply demarcated.

Voting behaviour in the Kurdish-inhabited provinces was largely independent of the parties' overt political programmes. It could happen that a chieftain switched to another party, bringing his allies and followers along and causing his rivals also to switch parties. Through their insertion into the Turkish political system, Kurdish tribal chieftains gained control of additional resources and could consolidate or strengthen their positions within their own tribal environment. Electoral politics reinvigorated tribal society, which proved to be highly compatible with formal modern politics.

Smuggling and Tribalism

The carving up of the Ottoman Empire after World War I resulted in a number of new borders cutting through Kurdistan. The prices of many essential and luxury goods had always differed between regions; the emergence of new states, with different policies, resulted in steeper price differentials across the borders. Much of what had in the past been normal legal trade now became smuggling – which made it more profitable. Many Kurds earned comfortable incomes by smuggling tea, sugar or sheep across international borders.

As long as the borders were not guarded very effectively, all men who knew the region had equal opportunities, and smuggling may, in fact, have contributed to economic levelling or at least have allowed vertical social mobility. Once effective surveillance was in place, smuggling demanded special skills, which led to the concentration of this resource in fewer hands. Specialists who knew how to pass through a minefield without detonating any mines were in great demand (along the Syrian-Turkish border), and the shepherds who best knew the high mountains of the border regions took a large share of the illicit cross-border trade into their own hands. Most profitable, however, were profit-sharing arrangements with the border police and the local gendarmerie officers. It was only certain people who were in a position to even attempt to conclude such arrangements without being apprehended at once. Tribal chieftains were best placed to do so.

Civil servants and especially law enforcement officers who were appointed to posts in Kurdistan soon found out that they could not do their work without the co-operation of at least some persons who held a form of traditional authority. If they attempted to bypass these authorities in dealing with the local population, they usually failed to penetrate through the walls of silence that shielded local society from their view. Soon they would learn that they could achieve much more by relying on one or more of the local chieftains as their guides. Almost inevitably they were thereby drawn into the power game of tribal society with its perpetual conflicts and rivalries. A 'reliable' chieftain might help them arrest a smuggler or bandit (who in many cases happened to be a rival) and get other work done, thereby furthering his own interests and harming those of his enemies.

Mutually beneficial relationships developed between state officials and 'traditional' authorities, most of them tribal chieftains. In important respects, the officials became part of local tribal politics, many of them becoming actively involved. Under these conditions, many officials appeared to be corruptible, and mutually beneficial co-operation easily developed beyond maintenance of the law. Tribal chieftains who had established profitable arrangements with the relevant officials came to monopolize an increasingly large share of smuggling. Thus they brought important economic resources under their control, strengthening their position within their tribes and enabling them to centralise their control over their tribes.

From around 1980 on, the smuggling trade developed rapidly. The traditionally smuggled goods – animals, tea, alcohol and electronic consumer goods – were supplemented with narcotics and political refugees, raising the risk but also, even more, the profits to be made. The guerrilla war being waged by the PKK and the recruitment of 'village guards' by the state constituted further complications that led to the emergence of new types of networks growing out of existing tribes. The functioning of these networks is, for obvious reasons, ordinarily hidden from view. From time to time, however, some of their activities have come to light. The most spectacular of the networks that were in part uncovered is the 'gang of Yüksekova' (*Yüksekova çetesi*), named after a town near the Turkish-Iranian border. There, a *korucu* tribe, several gendarmerie officers and a renegade ex-PKK fighter were together engaged in a profitable enterprise that combined the conduct of counter-insurgency with heroin trade and the extortion of rival entrepreneurs in the region (who were made to believe it was the PKK that extorted them, and thus they could also later be accused of supporting the PKK).[20]

Conclusion

Kurdish tribes show such a bewildering variety in size and forms of internal organization that it may seem misleading to refer to all by the same term. They share an ideology of common descent, endogamy (parallel cousin marriage) and segmentary alliance and opposition. These principles do actually operate at the level of the smaller sub-tribes, but they are contradicted by the political alliances and authority relations integrating these sub-tribes into larger wholes. In larger tribes, we often find leading lineages that are, at best, distantly related to the common lineages making up the bulk of the tribe, and their authority is often shored up by an armed retinue and/or by recognition by the state apparatus, which also implies ultimately violent sanctions.

The size and complexity of composition of tribes, as well as the authority relations within these, appear to change in response to two crucial variables. The first of these is the form and degree of indirect rule that the relevant state or states allow the tribes (which is itself the outcome of a process of continuous negotiation between society and state); the other variable consists of the available economic and ecological resource base. Mountain pastures, arable land and subject peasant populations were never the only available resource bases; caravan routes constituted another one (several tribes, most famously the Hamawand, specialized in protecting or robbing caravans) as did state military service. The establishment of modern, centralized states has not led to the dissolution of tribes, if only because they provided new resources that tribes could exploit. The new borders made smuggling an important source of income, and tribes appeared to be appropriate organizations to exploit this due to their internal solidarity and the strong authority of the chieftain over his followers. Electoral politics became a major mechanism of redistribution on a national scale, and for obvious reasons tribal chieftains were attractive partners for political parties. Political patronage strengthened the tribes and reinforced the chieftains' positions within their tribes.

Modernizing and centralizing regimes (most consistently Kemalist Turkey and Pahlavi Iran) have attempted to detribalize Kurdish society by physically removing the chieftains and sometimes deporting entire tribes. The successes of these measures appeared to be temporary only. When confronted with armed nationalist rebellion, both Iraq and Turkey established Kurdish militias to whom they delegated much power, thus reinvigorating some of the tribes and causing a resurgence of inter-tribal conflicts.

Both in peace and in war, Kurdish tribes have shown great resilience, and it is probably true that tribes have played more prominent social and political roles in the Kurdistan of the 1990s than they did a half century earlier.

Notes

1. Major sources on Kurdish tribes are the *Sharafnama* (a history of the Kurdish emirates compiled in the late 16th century), Türkay 1979 (a compilation of data on tribes from Ottoman documents), Hursid Pasa 1997 [1860] (written by an Ottoman member of the commission that delineated the Iranian-Ottoman boundary in 1848–52), Jaba 1860, Sykes 1908, Mayevski 1330/1914, Noel 1919, Gökalp 1992 (written in the early 1920s), 'Azzawi 1937–56, Razm-ara 1320, Hütteroth 1959, and the anonymous *Asiretler raporu* (the most complete list of Kurdish tribes in Turkey, compiled by one of the intelligence services, probably in the 1970s).

2. For an example of such changes over a relatively short period of time, see van Bruinessen 1983 (on the Shikak tribe).

3. See van Bruinessen, 1992, 'Tribes, Chieftains and Non-tribal Groups', for a more detailed survey of the range of forms of tribal organization in Kurdistan.

4. See Demirtas 1949, Gündüz 1997.

5. See the observations on the Bitlis, Baban and Jazira emirates in van Bruinessen 1992, pp. 161–80.

6. This is brought out clearly in the 16th-century Ottoman documents on the Tur 'Abdin region analysed in Göyünc and Hütteroth, 1997.

7. Van Bruinessen 1978, pp. 215–20; Tawahhudi 1359/1981.

8. This process is sketched in greater detail in van Bruinessen 1992, pp. 192–5.

9. Malcolm 1815, pp. 541–2. For a later but similar incident involving the Mukri tribe see Eskandar Beg Monshi 1978, pp. 1015–9.

10. Numerous examples in Edmonds 1957, the most striking one perhaps that of the Pizhdar tribe, pp. 217–220 and 228–59.

11. This is brought out in an interesting report prepared for Turkey's Chambers of Commerce and Industry in 1995. 1267 respondents in eastern Turkey, most of them locally prominent persons who were well-integrated into Turkey's political and economic life, were asked whether they had relatives or acquaintances who were with the PKK. Two thirds declined answering this questions, but 15 per cent (or 45 per cent of those who did give an answer) mentioned that they had a relative with the PKK (TOBB, 1995, pp. 19).

12. On the Bucak tribe see Sahin, 1995. Sedate Edip Bucak acquired great notoriety for his central role in the so-called Susurluk scandal, which involved the profitable but illegal cooperation of counter-insurgency forces, right-wing activists and organized crime.

13. Kodaman, 1987, pp. 21–66, cf. Duguid, 1973.

14. First (1970) describes how his own tribe, the Alevi Hormek, turned against the Shaykh Sa'id rebellion in 1925 out of resentment for the Sunni Cibran tribe, which played a leading role in the rebellion and which had in the past, as Hamidiye, oppressed the Hormek.

15. For the chronology of the events and the role of the tribes see Kinnane, 1964, pp. 59–81, Dann, 1969, pp. 198–9, 332–47, Jawad, 1981, pp. 50–4, 65–85, McDowall, 1996, pp. 302–13.

16. Besides the Zibari, Bradost and Lolan, the powerful Herki and Surchi tribes, who also had been in conflict with the Barzanis before, were among the first to be recruited as Fursan. Other tribes that followed played less prominent roles in the fighting.

17. Wimmer, 1997. For observations on the economic and political roles of the former *mustashar* and present warlords in Iraqi Kurdistan, see Leezenberg, 1997.

18. On the first Korucu tribes and their relations with the authorities and with other Kurdish tribes, see Dagli, 1989, Aytar, 1992, Wiessner, 1997, pp. 298–302.

19. The most notorious case is that of Sedat Edipt Bucak (cf. note 12 above) who has a private army of around 10,000 men, of whom only 350 to 400 were officially registered as 'village guards'. The figure of 10,000 armed men was reported frequently in the Turkish press, eg. in an interview with Bucak in the weekly *Aktuel*, no. 136, February 10–16, 1994, pp. 18–24. A report prepared by inspector general Kutlu Savas for Prime Minister Mesut Yilmaz in 1997 noted that Bucak used this force to establish his hegemony over Siverek district at the expense of other tribes, notably the old rivals Kirvar and Karakeçili. See Internationaler Verein für Menschenrechte der Kurden, 1998.

20. Fragmentary revelations about the gang of Yüksekova appeared in the press in the course of 1997. For a preliminary overview, see Berberoglu, 1998, pp. 143–71.

References

Anon, *Asiretler raporu*. Istanbul: Kaynak, 1998.

Aytar, Osman, *Hamidiye alaylarindan köy koruculuguna*. Istanbul: Medya Günesi, 1992.

al-'Azzawi, 'Abbas, *'Asha'ir al-'Iraq*. 4 vols. Baghdad, 1937–56.

Berberoglu, Enis, Kodadi Yüksekova. Susurluk, Ankara, Bodrum, Yüksekova fay hatti. *Istanbul*: Milliyet, 1998.

Bruinessen, M. van, *Agha, Shaikh and State: The Social and Political Structures of Kurdistan*. London: Zed Books, 1992.

—— 'Kurdish Tribes and the State in Iran: The case of Simko's revolt', in Richard Tapper (ed.), *The Conflict of Tribe and State in Iran and Afghanistan*. London: Croom Helm, 1983, pp. 364–400.

Dagli, Faysal, 'Asiret alaylari', *Ikibin'e dogru*, 12–11–1989, 8–13.

Dann, Uriel, *Iraq under Qassem: A political history, 1958–1963*. New York: Praeger, 1969.

Demirtas (Sümer), Faruk, 'Bozulus hakkinda', *Ankara Üniversitesi Dil ve Tarih–Cografya Fakültesi Dergisi* 7 (1949), 29–60.

Duguid, S., 'The politics of unity: Hamidian policy in Eastern Anatolia', *Middle Eastern Studies* 9 (1973), 139–156.

Eskandar, Beg Monshi, *History of Shah 'Abbas the Great (Tarik-e `Alamara-ye 'Abbasi),* translated by R. M. Savory. 2 vols. Boulder: Westview Press, 1978.

Firat, M. Serif, *Dogu illeri ve Varto tarihi.* 3rd printing, Ankara, 1970.

Gökalp, Ziya, *Kürt asiretleri hakkinda sosyolojik tetkikler. Hazirlayan: Sevket Beysanoglu.* Istanbul: Sosyal Yayinlar, 1992.

Göyünç, Nejat and Wolf-Dieter Hutteroth, *Land an der Grenze: Osmanische Verwaltung im heutigen türkisch-syrisch-irakischen Grenzgebiet im 16. Jahrhundert.* Istanbul: Eren, 1997.

Gündüz, Tufan, *Anadolu'da Türkmen asiretleri: Bozulus Türkmenleri, 1540–1640.* Ankara: Bilge, 1997.

Hursid (Pasa), Mehmed, *Seyahatname-i hudud. Gevrimyazi: Alaattin Eser.* Istanbul: Simurg, 1997 (originally published in 1860).

Hutteroth, Wolfgang, *Bergnomaden und Yaylabauern im mittleren kurdischen Hütteroth, Wolfgang, Taurus.* Marburg: Geographisches Institut der Universität, 1959.

Internationaler Verein für Menschenrechte der Kurden (ed.), *Bandenrepublik Türkei? Der Susurlukbericht des Ministerialinspektors Kutlu Savas.* Bonn: IMK, 1998.

Jaba, Alexandre, *Recueil de notices et de récits kurdes.* St.-Petersbourg, 1860.

Jawad, Sa'd, *Iraq & the Kurdish Question, 1958–1970.* London: Ithaca Press, 1981.

Kinnane, Derk, *The Kurds and Kurdistan.* London: Oxford University Press, 1964.

Kodaman, Bayram, *Sultan II. Abdulhamid devri Dogu Anadolu politikasi.* Ankara: Türk Kültürünevri Arastirma Enstitutu, 1987.

Leezenberg, Michel, 'Irakische Kurdistan seit dem Zweiten Golfkrieg', in Carsten Borck et al., *Ethnizität, Nationalismus, Religion und Politik in Kurdistan,* Münster, Lit Verlag, 1997, pp.45–78.

McDowell, David, *A Modern History of the Kurds.* London: I.B.Tauris, 1996.

Malcolm, J., *The History of Persia.* London, 1815.

Mayevski, Van, *Bitlis vilayetleri 'askeri istatistiki.* Istanbul: Matba'a-i 'askeriye -Süleymaniye, 1330/1914.

Noel, J. B., *Notes on Kurdish Tribes: On and beyond the Borders of Mosul Vilayet and Westward to the Euphrates.* Baghdad: Government Press, 1919.

Razm-ara, 'Ali, *Jughrafiya-yi nizami-yi Iran, vols. Adharbayjan-i Bakhtari, Kurdistan, Kirmanshahan, Pusht-i Kuh.* S.l. Tehran , 1320/1941.

Sahin, Osman, *Firat'in sirtindaki kan: Bucaklar.* Istanbul: Kaynak, 1995.

Sharaf Khan b. Shams al-din Bidlisi, *Sharafnama,* ed. by V. Véliaminof-Zernof. 2 vols, St-Petersbourg, 1860–62. French translation by M. Charmoy, 4 vols, St-Petersbourg, 1868–75.

Sykes, Mark Percival, 'The Kurdish tribes of the Ottoman Empire', *Journal of the Royal Anthropological Institute* 38 (1908), 451–486 (reprinted in M. Sykes, *The Caliph's Last Heritage: A short history of the Turkish Empire.* London: Macmillan and Co., 1915).

Tavahhudi 'Awghazi', Kalimullah, *Harakat-i tarikhi-yi Kurd bi-Khurasan dar difa' az istiqlal-i Iran.* Mashhad, 1359/1981.

Tobb Dogu sorunu: *teshisler ve tespitler. Özel arastirma reporu.* Ankara, 1995.

Wiessner, Gunnar, 'Grundfragen aktueller politischer und militärischer Entwicklungen in den kurdischen Provinzen der Türkei', *Orient* 38 (1997), 289–310.

Wimmer, Andreas, 'Stammespolitik und die kurdische Nationalbewegung im Irak', in Carsten Borck et al, *Ethnizität, Nationalismus, Religion und Politik in Kurdistan*. Münster: Lit Verlag, 1997, pp. 11–43.

Yalçin-Heckmann, Lale, *Tribe and Kinship among the Kurds*. Frankfurt am Main: Peter Lang, 1991.

SEVEN

Yazidi Tribes, Religion and State in Early Modern Iraq[1]

Nelida Fuccaro

The Yazidi Kurds of Iraq were (and still are) a group of agriculturalists and cattle breeders settled in the Mosul province. The greatest majority of the Iraqi Yazidis lived in the two enclaves of Jabal Sinjar and Shaikhan, the former located in the northwestern corner of the Iraqi Jazira and the latter between the city of Mosul and the mountainous areas of southern Kurdistan. For centuries, the community of Jabal Sinjar was able to maintain a strong local identity given the exceptional geographical location and economic resources of the Yazidi Mountain. Although Jabal Sinjar was situated in the middle of the arid Jazira plateau, it was relatively isolated from the surrounding environment and enjoyed abundant precipitation. The population of Jabal Sinjar included peasant communities who were tribally organized. The majority of the inhabitants of the Mountain were Yazidi who lived exclusively within a tribal system. The Shaikhan area, although less tribalized and more heterogeneous, represented the religious centre of Yazidism. Over time the local Yazidi society had developed strong links with the Yazidi religious establishment as the majority of Yazidi men of religion were settled in the area, including the Yazidi Mir, the supreme religious leader of the community. Among the Iraqi Yazidis, religious and tribal identity were closely intertwined and much more relevant for purposes of communal mobilization than language or racial affiliation. The Yazidi religion is a heterodox creed whose doctrinal backbone is influenced by Zoroastrianism and Dualism while many Yazidi rituals and religious practices are of Christian and Islamic origin as a result of the day-to-day contacts between Yazidis and other groups which developed in the fragmented society of northern Iraq. However, Yazidi/Muslim antagonism is clearly indicated by the fact that the most important symbol of Yazidi religious identity, *Malak Tawus,* or the Peacock Angel, was also the most tangible symbol of the Yazidis' dissociation from Islam as in the Muslim milieu it was considered a representation of the Devil.

The impact of British colonial rule on ethnic mobilization was particularly apparent in the Mosul province given that the area was populated by different linguistic, racial and socio-economic groups, which after 1918 came in contact with the realities of the colonial state established by Great Britain. In the north of Iraq were large settled Christian communities of various denominations (Jacobites, Syrian Catholics, Chaldeans and Nestorians or Assyrians), which since the Ottoman period had been in touch with Europe mainly through missions and consular representations. During the Mandate, ethnic mobilization in the Mosul province was central to the process of nation-building. It had a profound impact on Anglo-Iraqi relations as the development of the Assyrian and Kurdish questions would indicate. Since World War I the arrival in the Mosul province of large numbers of Assyrian refugees from eastern Turkey, who settled in the area under British protection, created the basis for local conflict and for the emergence or strengthening of political divisions along communal lines. To a great extent, the development of the Assyrian question substantiates the accusation often levelled against the British that they implemented policies of 'divide and rule' whose main outcome was the politicisation of communalism. British presence in the region also became closely associated with the emergence of new political aspirations among sections of the local Kurdish population. Shortly after the British occupation of Mosul in late 1918 Major Noel, a British official, was sent to the tribal areas of the province to test the viability of a Kurdish state. Although the project of creating a southern Kurdish confederation under British patronage collapsed after it became clear that cooperation between the British and local Kurdish leader Sheikh Mahmud Barzinji was not viable, Kurdo-British relations had a profound impact on Iraqi nation-building as exemplified by the prominent role played by the Kurdish question in the development of the dispute between Great Britain and Turkey for the Mosul *vilayat,* or province. [2]

While the Kurdish and Assyrian questions have been analysed with a certain consistency, the Yazidi Kurds are usually considered unimportant in the development of regional and intercommunal politics. Although it cannot be denied that the Iraqi Yazidis did not have as strong an impact on Iraqi political development as the Kurds and Assyrians did, they certainly represent a very interesting case study for the development of Iraqi ethnicity, both from the perspective of group mobilization and the impact of British colonial policies on communalism. First, Yazidi tribal and religious loyalties were tightly connected to a strong sense of localism, especially in the Yazidi enclave of Jabal Sinjar. To a great extent both Yazidi primordialism and localism were exploited by British colonial rule. Secondly, the Yazidis consistently failed to identify with mainstream Sunni Kurdish society, let alone with Kurdish political mobilization although they were ethnic Kurds. By contrast the members of the community identified socially and politically with local Christian groups whose leaders in the 1920s became widely involved in the arena of regional and national politics.

Ethnicity, Ethnics and British Colonialism[3]

In its modern paradigm, ethnicity is a dialectic process of confrontation closely connected to the establishment of modern nation-states. Thus ethnicity is primarily understood as ethnic mobilization, a phenomenon which is generally associated with the presence of modern political and socio-economic institutions. In this connection ethnic mobilization is a social, political and cultural 'resource' through which groups channel their demands and responses as a way of adaptation to changing political and socio-economic circumstances. Hence ethnicity as both an attribute and an analytical concept is a notion which exists only in opposition and relativities, and which stresses the socially and politically constructed nature of group behaviour.

The relationship between colonialism and the development of ethnic consciousness in Iraq, as elsewhere in the Middle East, is indeed complicated. Great Britain created the modern state of Iraq in 1921 when King Faysal was appointed to the headship of a parliamentary monarchy which came to embody the Iraqi state. King Faysal became the ruler of the three former Ottoman provinces of Baghdad, Basrah and Mosul under close British supervision. In this chapter I shall tackle the issue of ethnicity and colonialism as it developed in Iraq from a slightly different perspective. I will look at ethnic mobilization as it occurred in the Mandatory period in terms of the continuities it provided with the past, rather than considering ethnicity as a sudden break provoked by fast modernization. Although British colonialism fostered the emergence of new identities and started the process of adjustment, reframing and transformation of group loyalties, in the 1920s British rule had to come to terms with the socio-economic and political realities of the pre-modern period, which were particularly rooted in the rural areas. As an indication of the great degree of continuity with the past, new classes, groups and political affiliations emerged quite slowly and, in most cases, became apparent after the termination of the Mandate in 1932. Although Iraq was formally independent, its political development in the post-colonial period was still closely supervised by Great Britain under a system of advisorship which permeated all levels of state institutions.

The continuity between the late Ottoman and Mandate periods reflects the assumption that ethnicity is not exclusively a modern phenomenon and as such it was not 'created' by Great Britain. Ethnics or ethnic communities as socio-cultural groups had lived in northern Iraq for centuries under the umbrella of the multi-ethnic Ottoman Empire. As group consciousness was cemented by religion, language, kinship patterns, physical contiguity and socio-economic specialisation, ethnic difference was primarily based on primordial associations which were firmly rooted in localism. People generally identified with, and responded to, very local sources of power and authority: city notables, village heads, tribal or religious leaders who often functioned as intermediaries between the state and local society. Thus ethnicity as the existence of groups sharing elements of common culture, a sense of solidarity and myths of common ancestry which defined intergroup relations and relations between individuals and the state was by no means an imposition of the colonial period. During the British Mandate ethnic difference and established patterns of group leadership at a local level constituted the bases upon which ethnic mobilization developed in northern Iraq under new political conditions. The emergence of forms of Kurdish and Christian nationalism staged against the growing influence of the Arab Sunni elite in the colonial state, are a case in point. Political mobilization was promoted by the traditional leadership of these groups as they made extensive use of old communal solidarities and religious symbols in order to shape new concepts of legitimate nationhood.

The application to Iraq of the modernist paradigm of development of a national culture, as that of ethnicity, is rather difficult. As Ernest Gellner's theory of nationalism puts it, the static and ascriptive nature of group consciousness in the pre-modern period contrasts with the dynamic and vertical development of group mobilization during processes of state formation as a result of modernization. In Iraq modernization was not a prerogative of the Mandatory period for, to a certain extent, attempts at modernization started in the last century of Ottoman rule, notably during the reformist period known as Tanzimat (1839–76) which was continued under the Pan-Islamic policies of Sultan 'Abdul Hamid (1876–1909). During this period the Ottoman government made consistent efforts to centralize and rationalize the administration of the Arab provinces of the Empire along European lines. Although the Tanzimat reforms aimed at strengthening the existing political system rather than transforming the nature of Ottoman imperial rule, they set in motion unprecedented responses from many groups that felt threatened by the new policies of the government. During this period, group identities became active and instrumental as a response to the new measures enacted by the state. To a certain extent in the 1920s, group mobilization can be viewed not so much as a radical break with the past but as a process of adjustment to a quicker and more thorough pace of reforms. Ottoman centralization had a wide impact on the Yazidi communities of Iraq especially when considered in the context of the Pan-Islamic movement promoted by Sultan 'Abdul Hamid. It determined widespread conscription and conversion campaigns against the Yazidi communities of Sinjar and Shaikhan. In the last two decades of the 19th century many Yazidis were killed in the enclave of Shaikhan and the religious leader of the Yazidi community converted to Islam. In Sinjar, conscription campaigns, religious persecution and the more active presence of the Ottoman government among the local tribes promoted new tribal coalitions and a widespread religious revival which favoured the rise to power of prominent tribal leaders of religious background. These leaders played a prominent role in Yazidi affairs during the Mandate and became the main intermediaries between the population and the Mandatory administration. The last century of Ottoman rule also brought in crucial economic developments for the Yazidis of Jabal Sinjar. In the second half of the 19th century the Mountain became progressively integrated in a market-oriented economy as a reflection of the increasing commercialization of agriculture in the Mosul province. The Mosulite merchant classes, who had their representatives in Sinjar, invested large sums of money in agriculture and stock-farming. The integration of Sinjar continued further throughout the 1920s and 1930s as indicated by the growing importance of the area in the regional and national economy.

Localism and Essentialism[4]

In rural areas like Jabal Sinjar, religious and tribal loyalties, together with a strong sense of localism, survived the Ottoman period and became one of the most formidable hindrances to the process of nation-building. While more urbanized regions and especially the city of Mosul became the main recipients of colonial policies, British penetration in the rural areas was difficult and local communities became slowly, and often reluctantly, involved in the process of state formation. As an indication of this, the Iraqi state made the first consistent effort to call for a direct Yazidi participation into national affairs only in 1936 when the government attempted to enroll members of the community in the national army following the enforcement of universal conscription.

The persistence of localism in the context of the political and socio-economic modernization undertaken during the Mandate period highlights particularly well that dynamic opposition between communities and states which is considered essential for the development of ethnicity in its modern form. Seen from this perspective, the analysis of closely-knit communities like the Iraqi Yazidis gives an important insight into nation-building as developments which affected peripheral areas were often of the utmost importance in the definition of British colonial policies. The 1920 tribal disturbances, which jeopardized public security in the country, convinced the British government of the necessity to develop a cheap and less direct form of colonial control which resulted in the creation of the Kingdom of Iraq in 1921. Political developments in the tribal areas of Kurdistan affected substantially the course of British policy in Iraq as Kurdish separatism in the northern areas threatened the viability of a British-controlled Iraqi state. The writing of the history of Iraq without a Baghdad-centred approach has the advantage of highlighting continuities with the past, as the persistence of old solidarities was most noticeable in the rural areas, without underestimating the changes brought in by British colonialism. A localist approach also brings back many groups to the core of national development.

Studies of modern Iraq are often considered essentialist in relation to Iraqi social and political development as they support the idea that Iraqi society evolved out of dialectic oppositions (Kurds v. Arabs, Sunni v. Shi'i, cities v. countryside, tribes v. states). The employment of these categories is generally considered a reflection of an 'orientalist' historiography which takes at face value socio-economic and political constructs of the imperial powers. It seems, however, that an ethnic approach is *per se* essentialist as it focuses on groups as defined by their cultural and social boundaries. Furthermore, it analyses fragmentation rather that adopting a holistic perspective on social and political developments. Researchers interested in the colonial period face the dilemma of how to interpret the wide variety of sources coming from the British colonial administration which tend to explain in their own authoritative way political and social realities. However, for scholars interested in the development of the ethnic question these sources should represent strength rather than weakness, as often implied by the detractors of essentialism. Of course it is important to acknowledge the power of colonial constructs, especially when these constructs were supported by policies which *de facto* attempted to enforce them. However, categories indicating socio-economic or ethnic divisions were not created *ex novo* but,very often, reframed. For example, antagonism between the Yazidi Kurds and Muslim Arabs was by no means an invention of the colonial power; it overlapped the already existing dichotomy of heterodoxy v. Islam, which in the Ottoman period expressed Yazidi/Muslim antagonism in terms which were consistent with the realities imposed by an Islamic state. By contrast, a sense of Kurdishness did not emerge among the Yazidis of Iraq in the colonial period, although British policies possibly created the bases for the development of an all-encompassing Kurdish national movement.

It is true that the Yazidi community of Iraq is a subject of study particularly inclined to fit an essentialist cliché. The historiography of the community emphasises the Yazidis' isolation from state power and their strong communal boundaries was favoured by geographical seclusion, especially in Jabal Sinjar. The theme of tribes v. states also features prominently in accounts of Jabal Sinjar in which the history of the local Yazidi community is written primarily through episodes of warfare between the Yazidi tribes and the Ottoman state. New evidence on the late Ottoman and Mandate periods portray a fairly different picture, although resistance to the encroachment of state authority still emerges as an important feature of the Yazidi tribal ethos. The society of Jabal Sinjar was by no means exclusive to Yazidis as it was organised along communal lines: the Yazidi tribes included also Sunni Muslim and Shi'i heterodox sections and close socio-economic and political links existed between the tribes and Christian and Muslim communities settled in the area. Intercommunalism and exchange of religious practices with neighbouring groups was an accepted fact of life, as also indicated by the absorption of many Muslim and Christian rituals. Indeed, Yazidi identity reflected centuries of integration in the fragmented society of northern Iraq.

State Formation from a Yazidi Perspective: British Policies

The establishment of provisional borders with Turkey and Syria in 1919 (which ran very close to the main Yazidi settlement of Jabal Sinjar), the development of British tribal policies, the adoption of Air Control since late 1921 and the rationale which guided the establishment of the administration of the new colonial state at the local level were all aspects of British colonial policy which became particularly relevant to the development of the Yazidi areas under British mandatory control.

The definition of national boundaries with both Turkey and Syria was central to the process of nation-building in the northern areas of Iraq, and this became part of a general process of demarcation of British, Turkish and French spheres of influence in the region. Although Jabal Sinjar was included in the Mosul province under British administration since 1919, the temporary character of the delimitation of the borders with Turkey and Syria (fixed by international agreement respectively in 1925 and 1932), made the support of the local Yazidi tribes and tribal leaders essential for the nation-building policies of the British administration. In the 1920s the temporary character of the definition of the borders with Syria was especially problematic as since 1920 Jabal Sinjar had been bisected by a provisional frontier which placed one third of the land occupied rightfully by Yazidis under Syrian jurisdiction. Yet the whole of Jabal Sinjar was *de facto* administered by the British authorities of Mosul. Between 1920 and 1932, border disturbances occurred more and more frequently and usually involved local Yazidi tribes and Bedouin groups which tended to take advantage of the unclear frontier settlement. They would raid Yazidi villages and then withdraw to Syrian territory, as both British forces and the Iraqi police were not in a position to intervene in areas which were, theoretically, under Syrian jurisdiction. Apart from the economic losses suffered by the Yazidis of western Sinjar, the border dispute also had important implications for relations between the Yazidi population and the local Iraqi administration, which was perceived as unable to defend their interests. However, the presence of an international border bisecting Jabal Sinjar offered its Yazidi leadership a new bargaining power *vis-à-vis* the Iraqi state as on many occasions Yazidi leaders threatened to immigrate with their tribes to Syria.

The border issue clearly impinged upon British policy with regard to the Yazidi tribes. These policies reflected a system of informal control adopted by the Mandatory power in the rural areas and embodied the essentialist notion of tribes as opposed to states. The British created a special administrative and legal system for the tribal areas of Iraq through the Tribal Disputes Regulations first issued in 1916 which separated the administration of designated tribal regions from urbanized and settled areas. By early 1919, when Jabal Sinjar was included in the Occupied Territories of Iraq, Great Britain started to subsidise Hamu Shiru, a local Yazidi religious leader who was head of the Fuqara' tribe. He was put in charge of administration and public security for a monthly salary of Rs. 300. British tribal policies in Jabal Sinjar proved largely unsuccessful, although Hamu Shiru defended British interests in the area until his death in 1933. Hamu Shiru was not in a position to unite and successfully control all the tribes living in Jabal Sinjar as tribal units were politically very fragmented and continued to respond to the authority of different religious and tribal leaders. Since the 17th century, Yazidi tribalism had developed primarily as a response to the socio-economic and demographic development of Jabal Sinjar, which became an important immigration unit for many Kurdish groups coming from Iraqi and Turkish Kurdistan. Yazidi tribes were, in reality, small tribal confederations which included tribal sections (known as *bavik*) of different backgrounds and religious affiliations which had arrived more or less recently in the Mountain. As these sections developed as semi-independent political units under a loose tribal authority their members were inclined to shift allegiances very quickly according to circumstances. The appointment of Hamu Shiru to the paramountship of Sinjar in the 1920s did not substantially affect previous alliances at the level of the tribes. This is exemplified by the fact that the struggle between the Fuqara' chief and his old enemy Dawud al-Dawud, leader of the Mihirkan tribe, which had started in the 1880s, continued even after his appointment. However, the unclear border arrangements with both Turkey and Syria divided further political authority both among single tribal units and in intertribal context, as opposing factions would seek support on the other side of the border. This occurred to the extent that, in the late 1930s, after the enforcement of universal conscription, Dawud al-Dawud and Sheikh Khalaf Haskani emigrated to Syria with their followers while Hamu Shiru's successor, his son Khudaida, remained in Sinjar in an attempt to come to terms with the Iraqi administration.

The conflictual nature of British colonial policies in Jabal Sinjar became more apparent on administrative grounds. Policies concerning the development of a state administration in the area had a long lasting influence on the future development of Yazidi communal affairs. Although Hamu Shiru was subsidized by the government as Paramount Sheikh of Sinjar, in 1921 the British supported the establishment of an Iraqi administration in the Mountain assisted by permanent police forces dependent on the Iraqi Ministry of Interior. After 1921, British officials no longer had executive powers in the Yazidi areas although the Mandatory administration continued to support Hamu Shiru. By 1929, the power of British personnel was reduced further as their Iraqi counterparts assumed a more prominent political role in local affairs. The new administrative arrangements of Sinjar reflected the progressive devolution of administrative and political authority to the Iraqi government that was carried out by the Mandate at a national level. However, peripheral areas like Jabal Sinjar faced more pressures on the part of the Iraqi administration for a faster integration into the institutional framework of the Sunni-controlled Iraqi state, partly because of the still unresolved border disputes.

The presence of an Iraqi official who acted as the intermediary between the local population and the Iraqi government confined the British protégé Hamu

Shiru to the role of a mere contender in local tribal politics. The establishment of the authority of the government in Sinjar also had important repercussions on intercommunal relations as it negatively affected the local Christian community whose members were the main allies of Hamu Shiru. In previous decades local Christian traders who represented the capitalist class of Jabal Sinjar had helped the Fuqara' leader to build up his economic and political power in the context of the fast commercialization of agriculture and pastoralism in the Mosul province which started in the 1850s. The Sinjari Christians constituted a rather compact community who lived outside the Yazidi tribal system, and were concentrated in large villages usually controlled by Hamu Shiru (Balad Sinjar, the main administrative centre of the Mountain, Jaddala and Bardahali). The community also included groups of refugees who arrived in Sinjar in 1914/1915 as a result of Ottoman religious persecutions carried out in the Mardin and Nusaybin regions located north of the Yazidi Mountain. By the mid-1920s, a local secret organization known as Muslim League which was supported by some Iraqi officials, started to carry out a policy of terror against the local Christian community with the purpose of undermining the position of both Hamu Shiru and Great Britain on the Mountain. Although the the League's propaganda cannot be defined as Iraqi nationalist, it clearly attempted to use Islam in order to create a sense of identification with the Iraqi administration among certain sections of the population of Sinjar. While it seems that, to a certain extent, this propaganda succeeded in gaining the support of prominent Muslim merchants operating in Balad, it was not well received among those Muslim Kurds who lived integrated into the Yazidi tribes. By 1931, as a result of increasing friction between the local administration and large sections of the population of Sinjar, Great Britain, by then particularly concerned with relinquishing her Mandate over Iraq, attempted unsuccessfully to create a permanent administrative arrangement for Sinjar according to which Christian officials would serve on permanent basis on the Yazidi Mountain in the absence of suitable Yazidi candidates. This indicates the willingness on the part of Great Britain to enforce an Iraqi identity among the Sinjari Yazidis towards the end of the colonial period by making use of historical and socio-economic realities, which in the last century of Ottoman rule had favoured the rapproachment between Yazidis and Christians, especially after the enforcement of Pan-Islamic policies during the late Ottoman period. Clearly, the gradual encroachment of the Iraqi administration in Sinjar, which was most prominent in the local capital Balad Sinjar, favoured the development of a new political arena which increasingly staged conflicts among groups whose interests were based in the town as the growing Muslim/Christian confrontation over the issue of the nature of Sinjari administration would indicate.

Although after 1921 British control over Sinjar was rather loose, the Mandatory kept in check his vital interests in the area through the Royal Air Force. The Air Scheme, which was adopted by the Mandatory administration in October 1922, placed Great Britain in charge of the internal security and external defence of Iraq. In the northern areas it primarily supported British tribal policies by providing a force permanently in charge of rural peace-keeping in the region. In Jabal Sinjar, RAF planes proved to be particularly useful to quell tribal disturbances when the local police were unsuccessful, to deter anti-British propaganda coming from beyond the provisional borders and to maintain the strategic position of Great Britain in the region. The presence of the RAF also provided a means through which British officials based in Mosul closely followed Yazidi tribal affairs. A network of local informants dependent on the RAF command of Baghdad, called Special Service Officers, operated among the population of Sinjar on a regular basis. Their reports had a decisive impact on the formulation of British policies in the area. The enforcement of the Air Scheme often proved a double-edged weapon in the hands of the British in their dealings with the Sinjari tribes. If, on the one hand it assured the maintenance of public security and a vital provision of intelligence, on the other the employment of RAF planes for policing duties had very negative effects on the tribesmen's perception of the Mandatory power given the devastating effect of bombings. This is clearly shown by the reluctance with which the RAF undertook military operations against the Yazidi tribes in April 1925 at a crucial junction for the solution of Mosul question. As the dispute between Iraq and Turkey for the Mosul vilayat was referred to the League in June 1924, the future of Mosul province was made dependent on the desires of the local populations in accordance with the principle of self-determination which had guided the establishment of Mandatory systems in the Middle East. Clearly British military intervention in Sinjar before the final arbitration of the League seriously jeopardized the acceptance of British and Iraqi rule by large sections of the local population.

Yazidi Mobilization: Tribes, Communities and Religious Loyalties

The permanent establishment of representatives of the Iraqi government in Balad Sinjar after 1921, and the increasing intercommunal conflicts which developed in the town, had important repercussions on the development of tribal affairs in the rural areas inhabited by the Yazidi tribes. Major disturbances broke out in 1924–1925 which jeopardized public security and required RAF intervention. Interestingly, tribal resentment was not channelled against the government but against Hamu Shiru, whose autocratic attitude *vis-à-vis* tribes and tribal leaders living in the area deteriorated after the administrative rearrangement of 1921. During the disturbances, which had assumed the character of a military mobilisation against the Fuqara' chief, the tribesmen clearly showed that they did not have a clear concept of the authority of the government, although the role played by the British and local administration in the development of the hostilities was clearly felt by the tribal leaders who had become increasingly involved in colonial politics. The government was still perceived by many inhabitants of Sinjar as an extraneous power enforcing taxation and conscription, but was not yet viewed as an important actor in the development of tribal antagonism despite the increasing participation of British officials in the settlements of tribal and intertribal claims in accordance with the provisions of the Tribal Disputes Regulations.

The development of Yazidi tribal affairs during the Mandate was still profoundly influenced by the major tribal rearrangement of the early 1900s. By 1916 there existed an increasing awareness of religion as a factor shaping tribal politics in Jabal Sinjar as a result of the emergence of the Fuqara' tribe, a unit which included only Yazidi men of religion, and of the Yazidi revival led by the Fuqara' leader Hamu Shiru. Both were indirectly promoted by the religious policies of the Ottoman government during the Hamidian period. As a result tribal rivalries started to be expressed increasingly in religious terms, as the emergence of a 'Yazidi' versus a 'pro-Muslim' coalition would indicate. In the context of Sinjari tribal politics 'pro-Muslim' meant a particular attitude of the tribes *vis-à-vis* the Ottoman government rather than indicating any measure of political dominance of their Muslim sections. In other words, 'pro-Muslim' was indicative of the tendency of certain tribes to make use of the support of the government against centres of local tribal authority. At the beginning of the 1920s Hamu Shiru was still the leader of the so-called 'Yazidi' coalition which was supported by large sections of the pastoral tribes of the Qiran and Samuqa. His contender was the Mihirkani chief Dawud al-Dawud, the leader of the 'pro-Muslim' coalition whose family had often sought the support of the Ottoman government to extend its influence among the Yazidi tribes. Dawud, who controlled the northeast of Sinjar, was supported by the Haskan and Musqura tribes which also lived in the northern areas. Only the chiefs of the Habbabat tribe, who lived in Balad Sinjar and who had lost their paramount position in the town as a result of Hamu's rise to power, had changed sides during the Mandate. They severed their relations with the Fuqara' leader and started to support his rival Dawud al-Dawud. The 1925 hostilities developed as a confrontation between these two coalitions. Tribal unrest was not very dissimilar from that described in the Ottoman period as it clearly showed the segmentary character of Sinjar tribalism. During the disturbances, sections belonging to the same tribes split their allegiances and sided with opposing factions. For example, during the hostilities, two sections of the Qiran tribe living in the same village sided, respectively, with Hamu Shiru and Dawud al-Dawud despite the fact that the Qirani tribal leader Sheikh Khidr had consistently supported the Fuqara' leader. The old 'pro-Muslim' coalition headed by Dawud mobilized against the Fuqara' leader without any support on the part of the Iraqi administration which had been unsuccessfully involved in attempts at transferring part of Hamu' s subsidy to the Mihirkani leader. It seems that the growing interference of the British and Iraqi officials in Sinjari tribal affairs, the uneven distribution of rewards to Yazidi tribal leaders on the part of the mandatory administration (no leader was ever subsidized apart from Hamu Shiru) and British practices of removing important chiefs from Sinjar for long periods under the notorious section 40 of the Tribal Dispute Regulations, had all made more acute the conflicts between the two main coalitions and eventually led Dawud's refusal to enter into any negotiation with the Iraqi government which culminated in his flight to Syria in 1936. During the Mandate Yazidi mobilization at both communal and intercommunal levels was indeed very remarkable as a reflection of a changing political climate which became particularly evident towards the end of the Mandatory period. Yazidi political mobilization developed primarily as a reflection of the great deal of political activities which surrounded the non-Muslim communities of northern Iraq in the context of the Assyrian question. Furthermore, the Yazidi enclave of Shaikhan came increasingly under the control of the Iraqi authorities of Mosul who became very influential with the Yazidi Mir Sa'id Beg. Sometime in the late 1920s, the Yazidi religious leader started to be associated with Arab nationalist elements. Rumors circulated that he had approved of the transformation of the main sanctuary of Yazidism, the shrine of Sheikh 'Adi b. Musafir, into a Muslim *waqf*. Mainly as a reaction to the pro-Muslim and pro-Arab proclivities of the Mir of Shaikhan and his household, which seemed to threaten the survival of the entire Yazidi religious establishment, some tribal leaders of Sinjar started to plan the establishment of an anti-emirate on the Mountain, which would develop as the new centre of Yazidism. At the same time Yazidi tribal leaders such as Hamu Shiru and Khalaf al-Haskani became increasingly involved in the political activities promoted by the Assyrian community.

The construction of an Assyrian ethnic identity during the period of the British Mandate among those Nestorians who had arrived from Turkey to Iraq at the beginning of World War I, is an illuminating example of the ways in which a wide movement of politicization and primordialism developed in northern Iraq with the support of Great Britain and the League of Nations. Ideas of Assyrian self-determination shaped upon concepts of nationality expressed in racial terms and of territorial nationalism came to affect the Iraqi Yazidis who were progressively included in an enlarged 'Assyrian nation'. Since 1922, the Assyrian lay and religious leaders realised that their return to Turkey was no longer feasible. Thus they understood that the support of the non-Muslim inhabitants of northern Iraq was vital to the establishment of an Assyrian homeland in the area: an autonomous enclave under the protection of Great Britain or possibly of the League of Nations. The acquisition of political legitimacy necessitated the creation of a new myth, that of the ethnic, cultural and religious unity of the area in order to present Assyrian aspirations as part of a wider movement of self-determination which also included other non-Muslim groups. In this connection the 'Assyrian nation' started to be identified with a larger 'Christian nation' mainly for political purposes. Assyrian propaganda presented this nation as including all ethnic groups of semitic origin which historically were represented by the Eastern Christians living in northern Iraq. Claims to affinities between the Assyrians and the local Christian communities were largely unfounded. The Assyrians, as newcomers to Iraq, represented a distinct socio-economic unit that was by no means integrated in local society also because large numbers of Assyrian refugees were employed as soldiers and officers in the British-controlled Levies. Although there clearly existed doctrinal affinities with the other Christian groups, the Assyrian Church constituted an independent body whose proselytizing activities after the Chaldean schism of the 18th century had never extended to the Christian communities settled in the Mosul province. Membership in the 'Christian nation' was also extended to other non-Muslim groups and especially to the Yazidis, as they were the second largest non-Muslim minority living in the north of Iraq. In 1923, the Assyrian military chief Agha Petros Ellow who in the first half of the 1920s devised and publicized Assyrian plans of autonomy in the Mosul province, substantiated claims of ethnic unity of the populations of the region, not only Christians but also Yazidis and Jews, mainly on the grounds that they were all of 'Assyrian' origin. 'Assyrian' referred to the Assyrian Empire which flourished in northern Iraq in the first millennium B.C. The myth of a direct link between the non-Muslim population of northern Iraq and the old Assyrians was clearly a creation of a new national ethos which drew inspiration from beliefs already circulating in the area. It seems that the Chaldean priesthood in the past had much publicized the idea that the Yazidis were of 'Assyro-Chaldean' race given the close relations existing between Yazidis and

Chaldeans in the large Christian villages of the Mosul plain. In the 1840s the British archeologist Henry Layard, together with some Anglican missionaries, circulated this belief in Europe. Layard included the Yazidis of Jabal Sinjar among the supposed descendants of the old Assyrians on the basis of their physical resemblance with the heads portrayed in Assyrian reliefs.

Assyrian political mobilization developed first in 1922/1923 with the active involvement of Agha Petros Ellow in both British and League circles and was subsequently resumed towards the termination of the Mandate by the Assyrian Patriarch. He began to support the activities of Christian Hormuzd Rassam, a Mosulite Chaldean previously associated to Agha Petros, who in 1930 established the 'Iraqi Minorities (non-Moslem) Rescue Committee', a charitable organization based in London and used as a platform for the political aspirations of the Assyrians shortly before the termination of the British Mandate in 1932. Both in 1922–23 and 1930–32, Assyrian propaganda started to circulate in Yazidi areas and especially in Jabal Sinjar, where the local Yazidi leaders were still in close contact with Christian communities. Since 1923, Hamu Shiru and the most prominent Yazidi chiefs of Sinjar, with the exception of Dawud al-Dawud, participated in the activities of the movement. By and large the Fuqara' leader used Assyrian propaganda as a way to regain prestige among the Sinjari Christians with whom he had developed close economic and political relations in the past and whose position on Yazidi Mountain had been weakened by the activities of the Iraqi administration since 1921. Interestingly, in 1930 one of the main propagandists in favour of the Iraqi Minorities Rescue Committee was 'Abd al-Karim Qaraqulla, a Christian Mosulite trader who had substantial economic interests in Jabal Sinjar and who was closely associated to Hamu. Generally speaking, the Yazidi tribal leaders of Sinjar used the political activities of the Assyrians as a channel of communication with the League of Nations, to which, between 1930 and 1932, they submitted a number of petitions as part of the documentation presented by the Committee. The contents of these petitions focused on the abuses of the Iraqi administration in Sinjar and emphasized the necessity of new administrative arrangements which would give key positions to Christians. Clearly, after 1929 communications with the League had assumed a paramount importance, as British officials were no longer involved in communal affairs following changes in the administrative arrangements at a local, provincial and national level.

Parallel to the involvement with the Assyrian movement, the leaders of Jabal Sinjar started to voice their discontent against the religious establishment of Shaikhan as a result of the Mir's involvement with Iraqi nationalists, which was perceived as undermining the bases of Yazidi religious identity. The communal tension, which developed in 1931–32, resulted in attempts on the part of Hamu Shiru to create a new centre of religious authority in Sinjar. This clearly indicated the extent to which the Yazidi leaders of Sinjar had become independent from the religious authorities of Shaikhan following the developments of the colonial period. Although Hamu Shiru promoted himself as the custodian of the religious interests of the Yazidi community and advocated Yazidi religious reform, it became quite clear during the course of the development of the anti-mirate affair that Hamu Shiru had large economic interests at stake: the removal of Sa'id Beg meant that he could assure himself a share of the alms controlled by the Mir. Thus the Fuqara' chief made use of religious loyalties to increase his prestige and monetary reserves at a time when the decreasing influence of Great Britain in the area had negatively affected his position in tribal and communal context.

Conclusion

The Yazidi Kurds of Iraq undoubtedly emerged from the colonial period with uncertain identities: a reflection of the construction of new racial identifications with the Assyrians and of the development of communal tensions which had a religious base. The Yazidis' mobilization against the Iraqi state was clearly instrumental and resulted in structural and cultural adjustments among the community. The movement of religious reform promoted by the Sinjari leaders against Shaikhan and the enforcement of a Christian identity in the context of the politicization of the Assyrian movement can be also considered in this specific context. However, Yazidi ethnicity, in the sense of intercommunal mobilization, can be also seen in terms of the continuities with the Ottoman past especially when examining the role played by Islam in constraining Yazidis' relations with the many orthodox Kurdish communities at a time when the Kurdish question had become increasingly politicized.

Tribal and religious structures had survived the colonial period and, to a great extent, were strengthened by British policies which often had conflicting aims. It is through the conflicting nature of colonial rule that one can perhaps clarify further the issue of essentialism that has been discussed above. Society became more polarized along ethnic and communal lines not so much because the British were there and constructed new realities, but because the formula of Mandatory rule imposed the development of two parallel, albeit opposed, centres of power: the colonial and the Iraqi state.

The Yazidi example highlights:

1. The conflictual nature of British policies determined by the very nature of the Mandate system.;

2. The importance assumed by peripheral rural areas (and by their inhabitants) in the process of nation-building as after 1920 state power became increasingly identified with territorial control;

3. The high level of continuity existing between the late Ottoman and Mandate periods. In many ways the 1920s were, for large sections of the rural populations of Iraq, the years of adjustment to a faster process of reform in comparison with the late Ottoman period.

Notes

1. This chapter is heavily reliant on the author's work on the Yazidi community. See, N.Fuccaro, *The Other Kurds: Yazidis in Colonial Iraq* (London: IB Tauris, 1999); 'Ethnicity, State Formation and Conscription in Post-Colonial Iraq: The Case of Yazidi Kurds of Jabal Sinjar', *IJMES* 29/4 (1997), pp. 559–80; 'Die Kurden Syriens: Anfänge der nationalen Mobilisierung unter französischen Herrschaft, in, C.Brock, E. Salversberg and S. Hajo (eds.), *Ethnizität, Nationalismus, Religion und Politik in Kurdistan* (Verlag, Münster, 1997), pp. 301–26; *Yazidi: bibliografia analitica e studi* (Tesi di Laurea, University of Venice, 1998).

2. The only available publication which analyses Iraqi development from an ethnic perspective is L. Lukitz: *Iraq: the Search for National Identity* (London: Cass, 995). Works on Iraqi politics and society dealing with the colonial period which have been particularly useful are: A. Attar, *The Minorities of Iraq during the Period of the Mandate, 1920-1932* (Ph.D Dissertation, Columbia University, 1967; H. Batatu, *The Old Social Classes and the Revolutionary Movements of Iraq* (Princeton: Princeton University Press, 1978); C. J. Edmonds, *Kurds, Turks and Arabs*, (London: Oxford University Press, 1957); A. H. Hourani, *Minorities in the Arab World* (Oxford: Oxford University Press, 1947); J. Joseph, *The Minorities and their Muslim Neighbours* (Princeton: Princeton University Press, 1961); C. Kutschéra, *Le mouvement national Kurde* (Paris: Flammarion, 1979); H. C. Luke, *Mosul and its Minorities* (London: Hopkinson, 1925); D. McDowell, *A Modern History of the Kurds* (London: I.B Tauris, 1996); R. Olson, *The Emergence of Kurdish Nationalism and the Shaikh Said Rebellion, 1880–1925* (Austin: Texas University Press, 1989); P. Sluglett, *Britain in Iraq, 1914–1932* (London: Ithaca, 1976); R. S. Stafford, *The Tragedy of the Assyrians* (London: Allen & Unwin, 1935).

3. This section is based on both theoretical and empirical works dealing with ethnicity and nationalism. Among the most important are: B. Anderson, *Imagined Communities* (London: Verso, 1983); F. Barth, *Ethnic Groups and Boundaries. The Social Organization of Cultural Difference* (London: Allen and Unwin, 1969); L. Chabry and A. Chabry, *Politique et minorités au Proche-Orient* (Paris: Maisoneuve et Larose, 1984); P. Chatterjee, *The Nation and its Fragments* (Princeton: Princeton University Press, 1993); M. J. Esman and I. Rabinovich (eds.), *Ethnicity, Pluralism, and the State in the Middle East* (Ithaca: Cornell University Press, 1988); E. Gellner, *Nations and Nationalism* (Oxford: Blackwell, 1983); C. Geertz (ed.)*Old Societies and New States* (New York: Collier Macmillan, 1963); R. Owen, *State, Power and Politics in the Making of Modern Middle East* (London: Routledge, 1992); R. A. Schermerhorn, *Comparative Ethnic Relations. A Framework for Theory and Research* (Chicago: Chicago University Press, c. 1978); H. Sharabi (ed.), *Theory, Politics and the Arab World: Critical Responses* (New York/London: Routledge, 1990); E. Tonkin, M. MacDonald, M. Chapman (eds.), *History and Ethnicity* (London: Routledge, 1989); J. Hutchinson, A. D. Smith (eds.) *Ethnicity* (Oxford: Oxford University Press, 1996).

4. For what concerns the issue of localism this section draws a number of arguments from Gellner, *Nations and Nationalism,* pp.8–18. For a critique to essentialist approaches to Iraqi history see Introduction to S. Haj, *The Making of Iraq 1900-1963. Capital, Power and Ideology* (Albany: State University of New York Press, 1997).

PART FOUR

Emirates and Tribes:
Maghreb, Arabia and Iran

A Few Reflections on 'Tribe' and 'State' in Twentieth-Century Morocco

Kenneth Brown

To attempt to understand the meanings of 'tribe' and 'state' in the 20th-century context of pre-colonial, colonial and post-colonial Morocco would require detailed accounts of social and political structures, the ways in which power and authority have been legitimated, and the way these may have been maintained or transformed. What follows only intends to serve as a synthetic and schematic presentation of a few aspects of these matters, particularly the notion of 'tribe'.

From 1912 until 1956, the Moroccan Sultanate was under the control of French and Spanish protectorates. Since regaining its independence and sovereignty, the Sultanate has become a 'monarchy' – the Kingdom of Morocco – in which some aspects of constitutional democracy have been introduced. Nonetheless, like the Sultan of the past, today's King is the Commander of the Faithful and, as such, invested with supreme political and religious power and authority. At the beginning of the colonial period, 90 per cent of the Sultan's subjects were estimated to be rural. Most or all of these were said to be tribally organized. Today rural inhabitants comprise about 40 per cent of the overall population. Their identity as 'tribesmen' is problematic as, indeed, is the very terminology used to describe them.

In the anthropological literature on North Africa and the Middle East, the meaning of the Arabic term translated as 'tribe', *qabila* (*taqbilt* in Berber), is generally the following: an autonomous, genealogically structured group in which the rights of individuals are largely determined by their membership in corporate descent groups, such as lineages. Some writings on Morocco assume that this definition holds for the present as well as the past. Thus, group names such as Banu X or Awlad Y, the sons of X or Y, seem to imply common descent among members. However, other terms used to designate groups, for example 'Ahl A', literally 'the People of A', appear to lack implications of common descent. Some scholars who have done substantial research among rural Moroccans consider the assignation of the term 'tribe' to social groupings there as misleading. Thus, for example, D. Eickelman, who has studied the relevant literature extensively, argues that with regard to Morocco, *qabila* is best defined as a territorial notion rather than a genealogical one implying patrilineal descent from an eponymic ancestor. In his view, a Moroccan 'tribe' is fundamentally a territorial and administrative entity encompassing individuals who are perfectly aware of their quite heterogenous origins. As a consequence, a 'tribe' in Morocco is basically a strategy of social relations rather than a structure composed of such relations.

Regarding this issue of terminology and conceptualization, C. Geertz, H. Geertz and L. Rosen point out that ethnographers have been, in part, victims of the history of their profession. Thus, they have used terms implying structural regularities and consequences for practical behaviour (terms such as 'tribe', 'lineage', 'kindred' or 'settlement') which are not appropriate for the descriptions of the specific societies they study. A clear statement on the matter from the tradition of political anthropology comes from M. Gluckman, for whom tribal segmentation and cross-cutting alliances are often social processes which serve to maintain order in societies lacking government. However, he also suggests, on the basis of research by E. Peters amongst the Bedouin of Cyrenaica, that in feuding societies in which kinship by blood and marriage seem primordial proclaimed common descent may be falsified; i.e. that parts of genealogies may directly reflect topographical and ecological facts rather than genealogical ones. This is not quite the same as seeing tribes as strategies rather than structures, but it is an opening in that direction.

With regard to Moroccan society, the principle of common descent and segmentation has informed seminal studies by scholars such as J. Berque, E. Gellner, D. Hart, R. Jammous, and others, stretching back to E. Doutte, E. Durkheim, R. Montagne, E. Evans-Pritchard and E. Westermarck, some of the founders of modern social anthropology. All of these may be considered proponents, to some extent, of what is termed 'segmentary theory'. Other ancestors or adherents of this theory include the 15th century philosopher of history, Ibn Khaldun and important orientalists such as J. Wellhausen and G. Levi Della Vida. Contemporary studies of Moroccan society, particularly from the vantage point of history and political sociology (for example the works of G. Ayache, R. Bourqia, M. Guessous, A. Laroui, R. Leveau, P. Pascon, M. Tozy and J. Waterbury), also make use of, or criticize, the notion of tribalism and the now inevitable model of segmentary lineage.

It seems to me that three factors explain a tendency in Morocco to maintain 'tribal' allegiances based on real or fictive common descent: first, inheritance, whether based on Islamic law (*shari'ah*), or customary law (Arabic *'urf*, Berber *azerf*); second, vengeance and blood money; and third, the levying of taxes by the central power of the state. These may result from consensus and/or coercion. In all of these matters tribal affiliations may be significant and, at the same time, malleable. Thus, for example, in the Oued Dra'a region of southern Morocco, A. Hammoudi has shown that the 'tribe' is a fiscal unit, i.e. a group of individuals who are under the control of a given *qa'id*, or chief, who has been allocated or who has appropriated the right to exact taxes from that group. The internal organisation of the tribe, especially of its lineages, will be determined by or be a function of rights to land and water, taxation and vengeance. The categorisation of lineages presented by actors will depend on time, place, circumstances and interlocutors. Thus, the models of organization communicated to researchers should not be seen as objective statements of 'facts'. In the 'real' world, Hammoudi points out, there is no 'real' model of a tribal structure or organization.

The persistence of the discourse of 'tribal identities' throughout Morocco's history and, indeed, until the present day is, in any case, noteworthy. The notion of the 'tribe' appears as a construction composed of a mixture of the 'real' and the 'imagined', of 'structure' and 'strategy', a mixture kneaded together in specific circumstances for actual contingencies.

It seems clear from various Moroccan accounts that onomastic emblems – names and identities – may be forged for particular purposes or imposed by necessity. H. Rashiq, a Moroccan anthropologist, demonstrates this clearly in tracing the progression of his own family name over several generations, showing, among other things, how and why his father remoulded his name-identity several times in his own lifetime.

An additional caveat: Ibn Khaldun's categorization of the social structure of the medieval Maghreb, which many students of Moroccan society and history consider as implying a segmentary model, contains a dichotomy between the rural and urban populations, the former characterized by the solidarity (*'asabiya*) of common descent, the latter by a shared participation in urban culture (*'umran hadhari*). Nonetheless, N. Cigar has shown on the basis of written sources, which describe the urban population of 17th/18th century Fez, that the city was composed of the following 'tribes' and 'quarters' (*qaba'il* and *jihat*): the descendants of the Prophet, the Ashraf (*qaba'il al-ashraf*), the descendants of the original inhabitants of the city (converts to Islam?), the 'Bildiyyin' and the 'Lamtiyyin' and 'Andalusiyyin' (the last named identified by topography, i.e. quarters of the city). At the same time, those groups that surround the city are also called 'tribes', each of which has its own chief (*qa'id*) who is named or recognized as such by the Sultanate.

From my own research in the Berber-speaking region of the Jebel Bani in southwestern Morocco, I learned how the genealogical model is applied to the Ashraf. Thus, a self-proclaimed descendant of the Prophet Muhammad, through the Prophet's daughter Fatima and the Caliph 'Ali, once showed me a written genealogy to demonstrate his origins and his descent from Sidi 'Azza bin Ihda, a 'holy man' buried in the nearby oasis of 'Assa whose mausoleum is the object of a yearly pilgrimage-fair. The descendants of Sidi 'Azza are spread about the Jebel Bani. My informant came from a village in the area of the 'tribe' of 'Id Brahim, which had 22 Ashraf households; the heads of these households were called *igurramn*, the Berber term for 'holy men', on the basis of their genealogical affiliation to the 'tribe' of Sidi 'Azza. I was told that historically this lineage had occupied the area prior to its conquest by the 'Id Brahim. The latter had chased out all the earlier inhabitants with the exception of the holy men from the tribe of Sidi 'Azza, whom they allowed to remain after expropriating some of their property. The turbulent past of Morocco, with its attendant consequences for 'tribalism', is replete with such examples.

The historical movements of population within the countryside and into and out of the cities, the centres of political power of the Sultanate-state, the *Makhzan,* are all vastly complicated subjects. In this summary account, I simply want to propose an overview of some of the main characteristics of state-tribal relations over the past century. This comprises a dozen years before the French and Spanish protectorates over Morocco (1912–56), and almost a half century of independence.

Let me restate my view of 'tribalism' in Moroccan society: 'tribes' here do not fit the classical anthropological definition of relatively autonomous, genealogically discrete, structured groups of individuals with rights largely determined by membership in corporate descent groups, e.g., lineages. Generally, Moroccan 'tribes' have been territorial rather than genealogical entities, and their members have little or no awareness of their heterogeneous origins. Genealogies, nonetheless, whether real or fictive, may at times have been important, even wide-spanning. Tribal affiliations are at base strategies, rather than structures.

The pre-protectorate Moroccan state and government, the Makhzan, was headed since the 17th century by a charismatic, theocratic sultan of the 'Alawi dynasty, a descendant of the Prophet, and the Caliph and Commander of the Faithful – *Amir al-mu'minin*. Since independence in 1956, the formal terms have changed from 'Sultanate' to 'Monarchy' with the state (the Arabic term *dawla* replacing that of *Makhzan*) headed by the King (initially Muhammad V, then Hassan II, now Muhammad VI). R. Bourqia has shown that in the mid-19th century, 'tribes' on the margins of the Sultanate which combined transhumance and sedentary agriculture, like the Zayan and the Zemmour, could be and normally were mostly integrated and submissive to the state, although sometimes they resisted integration and submission. The relationship took the form of a kind of mutual accommodation between state and tribes. The Makhzan state was a way of doing things and a way of life, as well as an institution. It did not rule, on the whole, by means of coercion; it did, generally but not always, maintain military and administrative control over all or most of its territory, and its religious authority was recognized throughout. What M. Tozy has called the 'Caliphate Model' was characterized by a mixture of servitude, obedience, investiture, fear of chaos (*fitna*) and awe (*hayba*).

The Makhzan centralized symbolic power. The Sultan was both a secular and a religious leader. Religion, Islam, provided a systematic language of a culture and a cosmology shared at once by the ruler and his subjects. The Moroccan state appropriated symbols of orthodox and popular religious ideas and practises. The Sultan demanded and received his investiture from representatives of the population – the religious and secular elite – by way of a binding contract of recognition, the *bay'a*. The principles and activities linked to the Sultan's descent from the Prophet legitimated his authority as Commander of the Faithful. The presence of his Ashraf 'cousins' throughout the realm, along with the web of Sufi brotherhoods and urban corporations, also at times played important roles in binding together the Moroccan population under his sovereignty

A relatively powerful and authoritarian state, the Makhzan owed its authority and legitimacy to the royal charisma of the Sultan. That charisma had to be demonstrated to endure, and the ways and means of demonstration were elaborate and generally persuasive. These included annual expeditions (*harka*-s and *mahalla*-s), what C. Geertz has termed royal progresses through the territories of the realm. These made patent the symbols of power and served to mobilize troops and collect taxes. A theocratic state with an army and court at once peripatetic and centred in the cities, it comprised four capitals (Fez, Meknes, Rabat and Marrakesh) and four centres of higher urban culture (Fez, Rabat, Sale and Tetouan). The rule of the state had profound roots in the cities and extensive, if ill-defined, boundaries in the rural countryside where rebellions by regional leaders sometimes achieved relative autonomy.

Less accessible parts of the realm at times threw off the dominion of state control (entered into dissidence – *siba*); yet, even in those cases, a variety of institutions in the rural areas of the mountains and deserts made safe-passage feasible. These were mostly systems of protection known in the Berber-speaking areas as *tata, zetata, mezrag* and *'ar* . They provided the means for extensive routes of commerce along which merchants, often Jewish, were able to move in security. These rebellions and institutions of protection are usually described in the idiom of tribalism.

The impact and consequences of colonial rule over Morocco can be merely alluded to in such a brief article. As E. Burke has pointed out, there has been little recognition in the literature, indeed a 'selective amnesia' by scholars, concerning the transition to modernity of the Moroccan state under colonialism. The policies of the French and Spanish protectorates drew upon ideas of indirect-rule through established notables and institutions. Morocco was 'pacified' in the name of the ruling institution – the Makhzan; in the process, the rule of the state was intensified and expanded in unprecedented and permanent ways by the colonial powers. At the same time, the protectorates established and organized the practises of a modern administration. The consequences for the contemporary, independent state and the political, economic and social life of the country have been profound. These include the still incomplete transition from an absolutist state along the contours noted above to that of a quasi-constitutional and democratic monarchy and the establishment of a modern bureaucracy. Throughout the colonial period and up until the time of writing, the Sultan-King has endured and maintained, perhaps increased, his power. Some would argue that endurance was the principle goal and realization of the Sharifian dynasty and its state. That aim has been undoubtedly fulfilled in large measure thanks to the centralization and modernization wrought by colonialism.

Rule by a mixture of coercion, law and consensus by the monarchy and government since independence in 1956 has not been smooth, and indeed the regime's endurance sometimes seems miraculous. It has survived regional 'tribal' rebellions and attempted coups d'état; violently repressed riots; carried out large-scale arrests; kidnapped and assassinated political opponents; and largely domesticated leftist and Islamist movements. Its endurance has been painful and costly for many Moroccans, painful for both the rulers and the ruled, but especially for the latter. At the same time that the unifying factors of the modern world have had profound effects on the country, the regional and linguistic realities of diversity and class differences throughout society, in the urban and rural sectors, have imposed themselves on people's sense of identity and political consciousness with varying consequences.

Some 'facts' of change speak eloquently. In 1960, the rural population made up 71 per cent of the country's total. According to the 1982 census, 52.3 per cent of the total population of over 20 million was rural; in the late 1990s the rural population was estimated at 40 per cent out of some 30 million. Thus, massive rural exodus, rapid urbanisation, a lack of adequate economic infrastructure and social malaise have come to characterize Morocco's profile at the end of the 20th century.

What do 'tribal' identities mean in such circumstances? Of course, it is foolhardy to generalize – particularly in the light of the complex and paradoxical nature of the subject in the recent and not-so-recent past. Nonetheless, some seasoned observers of Moroccan society note that there is a relative dualism in this respect: for example, some institutions of the past have been revived for specific situations; tribal connections and alliances, as well as religious celebrations at saints' tombs linked to tribes, are used to preserve or enhance political, social or economic interests and privileges. For some, the 'tribe' remains a cultural framework which differentiates them from others and implies practical consequences for marriages, collective celebrations and elections. Perhaps the strategic aspect of tribal identity is stronger than ever. Such considerations may be reinforced by government practice. Thus, the Ministry of the Interior since independence may be said to have reinvented tradition, i.e. the qa'idal and tribal model, as a basis of rural administration.

In conclusion, the force of Moroccan 'tribalism', of primordial sentiments based on extended kinship and of strategic inventions and reinventions connected to notions of tribes, may continue to be enhanced by circumstances and contingencies. With a new monarch, perhaps a new form of monarchy, and an alternate form of parliamentary coalition government, presently led by a socialist opposition, the changing parameters and the rules of political life will inevitably be affected.

References

'Abdelraziq, A., *Usul al-hukm fi-l-islam*. Cairo, 1925.

Bennani-Chraibi, M., *Soumis et rebelles. Les jeunes au Maroc*. Paris: CNRS, 1994.

Brown, K. L., 'The Curse of Westermarck' in *Ethnos*, vol. 47:3–4, 1982, pp. 197–231.

Bourqia, R and S. G. Miller (eds.), *In the Shadow of the Sultan. Culture, Power and Politics in Morocco*. Cambridge, Massachussetts: Harvard University Press, 1999.

Cigar, N., Societé et vie politique à Fès sous les premiers 'Alawites (ca 1660/1830) in *Hésperis-Tamuda*, vol. XVIII , 1978–79, pp. 93–172.

Djait, H., *La Grande Désordre*. Paris: Gallimard, 1989.

Eickelman, D., *The Middle East and Central Asia: An Anthropological Approach*. Third edition. New Jersey: Prentice Hall, 1998.

Geertz, C., H. Geertz, L. Rosen, 'Meaning and Order in Moroccan Society'. *Three Essays in Cultural Analysis*. Cambridge: Cambridge University Press, 1979.

Gellner, E., *Saints of the Atlas*. Chicago: University of Chicago Press, 1969.

Gellner, E. and C. Micaud (eds.), *Arabs & Berbers*. London: Duckworth, 1973.

Gluckman, M., 'Political Institutions' in Evans-Pritchard, E. E. et al, *The Institutions of Primitive Society*. Oxford: Blackwell, first ed. 1956.

Hammoudi, A., 'Segmentarité, stratification sociale, pouvoir politique et sainteté. Réflexions sur les thèses de Gellner'. *Hésperis-Tamuda*, vol. XV, 1974, pp.147–77.

Hart, D., *Dadda Atta and his Forty Grandsons: the Socio-Political Organisation of the Ait 'Atta of Southern Morocco*. Cambridge: MENAS, 1981.

—— 'The Rgaybat: Camel Nomads of the Western Sahara' in *Journal of North African Studies*. London, vol. 3 (Winter 1998), pp. 28–54.

—— 'The Penal Code in the Customary Law of the Swasa of the Moroccan Western Atlas & Anti Atlas', *ibid.*, pp. 55–67.

—— 'Ibn Khaldun and the Beginnings of Islamic Sociology in the Maghrib' in *Arab Historical Review for Ottoman Studies* (AHROS), no. 7–8 (Oct. 1993), pp. 39–58.

Joffe, E. G. H. & C. R. Pennel (eds.), *Tribe and State*. Cambridge: MENAS, 1991.

Kably, M., *Societé, pouvoir et religion au Maroc des Mérinides aux Wattasides* (XIV–XV s.). Paris, 1984.

Leveau, R., *Le Fellah marocain. Defenseur du throne*. Paris: Presse de la fondation nationale des sciences politiques, 1976.

Levi Della Vida, G., *Les Sémites et leur role dans l'histoire religieuse*. Paris: P. Geuthner, 1938.

Mahdi, M., *Pasteurs de l'Atlas: Production pastorale, droit et rituel*. Casablanca, 1999.

Maspero, F. (ed) *Abd el-Krim et la Republique du Rif*. Paris, 1976.

Montagne, R., *The Berbers. Their Social and Political Organisation*. London: Frank Cass & Co. 1973. First published in 1931 as 'La vie sociale et la vie politique des Berbères' by la Société de l'Afrique Française.

Mottahadeh, R., *Loyalty and Leadership in an Early Islamic Society*. Princeton: Princeton University Press, 1980.

Pascon, P., *Le Haouz de Marrakech*, 2 vols. Tanger: Editions marocaines internationales, 1977.

Robertson Smith, W., *Kinship & Marriage in Early Arabia*. Beacon Press, original edition 1903.

Seddon, D., *Moroccan Peasants. A Century of Change in the Eastern Rif, 1870–1970*. Dawson, Folkestone, 1981.

Tozi, M., *Monarchie et Islam populaire au Maroc*. Paris: Presses de sciences PO, 1999.

Valensi, L., *On the Eve of Colonialism. North Africa Before the French Conquest, 1790–1830*. New York: Africana Publishing Co., 1977. Originally published as *Le Maghreb avant la prise d'Alger*. Paris: Flammarion, 1969.

Waterbury, J., 'Bargaining for Segmentarity', in E. G. H. Joffe & C. R. Pennel, 1991.

Wolf, E., *Peasant Wars of the Twentieth Century*. London: Faber & Faber, 1969.

NINE

Tribal Confederations and Emirates in Central Arabia

Madawi al-Rasheed

With the exception of three historical examples of political centralisation (emirates of Yamama, Banu Ukhaidhir and the Saudis), Central Arabia is perceived as not very state-friendly (Cook 1988: 676). This chapter examines attempts at political centralisation in Central Arabia. To do this it is necessary to first highlight the main characteristics of Arabian society.

To reduce the Arabian population to tribalism and nomadism is a misconception which, thanks to recent anthropological and historical research, has been partially corrected. The population was complex and varied in its social and economic characteristics. The tribes were only one social category among many others. Also, a pure form of nomadism had never existed as the sole mode of production among the tribes. The diversity of the Arabian population is best portrayed through an analysis of the social groups who occupied the desert and the oases.

Local terminology divides the population into two groups, the *badu* and the *hadar*. It is simplistic to translate the term *badu* as pastoral nomads. Although nomadism was an essential component of the notion of *badu*, it was not the determining factor which allowed a group to be so classified. Within the context of Arabia, all animal herders were *badu*, but not all *badu* were pastoral nomads. Some *badu* settled in the oases and continued to be identified as *badu*. The term *badu* referred to a cultural category which included both the pastoral and sedentarised nomads. Both shared a set of images of themselves with regard to their tribal origin, values and attributes. The *badu* often had elaborate genealogies defining their ancestors which they located in a distant past. They emphasised their *asl*, nobility, and the purity of their blood, believed to be uncontaminated by marriages with outsiders. The *badu* held a set of values regarding the ideal life style. They despised occupational specialization, which they regarded as humiliating and dishonourable. The true *badu* was someone who was able to enhance his ascribed status, i.e. his nobility by achieving a set of attributes. To have asl without these achieved attributes would immediately place individuals and groups outside the *badu* category. The *badu* valued their independence and resented submission to higher authority.

They were subdivided into lineages, each of which was led by a prominent sheikh. The sheikhs rose to positions of leadership as a result of their association with defending the lineage during times of external threat. Their reputation for eloquence, arbitration, wisdom and generosity contributed to maintaining a position of authority among members of their lineage. Although the *badu* recognised the authority of their own sheikhs, this authority was not perceived as oppressing, binding or requiring total submission.

Within the category *badu*, internal distinctions can be observed. There were those *asil badu*, a group consisting of the camel herders such as Shammar, Anizah, Dhafir, Murrah, Qahtan and Harb. Their nobility, coupled with the military superiority which their camels guaranteed in raids granted them the highest position in the status hierarchy. The sheep and goat herders were also *badu*, but from a group inferior to the *asil badu* as they lacked the means to demonstrate their military supremacy and maintain their independence. Often they lost their independence to the *asil badu* who imposed on them protection tax, *khuwa*. Payment of this tax was an indicator of the inferior status of the groups who paid it.

Although the *badu* practised nomadism, they were not totally dependent on it. Some *badu* tribal sheikhs owned agricultural land in the oases. This land consisted of palm groves often cultivated by oasis farmers and slaves. The sheikhs visited the oases to collect the produce and also to engage in trade in local markets. The oases were a retreat for the *badu* especially during the dry season. Some tribal sheikhs remained in the oases for an extended period of time while their herds were sent with members of their lineages to graze in the nearby deserts.

The fallacy that the *badu* were only those who herded camels, goats and sheep cannot be sustained as far as the Arabian population was concerned. The term *badu* was an encompassing cultural category partially dependent on the mode of economic production, but greatly influenced by social values. It is a term referring to the social identity of groups. The economic dimension is only one aspect of this identity.

The second category which described part of the Arabian population was *hadar*. The term referred to those who inhabited the oases, towns, and villages of Najd, Asir, Hijaz and al-Hasa. It included the tribal population of these settlements, especially those who ceased to own camels in the desert. The main distinction between the sedentarized *badu* and the *hadar* was related to the fact that the former continued to maintain genealogical and social links with their nomadic brothers, whereas the latter had lost such links and their orientation was directed towards the settlement itself. The *hadar* also included non-tribal groups, for example farmers, artisans and merchants, who had lost a connection with a well-identified tribe. They usually lived in small family units occupying a neighbourhood in the oases and towns. The Shi'a population of the oases of al-Hasa fell into this category of non-tribal *hadar*. The Shi'a families had a long history of sedentarization, which led to the weakening of tribal allegiances and marked genealogies (al-Hasan 1993 :7–10, vol.1). Moreover, the non-tribal population of Unayzah, an oasis in al-Qasim, were known as Khadiri; that is, *hadar* who were freeborn but who, for a variety of reasons, could not claim recognized tribal origins (Altorki and Cole 1989: 24). The presence of this non-tribal population is often ignored in scholarly work on Arabia. The literature is abundant on the tribal groups, but seems to have bypassed this important section of society. The reasons relate to the fact that non-tribals were politically and socially marginal. Travellers in 19th-century Arabia were fascinated by the 'courage' and 'chivalry' of the *badu*, the majority of whom were nomads, hence the detailed description found in such literature on their economic, social and political organization. However, in spite of their socio-political marginalisation, the Khadiri were economically active. It was among this group that farmers, artisans and merchants were drawn. Being outside the tribal value system, they were able to occupy an important economic niche, often held in low esteem by the *badu*. Their contribution to agricultural production, manufacturing and trade cannot be underestimated.

Political Organization and Emirate Formation

Arabian political organization followed two patterns. Loose tribal confederations existed among both the nomads and the sedentarized sections of the confederation, while centralized oasis-based polities, known as emirates, existed among the sedentary population of the various settlements in Najd, Hijaz, Asir, and al-Hasa. These two genres of political organization were interdependent. On the one hand, the tribal confederations contributed to the rise or demise of the emirates as a result of shifting political alliances dictated by economic interest. On the other hand, once an emirate became militarily and economically powerful, it was able to influence the course of alliances among the tribal confederations. Confederations were either broken or subjugated by the emirates. Emirate formation in Arabia prior to the establishment of the Saudi state in 1932 was an interplay between these two forms of political organization. At the heart of this interplay was the tension between a centralized polity based in an oasis and a decentralized political configuration among the tribes of Najd, al-Hasa, Hijaz and Asir.

Tribal Confederations

Tribal confederations were large political units held together by the idiom of kinship and elaborate genealogies, constructed as a rationale for group unity. They often consisted of a core and a periphery. The core included a group, often with a name and an epical ancestor. The group is referred to as *qabila*, or tribe which is subdivided into smaller sections, all claiming a common ancestor. We can identify a number of such tribes among the Arabian population; Anizah, Shammar, Mutair, Qahtan, Ajman, Murrah and Banu Khalid were among the best-known confederations. They all regarded themselves as *badu*, although some sections of these tribes were settled in the oases. The settlement of some *badu* sections in the oases was a phenomenon common among the Najdi tribes. In the Hijaz, where urbanization was more pronounced, the *badu* such as Ataiba and Harb remained nomadic and confined to the areas between Mecca, Madina and Jiddah. Tribal groups were also territorial units in the sense that they claimed communal ownership of the resources of a specific territory. The resources included wells, pasture and often entire oases. The tribe as a whole had communal ownership of these resources. They frequented markets in the oases and engaged in the exchange of their animal produce for agricultural products and manufactured items. In general, tribal territory was not marked by clear geographical boundaries, but fluctuated as a result of the changing strength of the confederation. The core of the tribal territory remained constant and defined by custom and tradition.

Each section of the tribal core was led by a prominent sheikh. Sheikhs played the role of mediators, political leaders, judges and negotiators with other groups. They were drawn from noble lineages who were associated with wisdom, military skills and generosity. There were no clear rules for succession to the office of sheikh. Members of a particular lineage assumed the role of leadership, but had no monopoly over it. A sheikh negotiated his supremacy within his section, the consensus of which was important for him to stay in office. Within a tribe, sheikhs of different sections occasionally came together to discuss issues relating to the whole tribe such as migration routes, economic resources and political alliances. Once in a while a prominent lineage sheikh would rise in power and would be able to assume leadership of the whole tribe. The al-Shaalan of the Anizah and the al-Rashid of the Shammar were cases of sheikhs rising beyond their tribal section to be recognized as heads of the tribe. The authority of a tribal sheikh rested on a combination of tradition and coercion. Tradition in the form of recognized noble descent granted a lineage supremacy; however, descent alone was not enough for establishing the hegemony of an individual. His military skills in battle were often far more important than mere blood ties. The role of the tribal sheikh was crucial for establishing the hegemony of a particular confederation. The presence of such strong sheikhs was more common among the Najdi tribes than among the Hijazi ones. The Hijazi Harb tribe, for example, controlled the Jeddah-Mecca route, but lacked a paramount chief to control all the tribal sections. In this respect, Hijazi tribes had no extended pattern of hierarchical organization (Alangari 1998: 53).

An important characteristic of tribal confederations was their fluidity. To overemphasize tribal solidarity, believed to emanate from kinship and genealogy, is a long held misconception relating to these confederations. Ibn Khaldun's description of *'badu asabi'* (solidarity) was perhaps behind the glorification of tribal cohesion, an assumption dominating the anthropological literature of the 1950s (Ibn Khaldun 1987). An historical analysis of intertribal relations shows that Arabian tribes were not solid units, but loosely organized groups who occasionally overlooked their genealogical unity in the pursuit of economic and political interests. Their alliances were not always dictated by the rules of segmentation and the underlying bond of kinship. Although kinship solidarity was cherished, historically it remained the rhetoric which masked a sense of pragmatism on behalf of the various segments comprising a tribe. The historical context of intertribal relations was far more important than kinship solidarity. Political action was motivated by economic necessity rather than idealised solidarity. Often external factors played a far more crucial role in determining political alliances. It was not uncommon for a tribal section to ally itself with an outside power, thus threatening the survival of the whole tribe. As tribal sections often drifted towards more profitable alliances with other groups, this resulted in the weakening of the tribal confederation.

In situations where common interest between a sheikh and the various tribal sections was identified, these confederations became more solidified and were able to endure the underlying threat of fission. Moreover, they became capable of territorial expansion, thus leading to the emergence of a political structure relatively more durable than the tribal confederation, though by no means permanent. This political structure is referred to here as the emirate, a centralized polity with a base in an oasis.

The Emirates

Contrary to Ibn Khaldun's assumption that dynastic rule needed both tribal solidarity and the legitimation of a religious ideology, we find that Arabia exhibited a mixed pattern. By 1900, Arabia had witnessed two types of emirates: those founded on the basis of the support of a strong tribal confederation, henceforth referred to here as tribal emirates, and those founded solely on the basis of religious impetus, but later needing the tribal element for control and expansion (of the type described by Ibn Khaldun). These are referred to as religious emirates.

The Rashidi Emirate (1835–1921) was an example of the tribal type. The first SaudiWahhabi emirate (1744–1818) and the Riyadh-based second emirate (1824–1891) were examples of the religious type. Both tribal and religious emirates depended on tribal confederations for their consolidation. The only difference pertains to the source of authority underlying the polity. Tribal emirates were backed by the supremacy of a tribe, for example the Shammar in the case of the Rashidis, without invoking a religious legitimation formula. The reformist Wahhabi movement represented the underlying rationale behind Saudi power in the 18th and 19th centuries in the absence of a strong identification with a tribal confederation.

With the exception of their sources of authority, both religious and tribal emirates shared common characteristics. They were political structures sprung out of the interaction between two interdependent sections of Arabian society, the *badu* and *hadar*. It is because of the ancient economic, social and kinship symbiosis between the *badu* and *hadar* that a political structure, the emirate, rose to confirm an already existing interdependence. Emirate formation was a political response to sanction an already established historical reality marked by the interconnections between two categories of the population, the *badu* and *hadar*, mistakenly portrayed as separate.

Arabian Emirates varied in size and strength. In the 18th and 19th centuries, some developed into regional power centres (e.g., those of Mecca, Deraiyya/ Riyadh and Hail), incorporating several settlements and tribal confederations. Others remained localized webs of authority within the confines of a single settlement and a tribal lineage (e.g., Uyayna, Buraidah, Unaizah, and Abha).

The Saudi-Wahhabi emirates of the 18th and 19th centuries (1744–1818 and 1824–1891) owed their establishment to two equally important factors: first, the presence of an oasis-based leadership and second, the presence of an umbrella religious ideology. The Saudi rulers of Deraiyya had no claims to leadership beyond this oasis on the basis of the support of a tribal confederation. Accounts of their rise to a position leadership emphasized that before 1744, they ruled over the settlement of Deraiyya as local rulers. In this respect they were similar to the many oasis amirs who assumed a position of leadership among the various settlements in Najd. For example, in the neighbouring oases of Uyayna, Riyadh, Tharmada and Kharj, the following rulers (*amir/rais*) were identified: Uthman Ibn Muamar, Dahham Ibn Dawas, Ibrahim Ibn Salman, and Zayd Ibn Zamil (Cook 675; al-Juhany 1983: 189; Lam al Shihab: 36). Evidence suggests that on the eve of the Wahhabi movement, Deraiyya was smaller in fame, sophistication and wealth to its neighbouring settlement, Uyayna (al-Juhany 1983: 252).

How certain amirs and lineages rose to position of leadership in the oases was a complex issue, which cannot be easily answered from the scarce historical evidence at our disposal. The emergence of an oasis leadership was perhaps determined by a combination of economic, social and political factors. It seems that settlements belonged to the lineage which had founded them. Some lineages became prominent as a result of seizure of cultivated land in an oasis. If this happened to be combined with engagement in local and regional trade, more grounds for fame tended to be established. Ownership of land and wealth from trade distinguished lineages within the confines of a settlement. The authority of certain lineages was enhanced by economic wealth. Any meagre surplus originating from agriculture or trade would have increased the chances of a lineage becoming a sort of a distinguished category of elite/nobility in the oasis. Yet, economic wealth alone could not fully explain how a lineage in an oasis assumed political leadership. We know that in the 19th century the oases of al-Qasim had well-established merchant families, but not many of those families were able to convert their material wealth into political leadership. The merchants of the oasis of Unaizah were an example of this pattern (Altorki and Cole 1989). An oasis leadership must have been dependent on its ability to rise above other groups by virtue of political and military qualities (al-Juhany 1983: 179). The ability to mediate between the various groups who inhabited the oasis, protect the settlement from attacks by other settlements and tribal confederations, and more importantly the ability to coerce other groups in the settlement were far more crucial factors behind the consolidation of an oasis leadership. In short, oasis amirs were amirs because they mediated between groups or coerced other groups, including members of their own lineage. One would argue that coercion would not have been possible without a degree of economic surplus. However, in the oases of Arabia coercion depended on both material and symbolic capital. The material capital consisted of wealth converted into weapons, slaves and bribes, all important for the consolidation of a leadership and the expansion of its sphere of influence beyond the single settlement where it originated. The symbolic capital consisted of a mixture of genealogical heritage, and reputation for valued attributes (al-Rasheed, 1991: 90). Without the symbolic capital, it was difficult to establish leadership on the basis of economic wealth alone. The Arabian society of the time had no tolerance for the 'nouveux riches'. Wealth was not automatically converted into political assets.

Deraiyya was a small settlement with a mixed population, consisting of farmers, merchants, artisans, minor *ulema* and slaves (Lam al Shihab: 145). In 1744, Mohammad Ibn Saud was the amir, who held the settlement together under his authority. The settlement recognized this authority as a result of a combination of factors: his residence in the oasis and his ownership of agricultural land (date palms), vital resources (wells) and *hima*, protected land around the settlement. These were the material basis for the authority of the Saudis in Deraiyya. Political skills of mediation and ability to defend the settlement against other amirs and tribal sheikhs were important complementary attributes. In return for tribute from members of the settlement, the oasis amir became the defender of the inhabitants who served as a military force, enhanced by the amir's own slaves. Collection of this tribute enhanced political leadership; it distinguished the amir and his lineage from other lineages in the settlement. It was not uncommon for a single settlement to comprise two or more distinct units, each living in a walled quarter with its own recognised *amir/rais*. After a period of tension and competition, one quarter under the leadership of an ambitious amir would overcome the others and impose tribute on them (al-Juhany, 1983:175).

Saudi leadership in Deraiyya is best described as a traditional form of rule common in many settlements in Arabia at that time. When the religious reformer Mohammad Ibn Abdul Wahhab started preaching in the neighbouring oasis of Uyayna, the amir of Deraiyya enjoyed limited authority over the settlement. With the exception of his collection of tribute, the executive authority of an oasis ruler was weak as he did not have a strong police force to carry out his decisions and especially not against the interests of other prominent families in the settlement (al-Juhany, 1983:179).

It seems that the Saudi leadership lacked two dimensions: first, identifiable undisputed noble tribal origin which would have guaranteed a strong association with a tribal confederation, and second, excessive wealth which would have promised prospects for expansion of authority over other settlements. The al-Saud seemed to have been sedentary for a long period of time not only in Deraiyya since the 15th/16th century, but in an oasis in al-Hasa before then (al-Juhany, 1983). They may have had some surplus wealth due to the collection of tribute from the settlement, but this does not seem to have been a distinguished characteristic since historical accounts, including the Najdi pro-Saudi chronicles, do not draw our attention to it.

Given the limitations of the Saudi leadership (lack of tribal association and wealth), it is not surprising that the Wahhabi reformist movement appealed to Mohammad Ibn Saud as it provided an alternative source of legitimation. Mohammad Ibn Saud adopted the movement because it seemed to promise an opportunity to compensate for the limitations of his rule.

The historical alliance between the Wahhabi religious reformer and the ruler of Deraiyya set the scene for the emergence of a religious emirate in central Arabia. Without Wahhabism, it is difficult to imagine that Deraiyya and its leadership would have assumed any political significance in Central Arabia. There was no tribal confederation to support any expansion beyond the settlement. The settlement itself did not have sufficient manpower to initiate conquest of other oases or tribal territories. In the middle of the 18th century, Deraiyya had been within the sphere of influence of Banu Khalid, the strong tribal confederation of the al-Hasa, similar to other settlements in southern Najd. From the early days of Saudi-Wahhabi expansion, the crucial element was to gain submission to the tenets of Wahhabi Islam among both the sedentary and nomadic population. This submission led to the creation of a quasi-tribal confederation with which to conquer further territories in the absence of an identifiable 'Saudi' tribal confederation.

Although Wahhabism provided a novel impetus on the basis of which political centralisation took place, the Saudi-Wahhabi emirate exhibited structural characteristics already manifested in Arabia. Expansion by conquest was the only mechanism available for emirates to rise above the limited confines of the specific settlements where they had sprung. The Saudi Wahhabi emirate was no exception to this rule. Wahhabism provided a legitimation formula under which conquest of new territories became justified. The spread of the Wahhabi call, the purification of Arabia from unorthodox forms of religiosity and the enforcement of the Shari'a among Arabian society were fundamental demands of the Wahhabi movement.

Saudi historical narratives emphasize that the amir of Deraiyya put the Wahhabi reformer, recently expelled from Uyayna under his wing as he accepted to execute these demands. This emphasis, however, is misleading as it does not take into account the limitations of the Saudi leadership at that time. In fact, Wahhabism impregnated the Saudi leadership with a new force, which proved to be crucial for the consolidation and expansion of Saudi rule. Wahhabism promised this leadership clear benefits in the form of political and religious authority and material rewards, without which the conquest of Arabia would not have been possible. The Saudi adoption of the movement was not crucial for the spread of Wahhabism in Arabia since this leadership initially lacked the means to do so. It is more accurate to argue that Wahhabism was crucial for the consolidation of the Saudi leadership, which began to rise above other contemporary oasis leaderships in the region.

The expansion of the Saudi-Wahhabi realm beyond Deraiyya was dependent on the recruitment of a fighting force ready to spread the religious message of the reformist movement and Saudi political hegemony. The population of the oases in southern Najd were the first to endorse Wahhabism and respond to its call for jihad against the 'unbelievers'. Settled Najdis between the age of 18–60 were its conscripts, the backbone of the Saudi-Wahhabi force. Some accepted Wahhabism out of conviction, others succumbed to it out of fear. Wahhabi religious specialists (imams, *ulamas* and *qadis*) were sent out to the oases to spread the message. Those who willingly accepted Wahhabism were spared future atrocities. They were required to swear allegiance, *bay'a*, to its religio-political leadership and demonstrate their loyalty by accepting to fight for its cause and pay the *zakat* to its representatives. Those who showed resistance were subjected to raids threatening their livelihood.

The same method of recruitment was used among the tribal confederations. Preaching and raids progressed simultaneously to swearing allegiance to the Saudi leadership. While control over the oases was easier to maintain, the allegiance of the various Arabian tribes proved most difficult to sustain. The tribes had been more experienced in evading central authority due to their mobility and tradition of autonomy. However, once they had been subjugated, they proved to be an important fighting force to spread the message of Wahhabism.

The Saudi-Wahhabi emirate depended on maintaining a balance between a central religio-political leadership and the tribal confederations. The leadership strove to achieve a firm grip over the population by imposing various mechanisms of control. Given that the Saudi mixed armed force was better at prolonged raiding than at prolonged occupation (Cook, 1988: 671), punitive raids, regular taxation, and the appeal of various material and non-material rewards ensured tenuous control over distant settlements and territories. The ferocity of raids against those who were regarded as outside the realm of true Islam spread fear among the population and encouraged the acceptance of Saudi-Wahhabi rule.

Coercion alone, however, would not have guaranteed the same level of expansion that was achieved by the Saudis by the end of the 18th century. Wahhabism promised salvation not only in this world, but also in a distant future. One cannot underestimate the religious factor which was an important motivating force for submitting to a political leadership, whose stated objective was to guarantee the return to a pure form of religion. We cannot rule out the level of religious motivation among those who willingly accepted the tenets of Wahhabism. Submission to the teachings of Wahhabi Islam promised not only immediate evasion of atrocities, but also spiritual rewards. The regular payment of *zakat* to the Saudi-Wahhabi leadership was a token of political submission, but also an expression of fulfilling a religious duty. While this religious duty might not have been strong among the tribal confederations, it was definitely apparent among the oasis population of southern Najd whose allegiance to the Saudi leadership had been resting on more solid grounds. The religious awareness/zeal of those converted into Wahhabis cannot fully explain the expansion of the emirate, but at the same time it cannot be reduced to insignificance. To account for the consolidation of the Saudi-Wahhabi emirate against inherent decentralizing tendencies in Arabia, emphasis should be given to the religious motivation of the sedentary Najdis, who found in the developed Wahhabi *fiqh* real solutions to their practical problems.

We can also point to the appeal of the doctrine of *tawhid* to the tribal confederations, especially the nomadic sections. Those may not have had the same fascination as the sedentary population with Islamic rituals or with Islamic law (as they had their own tribal custom to deal with conflict and transgression), but we can claim with certainty that the doctrine of *tawhid* did actually strike a nerve amongst them. It certainly did not fall on deaf ears. Even those tribal confederations who fought against the Saudi-Wahhabi political agenda could not resist the temptation of *tawhid*. For instance, in spite of its ferocious resistance to political Wahhabism, the Shammar tribe accepted the doctrine of *tawhid* in the 18th century.

Armed with this religious motivation, the first Saudi-Wahhabi emirate began to expand in Arabia. Four factors facilitated the process. First, disunity and rivalry among local oasis amirs meant that the Saudis could defeat them one by one. Second, internal familial disputes among members of the oases' ruling groups weakened their resistance and enabled the invaders to use dissidents for their purposes. Third, the migration of Arabian tribes to more fertile regions in Iraq and Syria aided the conquest. And fourth, the peaceful adoption of Wahhabism by a number of groups provided grassroot support for the expansion even before it took place (Abdul Rahim, 1976: 73).

The expansion of the first Saudi-Wahhabi emirate resulted in the creation of a political realm with fluctuating boundaries. A permanent political leadership was provided by the descendants of the al-Saud under Wahhabi legitimation. However, there were no mechanisms other than raids to ensure the durability of the polity, nor of its boundaries. With this political system tribal confederations retained their ability to challenge Saudi-Wahhabi authority. Withdrawing the payment of *zakat* and organising counter-attacks on groups and territories within the Saudi-Wahhabi sphere of influence were recurrent challenges to this authority. Although there were rudimentary attempts at formalizing political, economic and religious relations within the emirate, these remained insufficient to hold the constituency together. There was a vague recognition of belonging to an Islamic *umma*, but this did not preclude attachment to more specific tribal/regional identifies. The emirate was a political entity which needed to revitalize itself through continuous raids and plunder. Raids were rituals of rejuvenation, injecting fresh blood into the realm, especially when it was on the verge of disintegration. While these raids initially guaranteed expansion, later they proved detrimental to political continuity as the population began to resent their devastating effects. When the Ottoman empire responded to the Saudi-Wahhabi challenge by sending the troops of Mohammad Ali into Arabia in 1811, tribal confederations which had already suffered the punitive raids of the Saudis responded by switching their allegiance to the foreign troops. The disintegration of the first Saudi-Wahhabi emirate was completed with the destruction of their capital, Deraiyya, in 1818 and the capture of the Saudi ruler Abdullah by Ibrahim Pasha.

A second attempt at re-establishing Saudi-Wahhabi authority began in 1824 when Turki Ibn Abdullah installed himself in Riyadh, south of the old capital. Turki endeavoured to again enforce recognition of Saudi authority in the al-Hasa region in 1830. Although he was a strict Wahhabi imam, he was careful not to antagonize the Ottoman-Egyptian troops who were still in the Hijaz, guarding the security of the pilgrimage caravans. However, the greatest challenge to Turki's authority came from internal dissension within his own family. In 1831 Turki faced the challenge of Mishari, a cousin whom he had appointed governor of Manfuha. In 1834, Mishari successfully plotted the assassination of Turki while the Saudi forces were occupied in a war with Qatif and Bahrain. Turki was killed while coming out of the mosque after the Friday prayers. His son Faisal returned to Riyadh and defeated Mishari. He became ruler of the emirate until his death in 1865. After Faisal's death, his four sons Abdullah, Saud, Mohammad and Abdul Rahman competed with each other over leadership, which proved to be detrimental for Saudi leadership in Arabia. Abdullah, the eldest son, became imam in Riyadh, but his half brother Saud resented his exclusion from power and began a campaign to undermine his brother's authority. He started a series of contacts with the rulers of Asir and Aridh. He also negotiated an alliance with the Murrah, Ajman and Dawasir confederations. These tribal confederations were trying to maintain their autonomy by allying themselves with Abdullah's rival brother. The internal struggle between the Saudi brothers was fuelled by the desire of the various confederations to free themselves from Saudi domination (Abu Aliya 1969: 156–97). A weak second Saudi-Wahhabi emirate was maintained until it was finally defeated in 1891 by the Rashidi emirate of Hail.

While the disintegration of the first Saudi realm was partially attributed to the intervention of the Ottoman empire, the second realm collapsed as a result of two factors. First, the fragile Saudi leadership of the second half of the 19th century was plagued by internal strife among members of the Saudi family. Second, the increasing power of a rival central Arabian emirate to the north of the Saudi base was able to undermine Saudi hegemony at a time when the Saudis disputed among themselves for political leadership. In 1891, the Saudi ruler Abdul Rahman was expelled from Riyadh by the Rashidis of Hail. He took refuge first among the Murrah tribe of the Empty Quarter and later settled in Kuwait under the patronage of the al-Sabah and with a stipend from the Ottoman government. In 1902 Abdul Rahman's son Abdul Aziz, the founder of the present state, re-emerged in Arabia and captured Riyadh from its new rulers, the Rashidis. The capture of Riyadh marks the beginning of the present Saudi polity.

The Saudi-Wahhabi emirates were religious polities characterised by the co-existence of a central religio-political leadership and semi-autonomous or autonomous tribal confederations. A stronger leadership at the centre tended to weaken the tribal confederations and make them submit to its rising power. A weaker central leadership was always accompanied by the tribal confederations' increasing ability to defy this power. The tension between the emirate and the confederations was resolved by resorting to coercion, a mechanism which guaranteed the momentary regeneration of the central power, but could not sustain it for a long period. The confederations always retained their ability to switch allegiance and openly challenge the Saudi-Wahhabi emirates. This led to a precarious relationship between the leadership and its constituency. Neither political nor social cohesion was established to bind rulers and ruled. Even at the height of Saudi-Wahhabi hegemony towards the end of the 18th century, religious ideology alone was not capable of generating this cohesion. The expansion of the emirates created 'spheres of influence' rather than effective control over confederations and distant territories. Religion was obviously an advantage. It was a rationale for legitimation, and an organizing mechanism for the economy and the Saudi-Wahhabi army. But the strength of the decentralizing tendencies could not be easily overcome. Alternative tribal/regional identities continued to surface at times when the leadership was weak. These undermined the viability of the emirates and eventually led to their decline. This decline was assisted by foreign intervention during Mohammad Ali's campaign in Arabia at the beginning of the 19th century, and later by competition and rivalry at the level of leadership during the second half of the 19th century.

The Rashidi Emirate (1836–1921)

In addition to the Saudi-Wahhabi religious emirates, Central Arabia had known attempts at political centralization based solely on tribal foundation (al-Rasheed, 1991). The Rashidi emirate was a polity deriving its legitimacy and power from one of Arabia's large tribal confederations, the Shammar. The impetus for centralization came from an oasis-based leadership, that of the Rashidis, a tribal section which had already settled in Hail, an oasis in northern Najd. The Rashidis represented a tribal nobility, ruling as amirs over the Hail mixed population of Shammar tribesmen, Bani Tamim sedentary farmers and merchants, and non tribal groups of craftsmen, artisans and slaves. Shammar nomads frequented Hail for trade and regarded the oasis as falling within their tribal territory. The presence of the Rashidis in the oasis was an extension of the tribes's claim over it. Since the mid-19th century, Hail served as a base from which the Rashidis expanded into north Arabia and southern Najd. While the Saudi-Wahhabi emirates expanded under the banner of a religious legitimation, the Rashidis spread their influence over other oases and tribal confederations on the basis of the support of their own tribe. The conquests of the Rashidi emirate were in fact a mechanism for spreading Shammar hegemony over others. When this expansion gathered momentum in the middle of the 19th century, it was initially orchestrated by Shammar tribesmen who, under the leadership of the amirs of Hail, provided a military force held by the idiom of tribal solidarity. Shammar tribal sections were the backbone of the force, which conquered oases outside Shammar tribal territory. They also subjugated weaker tribal confederations who became their vessels. In the case of the Rashidis, the emirate and the confederation were initially one polity. This was an important factor distinguishing Rashidi authority from that of the neighbouring Saudis in southern Najd. The Rashidis did not have to 'convert' the Shammar to their cause, but acted in conjunction with them to spread the tribe's hegemony. The Rashidi amirs were themselves drawn from the tribe and were tied into marital alliances with it. In contrast, the Saudi leadership in Riyadh lacked the tribal depth, hence its dependence on the alliance with Mohammad Ibn Abdul Wahhab and his followers.

The motivation for the Shammar to rally behind the Rashidi leadership should be understood within the context of Arabia in the middle of the 19th century. It would be simplistic to argue that tribal solidarity was the sole motivating force behind the confederation's support of this newly emerging leadership. Shammar support arose out of their fears at that time. The tribe had witnessed the growth of the first Saudi-Wahhabi emirate, which had defeated some Shammar sections and forced them to migrate to Mesopotamia towards the end of the 18th century. Furthermore, in 1818, the Shammar were attacked by the Ottoman Egyptian troops who regarded their territory as part of the Saudi domain. The Egyptian presence in Arabia created uncertainty among the Shammar, who felt the desire of these troops to encapsulate them. By supporting the Rashidis, the Shammar were seeking a leadership which would guarantee their security and autonomy *vis-à-vis* local and foreign rivals. In backing the Rashidis, who were connected genealogically to the Abde section of the Shammar, the tribal confederation laid the foundation for organizing its defence and strengthening a unity which had been previously resting on the rhetoric of common origin and tribal solidarity. The centralization of power in the hands of the Rashidis stemmed from this context of political upheaval, military turmoil and foreign intervention in Arabia. Subsequently, the Shammar were able to resist encroachment on their territory not only by the Egyptian troops, but also by the re-established Saudi-Wahhabi emirate in Riyadh (al-Rasheed, 1991:47)

With the consolidation of Rashidi leadership, the amirs began to rely less on the Shammar and more on a mixed force of slaves and conscripts from the oasis. This was a development dictated by the inability of the leadership to keep a firm control over its own tribal sections. The partial shift towards a permanent non-tribal military force was an indication of a change in the power of the amirs. Initially the amirs were tribal sheikhs comparable to other Shammar sheikhs, but later their power increased as they became a sedentary nobility with its own political ambitions. This pattern was consolidated with the leadership of Mohammad Ibn Rashid (1869–1897), whose expansion in Central Arabia reached an unprecedented level in the history of the emirate. His domain was extended from the borders of Aleppo and Damascus to Basrah, Oman and Asir (A. Musil, 1928: 248). The al-Qasim region and the Saudi-Wahhabi capital Riyadh were incorporated into this domain. Representatives and governors were appointed in the conquered areas.

The Rashidi emirate relied on four groups for its expansionist campaign in Arabia. First, its leadership summoned the sedentary and nomadic Shammar to fight their rivals, who were designated enemies of the whole tribe. Skirmishes against the Shammar sections acted in favour of Mohammad Ibn Rashid in his mobilization of this tribal force. Second, other non-tribal confederations took part in his campaign, as they were motivated by the prospect of booty. Third, the amir's slaves and bodyguard formed a solid core in his military force. And fourth, conscripts from the towns and oases of Jabal Shammar provided a reliable military force which was used regularly for expansion. Their participation guaranteed the predominance of Hail, both economically and politically.

This expansion, however, did not lead to establishing firm control. The scanty resources of the region, coupled with the poverty of the transport infrastructure, militated against the full integration of these areas in a single unit. It is more accurate, therefore, to describe this expansion as spreading influence rather than direct control over conquered territories. In this respect, the Rashidi emirate exhibited a pattern similar to that predominant in the first and second Saudi-Wahhabi emirates. Both polities engaged in raids and conquest without being able to hold the conquered territories for an extended period of time. While control over the core of the emirate was relatively easy to maintain, the conquered territories represented a periphery difficult to supervise regularly and integrate thoroughly. While in the Saudi-Wahhabi emirates the payment of *zakat* was an indication of a group's submission to its authority, the payment of *khuwa* (tribute) to the Rashidis guaranteed their control over other groups. Tribute was a tax levied not upon the collector's own community, but rather upon a conquered group which remained more or less autonomous (A. Pershit, 1979: 149–56). Both leaderships, however, resorted to regular raids as a mechanism ensuring the payment of either *zakat* or *khuwa*.

While initially the Rashidi emirate was characterized by full integration between the leadership and the Shammar tribal confederation, expansion brought about the recurrent tension between a central power and its diversified and semi-autonomous constituency. The Rashidi constituency included in addition to the Shammar other weakened tribal confederations, and the population of oases outside their traditional tribal territory. While frequent raids against rebellious tribes continued to be a power maintaining strategy, a redistributive economy was put in place. The amirs of Hail collected tribute from weakened groups to be redistributed among others, as rewards for loyalty and participation in the leadership's military campaigns. In order to maintain their position in Hail, the Rashidis spent lavishly on their followers and gave them various gifts. Tribal sheikhs visited the oasis and received handouts in cash and kind. The subsidy system functioned as a mechanism for the circulation of wealth, thus promising loyalty in return for material gains. Subsidies from the centre to the periphery created economic integration between the Hail leadership and its constituency. More importantly, they created dependency on the revenues of the amirs among the sedentary and nomadic population, who became incorporated into their political realm.

Economic integration between the leadership and its constituency was partially achieved in the Rashidi emirate, but military and political integration were difficult to create and maintain over an extended period of time. Tribal confederations who paid the *khuwa* remained more or less autonomous. The amirs of Hail had no monopoly over the means of coercion as it was difficult to break the military strength of the various confederations which came under their authority. The military strength of tribes was occasionally neutralized by frequent raids and subsidies, but in the long term, these strategies failed to guarantee loyalty.

Control over oases in Jabal Shammar was, however, a different matter. Hail, the urban core of the emirate, remained loyal to the Rashidi leadership as long as this leadership was capable of defending its interests. The merchants, artisans and agriculturalists supported the leadership because it was able to guarantee the safe passage of trading and pilgrimage caravans, thus allowing the flow of trade between Hail and the outside world to continue. An amir who extended his authority over the tribal confederations in the desert created secure conditions for travel between Arabia's trading markets, thus benefiting the merchants and artisans of the sedentary communities. The loyalty of the oasis population was highly dependent on this factor. The Hail population withdrew its support only when the Rashidi leadership of the first two decades of the 20th century became incapable of extending protection outside the walls of the oasis, due to the rising influence of Abdul Aziz Ibn Saud after 1902. Some Hailis switched allegiance and negotiated with the rivals of the Rashidis under economic pressures which led to disturbing economic relations between Hail and its surroundings. During the economic and military siege of Hail by Ibn Saud in 1921, the religious and economic elite of the oasis switched allegiance to the newly rising Saudi power, a strategy which among other variables led to the collapse of the Rashidi emirate.

The decline of the Rashidi polity can be attributed to several factors. Rivalry between Britain and the Ottoman empire in Arabia resulted in upsetting the balance between local Arabian power centres. The Rashidi amirs continued to be allied with the Ottomans even after several tribal confederations and local amirs sided with Britain. As the Ottomans lost the First World War, the local Rashidi allies felt the rising pressure of the Saudis who had secured a firm alliance with Britain. This factor alone could not fully explain the demise of Rashidi power in 1921. But the instability of Rashidi leadership, which manifested itself in internal rivalry between the various Rashidi branches, added to their already disadvantaged position in Arabia. A weakened leadership was not able to maintain the loyalty of the various tribal confederations who shifted their allegiance to a more powerful centre, that of the Saudis. The emirate lost control over its tribal periphery; its leadership witnessed the shrinking of its territories without being able to reclaim them. The fact that the Rashidis had no monopoly over the use of coercion meant that autonomous and semi-autonomous confederations retained their ability to undermine their leadership. These confederations remained a potential threat in the absence of any mechanism to contain their tendency to either directly challenge Rashidi authority or passively resist by withdrawing support needed at times of external threat.

As the emirate included both sedentary and nomadic groups, maintaining the economic interests of these two sections generated contradictions which could not be resolved without antagonizing one or the other. The prosperity of the oases depended on pacifying the nomads to secure safe trade. But pacifying the nomads meant depriving them of a supplementary source of income, which consisted of extracting protection tax from caravans or raiding them; both activities undermined the viability of the economy of the sedentary population of the oases. This contradiction was dealt with efficiently by the strong Rashidi leadership of the late 19th century. Nomads were pacified by raids and bribes. But in the 20th century these strategies were no longer possible, given the economic and political pressures exerted on the Rashidis by the consolidated Saudi leadership.

Although the Saudi-Wahhabi and Rashidi emirates differed in their legitimation formula, both polities were plagued by tension arising from the coexistence of a central power and a decentralized political and economic tribal infrastructure. Until 1900, the Saudi and Rashidi leaderships strove to resolve the tension by resorting to similar strategies, but both failed to secure political integration between the core of the emirate and its periphery. Both

Najdi emirates remained fragile political configurations with boundaries in a permanent state of flux.

I propose an understanding of the rise of Central Arabian emirates in terms of two certainties, documented in the past and continued to be exhibited until later in the 20th century. These are the certainties of sedentary/ nomadic interaction and the inseparability of the *badu/hadar* culturally, politically, economically and socially. While not underestimating demographic, religious, military and economic factors, the rise of an emirate was, above all a, function of the interdependence between the *badu* and *hadar*; emirates were attempts to cast a political unifying umbrella on an already established symbiosis, which had been in place for centuries.

That emirates rose and fell, amirs fought battles amongst themselves and against others, and raids were endemic has been interpreted as a manifestation of chaos in Arabia. Today modern states rejuvenate their hegemony by resorting to violence. In the last decade of the 20th century, consider the USA and Iraq to have a clear indication of how regular, theatrical violence contributes to the consolidation of power even in an age where such practices are supposedly under control. If the use of violence is to indicate chaos, then present day Arabia is experiencing a more 'chaotic' political life at the end of the 20th century than that experienced during the age of emirates, an age of social, political, religious, and economic diversity.

References

Abdulrahim, A. *al-Dawla al saoudiyya al oula, 1745–1818*, Cairo, 1976.

Abu 'Aliya. *Tarikh al-dawla al sao'udiyya al thaniya, 1840–1891*, Riyadh, 1969.

Abu Hakima, *Lam' al-Shihab fi Sirat Mohammad ibn Abdul Wahab*, Beirut, 1967.

Alangari, H. *The Struggle for Power in Arabia*, London: Ithaca, 1998.

al-Hasan, H. *al-Shi'ia fi al mamlaka al 'arabiyya al saoudiyya*, volumes I and II. Mu'assasat al-buqai' li ihia' alturath, (n. p.) 1993.

al-Juhany, U. *The History of Najd prior to the Wahhabis: A Study of Social, Political and Religious Conditions in Najd during three Centuries*. Ph.D Thesis, Washington: University of Washington, 1983.

al-Rasheed, M. *Politics in an Arabian Oasis*, I.B. Tauris, London, 1991.

Altorki, S. and D. Cole. *Arabian Oasis City: The Transformation of Unayzah*, Texas: University of Texas Press, 1989.

Asad, T. *The Bedouin as a Military Force: Notes on some Aspects of Power Relations*, in C. Nelson (ed.), *The Desert and the Sown*, Institute of International Studies, Berkeley: University of California, 1973.

Cook, M. *The Expansion of the First Saudi State*, in C. E. Bosworth (ed.), *The Islamic World from Classical to Modern Times*, Princeton: Darwin Press, 1989. W. Facey, *Dirriyya and the First Saudi State*, London: Stacey International, 1997. Ibn Khaldun, *The Muqqadimah*, translated by F. Rosenthal, Princeton: Princeton University Press, 1987 (1967).

Lorimer, J. *Gazeteer of the Persian Gulf, Oman and Central Arabia*, volumes I and II, Calcutta, 1908. A. Musil, *Northern Neged*, New York: AMS Press, 1978, 1928.

Pershit, A. *Tribute Relations in Political Anthropology: the State of Art*, edited by S. Seaton and H. Claessen, the Hague, 1979.

Vassiliev, A. *The History of Saudi Arabia*, London: Saqi Books, 1998.

Wallin, G. *Narrative of a Journey from Cairo to Medina and Mecca by Suez, Araba, Twaila, al-Jauf, Hail and Negd in 1854*, Journal of the Royal Geographical Society, volume 24:115–201.

TEN

The White Tent programme: Tribal Education Under Muhammad Reza Shah

Farian Sabahi

This chapter examines the White Tent programme which took place in Iran and brought education to nomads between 1953 and 1979; that is, from Mosaddeq's fall to the Islamic Revolution, after which this programme continued but the banner on the white tent was taken away.[1] Those urban teachers who in the 1950s were sent among nomads could not get used to living in a tent, moving from winter to summer pasture, without a chance to receive a doctor's attention in case they fell ill. According to the Iranian government, nomadic life was supposedly harsher than in the villages; only nomads could cope with such difficulties and, therefore, only nomads could be teachers in their own tribes.[2] However, foreign visitors witnessed among nomads little sickness, an active outdoor existence, and acceptable hygienic conditions:

> every morning pots and pans were carried down to the stream and scrubbed with sand, than boiled for several minutes. Milk was covered while it cools, and even the dirt floor of the cook tent was swept several times a day with bunches of twigs. The only vessel not washed daily was the battered stone pot holding the culture from which yogurt was made.[3]

To examine nomad education in context, it is necessary to study the successive plans in this regard, from the *Ashiret Mektebi Humayun* (the Imperial School for Tribes) in the Ottoman Empire, which was a historic precursor, to the first steps toward nomad education, the US Point Four and the White Tent Programme.

Implementation of the programme, its results and evaluations, will also be analysed. As for the Literacy Corps, my focus will be more on the impact on the teachers than on the pupils. The written material I am going to quote in the following pages has mainly been found, under particularly fortunate circumstances, in the Unesco archives in Paris. In fact, I was given many documents which the archivist was throwing away as 'old and useless'.

To begin with we have to clarify terminological ambiguities. Dealing with words has been like walking through a minefield. 'Tribe' is a protean notion.[4] Academics and governments use an ambiguous and confusing terminology. For instance, many official documents mention 'tribes' meaning 'nomads', possibly because 'through its propaganda machine' the Pahlavi government 'controlled the language of communication' and, since 1960s, ruled out the existence of nomads.[5] However, tribes are not always nomadic: in Fars the Qashqai are both characterized by nomadism and tribalism, while the Mamasani have a tribal structure but are settled and therefore not nomads; leading a nomadic life without having a tribal organization, the Komachi of Kirman had no claim to fame, did not attract the Government's attention and were therefore allowed to exist.[6]

Scholars and Iranian officials published many lists of tribes, which they classified by ethnic affiliation based on language and/or supposed origins, or by province and/or by socio-political structures.[7] Though English words cannot easily apply to other cultures, several definitions of 'tribe' have been attempted, beginning with 'the loose equation of *tribe* with *primitive society*, once applied to the pre-colonial populations of many parts of the world'.

According to a second definition, tribe is 'a particular type of society intermediate between simple hunting bands and more complex chiefdoms and states'. And, finally, a third notion of tribe describes it as a 'political group defined by territorial boundaries and by accepted mechanisms for the resolution of internal disputes'. For the purposes of this study I shall use Richard Tapper's definition of 'tribe' as: a state of mind, a construction of reality, a model for action, a mode of social organization essentially opposed to that of a centralized state.'[9]

Regarding numbers, according to an official document published in Iran in 1965, 400,000 people were classified as 'tribal' meaning 'nomads'. Among these 400,000 people, 50,000 were children of school age, 250,000 were illiterate adults between 15 and 45, three out of four migrated during winter towards the southern areas of Fars and during summer to the hills and mountains in the northern part of this region, whilst in spring and autumn they had their camp between the two pastures.[10] However, these official numbers look completely unreliable if compared to the data provided by Lois Beck just prior to the Islamic Revolution: the estimated tribal population (but not nomads) counted 3 million Kurds, 2 million Baluchis, 570,000 Bakhtiyaris, 500,000 Lurs, 400,000 Qashqais, 315,000 Turkomen, 300,000 Shahsevan, 150,000 Arabs, 20,000 Basseri and 200,000 others.[11]

The Imperial School for Tribes (*Ashiret Mektebi Humayun*) in the Ottoman Empire

At the end of the 19th century the Ottoman Empire lost some two fifths of its land and one fifth of its subjects as a consequence of the Balkan crises and of the Treaty of Berlin (1875–1878). Whilst ethnic minorities were threatening further defections, nomad tribes were a major menace to the central state. Besides escaping conscription and the payment of taxes, tribes

> posed a three-way drain on the treasury: raids against cultivators and townsmen reduced producers' ability to pay taxes; fear of raids diminished economic productivity by reducing the area under cultivation and restricting trade; and the cost of providing security forces to deter raiding was high, while such forces were only intermittently successful against the more mobile tribes.[12]

The Ottoman central government tried to oppose separatist movements by promoting Pan-Islamism and Ottomanism (the Tanzimat notion of Ottoman patriotism). While the imposition from above of such supranational ideologies did not seduce tribal people, the creation of the Imperial School for Tribes (*Ashiret Mektebi Humayun*) was a major attempt to 'integrate its tribal communities into the political life of the state' and, for the restless socio-political context in which it was set up, prefigures the Iranian White Tent programme.[13]

The *Ashiret Mektebi Hmayun* was created in October 1892 by order of Sultan Abdul Hamid II (r. 1876–1909) and until its closure in 1907 tried to enroll children from the frontiers of the Arab provinces and the eastern Anatolian and Kurdish areas, aiming at fostering 'an allegiance to the Ottoman state within one of the most alienated segments of its society: the empire's tribes'. In order to 'provide an Ottoman education for the sons of leading tribal notables', boys between 12 and 16 years old were educated at the five-year boarding school which sought to create a corps of 'intermediaries between the state and its tribes'. Such a group was inspired by a similar body loyal to the empire, formed by the offspring of urban notables who were educated in Istanbul and then granted posts within the Ottoman government.[14]

First Steps Towards Nomad Education in Iran

Both Muhammad Reza Shah and his father aimed at subjugating tribes and sedentarizing nomads in order to transform them from 'a threat to the national integration of a state' and 'a cultural anachronism' into loyal citizens, moving their devotion from their chiefs to the sovereign and the central government.[15] Killing their leaders and disarming their followers in the 1920s, Reza Shah carried on pacification and detribalization policies. In 1928 the tribal dress was outlawed and those who did not comply with the law were harshly punished. Then, the Pahlavi government drafted young tribesmen into the army and obliged them to serve in distant areas. In the 1930s a brutal policy of forced sedentarization took place without providing any means for settlement or farming. By blocking mountain passes, the army prevented nomads from migrating from winter to summer quarters and vice versa; only bribes and dangerous migrations at night succeeded in saving nomads from heavy losses. In 1941 Muhammad Reza Shah's ascent to the Peacock Throne was followed by a return to nomadic pastoralism, but between 1950 and 1970 nomadic tribes were attacked again, mainly through a policy of settlement, the nationalization of pastures included in the White Revolution, economic neglect, impoverishment and consequent mass migration to urban areas. In 1963, for instance:

> The Government has undertaken to disarm some of the most populous tribes, including the Qashqai and the Kurds. Echoes of the revolutionary reform programs may also be heard in urban areas.'[16]

And:

> The Iranian Armed Forces have been put to a substantial test. Armed tribal
> disorders in Fars began in March and were met by the despatch of 16
> battalions of troops. The policy direction of the Government and the
> military conduct of the campaign were not always well managed, but the
> rebel tribes were contained and the situation now appears stabilized. Units
> appear to have eventually carried out their missions with only minor
> dissidence and no reported defection.[17]

Tribal chiefs were also often exiled. For instance, Malek Mansur, one of the
hereditary chiefs of the Qashqais, spent eight years abroad. A 'superb
horseman and marksman', he graduated in England at the Agriculture College
of the University of Reading and then took a degree in law at Oxford. In the
early 1950s his story was reported in the *National Geographic Magazine* by an
American couple he hosted in Iran, providing them with the luxury of tribal
life, from caviar for breakfast to Coca-Cola 'encased in a box of crushed ice'.[18]

Among the attempts of the Pahlavi to subjugate the tribes and mould the
young generation, education was considered the most adequate means. Persian
language and Iranian history were instruments conveying a sense of
nationalism which could possibly undermine tribal society. In this context,
the White Tent programme had thus a twofold aim: educating young people
in order to transform them into useful manpower which could help Iran to
become a major industrialized country and, secondly, settling pastoral nomads
by offering them an alternative to nomadic pastoralism. However, at that time
literacy was not important to nomadic life: the amount of education
considered necessary was linked to carrying out rites of passage such as
marriages, whilst all other contracts were normally performed orally.[19]

In 1948, just a few years before the implementation of the White Tent
programme, three boarding schools for children of pastoral nomads were set
up in the towns of Fassa, Firuzabad and Shiraz. However, due to financial
problems, two years later the programme came to an end. In 1949, moving
schools for nomads were suggested by American consultants involved in the
'Seven-Year Development Plan for the Plan Organization of the Imperial
Government of Iran'. In 1951 Glen Gagon, the Point Four Education Adviser
for Fars, met Muhammad Bahmanbegi, the graduate son of a tribal chief, and
put him on the Point Four payroll.[20]

The US Point Four

'Point Four' was the first United States development programme for technical cooperation. In his inaugural address on 20 January 1949, President Truman pointed out four major lines in American foreign policy. The fourth and last point of his speech stated that the United States should embark on a programme aimed at sharing the American scientific and industrial achievements with underdeveloped countries in order to 'realize their aspirations for a better life.'[21] Reactions to Point Four differed, but the Tudeh party demanded that its aid programmes be rejected, in a surging tide of 'Communist-inspired anti-foreignism', whilst Prime Minister Mossadeq defined Point Four as the Iranian tarantula jumping up and down and thus frightening people though it had never been known to bite anybody.[22]

The programme, thereafter known as Point Four, underwent many different managements. At the beginning it was administered by the Technical Cooperation Administration, which referred to the Department of State. In the summer of 1953 it was transferred to the Foreign Operations Administration, an entity independent of the Department of State. Two years later, on 30 June 1955, the Foreign Operations Administration ceased to exist and the International Cooperation Administration, a new and semi-autonomous agency, took charge of Point Four.

At any rate, people in the field were only marginally influenced by these changes.[23] Needless to say, Point Four had a direct impact on Iran. An agreement was signed on 19 October 1950 at Abayaz Palace in Tehran by Ambassador H. F. Grady and the Iranian Prime Minister, General Ali Razmara. The agreement regarded the establishment of a joint Iranian-American commission for rural development, and called for cooperation in a programme towards the involvement of American experts in Iranian villages for the improvement of health, education and agriculture.[24]

According to William E. Warne, director of Point Four in Iran from 1952 to 1955, its major achievement in Iran took place within the educational system. In fact, in the first four years of activity, Point Four trained 12,000 elementary and secondary teachers and 55 supervisors for rural schools. Furthermore, for demonstration purposes, Point Four built 200 village schools equipped with windows, blackboards, wells and sanitary facilities, and restored 200 schools in bad conditions.[25]

Point Four was relevant to the White Tent programme because in July 1951 Bahmanbegi started cooperating on the subject of nomadic education within its Educational Division, composed of American graduates of Brigham Young University. Gagon offered tents and classroom supplies for mobile schools which would have moved with the nomads, while Bahmanbegi was involved in looking for teachers and salaries, which were paid for by 117 wealthy Qashqai families.[26] However, finding 100 teachers among tribes was not an easy task, and Bahmanbegi was thus obliged to choose some from villages in tribal areas.[27]

Aims

'Except for the teachers,' Bahmanbegi declared in an interview, 'I tell our students, "Don't *go* back to your people, *look* back at them as you make your way in life. The real power to help them lies not in the black tents but where the money and decisions are made – in government, industry, the professions. Aim there, and in time your people will have a better life."'[28] Education therefore meant settlement, perfectly in line with the aims of the government's planners who, embedded with ignorance and prejudice against nomads and tribes, wished to transform them into 'more useful and productive citizens'. As showed by an official document, with the White Tent programme the Ministry of Education aimed at providing:

> the basic opportunities for education as a means of increasing the resourcefulness and latent talents of the tribal population and increase their scope and horizon to a level sufficient to make them aware of the social and economic benefits of settlement.[29]

Points Two and Three of the same document stated that 'education, once a privilege of the leaders, was to be spread among the whole nomadic population in order to forge strong bonds of national unity by wide infusion of the Persian language'. 'Raising living standards, self confidence and economic productivity of the tribes by creating in them the ability to understand and absorb the benefits of science and technology' was stated in Point Four. And, finally, Point Five aimed at destroying 'the remaining tracks of feudal power and anti-state individualistic tendencies'.[30]

Needless to say, various sources give slightly different versions of the story.

According to a Unesco expert who visited tribal areas near Shiraz in 1960, the first goal of nomadic education was literacy, whilst sedentarization was seen as long-term objective motivated by the conditions of tribal life, supposedly harsher than in the villages:

By means of a simple programme of social studies, the tribal school endeavours both to secure a gradual adjustment of the pupils to the habits, customs and behaviour patterns of a settled village or urban community, and to inculcate a sense of loyalty and respect for the laws and constitution of Iran.[31]

However, the sight of nomadic children riding over the crest of a barren hill prompted the Unesco expert to doubt the purposes of the White Tent programme and led him to the following relevant remark: 'For God's sake, leave these people alone!'[32]

The Implementation of the Programme

Between its establishment in the early 1950s and the Islamic Revolution of 1979, The White Tent programme taught 111,819 students (32,406 girls and 79,413 boys).[33] It was set up in a period when tribes had been restless and the Qashqai, for instance, were struggling for autonomy. Conflicts were partly toned down by Mosaddeq, Prime Minister from 1951 to 1953, who was remembered in Fars as the popular governor of the 1920s. Having promoted Iranian nationalism against foreign influence and economic exploitation, Mosaddeq was considered as a possible alternative to the Shah, whose anti-tribe approach had always been feared.[34] After Mosaddeq's fall, Bahmanbegi took position against a possible uprising of the Qashqai. This last factor and Bahmanbegi's involvement in an American programme were among the reasons which eventually led to the withdrawal of financial support by tribesmen.[35]

On 1 August 1953, 109 teachers started a six-week training course in Shiraz, which 105 completed. Due to the difficulties of nomadic life with which urban men were thought not to be able to cope with, only members of nomadic tribes were recruited. Those who already had a little education were chosen, further educated for a year, and then sent out to their mission. In January 1954 they began teaching in 73 tent schools. By September 1954, 1,164 pupils were enrolled in 78 schools.[36]

Students attending the Tribal Teachers Training School received a wage of 600 *toman*. Once graduated, their annual salary went up to 15,000 *toman* if they taught in Fars and 19,000 *toman* if they were assigned to a different part of the country.[37] According to Wright's account covering the area of Doshman Ziari, Mamasani, the first teachers belonged to important tribal families:

In the first year the Seyyid from Kolah Siah passed the course and set up a tribal primary school in Gha'edan, a satellite village of Kolah Siah. In the next two years, two more Seyyids from Kolah Siah, a son of the headman of Gha'edan, a son of the headman of Mashayekh, a son of a *khan*, a boy from Balutak and another from Darreh Gorg became tribal literacy teachers.[38]

The headman (*kadkhoda*) was the tribal leader's (*khan*) representative in the village. From the 1890s to 1959, he was in charge of assessing each family's crop and collected the 20 per cent due to the *khan*, 5 per cent for the *khan*'s assessor and 10 per cent for himself. After 1959 the Agriculture Department took tax collection under its own auspices and, from 1963, the *kadkhoda* and the *khan* lost relevance and were replaced by the gendarmes as representatives of the central government.[39]

In 1962 women were admitted to the Tribal Teachers Training School and, 11 years later, 270 female teachers finished their degree. By 1978, 3,834 teachers graduated and 1,000 tribal men and women were attending.[40] As a consequence of the appearance of women teachers, all sort of superstitions were spread: 'If a girl picked up a pen the world would end, if the girl from Gha'edan went to Shiraz a taxi would steal her.'[41]

In 1967 Bahmanbegi set up in Shiraz a Tribal Boarding High School for secondary education which was established by a royal *firman* and first enrolled 40 students chosen from among primary school graduates. Four of them started teaching in an elementary school and 34 entered university. In 1974, 64 students passed their final exam and 58 started to attend university. In 1975 all students successfully ended their course of study and their brilliant performances permitted 50 out of 52 to be admitted to university.[42]

In 1978 the total number of tribal students in the high school and guidance cycle was 916. A further 442 students were attending the seven guidance-cycle schools set up among some of the settled tribes: the Doshman Ziari, the Javid Mamasani, the Amaleh Qashqai and the Arabs. Drawing techniques, typing, basic auto-mechanics, repairing of radios, televisions and telephones, photography and film making were among the subjects taught.[43]

Results

According to a publication of the Ministry of Education, nine factors contributed to the success of the White Tent programme. Here, as in other official publications, 'tribal' should read 'nomadic':

1. The initiative came from within the ranks of the tribesmen (*nomads*) themselves. The elders of the tribal (*nomad*) population accorded full support and co-operation to the programme.

2. Experience showed that the best results could be obtained by using tribesmen (*nomads*) for teachers though they may be less qualified. And the policy adopted for teachers was based on the results of this experience.

3. Permanent school facilities would not cope with the peculiarities of tribal (*nomadic*) life. Thus mobile schools suited to the migratory nature of the tribesmen (*nomads*) were used. But a quarter of the school facilities have gradually became permanent. These permanent units are used for back stopping and staff support for the other schools. They are introducing elements of stability in the tribal (*nomadic*) way of life, because they have induced a portion of the tribal (*nomad*) population to settle down. The results obtained from the permanent schools and the settled population act as effective inducements for others to follow their example when they observe the socioeconomic benefits of settled life.

4. The teaching and action plan has been adjusted to the movements of the tribesmen (*nomads*).It is because of this objective that the vacations are not held during summer as normal schools. The school vacation is usually held during the Spring season when they are most active in their movements.

5. The rate of turnover and transfer are very low. This is because teachers are usually chosen from the same tribes (*nomadic groups*) they are required to teach. In this way the teachers are well known in the tribal (*nomadic*) community. Responsibility can be easily pinpointed. The teacher knowing he is a permanent figure of the tribe (*nomadic group*) and being in his own home will be more conscious of his work. The fact that parents share in the honours of the teacher strengthens this tendency.

6. As the tribal (*nomad*) teacher lives in his own home he is spared the expenses of living independently. Thus he is in a position to save a considerable portion of his 500 toman monthly salary.

7. Perhaps the most important factor contributing to the high level of efficiency by teachers and the alertness and keen sense of love for learning displayed by the school children is the effective means of supervision. All the classes held under the tents are visited during the year. All children are examined in all subjects. The results of the inspections are made public to the entire tribal (*nomad*) population. Good performance by the teacher brings honour to members of his tribe (*nomadic group*). Those with below standard ratings cause shame to their brethren.

8. To further encourage hard work, teachers and students of the best schools are invited to visit Shiraz for three days during which they are given the opportunity for examining the most recent progress made in the city. All tribes (*nomadic groups*) look up on this event as a great honour brought to them.

9. As mentioned earlier there is no corporal punishment, The individual sense of dignity is highly respected. Moral support and continuous encouragement prevails to the highest degree. The class atmosphere is so cordial and conductive in study that many children come to the white tents during vacation time.[44]

The above propaganda pointed out some assets of tribal education. Compared with other educational programmes such as the Literacy Corps, the White Tent project certainly had an advantage: teachers taught and lived with their own tribes, migrating from summer to winter pastures and vice versa. Since teachers normally lived with their own families, their salary of 500 *tomans* a month contributed to tribal economy. In the case of female tribal teachers, their pay often exceeded their father's income; they had been trained to face a class, talk to parents and sometimes, though always escorted by their husband or brother, had lived in distant tribes. As a consequence, women teachers were more direct in their stance, enjoyed prestige and decisional power, while: 'their income gave them a new place in the society, and a few of them would join men's gatherings in their house and speak at those gatherings.'[45]

Tribal teachers knew the habits and customs of their own people better than anyone else. This knowledge was also Bahmanbegi's strength, who 'realized that only through education his people could break the vicious circle of stagnation and poverty'.[46] In 1945, well before the implementation of this programme, Bahmanbegi had written *Orf va adat dar ashayer-e Fars* ('Customs and Traditions Among the Tribes of Fars'), on the basis of his personal experience interpreted through the lenses of his French education. He described different aspects of tribal life and suggested that an enlightened policy to settle the tribes would have provided health care, roads, schools, and a general and respectful amnesty.[48]

However, the White Tent was challenged by several problems. First, imposing the urban curriculum in tribal areas resulted in learning difficulties. Tribes still resented the policy of forced settlement and were not very keen towards government officials. Covering educational topics not related to husbandry methods, the programme itself conveyed the idea that tribes had to settle because otherwise they could not fit in a modern country. For a certain period, the tribal families involved had to pay for the teacher's salary, which was lower than the regular teacher's, but this factor raised resentment both from the nomads and the teachers.[49]

Evaluations

The White Tent programme aroused a great deal of interest. On 16 September 1971, *The International Herald Tribune* published the article *A Nomad Who Put Schools in Tribal Tents,* by Naomi Barry reporting from Shiraz. The article began with Bahmanbegi's 'Oriental tale': There was a giant of a man who decided that the children of the nomadic peoples should learn to read and write and do problems in arithmetic as they wandered the tribal trails.[50]

Barry explained how Bahmanbegi challenged the traditional Pahlavi view, according to which education could not be provided until tribes had settled down. Bahmanbegi first wrote to the Ministry of Education in 1946, stating that 'tribes needed education because their ignorance was dangerous to the country'. He did not receive answer and only later he decided to pursue a different strategy, first by convincing the Ministry of Education to prepare and hire tribal teachers instead of urban graduates who could not cope with harsh conditions, secondly by collecting $20 a month from 100 tribal families to pay for the programme, and finally by asking Point Four for 'material such as blackboards, chalk, pencils and notebooks'.

Barry reported on Bahmanbegi examining a class of 27 young nomads aged 10 to 13. Among them a 10-year old girl, 'boldly self-reliant and beautiful', stood out:

> She wore the traditional costume of long flowered skirt, printed apron, and white diaphanous scarf on her dark hair. She was asked the meaning of an esoteric word in Farsi. She gave the right answer and supplied four other words from the same root. Then she declaimed a poem commemorating the day the veil was legally put aside.

Barry's article ends with a sadly realistic remark about the limited access to further education granted to tribal students: only 110 out of 700 applicants were accepted at the new Tribal High School in Shiraz. Journalists and Unesco experts were fascinated by tribal life and by the natural scenario:

> After three or more hours of rough riding we would rattle over the brow of the mountain and see below us an Old Testament scene of black tents pitched near a stream in the midst of a grazing area and, in sharp contrast, the white tent of the school with the national flag fluttering on top. On either side of the valley an assortment of sheep, goats, donkeys, camels and horse cropped the sparse vegetation. Their sole attendant would probably be a tiny girl, invariably nursing a newly born kid or lamb.[51]

And, again, the foreign spectator was amazed by the sight of a young Qashqai girl:

> Perched high above the ground on the top of an enormous bundle of baggage on the back of an aristocratic camel, reading a book held in one hand and guiding the camel with the other as the long string of the caravan moved to pastures.[52]

These two last quotations have been drawn from *A Report on a Visit to Tribal Schools in the Shiraz Area*, written in 1960 by the Unesco expert J. W. Dunhill. To the extent of my knowledge, only one other report was written on the White Tent programme by Unesco experts: *L'éducation pour les tribus en Iran*, dated December 1974 by H. Varlet. The different period in which the above-mentioned reports were written gives the opportunity to find out to what extent the situation had changed.

Dunhill's report is a survey of the teachers' preparation for tribal tented schools. It was carried on the occasion of the Sharestan Leaders Conference and did not claim to be objective but rather to have been influenced by the author's Scottish background. After having listened to the recitation of some of Sa'adi's and Ferdousi's poems, Dunhill declared that 'the achievements managed by these tribal children is probably the most astonishing single feat of education I have ever seen'.[53] He drew a comparison between the humble conditions of tribal education and the sophisticated and expensive equipment used in industrialized countries, where teachers sometimes complained about the 'texture of paper in the children's exercise books'. Since improvements could be achieved 'at very little extra cost', Dunhill recommended additional financial support and material aid in terms of a first aid box and the following equipment:

A satisfactory, light, portable blackboard in a protective case, an improved composite text book, radios for each school, supplies of paint boxes and brushes, a selection of attractive charts, wall maps and illustrations to enrich the restricted experience of these tribal children and a set of handicraft tools to promote creative expression.[54]

Since too much material would have been inconvenient from the logistic point of view, especially during seasonal migrations, Dunhill realized it would have been 'unwise to over-elaborate the arrangements'. He rather recommended more opportunities for creativity in terms of handicrafts and modelling, a continuous link to tribal life and the environment during classes, a promotion of girls' attendance, association between tribal and settled pupils within social activities such as games and competitions, educational trips to 'factories, civic services, museums and other facets of urban life'.[55]

In his report Dunhill also recommended secondary, vocational, technical and adult education. He foresaw the possibility of finding accommodation for students in 'well directed hostels or approved lodgings with good, wholesome families in such towns as Shiraz and Esfahan'.[56]

Last but not least, Dunhill aptly suggested that tribal teachers should have kept a daily diary in order to provide interesting material for historians.[57]

A second Unesco report was written in 1974 by Henri Varlet. He considered the Iranian programme on tribal education a remarkable success whose costs had to be carefully monitored for three reasons.[58] Since the population growth among tribes was high, in the following years it would be hard to cope with growing numbers and, therefore, to spread primary education among all tribes. Secondly, the curriculum had to be adapted more and more to tribal life. Finally, adult education had to be tackled, keeping an eye on topics such as herding, pastures, separation between herds and human dwellings, water conservation for consumption, and corporal and food hygiene.[59]

According to Wright, who did her fieldwork west of Shiraz in the tribal area of Doshman Ziari, Mamasani from 1974 to 1976, before the implementation of the educational reforms, villagers had rural teachers based in the *khan*'s house and only those children whose fathers were heads of the 'tribe' were allowed in the *khan*'s house and received an education. Bahmanbegi, who belonged to a minor clan, went to the four Qashqai brothers to discuss his educational programme. However, since they thought it would have enhanced Bahmanbegi's personal status and promoted the state system versus the tribal one, they refused to join the White Tent programme. Thus, Bahmanbegi coopted pupils from minor clans. The children had no hesitation in going to school, all of them attended, then took their exams and entered the Teacher Training College.

As a consequence of the White Tent programme, nomadic society underwent a transformation. As in the case of the Literacy Corps, I mainly concentrate on the impact on teachers and their families. Since young men and women employed in nomadic education received the same wage and generally made far more money than their parents - who were occupied in a diversified economy composed of husbandry, vineyards and farming - they obtained economic independence and became influential in tribal affairs.[60]

Drawing a comparison between nomad teachers and the Literacy Corps, the economic and social impact was larger for the first group whilst, as shown by the interviews, in the case of some literacy corpsmen the rural experience raised radical political ideas. In fact, literacy corpsmen generally belonged to urban middle class families; enrolling in the corps was an alternative to the army, and the monthly wage did not contribute enormously to the income of their families who were not, needless to say, employed in nomadic pastoralism, but were usually integrated in urban economy. Furthermore, these two educational programmes had a different political impact. Since the Islamic Revolution of 1979 was largely an urban phenomenon and the organization of revolutionary events took primarily place through Shi'i mosques and urban bazaars, nomads only played a marginal role. Nomad teachers may well have been less involved in revolutionary politics than urban teachers.[61] Due to their early politicization in the urban milieu and to the further development of their critical views during their term in rural areas and through liaisons with other colleagues in leisure time, some literacy corpsmen played a part in the events of 1978–79.

In the case of female teachers, their economic independence was accompanied, as in the case of the Women's Literacy Corps, by wider capacity to decide their own futures. In the mid-1970s there was a time in which women employed as teachers did not want to marry the men they had been engaged to since childhood. The reason was that women teachers were supposed to work in different areas, but on the condition that they moved with their husband-teacher. The concept of *ekhtiar* (the capacity to make decisions by yourself) was still in the hands of the husband. According to Wright's account, the potential wife's question was: 'How much *ekhtiar* is he going to give me?' And the most probable answer was: 'If he is a teacher, probably more'. Since finding an educated wife was not easy, this situation was a terrific incentive for men to become teachers too.

Further Developments

The programme was extended to illiterate adults, tribal education was implemented beyond Fars, and outstanding students were given a chance to go into further education. In 1972 the Office of Tribal Education was given the opportunity to expand its programme to all tribal areas of Iran. In 1978, 3,375 tribal teachers were employed in different parts of the country and 90,151 pupils were studying in the white tents. Teachers were sometimes sent to tribes far from their own. In such circumstances the educational output was said to be higher, mainly because 'the lack of tribal and personal business' allowed a 'single-minded concentration on their teaching duties'. However, pride played an important role and those who were teaching within their own tribe were said to be 'trying to perform better than the teachers of other nearby tribes'.[62]

A further development of tribal education was that fellowships were granted to the best students by a joint programme involving the Plan Organization, the Ministry of Education, the Armed Forces, the Pahlavi University and some charities. The aim was to allow them to attend higher education and, eventually, to become 'physicians, midwives and lawyers for serving the tribesmen'. In 1973, a joint programme of the Imperial Institute for Social Welfare and the Pahlavi University selected some graduates from the Tribal School and trained them a para-medics and veterinarians. In 1978, 60 of them were working in tribal areas and, additionally, 30 finished their training in veterinary medicine. In 1977 the World Health Organization Congress on Health Problems of the Middle East was held in Shiraz. In 1978, 55 women from the Fars tribal area graduated as midwives.[63]

In 1972, the Office of Tribal Education set up a Carpet Weaving School in Shiraz, which it assisted by providing the initial capital. Elderly tribal women were hired as instructors and around 50 tribal girls and young women enrolled each year. For a period of 12 months they learned how to spin and dye wool, weave tribal rugs, *gelim*s, bags and other handicrafts according to traditional patterns. Upon finishing this course, they went back to their families and opened their own workshops.[64]

Within the Pahlavi regime's policy of settling the tribes, in 1972 the Office of Tribal Education established in Shiraz a boarding vocational school which admitted 100 boys every year. They were trained for two years in the fields of masonry, carpentry, lathing, electricity, auto-mechanics, metal-working and plumbing, thus providing the skills needed in a settled village.[65] Libraries 'on wheels', were also created to serve tribal areas.[66]

Finally, in 1975 the Governor-General of Fars established tribal mobile stores where tribal people could buy products and sell their goods at better prices than those by merchants.

Conclusion

To sum up, the Iranian tribal educational programme sought to incorporate dispersed nomadic and semi-nomadic population into the wider gamut of national life. It triggered social change, notably among the teachers' population, and affected their social and political views. One indication of this incorporation was the role played by the tribal population in the revolutionary process which brought about the demise of Muhammad Reza Pahlavi's monarchy. It should be pointed out, however, that only at the very end the tribal population joined the revolutionary ranks. Interestingly, some of the educated and professionally trained tribal youth shared leftist feelings and were engaged in revolutionary activities. In particular, some of the teachers involved in the tribal educational programme sponsored by the United States in southwestern Iran were reported to have manifest leftist leanings.

Notes

1. This chapter relies on a section of my PhD dissertation, *The Literacy Corps in Pahlavi Iran (1963–1979): political, social and literary implications*, discussed in July 1999 at the School of Oriental and African Studies, Lugano: Editrice Sapiens, 2001.

2. Ministry of Education, *Tribal Education in Iran,* Tehran, 1978, p. 2.

3. J. and F. Shor, 'We dwelt in Kashgai Tents. An Adventurous American Couple Shares Everyday Life in Camp and Saddle with Nomad Shepherds of Iraq', in *National Geographic Magazine*, January, 1952, n. 51, p. 829.

4. G. R. Garthwaite, ' Tribes, Confederation and the State: An Historical Overview of the Bakhtiari in Iran', in, R. Tapper (ed.), *The Conflict of Tribe and State in Iran and Afghanistan*, New York: St. Martin's Press, 1983, p. 316.
   –'Khans and Kings: Dialectics of Power in Bakhtiyari History', in, M. E. Bonine and N. R. Keddie (eds.), *Continuity and Change in Modern Iran*, Albany: State University of New York Press, 1981, pp. 159–72.

5. R. Tapper, 'Change, Cognition and Control: Reconstruction of Nationalism in Iran', in, C. M. Ham (ed.), *When History Accelerates. Essays on Rapid Social Change, Complexity and Creativity*, London, Athlone Press, 1994, pp. 189–0.

6. D. Bradburd, *Ambiguous Relations: Kin, Class and Conflict among Komachi Pastoralists*, Washington DC, Smithsonian Institute, 1990. 'Being There: the Necessity of Fieldwork', Washington DC, 1998.
   'Size and Success: Komachi Adaptation to a Changing Iran', in M. E Bonine and N. R. Keddie, 1981, pp. 123–37.

7. R. Tapper, *Frontier Nomads of Iran. A Political and Social History of the Shasevan*, Cambridge: Cambridge University Press, 1997, p.11.

8. R. Tapper, ibid., p.5. The first definition is common in popular English usage, the second derives from M. Sahlins, *Tribesmen*, Englewood Cliffs, Prentice-Hall, 1968, and the third from E. E Evans-Pritchard, *Witchcraft, Oracles and Magic among the Azande*, Oxford, 1940.

9. Tapper, 1997, p. 9.

10. Ministry of Education, *Tribal Education in Iran,* Tehran, 1965, p. 1.

11. L. Beck, 'Revolutionary Iran and its Tribal People', in MERIP, n. 78, May 1980, p. 16. These populations estimates partly derive from R. Weeks, *Muslim Peoples: A World Ethnographic Survey*, Westport, CT, 1978.

12. E. Rogan, 'Ashiret Mektebi: Abdulhamid II's school for tribes (1892–1907)', in *International Journal of Middle Eastern Studies*, No. 28, 1996, p. 84.

13. Ibid., p. 83.

14. Ibid.

15. Tapper, 1997, p. 191.

16. Secret airgram from S.W. Rockwell at the American Embassy in Teheran to the Department of State, dated 9 February 1963, n. A-507, Subject, 'Quarterly Progress Report on Internal Defence Plan for Iran', kept at NARA Defence Iran.

17. Secret airgram from J. C. Holms at the American Embassy in Teheran to the Department of State, dated 27 August 1963, n. A-507, Subject, 'Reliability of the Iranian Officer Corps', kept at NARA Defence 6 Iran.

18. Shor, 1952, pp. 832, 805.

19. P. Barker, 'Tent Schools of the Qashqa'i: A Paradox of Local Initiative and State Control', in,M. E Bonine and N. R. Keddie, 1981, pp. 110–11. From 1973 to 1975 the author, an ex-Peace Corps officer, was a teacher at the Tribal High School in Shiraz, and was closely linked with Muhammad Bahmanbegi and the Office of Tribal Education.

20. Barker, 1981, p.118. In 1956, while at Brigham Young University, Gagon wrote his MA thesis, *A Study of the Development and Implementation of a System of Elementary Education for the Ghasghi (sic) andthe Basseri Nomadic of Fars Ostan, Iran.*

21. W. E. Warne, *Mission for Peace. Point Four in Iran,* Indianapolis, 1956, p.16 (reprinted in 1999, Bethesda, Ibex).

22. C. Hendershot, White Tents in the Mountains: A Report on the Tribal Schools of Fars Province, Tehran, US AID, 1965, pp. 8, 21, cited in S. Shahshahani, 'Tribal Schools of Iran: Sedentarization through Education', in *Nomadic People*, 36/37, 1995, p. 154.

23. Warne, 1956, p. 12.

24. Ibid., p. 18.

25. Ibid., pp. 180–81.

26. Hendershot, pp. 7–9.

27. Hendershot, p. 90.

28. W. Graves, 'Iran: Desert Miracle', in *National Geographic Magazine*, 1975, p. 40.

29. Ministry of Education, *Tribal Education in Iran,* Tehran, 1965, p. 5, 7.

30. Ibid., 1965, p. 7.

31. J. W. Dunhill, *A Report on a Visit to Tribal Schools in the Shiraz Area,* n. p., 1960, p. 1. This report was received by the Unesco headquarters in Paris with a letter dated 9 November, 1960 which was no longer kept with the report.

32. Ibid., p.3.

33. Ministry of Education, *Census,* Tehran, academic year 1977–78 (1356–57), quoted by S. Shahshahani, 1995, p. 145. According to S. Rassekh (Chief of the Social Affairs Section of the Division of Economic Affairs of the Plan Organization), *Education. Third Plan Frame,* Tehran, August 1961, p. 8, only 6,000 children were so far enrolled in the tent schools.

34. Barker, 1981, pp. 114–15.

35. S. A. Wright, Identities and Influence: *Political Organisation in Doshman Ziari, Mamasani, Iran*, PhD dissertation, Lincare College, Oxford, 1985, p.333.

36. G. S. Gagon, *A Study of the Development and Implementation of the Elementary Education for the Ghasghi (sic) and Basseri Nomadic Tribes of the Fars Ostan, Iran*, MA Dissertation, Brigham University, 1956, pp. 91–2, quoted in Barker, 1981, p. 120. The Ministry of Education, 1965, p.5, gives different data: 112 teachers joined the six weeks training course and 106 completed it.

37. Wright, 1985, pp. 335–6.

38. Ibid., p. 334.

39. Ibid., pp. 58, 339.

40. Ministry of Education, *Tribal Education in Iran,* Tehran, 1978, p. 2–3.

41. Wright, 1985, p. 334.

42. Ministry of Education, *Tribal Education in Iran,* Tehran, 1978, p. 6.

43. Ibid., p. 5–6.

44. Ministry of Education, *Tribal Education in Iran,* Tehran, 1965, pp. 9, 11.

45. Wright, 1985, p. 34.

46. Ministry of Education, *Tribal Education in Iran,* Tehran, 1965, p. 3.

47. M. Bahmanbegi, *Orf va adat ashayer-e Fars,* Teheran, 1324 (1945). French translation in V.Monteil, *Les tribus du Fars et la sédentarization des nomades,* Paris, 1966.

48. Monteil, 1966, pp. 136–7.

49. J. S. Szyliowicz, *Education and Modernisation in the Middle East,* London, 1973.

50. N. Barry, 'A Nomad Who Put Schools in Tribal Tents', in *The International Herald Tribune,* 16 September 1971, p. 5.

51. Dunhill, 1960, p. 2–3.

52. Ibid., p. 8.

53. Ibid., p. 5, 7.

54. Ibid., p. 54.

55. Ibid., p. 9.

56. Ibid., p. 7, 10.

57. Ibid., p. 10.

58. Varlet, 1974, pp. 19–20.

59. Ibid., pp. 17–19.

60. Dunhill, 1960, p. 6.

61. L. Beck, 'Tribes and the State in Nineteenth and Twentieth Century Iran' in P. S. Khoury and J. Kostiner (eds.), *Tribes and State Formation in the Middle East,* Berkeley: The University of California Press, 1990, pp. 208–209.

62. Ministry of Education, *Tribal Education in Iran,* Tehran, 1978, p. 12.

63. Ministry of Education, *Tribal Education in Iran,* Tehran, 1978, p. 10.

64. Ministry of Education, *Tribal Education in Iran,* Tehran, 1978, p. 9; Varlet, 1974, p. 8.

65. Ministry of Education, *Tribal Education in Iran,* Tehran, 1978, p. 9.

66. Ministry of Education, *Tribal Education in Iran,* Tehran, 1978, p. 9–10.

67. Ministry of Education, *Tribal Education in Iran,* Tehran, 1978, p. 10.

68. Beck, 1980, pp. 16, 20.

PART V

Tribes, Colonialism and Nationalism

The Social Ontology of Late Colonialism: Tribes and the Mandated State in Iraq[1]

Toby Dodge

Treating obscure bureaucrats as expressions of the Zeitgeist has far-reaching metaphysical implications. It implies that vested ideas, rather than vested interests, are the great determinants of human behaviour; it denies that men can see complex things – societies, economies, polities – 'as they really are', without invoking elaborate theories to explain their chaotic impressions; and it dismisses 'common sense', the last refuge of the pragmatist, as low-grade ideology: a rag bag of rules of thumb, culled from forgotten thinkers. A universe which is full of puppets dancing on intellectual strings leaves little room for heroic individuals exercising free will or heroic masses reacting to changes in the mode of production.[2]

Introduction

The modern Iraqi state was built by British colonial civil servants, in collaboration with Iraqi politicians, during the period from 1914 until, at least,

1932, the year that Iraq achieved her formal independence and entered the League of Nations. The state institutions that came to dominate Iraqi society and the nature of these institutions' relationship with the tribal population were initially constructed, and then directed, under British tutelage. Hence, British conceptions of tribes played a crucial role in the growth of the Iraqi polity and its relations with the state. A close examination of British tribal policy sheds light on the evolution of state-society relations in Iraq, as well as on British attitudes to tribal social structures across the Empire from which these colonial civil servants came.

Previous scholarship on the interaction between the British (at the heart of the nascent Iraqi state) and the tribes (in the rural areas), can be divided into two broad and overlapping approaches. Traditional historiography on the Mandate has been organized around an unproblematized understanding of British Imperialism. At the end of a gruelling war, the British state was short of funds and needed to find collaborators within Iraq to minimise its costs and so allow it to control this newly conquered part of the Middle East. The key agent, i.e. the colonial state, was aware of its limitations but was perceptive enough to recognize which group within Iraqi society was best suited to fill the role of willing helper. The British picked the tribal sheikhs for this role. They arrested the sheikhs' long-term decline in the face of modernity by restoring the sheikhs' position as key sources of local power within rural society. The broad sweep of this argument is reproduced in an unproblematized manner in most work on this period, with varying degrees of detail.[3]

It is tempting to explain Britain's role in Iraq as based purely on the pursuit of strategic interests. But using such a narrow epistemological framework to interpret the varied and detailed archive material leads to a reductive and mono-causal understanding of British attitudes to, and their effect upon, tribal structures. More recent scholarship shows the influence of an innovative Foucaultian approach to the deployment of social categorisation under the mandated state.[4] The one-dimensional projection of instrumental reasoning has now been tempered by conceiving of the apprehension of Iraqi society as being heavily dependent upon modern methods of quantification. This led to the creation of rigid social boundaries around ethnic, religious and tribal distinctions.[5] The forced modernity imposed on Iraq by the British was certainly transformative, but its effects were not always the results intended by those who were formulating and implementing policy.

This approach can be built upon by developing an explanation of Britain's role in Iraq that places the furtherance of interests, however defined, in their social and historical context. We can historicize the mandated state's attitude towards tribes by attempting to identify the social perception of those who staffed its main institutions and formed its policy. By doing this we can then better understand their agency – both conscious and unconscious.

The Ontology of the Social

Social practices are rarely, if ever, transparent to either those charged with implementing and sustaining them or to those caught up in their constraints.[6] Agents in the modern world are restrained by discursive structures, both ideational and material, that are beyond their control and immediate understanding. The thinking and indeed actions of the India and Colonial Office officials in Iraq were a reflection of the societies they were socialized within, reflections both of the English metropolis and its warped reproduction through the prism of Empire.

The approach of these officials can be analysed in Gramscian terms. In this sense the discourse that shaped their perceptions was diffuse in its structure. The 'common sense' assumed of individuals who are deployed to navigate themselves through an unfamiliar society is, on closer inspection, a complex and contradictory discourse. It may, at any one time, hold competing visions in a muddled symmetry, swinging between these in an ontological reductionism as they try to explain different facets of the social world.[7] In the case of Iraq, the majority of colonial officials perceived the area as under-developed or pre-modern, and so would tend to see the social structures as different from their own. A collective ontological perception of society could become dominant because rural Iraq would – within European discourse – represent a pre-modern sphere, unchanged by modernity's drive to individualisation.[8]

The opposition to this would see the Iraqi population as simply that most universal of categories: individuals, rationally prone to maximising their own utility. The collective social structures so fiercely defended by some were judged by this outlook to be not only anachronistic but as already in a condition of partial and unstoppable disintegration. The state they were involved in building had then to aid this process and form direct links with individuals across the rural areas of Iraq.

Within British policy towards tribal communities there were strong tensions between this collectivist approach, i.e. ruling the country through sheikhs and tribal structures, and an individualist approach, i.e. breaking down the already weakened communal allegiances. The removal of collective structures for the later position would become a prerequisite for the normative passage to modernity based upon individualization and the increased power of government.

Town and Country in Iraq

The British staff's comprehension of Iraqi society was heavily dependent upon the imposition of rigid boundaries. It was the urban-rural divide that primarily structured their understanding of the emerging polity. The gulf between the urban-based effendi and the rural tribesmen was the key organising trope around which society was conceived. The *ulema* for example, were not only chastised for being Persian but also for being exclusively 'town dwelling'.[9] Najaf was described with an imagery which subconsciously alluded to the horrors of urbanization and that would not have been out of place in a Dickensian novel. The picture painted was of crowded towns where poverty and 'oppressive wealth' lived side by side.[10]

This anti-urbanism can be partly explained by the fact that Baghdad was the main centre of Arab Nationalism in Iraq. But ideationally the demonising of the cities and their population can be traced back to England.[11] The rise of 'ruralism' in popular British discourse in the 1800s and its great influence after World War One was the cultural background to the Colonial Office employees harbouring such a passionate distaste for urban Iraqis. We can identify similar attitudes and approaches in colonial discourse in both India and Africa. The whole notion of the 'martial races' is structured around the virile qualities of soldiers who have remained untouched by the emasculating effects of modernity and the city.[12]

The notion of the 'Noble Savage', deployed by Rousseau to rail against injustice in Europe, was easily adapted by those who saw the effects of modernity as undermining man's 'natural' abilities and constraining him through complexity and regulation.[13] Although initially constructed as an internal critique of European society, it found its material form in British interactions with the Bedouin.[14] At base, capitalism was seen as negative, destroying stability and tradition and entrapping the essence of man within a selfish and commodified world.[15] To the British the noble Bedouin, untouched by all that was negative about the modern day, stood in stark contrast to the city dwellers who appeared to have succumbed to the temptations of modernism.

In Iraq this anti-urban discourse was predominant. Sir Henry Dobbs, the longest serving High Commissioner under the Mandate, when reviewing the principles that drove his approach, claimed Iraq was unique because:

'The country men, including the inhabitants of the villages, are almost all tribal, unlike the cultivators of Egypt or India or even Persia ... In this respect I doubt whether the conditions of any other country in the world, even of Afghanistan, resemble those of Iraq.'[16]

For Dobbs, as for his staff in Iraq, the prevalence of what he identified as tribes indicated that here was a society only lightly touched by modernity. The tribal system still held sway because capitalist penetration was limited. The notion of rural Iraq was in contrast to the evils of urbanism. This polemical vision was sustained by stressing the difference that separated the two spheres. The Iraqi population had no national spirit because it was 'split by an effendi-tribal breach.'[17] This was mutual and all-powerful, as the propertied and conservative classes regarded the tribesmen as 'little removed from savages'[18] and the tribesmen possessed an 'almost instinctive hostility to Arab 'effendis' in positions of authority.'[19]

For the British the towns had been homogenized into the effendi class and the rural areas into tribesmen. Apart from the unsustainability of such a caricature there is strong evidence that the divide itself was empirically hard to substantiate. Due to the rapid growth of Baghdad's population, 'many townsmen were of relatively recent tribal origin', with some of them retaining their tribal customs and social organisation.[20]

Previous work on Iraq has noted the dichotomy between town dwellers and rural society at the centre of the British conception of Iraq,[21] but this has been interpreted as a conscious effort to categorise and divide society, making it easier to dominate. A closer reading of the archival material, however, gives no support to this position. The officials concerned saw the division as real and they continually worried about its effects on the present and future governments of Iraq.[22] Many of their policy initiatives had the stated outcome of trying to lessen the ramifications of a fractured society. Far from consciously trying to create such divisions they saw these divisions as a negative but pre-existing fact of social relations. Their perception of the divided nature of Iraqi society was much more a subconscious product of their own discursively structured understanding than a conscious policy of rule.

The anti-urbanism at the core of British discourse was combined with a strong unease about the penetration of capitalism into the rural areas. The vehicle for this was the commercial landowner, resident in the cities and motivated by profit with no interest in the welfare of the *fallaheen*. This person was seen as the tool that would eventually destroy the tribal structures that held sway over rural Iraq. For the Divisional Adviser in Dulaim the big-time capitalists already established there were 'parasites on society', positioned in opposition to the tribes, who 'despised the work of the fallah.'[23] An explanation for the constant unrest around land issues in the Muntafiq centred on the imposition of commercial property rights and landlords by Medhet Pasha. From 1920 these landlords 'allied themselves with the extremists and with the merchants of the town known for their talent for intrigue.'[24] Dobbs, in explaining why the Saduns were the core reason for the Muntafiq instability, describes them as 'never truly tribal', 'urban dwelling' and finally Sunni 'city overlords'.[25]

The Nature of Rural Society in Iraq: What Was a Tribe?

For British administrators 'tribal' and 'rural' were most frequently collapsed into one category. The tribal nature of the rural population was the first and dominant category of understanding. For Stephen Longrigg, Political Officer and then Inspector-General of the Revenue Department, 'tribal loyalties prevailed everywhere'. A. T. Wilson, the second High Commissioner in Iraq, recognized the 'peculiar complexity' of Iraq, but then went on to describe this in terms of pastoral tribes, i.e. partly nomadic and sedentary groups who were organised on tribal lines.[26] Official estimates of the numbers of tribespeople in Iraq ranged from the High Commissioner's estimate in 1919 of three quarters of the population, to the 1926 assertion by Kinahan Cornwallis (responsible for overseeing tribal policy at the Interior Ministry) that 'settled tribes ... constitute practically the whole of the rural population of Iraq'.[27]

The conceptual homogenizing of a diverse society was driven by the presuppositions of the collective social ontology with which the staff were working. Following Foucault's approach it can be seen that an understandable 'truth' was being created by the suppression of other competing truth claims. The homogeneous category of 'tribe' was given meaning by marginalising other more ambiguous categories. The space for such a category within the societal vision of the British in Iraq was also bounded by the urban other. The tribe became a receptacle for all that the urban was not.[28]

Layne has identified the creation of such an essentialist category within current anthropological literature,[29] but we find similar if not identical practices occurring in the 1920s in Iraq. What Layne labels the 'pigeonhole model' of identity was working effectively in colonial mentalities. Units of analysis had to be clear and unambiguous, enframing individuals within models of collective identity. The rigidity of the frame and its comparability to other enframed groupings make it difficult to conceive of people belonging to more than one group. Layne is right to identify the origin of enframing in the scientific revolution of the 17th and 18th centuries. But the late colonial discourse at work in Iraq injected this fairly rigid rationality with a romantic conception of its contents.

The ramifications of this approach meant groups or individuals outside urban areas that did not fit into this single category were very difficult to deal with and so were either forcibly integrated or overlooked. The High Commissioner, his staff and the advisors to the government in Baghdad acknowledged the variations of economic and social conditions across Iraq. But the rigid definition applied to rural social structures was all-pervasive. Although tribal disintegration was identified and a major point of discussion, the rigid categorisation of rural areas led to it being understood in terms of the creation of new collective groupings. 'Tribal fragmentation' up until 1932 was seen by the majority not to have resulted in the growth of overt individualisation but in the creation of smaller tribal units and the growth of 'petty sheikhs'.[30] Even on the rare occasion that rural populations were identified as having broken away from the tribal system, those planning the future constitution of Mesopotamia concluded that they could be treated 'in the same manner as tribal districts'.[31]

The idea of 'tribe' was primarily defined externally for the unit itself. The unit was certain to exist, juxtaposed against the non-rural sections of society and more tangibly by other tribes competing for land and government resources, but there was limited investigation into the internal coherence and structure of the collective.[32] A romantic theme of mutual brotherhood ran through the descriptions of tribal life and identity. A. T. Wilson strikes a familiar note when describing the 'unsophisticated' Arab, Kurd or Persian's deeply held loyalty to family and tribe. Although practical, thorough and sustained until death, it appeared to Wilson to be beyond rationality, 'largely independent of admiration or affection for individuals' but giving 'unity and stability to their philosophy of life.'[33] Of all the colonial officials in Iraq, John Glubb had the most intense and extended exposure to the everyday life of both nomadic and sedentary Arabs. Although his exposition of tribal cohesion was, naturally, more detailed and anchored in experience, his understanding was still shot through with romanticism. His written work can be read as an extended homily to a dying and nobler way of life, based on honour and virility.[34]

The tribe was described as a democratic system of equality. Leaders were naturally selected on the basis of strength of character. The individual member gained his definition through the collective. But when the organisation broke down, its members degenerated and became lesser beings. Assistant Political Officer Mylles, when comparing the members of the Dulaim to the Agadat, describes them as 'twice the men', 'chiefly because the tribal organisation is still strong'. The Agadat suffered because their 'tribal spirit' had been broken by the Turks.[35]

The social plane which these groupings existed on was perceived by the British as one structured by anarchy. If the internal life of the tribe was characterised by respect and co-operation, then the external world was more Hobbesian in character. Inter-tribal relationships were defined by the lack of a sovereign state structure to guarantee order. The feeble nature of the Ottoman government had left these groupings to evolve in a violent atmosphere where collective security was the only guarantee of survival.[36] It was the internal cohesion that guaranteed the external nature of the organization. The tribes had been unencumbered by the imposition of external authority. This had left them in a state of nature relying on their natural abilities and the solidarity of their comrades.

Defining the Sheikhs of Iraq: A Romantic Vision Transformed by Rational Imposition

If the dominant vision of rural Iraq was the tribe, then this vague and chimeral collective could only be understood in terms of its sheikh. In the figure of the sheikh, we find the powerful contradictions thrown up when the romantic vision of how Iraqi society should be was imposed upon the material realities of the society the British Imperial power was attempting to rule through its own discursive creation. In trying to impose policy through the authority of the sheikh, an authority already perceived as consensual, they radically changed the nature of this individual's position *vis-à-vis* the rest of the population.[37] The irony of the situation was that the dominant conservative British discourse of ruralism transformed the material realities of Iraqi society by using the allocation of rational administrative methods and the very modern coercive technologies of air power.

This discursive vision was not hegemonic and so caused a continuing and sometimes bitter debate about whether authority and order could be transmitted through the tribal system. For some people, the office of the sheikh had failed to have any meaning long before British troops landed in 1914, while for others its weakness was personified by the 1920 revolt and the ignominious exit of some sheikhs from their supposed areas of influence to British held towns. But the power of the collective romantic discourse meant the vision championed by Sir Henry Dobbs won. This vision focused on the sheikh as the linchpin of rural society and the key to a passive countryside. The mismatch between this powerful ideational construct and the material realities on the ground meant British policy continually threw up aberrations and contradictions. But the fact that Dobbs' approach triumphed and led to a restructuring of Iraqi society was testament to its power to deliver ideational coherence in the face of material contradictions.

The romantic vision through which the British created a notion of rural Iraqi reality was centred upon the figure of the sheikh. The sheikh personified the tribe,[38] its authenticity and character, with those below him not registering in British perceptions or policy. On one level this was explained in terms of ability: those lower down the social hierarchy simply did not have an opinion worth consulting. When it came to gauging the views of tribal populations, the notion of consulting the 'rank and file of the tribesmen, shepherds, marsh dwellers, rice, barley and date cultivators of the Euphrates and Tigris, whose experience of statecraft was confined to speculations as to the performances of their next-door neighbours',[39] was considered ridiculous. Instead, Bell recommended consultations with their immediate chiefs.[40]

Problems arose for both the Iraqis and the British when populations labelled 'tribal' failed to have an identifiable sheikh. For the Iraqis this meant they did not register within the government's vision and had no access to state largesse. For the British these groups appeared sinister, uncontrollable and a source of instability:

'Early in May a large band of miscellaneous tribesmen from the Muntafiq numbering about 5,000 tents crossed into the Sirah Nahiyah of the Kut Division. Trouble was anticipated as the tribesmen were armed and had no recognized headman ...'[41]

A tribe that failed to have a sheikh of recognisable stature was below standard: too deficient to be treated as autonomous.[42]

For the British an 'authentic' or ideal tribe would be hierarchically divided into three categories. At the very peak of tribal authority and the main point of contact with Baghdad would be the paramount sheikh, who, in theory, controlled a whole tribal confederacy, like Ali Sulaiman who ruled the Dulaim on the upper Euphrates or Ibn Suwait who was the paramount sheikh of the Dhafir. The position was supposed to have been inherited 'in accordance to tribal tradition'.[43] Beneath the paramount were the 'big sheikhs' or sheikhs of tribes that made up the confederacy, and beneath them the head of the tribal sub-section. These two categories were not universally applicable. Some tribes did not have sheikhs, and the role of the tribal sub-head was often confused with that of the sarkal. [44] The role of these two positions was lower in status than the paramount. So much so, that the High Commissioner went to great lengths to discourage all but very minor dealings between the British staff, the Iraqi government and tribal sub-sections.

In this idealised tribal organization a loose form of democracy permeated the three levels of the tribe. The sheikh dominated and came to represent this structure by force of personality and natural intelligence. The British saw the whole collective organised around a community of interest. [45] The sheikh could thus be identified and admired for his position. Bell amongst others frequently referred to this group as 'great personalities' and 'aristocrats', [46] with the system generally being maintained in a 'natural equilibrium.'

The sheikhs' offspring were not only 'born to rule', but were also physically much more suited to take their place in the nascent army of the Iraqi state. When he was recruiting for the Iraqi army in 1929 the Inspector General requested that Assyrian tribal boys should be sought out for admission to the Military College. These boys were required to bring with them a certificate of their social status, 'completed by an official not lower than a Qaimmaqam (stating that) the candidate is a son of a sheikh or head of a tribe.' [47]

The sheikh and his relatives became a receptacle for the colonial romantic vision. This is typified by Captain Holt's description of Sheikh Mahmud's surrender to British forces in May 1931. As a long-time Oriental Secretary to the High Commissioner (the post held by Gertrude Bell until her death), Holt played a key role in forming policy and disseminating information from Iraq to Britain and India. Sheikh Mahmud, on the other hand, had been the major challenge to British and then Iraqi state dominance of Kurdistan since 1920. [48] Upon Mahmud's capture Holt wrote a note detailing his history, a note which was full of romantic imagery and underlined by a lament for times past.

Holt describes the first engagement Mahmud had with Turkish forces during the battle of Shu'aibah in April 1915. Mahmud, 'like many other tribal chiefs of ancient lineage', had arrived with his feudal levies to do battle with the foreign invaders. Then, after prayers:

> believing that the age of chivalry was still with them, they swept forward on their gaily caparisoned horses to drive their enemies back into the sea which, it was said, was their home. Taunts and challenges were shouted at the still invisible enemy but only the shriek of shrapnel answered and a dozen saddles emptied and a score of horses fell. Ardour was daunted, home became dearer than glory and life on earth more blissful than the

hope of Paradise and the hosts of chivalry melted away; each man the richer by at least two rifles taken from the Turkish wounded. [49]

Describing Mahmud's final surrender to the British, Holt's admiration for the man and the passing of what he represented, is evident from his gushing prose:

'As he rode to captivity after his surrender at Penjwin the Kurds streamed down from the villages on the hill sides to cluster round him and to kiss his hand and the eyes of many were filled with tears as they bid him farewell.'

'His tyranny is the will of a tyrant but it is mellowed by the generosity of a prince. If he is cruel, where are the witnesses? Not among the villagers who press around to kiss his hand in the hour of his defeat, nor among the officers of the Royal Air Force who have fought against him (and of whom two have been his prisoners), who are all eager to say a cheery word of comfort to him.'

'An outlaw brigand, let that be granted, so were Garibaldi and Mustafa Kamal. But when all has been said on both sides perhaps the wisest judgement is that his greatest fault is that he was born a century too late.'[50]

Here, in an official report circulated as far afield as Whitehall and New Delhi, we find the romantic lament for a chivalrous hero of old. Mahmud is described as a figure who would not have seemed out of place in Sherwood Forest, battling the negative forces of modernity and 'progress' with common decency and courage. It was this romanticised figure of the tribal sheikh that gave the British their coherent view of Iraqi rural life. This dominant conception of the structure of Iraqi society had the most powerful effect on how the British deployed their military power and financial largesse. The sheikh delivered comprehension of an alien world and provided a material order. The immediate goals and long term policies of the Mandate state were imposed on Iraq through what was seen as the sheikh's social power. It was this combination of a romantic vision and a rational method that drove the British approach to Iraq.

The tensions involved in ruling through this romantic discourse can be seen in the mechanics for official recognition of tribal sheikhs and the administration's efforts to secure them in their positions. Tribal sheikhs were divided by colonial officials into 'nominal' and 'recognized'. Both categories of sheikhs were seen to possess the degree of social stature needed to control a given area, as they were the pinnacles of organic and authentic social structures. However, official recognition was dependent upon the suitability of the individual to rule in a manner that conformed to British notions of administration and delivered guarantees of order. Thus, two types of sheikh were identified, and although both sprang from Iraqi society those favoured by the British were the ones who delivered what was needed of them, and they were built up as romantic figures.

For a sheikh, government recognition brought with it responsibility, reward and prestige. For guaranteeing the good behaviour of the tribe or a particular section, a sheikh received a monthly subsidy and, in some cases, the right to regulate the movement of all the Bedouin out of his designated area to markets and urban centres. Fahad Beg ibn Hadhdhal, for example, received a subsidy of Rs. 12,000 a month.[51] The office of recognized sheikh clarified and strengthened his position, as his nearest rivals were ordered to submit to his authority under threat of state intervention. They would only gain recognition and a place within this hierarchy if they agreed to his authority:

Jaid ibn Mijland of the Dahamshah ... has been informed in the presence of Fahad Beg and his son Mahrut that Fahad has been recognized paramount Sheikh of the ʿAmarat, of which the Dahamshah are part, and has the right to grant passes for the purchase of supplies, Jaid is expected to be loyal to the King, to recognize the paramountcy of Fahad, to have no dealings with ʿIbn Saʿud and to help Fahad in carrying out his obligations to Government. Though he is to be treated as Sheikh of Dahamshah, he is not to be given official recognition until it is seen whether the reconciliation with Fahad is genuine. Jazzaʾ al Mijlad has been released on security of Rs. 5,000, but will not at present be allowed to leave Baghdad.[52]

Rationalism as a method of governing was deployed to give definition to romantically constructed categories of collective organisation. The state in Iraq, although ruling through what it perceived as indigenous institutions, had by the act of utilising them, changed them. What had previously been 'fuzzy' communities had now become rigidly defined.[53] By imposing precision on the role of sheikh, by demanding an instrumental relationship between him and members of his tribe, the role of the sheikh was necessarily transformed.

Even when accompanied with generous financial rewards, 'natural' candidates for the now onerous position of recognized sheikh were surprisingly difficult to locate. An intelligence report for 1923 details how the coercive power of the state was deployed to give material reality to the discursive vision of Iraq. Khashan al Jaziʾ, the 'nominal Sheikh of the Barkat', was summoned to Samawah to see the Qaimmaqam.[54] His adamant refusal to accept responsibility for any section of the tribe including his 'own village' was greeted with incredulity which increased when other figures of responsibility in the district acted likewise:

'It is probable that he was merely sent in by the tribe to find out what were the intentions of the Government ...'[55]

'On the 24th 'Azzarah al Ma'jun, nominal Sheikh of the Sufran, reported. He declined to take responsibility for the 'Atawah and Fallaha sections, but said he would guarantee the rest ...'[56]

'It was considered that he had not attempted to comply with the conditions imposed upon him. On November 30, bombing was begun and on December 1, the Sufran headman came in and accepted ... terms'[57]

The 'nominal sheikh' called in by the Qaimmaqam was not merely bloody-minded in resisting government demands but may have been unable to deliver the type of order required. After the area had suffered the shock of aerial bombardment, the population had no choice but to deliver the individuals identified by the administration as their leaders. These individuals then acted as the liaison between government and tribe. The sheikh was designated as responsible for the behaviour of every member of his tribe. In return he became a conduit for government resources no matter what his original status within the tribe was. Authority, therefore, was given to an individual and enforced by air power. The tension between the romantic vision of tribal life and its instrumental applications through the figure of the sheikh drove Britain's approach to the tribes. The collective perception of Iraqi society was subconscious but it structured the conscious policy of how Iraq was to be ruled.

Where those individuals who were identified as sheikhs or sarkals became unruly or troublesome, they were replaced by more suitable candidates. But because instrumental concerns were shaped by a discursive vision, the replacement had also to come from the sheikhly stratum. For example, when Hamudah of the al-Hasan became an outlaw, his nephew was placed on his land. A problem then arose when Hamudah wanted to make peace with the government:

'His character and record forbid his reinstatement in his old position, while to leave him at large, nursing a bitter grievance and dispossessed of his lands would be to sow the seeds of certain trouble in the future.'[58]

If, despite government recognition, sheikhs proved unable to restrain the population under their control, they ran the risk of having their tribe de-recognized and their lands allotted to others.[59] It was not the system of tribal organisation or sheikhly power that was at fault but the individual personalities of the 'defective' sheikhs or the 'untribal' nature of their tribes. Clearly, social realities were being created on the ground, which in the case of Sheikh Sultan was the threat of his tribe being disbanded and its members merged with another because of its lawlessness.

As the Iraqi state became more established and monetary pressure became greater, subsidies were replaced by grants of land. The designated sheikhs quickly learnt what was required of them and how they could manipulate the key concerns of the British. Ali Sulaiman, the paramount sheikh of the Dulaim, upon learning that his subsidy was to be cut, argued that it was not the monetary value that concerned him but he valued it for the prestige that it brought him in that he appeared to his tribes as a valued servant of Government.

> Taking a broader view he then went on to explain that the tribes judge by what they saw and that the fact that he ceased to draw an allowance without receiving any recognition from his past services would be taken to mean that he no longer retained the confidence of Government although of course he was satisfied that this was not the case. His prestige would suffer accordingly and his advice would not be listened to so readily. He presumed that Government was aware that many of the tribes were far from satisfied and that there was a considerable amount of talk abroad that a return of Turkish officials would be an improvement on the existing regime. The last thing in the world he wanted was *thaurah* and all his influence would be thrown into the scales to prevent this. He could not help feeling however that the Government forces in this area were small to cope with any disturbances which might arise and consequently anything which led to a reduction of his own influence he viewed with a certain amount of misgiving.[60]

The shallow foundations of sheikhly authority became increasingly apparent after the chaos of the 1920 revolt subsided. The case of Ali Sulaiman not only highlights the wider problem in Iraq but also the divisions within the Mandate administration on the perception of tribal structures. In 1922, Yetts, a divisional advisor, saw Sulaiman as a potential pillar of government control:

'... if a place can be found in the body politic for the type which Sheikh Ali Sulaiman represents with their rights clearly defined the whole-hearted support of this class can be counted on.'[61]

But by 1924 it was apparent that the ability of Ali Sulaiman to wield, on his fellow Dulaim tribesmen, the type of influence needed by the British was doubtful. After the 1920 uprising several sectional leaders had recognized Sulaiman as their paramount sheikh in an attempt to avoid British retribution for their part in the disturbances. But four years on he was unable to collect revenue from sarkals without government support. The Administrative

Inspector in Dulaim saw Sulaiman as a hindrance to state control with little or no influence.

'Ali Sulaiman may be regarded in Baghdad as paramount Sheikh of the Dulaim but to the Liwa authorities it is painfully obvious he relies more and more on Government support to keep up his position. One issue seems clear that with gradual disintegration of the tribal system it will be increasingly difficult to find room in the numerous constituencies of the Dulaim Confederacy for both the Sheikh and Sarkal. The Sarkal has long regarded the Sheikh as an incubus which he will sooner or later throw off. At present he is waiting for a sign from Government.'[62]

Cornwallis, the advisor to the Ministry of Interior, supported this view. Arguing against the position of the High Commissioner, Henry Dobbs, that Sulaiman was necessary for the preservation of order near to the Syrian border, he stated that the main force for law and order in Dulaim had long since been the Liwa police.[63]

The High Commissioner responded to this interpretation of policy with great vigour,

'The position which I take up is that it is essential to preserve the authority of 'Ali Sulaiman over the *badu* portion of his tribe for the purpose of making the desert routes safe and that it is almost impossible to do so if his authority over the more settled portion of his tribe is undermined. He can't well become a mere 'rentier' with regards to the settled portion, without losing his hold over the *badu* portion also; for there is no very clear dividing line between them. Another reason for not lessening his authority over the settled portion is that we have no adequate machinery except the Sheikhship for controlling the Dulaim in their relations with the Aqaidat which are so important from the point of view of our relations with Syria.'[64]

For Dobbs, Ali Sulaiman's power was a natural facet of his position within his tribe. Any reduction in Sulaiman's power was therefore caused by external influences. In this case Dobbs saw it as a direct consequence of state interference. To this end, he argued, the police should be kept out of Dulaim affairs in all cases but those of murder. Everything else should be referred to Sulaiman for resolution so his power as a tribal sheikh could then return to its natural level unencumbered by the negative incursions of modernity in the form of employees of the state.

The policy of subsidising sheikhs came under repeated attack from the Iraqi cabinet. As Britain placed strict budgetary restraints on the Iraqi government the money spent on underwriting the sheikhs became a contentious issue.[65] Cornwallis was aware of this and the ramifications it had for policy:

The main point ... is to maintain the authority of all the sheikhs and to use it to reinforce the Police. This is the policy which Administrative Inspectors and I have always adopted. It is not a policy of which any Arab townsman approves and though it has been outwardly accepted as a necessity, one must always be on the lookout for attempts to run counter to it.[66]

The clash in perspectives between the British advisors and the urban politicians was, in this and many other cases, put down to the townsmen's ignorance and fear of anything outside their metropolitan domain. This itself sprung from a collectivist social ontology which exaggerated the urban-rural divide. It was this that allowed Cornwallis and Dobbs to override cabinet concerns about budgets or the power of sub-state actors.

Henry Dobbs and his staff gained their ideational understanding of Iraqi society through a discourse which romanticised the tribes as an egalitarian collective of actors personified by their sheikh. But by using this idea to bring order to Iraq they fundamentally transformed its material reality. By rationally defining the romantic vision of tribe they turned a fuzzy and overdetermined structure into an enumerated and rigidly defined one. The sheikh became key to the instrumental use of the tribe. Whatever his role had been before he was identified by the British, he now became the key interlocutor between rural society and the Mandate state. If he failed to carry out the tasks assigned to him, the coercive power of the state was deployed to bring him, and more importantly his tribe, into line. Air power was used to create the facts on the ground that the British believed were already there.

Conclusion

The predicted future of tribal organizations in Iraq is a strong indication of how these social structures were perceived. For example, two of the most prominent historians of the Mandate period, Batatu and Sluglett, when describing tribal disintegration tend to ascribe unilinear notions of development to Iraq and, by implication, to the wider non-Western world. Sluglett sees 'tribal disintegration' as inevitable and caused by the 'natural forces arising from the process of sedentarisation'.[67] Batatu considerably broadens the reasons for the erosion of tribal loyalties to include, '... river navigation (1859), the appearance of the electric telegraph (1861), the attendant deepening of English economic penetration and tying Iraq to the world of capitalism, the opening up of state schools (since 1869), the development of the press (especially after 1908), and the repeated attempts by the Turkish governing authorities between 1831 and 1914 to gather all the means of power into its hands ...'[68]

The implication of both approaches was to see tribes' subjective loyalty to a grouping or objective social organisation, as anachronistic. For both Sluglett and Batatu these organisations could not possibly survive the onward march of modernity and capitalism. They both saw tribalism as inescapably linked to pre-capitalist social relations and so destined for destruction.

Interestingly, this conception of tribes as doomed to inevitably succumb to the onward march of progress was a theme that united most of those in government service across the Empire. Lord Lugard, the great promoter of tribal organization, had a rigidly evolutionary view of how societies developed. For him, African society could be divided into three groups. At one end of the evolutionary road to development were 'advanced communities' and at the other 'primitive tribes' who recognized no chief and were still in the patriarchal stage of social organisation.[69] In between were the organized tribes that Lugard saw as the best basis for social life in Africa. The 'Europeanised Africans' whom he despised were excluded from this model of gradual development because they were aberrations; they had stepped out of the natural order of things, had tried to move too fast, and in the process had lost authenticity.

For Lugard, then, the process of tribal disintegration may have been lamentable and its progression slow but it was, finally, inevitable. 'These processes of natural evolution ...' can 'be traced in every civilisation known in history'.[70] What they resulted in was, finally, overt individualisation and 'a disintegrating effect on tribal authority and institutions, and on the conditions of native life.'[71]

What made Africa different from the general flow of evolutionary history was a process driven with undue haste by European intervention. It was, thus, up to the Europeans to regulate the process as much as possible and to impose constraints on a dynamic process that they themselves had created.

A variety of such views could be found amongst the colonial staff in Iraq from 1914 to 1932. From Sir Henry Dobbs, the most ardent defender of the sheikh and his tribe, to Sir Ernest Dowson, the land expert and passionate promoter of individualism, the life span of the 'tribe' was seen as, inevitably, limited. Its demise was unstoppable. The reasons for this process of decline, and whether or not it was a good thing, divided the opinion of those in Iraq.

In the early stages of British intervention in Iraq it was the policies of the Ottoman Empire that were seen as causing tribal disintegration. The Ottoman state, weak but devious, had planted the seeds of disunity amongst the once great tribal federations.

'Instead of utilising the power of the sheikhs, the Turks pursued their classic policy of attempting to improve their own position by the destruction of such native elements of order as were in existence.' 'To recognize local dominion and yoke it to his service was beyond the conception of the Turk, and the best that can be said for his uneasy seat upon the whirlwind was that he managed to retain it'.[72]

The Ottoman state was personified by the 'feeble Turkish tax gatherers' who brought with them the contaminating effects of modernity. The results were 'endless bickering' amongst the tribes and ' ... the tendency towards levelling, division, disunity.'[73] For Longrigg this led to the visible decline in the lifestyle and character of the tribesmen as they struggled to adjust their lives to the new and unfamiliar situation.

Once the mandated state had been established it became obvious to the British personnel that the onward march of modernity was unstoppable. It seemed to them that their very presence and the order and stability which they brought would eventually change Iraqi society. Although there was broad agreement that this was bound to happen, attitudes towards the process and estimates of how long it would take were far from uniform. Again the divisions over this issue can be categorised by looking at the social ontology that structured the different interpretations. For example, as Sir Ernest Dowson travelled through Iraq compiling his report on land tenure regimes, he identified a general process of increased tribal sedentarization and decreased tribal cohesion and authority. This he directly linked to the spread of government authority:

'... Everywhere I was advised tribal disintegration was accelerating, everywhere the tribesman was becoming an individualist and wanting his individual holding.'[74]

For Dowson this was a positive process; the rational individual, liberated from the constraints of the tribal system, could now pursue his or her life with all the freedom that a modern state and civilisation allowed them. All that had happened was the restraints of the pre-modern world had been lifted from the shoulders of the individual, leaving them to flourish.[75]

The opposite position to Dowson was well represented by John Glubb. He recognized that the tribal system was in decline. The cause of its terminal ill-health was, for Glubb, the arrival of technology. It was the car, the road and the aeroplane that killed the tribal system.[76] But far from seeing this as the welcome effect of 'progress', Glubb laments the passing of what he labelled the 'patriarchal system'. For although, according to Glubb, patriarchy was referred to with 'contempt' by Europeans. . . 'it had many advantages. Basically it was founded on the mutual love of the governor and the governed.'[77]

Glubb, like many of his colleagues, was deeply uneasy about the disruption he was causing. In a diary entry in April 1923 he rails against Woodrow Wilson, the British press and politicians who ' . . . continue to demand that the nations of Asia and Africa should make a clean cut with their past, and at one fell stroke, adopt the mentality and traditions of the Western democracies.' He concludes, 'Would it not be more practical, as well as more polite, if we left these nations to govern themselves in their own way?'[78] For Glubb and many of his colleagues the legacy they brought to Iraq, the modernity that destroyed the tribal system, was far from straightforward, bringing in its wake many consequences they believed to be negative.

Yet the diverse interpretations detailed above were all united by a common conclusion: the inevitable demise of the tribe. Even a cursory glance at present-day Iraq shows that the obituaries for tribal allegiances and the figure of the sheikh, however defined, seem extremely premature.[79] So what was it about a diverse range of scholars and colonial officials with divergent views that allowed them to agree on this one issue, the unsustainability of tribes, whether as social groupings or as objects for identity definition and loyalty?

Both broad approaches identified above were ultimately reductionist in their ontology. In order to impose meaning upon the concept they were using (in this case the notion of tribe), other categories were either collapsed into or dominated by it. For example, Dowson sees the individual as the ultimate and sovereign unit of analysis. The individual's agency explains her or his actions and the social groupings these people choose to be a part of. For this model, as for Dowson and Batatu, the persistence of tribal units and allegiances in Iraq was wrong. Rational individuals in a capitalist system would not choose to have their options constrained by the existence of a tribal structure through which social interactions were arranged. For Dowson the tribes were slowly and irrevocably disintegrating, driven away by the demands of individuals for autonomy. Batatu, on the other hand, looks to the British for the explanation of why these anachronistic tribal structures did not disappear with Iraq's integration into the world capitalist system. It was the colonial state that stopped the unilinear development of capitalism, and had stepped in, with its own interests in mind, to artificially bolster the sheikhs and the tribal system.[80] This was to be a system which hampered the development of Iraq, long after the Mandate was over.

The other way of analysing the demise of tribal structures is that expressed by both Glubb and Dobbs. Here the tribe as a social unit was the ultimate causative structure. Individuals in Iraq gained their agency within the confines of the larger unit. The unit was rigidly defined with no room for ambiguity. It has been pointed out by Layne that this approach constructs tribespeople as '... a distinct and unique social type ... If viewed from the point of view of an organic model of culture in which a culture is likened to a body, if any one of these elements were to be missing, say tent dwelling, the culture is maimed.'[81]

For Dobbs and those with his social perception, the essence of the tribe was not only its rural setting and collective organisation but also its essence as a pre-modern, anti-capitalist way of living. Dobbs and the majority of the British administration accepted but did not welcome the inevitable triumph of modernity. It was because of this that the sheikh, the tribe and the essence of what Iraq was to them was bound slowly to disappear as it got swallowed up in the pernicious mediocrity of the modern world. The tribal system viewed in this way could not change, it was static, if it reacted (as it must) to the new circumstances within which it found itself, it must ultimately perish.

A third way of viewing the notion of tribe, the role of the individual and the effects of modernity, would be to see social structures and individual agency as distinct and very different entities. Social structures were certainly greater than the sum of their parts, i.e. individuals, and so could not be reduced to them. But it is also clear that individuals have a relative (if limited) autonomy in the way they relate to the structure they find themselves born into. The society that the Iraqi individual was born into 'always already' pre-existed her or him. But the individual in acting within these various social structures, in this case the tribe, had the possibility of changing them as they reproduced them: '... (If) society is already made, then any concrete human praxis or, if you like act of objectivation, can only modify it; and the totality of such acts sustain or change it.'[82]

To seek to judge what category was more factually accurate – the individual or the tribe – is to ask the wrong type of question. Society cannot be identified separately from its effects, i.e. the actions of humans, but social structures have a material dimension and cannot be reduced to the human consciousness they are dependent upon. The tribe cannot, then, be judged as an objective structural relationship without doing damage to explaining its power and significance. As Iraqi society changed, the tribe became equally important as a reference of apparent social certainty in a confusing and rapidly changing world. Crucially, because tribal loyalties were based on how people saw themselves as well as on the tribes' collective role as organised structures, they continued to persist and remain salient to people's lives long after the structural framework within which these identities were created had been transformed by new structural realities.

Notes

1. Earlier versions of this paper have been presented at the Middle East History Seminar, School of Oriental and African Studies, the Middle East Studies Association 32nd Annual Meeting, Chicago, the Centre for Middle Eastern and Islamic Studies, University of Durham and the Middle East Studies Forum, Birkbeck College. I would like to thank participants at those meetings as well as Clare Day, Nick Hostettler, Roger Owen, John Sidel and Charles Tripp for their comments.

2. Clive Dewey, *Anglo-Indian Attitudes: The Mind of the Indian Civil Service*, Hambledon Press, London, 1993, pp. vii-viii.

3. This school of thought has in Hanna Batatu its most detailed and polemical exponent, see, *The Old Social Classes and the Revolutionary Movements of Iraq. A Study of Iraq's Old Landed and Commercial Classes and of its Communists, Ba'thists and Free Officers*, Princeton: Princeton University Press, 1989, p. 88. Also see Helmut Mejcher, *Imperial Quest for Oil: Iraq 1910-1928*, Oxford: Ithaca Press for St Antony's College, 1976, Mohammad A. Tarbush, *The Role of the Military in Politics. A Case Study of Iraq to 1941*, Routledge, Kegan Paul PLC, London, 1985, pp. 25, 41, and Marion Farouk-Sluglett and Peter Sluglett 'Iraq Before the Revolution of 1958', in Marion Farouk-Sluglett and Peter Sluglett, *Iraq Since 1958, From Revolution to Dictatorship*, I.B. Tauris and Company, London, 1990, pp. 32–33. To some extent the exception to this can be found in Peter Sluglett's, *Britain in Iraq 1914–1932*, London for St Antony's College: Ithaca Press, Oxford University, 1976.

4. See Samira Haj, *The Making of Iraq, 1900–1963, Capital, Power and Ideology*. New York: State University of New York Press, 1997, and Roger Owen, 'Class and Class Politics in Iraq before 1958: The Colonial and Post-Colonial State,' in Robert A. Fernea and Wm. Roger Louis (eds.), *The   Iraqi Revolution of 1958, The Old Social Classes Revisited.* London: I.B. Tauris, 1991. In Haj's case the influence of Foucault appears to have been mediated through the Subaltern Studies school of Indian historiography; in Owen's case through the work of Timothy Mitchell.

5. Haj, ibid. , pp. 146–7 and Owen, ibid., p. 158.

6. This is not to ignore the fact that there are obvious differences in power relations between different individuals and groups in any given circumstances.

7. See Antonio Gramsci, *Selections from the Prison Notebooks*, edited and   translated by Quintin Hoare and Geoffrey Nowell Smith, Lawrence and Wishart, London, 1971, pp. 327–330 and Stuart Hall, Bob Lumley and Gregor McLennan, 'Politics and Ideology: Gramsci,' in Gregor McLennan and the editorial board of the Centre for Contemporary Cultural Studies. *On Ideology*, London: Hutchinson and Company, 1977, p. 49.

8. For the deployment of the argument in the African case see Tim Youngs, *Travellers in Africa British Travelogues, 1850–1900*, Manchester: Manchester University Press, 1994, pp. 5, 41–43, 201.

9. Stephen Hemsley Longrigg, *'Iraq, 1900 to 1950. A Political, Social, and E c o n o m i c History*, Oxford: Oxford University Press, 1953, p. 10.

10. Public Records Office (PRO) Colonial Office (CO) 696/1, Vol. 1, Reports of Administration for 1918 of Divisions and Districts of the Occupied Territories in

Mesopotamia, Shamiyah Division Annual Administration Report, 1 January to 31 December 1918, p. 65. Also see PRO Air Ministry Overseas Commands (AIR) 23/382, I/130, Intelligence Reports on Internal Politics, Baghdad, 1930–1932, p. 26a.

11. See Martin J. Wiener, *English Culture and the Decline of the Industrial Spirit. 1850–1980*, London: Penguin Books, 1992, p. 6.

12. See V. G. Kiernan, *The Lords of Human Kind. European attitudes to the Outside World in the Imperial age*, Penguin Books, Middlesex, 1972, p. 55.

13. See Kiernan, ibid., p. 23.

14. See Kathryn Tidrick, *Heart Beguiling Araby, The English Romance with Arabia*, I.B. Tauris and Co., London, 1981, p. 30, and James Morris, *Farewell the Trumpets, An Imperial Retreat*, London: Penguin Books, 1978, p. 264.

15. See Youngs, ibid, p. 89.

16. Henry Dobbs to Louis Amery, Secretary of State for the Colonies, 4 December 1928, Box 427/13/127, *The Sudan Collection*, Durham University Library, p. 4.

17. PRO CO 730/40, CO 33280, 4 July 1923, *Local forces in Iraq*, Minutes, by Meinertzhagen, 10 October 1923, p. 734.

18. PRO CO 730/1, Vol. 1, Despatch 9829, Mesopotamian Intelligence Report No. 4, dated 31 December 1920, Proceedings of the Council of Ministers.

19. Box 303/1/67, Sudan Archives, Durham University Library, P. 8253/19, Despatch from the Civil Commissioner, Mesopotamia, to Secretary of State for India, No. 344436/75/19, Office of the Civil Commissioner Baghdad, 15 November 1919, p. 7.

20. See Batatu, ibid., p. 13, and Faleh A. Jabar's chapter in this volume.

21. See Batatu, ibid., Haj, ibid., p. 146 and Owen, ibid., p. 158.

22. See for example PRO CO 730/14, p. 189, *Report by His Britannic Majesty's Government on the Administration of Iraq for the period April 1923–December 1924*, London, Published by His Majesty's Stationary Office 1925, Colonial No. 13, Section 28, Report by His Britannic Majesty's Government to the Council of the League of Nations on the Administration of Iraq for the Year 1925 Colonial No. 21, issued by the Colonial Office H. M. Stationary Office, London 1926, p. 138, CO 730/1 Iraq Vol. 1 Despatch No. 9829, CO 730/40, CO 33280, 4th July 1923, Letter from Dobbs to Devonshire, 20 June 1923, p. 739, CO 730/57, CO 3271 Letter from Dobbs to Devonshire, 10 January 1924, to name but a few.

23. PRO CO 730/5, CO 50265, 10th October 1921. Report of Divisional Adviser, Dulaim 15th August to 31st August, p. 245.

24. The Baghdad High Commission Files (BHCF), Indian National Archive, New Delhi, File No. 19/1, Vol. No. IV, Intelligence Report No. 16, Baghdad 15 August 1922.

25. BHCF, File No. 6/34/55, Finance: Revenue, D. O./8165, From the Secretariat to the High Commissioner, to S. H. Longrigg, 14 July 1926, p. 57.

26. Longrigg, *Iraq, 1900–1950*, ibid., p. 8 and A. T. Wilson, *Loyalties, Mesopotamia*, Volume II, 1917–1920, *A Personal and Historical Record*, London: Oxford University Press, June 1931, p. 78.

27. Box 3030/1/67, Sudan Collection, Durham University Library, P 8253/19, Despatch from the Civil Commissioner, Mesopotamia to the Secretary of State for

India, 15 November, 1919. Also see PRO CO 730/95, Iraq 1926, Vol. No. 4, Despatches August to September, Secret From Dobbs to Amery, September 1926.

28. Michel Foucault, *The Archaeology of Knowledge and the Discourse on Language*, Barnes and Nobles Books, New York, 1993, pp. 48–9.

29. See Linda L. Layne, *Home and Homeland. The Dialogics of Tribal and National Identities in Jordan*, Princeton: Princeton University Press, 1994, p. 6.

30. See for example PRO CO 696/1, *Iraqi Administration Reports 1917–1918*, p. 10. This describes the riverine tribes around Samarra as forming 'a swarm of tiny self-contained communities, owing no allegiance or connection one with other or with outside tribes ... in all the tribes inhabiting this district number 64.'

31. India Office Library (IOL) L/P&S/10/756, Political Department, India Office, 1 November 1919, B. 335, *The Future Constitution of Mesopotamia*, p. 79, by C. C. Garbett.

32. Longrigg, *Iraq, 1900 to 1950*, ibid., p. 23.

33. Wilson, ibid., Vol. II, p. 71.

34. For a wonderful example of this see, John Glubb, *Arabian Adventures. Ten Years of Joyful Service*, London: Cassell, 1978, p. 97.

35. The Agadat or Aqaidat, Albu Kamal, whose paramount sheikh was 'Abdul Karim Pasha al Nijris, were based on the Euphrates as far west as Dair al Zor. See IOL, L/P&S/10/621, P6705, *Notes on the Tribes and Shaikhs of Anah-Albu Kamal District*, by Captain C. C. Mylles, APO, 1920, p. 7. A similar perception is to be found in Major C. F. MacPherson's description of the Bani Hasan in the Hillah district in 1917. They were 'a bad lot and a low class of Arab.' Adding in support of this classification that they were 'split up into innumerable small sections, independent and owing allegiance to no one.' *Administrative Report by Major C. F. MacPherson, Political Officer, Hillah District, 1917*, in PRO CO 696/1, *Iraq Administration Reports, 1917–1918*, p. 106. Also see John Glubb, *Arabian Adventures*, ibid, p. 65, who when comparing the semi-settled Dulaim to the Anaizi, comments ' ... there was about him (the Anaizi) an indefinable air of aristocracy, as compared to with the Dulaim yokels.'

36. See for example, PRO CO 696/1, *Iraq Administration Reports 1917–1918*, p. 119, Hillah Division, *Review of District Administration Reports*, 1 January to 31 December, 1918.

37. See Batatu, ibid., pp. 77, 99, 110.

38. D. G. Hogarth, *Arab Bulletin, Bulletin of the Arab Bureau in Cairo*, No. 1, 1916, Number 32, November 26, Archive Editions, 1986, p. 489, argues that the unity of the Anazeh can only be defined by their 'veneration for the Sheikh of the Tayyar house ...'

39. Gertrude Bell, *Mesopotamia: Review of Civil Administration*, PRO Foreign Office (FO) 371/5081, E13898, p. 150.

40. Bell, ibid, p. 197.

41. BHCF, File Number 19/1, No. 5, *Intelligence Report No. 11*, Baghdad 1 June 1923, p. 4, paragraph 412. This lack of control resulted in the threat of aerial action on the supposedly leaderless tribespeople. For a similar event and reaction see, PRO AIR 23/546, dated 4 June 1923, Operations in Basrah, Amarah and Nasiriyah, Part II.

42. Dobbs claimed in May 1920, 'the really important tribes and their leading divisions are well known.' See IOL, L/P&S/18 B. 342, Mesopotamian Constitution.

Memorandum by Mr. H. R. C. Dobbs C.S.I., Foreign Secretary to the Government of India, on the proposals of the Bonham-Carter Committee, 26 May 1920, p. 3.

43. IOL, L/P&S/10/761, P. 2581, Memo No. 7442, dated 5 December 1920, from the Political Officer, Nasiriyah Division.

44. The categories of Sub-sheikh and Sarkal are separated in British definitions by their differing roles and authority. The Sarkal is seen as more of an economic and rational category and so less authoritative within the tribe. For a detailed study of the role sarkals played in the agricultural production in Iraq see Albertine Jwaideh, 'Aspects of Land Tenure and Social Change in Lower Iraq During Late Ottoman Times', in Tarif Khalidi (ed), *Land Tenure and Social Transformation in the Middle East*, Beirut: American University of Beirut, 1984, pp. 343–49.

45. See Sluglett, ibid., p. 240. For further examples see, BHCF, File Number 6/34/22, Heading Finance, Subject Mr. S. H. Longrigg's note on Revenue Policy in Iraq. Note by the High Commissioner, 10 July 1926, pp. 43–44. In this, Dobbs argues vehemently that any sheikh's desire to oppress his tribesmen ' … is much more effectively restrained by tribal custom … ' 'The position of the tribal sheikh depends so much upon the acquiescence and good will of his tribesmen, that he cannot afford to oppress them or rack rent beyond a certain limit … '

46. See for example, *Bell's letter to Sir Valentine Chirol*, 29 January 1918, Box 303/4/189, Sudan Archive, Durham University.

47. See BHCF, File No. 4/75, Heading the Iraqi Army, No. CRIA/423(A)2. 34/2.' Iraq Army HQ, 23 June 1929, signed by the Inspector General 'Iraq Army, p. 14. Also see BHCF, File 4/14/19 II. Subject: Iraqi Army Personnel. Miscellaneous, p. 4. Ministry of Defence, 13th April 1932, No. 3147 From the Inspector General Iraq Army to F. H. Humphrys, the High Commissioner.' Courage and character, not education, are … the prime requirements at present and they are most likely to be found in the sons of sheikhs – desert or Kurdish – and possibly Assyrian officers.'

48. For a more detailed account of his continuous rebellion see Sluglett, op. cit.

49. PRO, CO 730/163/6, 1931 Iraq, No. 88069 (Part 2.) Sheikh Mahmud. Report by the Air Officer Commanding 'Iraq on the operations in Southern Kurdistan against Sheikh Mahmud from October 1930–May 1931. Note by Captain V. Holt on Sheikh Mahmud, pp 44–77.

50. Ibid., p. 77.

51. BHCF, File No. 19/1 Vol. 6, *Intelligence Report* No. 23, 1 December 1923, p. 6, para 851.

52. BHCF, File No. 19/1 Vol. 6, *Intelligence Report* No. 23, 1 December 1923, p. 6, para 852.

53. See Sudipta Kaviraj, 'On the Construction of Colonial Power. Structure, Discourse and Hegemony', in Dagmar Engels and Shula Marxs, *Contesting Colonial Hegemony. State and Society in Africa and India*, British Academic Press, London, 1994, pp. 21–32.

54. The Barkat were part of the Beni Huchaim confederation that played an extensive role in the 1920 uprising. They were based along the Euphrates between Samawah and Fallujah in Muntafiq *liwa*(governorate), Samawah *qadha* (district)

55. BHCF, File No. 19/1 Vol. 6, *Intelligence Report*, No. 24, 15 December 1923, pp. 4–5, para. 875.

56. Ibid.

57. Ibid.

58. BHCF, File No. 19/1 Vol. 5, *Intelligence Report,* No. 12, 7 June 1923, p. 1, para. 432.

59. In 1920 Sheikh Sultan was fined 50 rifles in punishment for one of his tribes' firing on a government official. F. C. C. Balfour, Lieutenant Colonel, Military Governor and Political Officer, comments, 'If the terms are not complied with the tribe must be severely dealt with. They are people of no importance except on account of their habitual lawlessness and should, I think be broken up altogether and their lands on the Abu Ghuraib taken from them.' PRO, FO 371/5072, p. 75.

60. BHCF, File No. 7/22/15I, Heading: Ministry of Interior. Sub-Head: Dulaim Liwa, Subject: Sheikh Ali al Sulaiman, Chief of the Dulaim tribes, D.O. No: 203, From: L. M. Yetts, Office of the Divisional Adviser, to: Cornwallis, 30 January 1922, pp. 11–12.

61. BHCF, File No. 7/22/15I, Heading: Ministry of Interior. Sub-Head: Dulaim Liwa, Subject: Sheikh Ali al Sulaiman, Chief of the Dulaim tribes, D.O. No: 203, From: L. M. Yetts, Office of the Divisional Adviser. To: Cornwallis, 30 January 1922, pp. 11–12.

62. BHCF, File No. 7/22/15I, Heading: Ministry of Interior. Sub-Head: Dulaim Liwa, Subject: Sheikh Ali al Sulaiman, Chief of the Dulaim tribes, Extract from Revenue Report of the Administrative Inspector Dulaim Division for the period 27th August to 13 November 1924, pp. 89–90.

63. BHCF, File No. 7/22/15I, Heading: Ministry of Interior. Sub-Head: Dulaim Liwa, Subject: Sheikh Ali al Sulaiman, Chief of the Dulaim tribes, No. C/2779, To: Secretary to the High Commissioner, from: Adviser to Interior, Cornwallis, 9 December 1924, p. 92.

64. BHCF, File No. 7/22/15I, Heading: Ministry of Interior. Sub-Head: Dulaim Liwa, Subject: Sheikh Ali al Sulaiman, Chief of the Dulaim tribes, From H. Dobbs, to: Cornwallis, Adviser, Interior, 17 October 1925, pp. 103–5.

65. 'The Budget was further considered at the following meeting, April 23rd. A somewhat heated debate took place on the priority of payments of subsidies to tribal Sheikhs. Yasin Pasha took the lead in opposing the payment of any subsidies and was supported by Nuri Pasha and Naji Beg. 'Abdul Latif Pasha held the same view but qualified it by saying that the matter should be left to the Ministry of Interior. The Minister, 'Abdul Muhsin Beg, was of the opinion that the 'Iraq Government was not in a position to abolish subsidies.' BHCF, File No. 19/1, Vol. 5, *Intelligence Report* No. 9, 1 May 1923, p. 2, para. 315.

66. BHCF, File No. 7/22/15I, Heading: Ministry of Interior. Sub-Head: Dulaim Liwa, Subject: Sheikh Ali al Sulaim, Chief of the Dulaim tribes, D.O. No. C/3079, From: Cornwallis, to: Dobbs, 21 October 1925, pp. 108–9.

67. Sluglett, ibid., p. 239.

68. Batatu, ibid., p. 22.

69. Lord Lugard, *The Dual Mandate in British Tropical Africa*, Frank Cass & Co. Ltd, London, 1965, p. 75.

70. Lugard, ibid., p. 281.

71. Ibid., p. 215.

72. Gertrude Bell, *Mesopotamia: Review of Civil Administration*, 9 November, 1920, PRO FO 371/5081, paper E13898, p. 94.

73. Longrigg, *Iraq, 1900 to 1950*, ibid., p. 25.

74. BHCF, File No. 6/34/65, Date opened January 1931, Subject: Report by Sir Ernest Dowson – on land settlement in Iraq and allied subject, Government of el 'Iraq. An Inquiry into Land Tenure and Related Questions with Proposals for the Initiation of Reform, by Sir Ernest Dowson, p. 20.

75. This view springs from the same philosophical heritage as James Mill's on India where the progress of any country can be judged by the level of encouragement of rational thought and individual action. This conception of tribal disintegration finds support throughout the Mandate period. For example ' ... disintegration has already begun and reflects the desires of the people themselves, who are openly averse to the tyranny of the tribal confederation ... ' Shamiyah Division, Annual Administration Report, 1 Jan–31 Dec 1918, Vol. 1, Reports of Administration for 1918 of Divisions and Districts of the Occupied Territories in Mesopotamia, PRO CO 696/1, Iraq Administration Reports 1917–1918, p. 72. Also 'After the events of the past two years there can be little doubt that the paramount sheikh, if left to his own devices, quickly loses his paramountcy. Tribesmen are very human, and they object to the imposition of autocratic rule by one who is, in most cases, their enemy and, in nearly all, covets some portion of their land.' Administration Report of the Suq al Shuyukh for the year 1921. By Mr. G. C. Kitching, Assistant Divisional Adviser, CO 696/4 'Iraq Administration Reports 1921–22, p. 56.

76. See for example J. B. Glubb, *The Story of the Arab Legion*, London, Hodder and Stoughton, London, 1946, p. 8 and *Arabian Adventure*, ibid., p. 65. The dominant view was that the tribal system was killed by the effects of modernity and the advance of 'civilization' and urbanization. See for example, *Report on 'Iraq Administration*, October 1920–March 1921, Published by His Majesty's Stationary Office, London, p. 19 and IOL L/P&S/10/619, File No: P433 1919 2 December 1918, *The Future of the Tribal System by the Assistant Political Officer*, Hillah, p. 526.

77. Glubb, *Arabian Adventures*, ibid., p. 65.

78. Diary entry for April 1923 quoted in Glubb, ibid., p.73.

79. See for example see Amatzia Baram, 'Neo-Tribalism in Iraq: Saddam Hussein's Tribal Policies, 1991–96,' *International Journal of Middle Eastern Studies*, 29 (1997), pp. 1–31.

80. See Batatu, ibid., pp. 24, 82, 87, 88–99.

81. Layne, ibid., p. 13.

82. Roy Bhaskar, *Reclaiming Reality, A Critical Introduction to Contemporary Philosophy*, London: Verso, 1989, p. 76.

TWELVE

Tribes and Nationalism: Tribal Political Culture and Behaviour in Iraq, 1914–20

Thair Karim

This chapter is a re-examination of the politics of tribalism versus nationalism during Iraq in the period 1914–20. The study involves a re-analysis of formative historical events in modern Iraqi history, particularly the 1920 uprising by sections of the mid-Euphrates tribes, which subsequently has been represented in most accounts as a rebellion militating for nationhood.

The main argument put forward in this chapter is that nationalism during this period was no more than a vague ideological construction. This construction was projected onto the events of that period, partly during it but mostly after the establishment of the Iraqi state. While many social scientists, journalists and political activists have accepted uncritically the nationalist representation of this episode, this study is an attempt to deconstruct such nationalist discourse from a historical perspective. This, obviously, has implications for other contemporary power-oriented and power-motivated nationalist discourses as well.

This study puts forward the view that the 1920 rebellion was merely a form of jockeying for politico-economic position which was purposefully instituted by middle-rank Euphrates chieftains in a period when British plans for state formation were already underway.

283

Constructing Nationalist History and Heroes

Almost all Iraqi political activists and social scientists refer to the so-called '1920 revolution' as the first historical act by which 'the Iraqis' fought the British, thereby creating the Iraqi state. Nationalist historiography in particular has been tireless in telling and retelling episodes of the troubled year 1920, finally producing a popular stereotype of nationalist representation and nationalist history.

Most Iraqi writers and scholars, as well as many non-Iraqi students of modern Iraqi history, have invariably characterized the events of the summer and autumn of 1920 against the British as the epitome of the nationalist and revolutionary spirit that gave rise to the Iraqi state. Apart from the coup of July 14, 1958 and Saddam's 'historical deeds', it seems that no episode in the history of this country has been as revered as the 1920 rebellion. Writers taking this view include not only the Soviet historian Kotolov, who flung the door open for further emotive pride and historical glorification particularly on the part of Marxist writers and political activists, but also western writers sympathetic to the uprising who have tended to overvalue its 'anti-imperialistic liberation uprisings'.

The renowned British officer T. E. Lawrence was perhaps the first to portray the 1920 rebellion as a product of national aspirations in Iraq. Lawrence's view was mainly determined by the settling of political scores between him and those leading figures of the Indian colonial office who became the first civil servants in Iraq – above all, Arnold Wilson. Lawrence had a vested political and prestige-preserving interest in proving himself right and debunking the views espoused by Wilson and Sir Percy Cox, both of whom were strongly opposed to the ideas advocated by the Arab Bureau in Cairo with which Lawrence was associated. Apparently, Lawrence's explanation of the causes and nature of tribal rebellions was readily embraced in an intellectual context which viewed such rebellions as manifestations of emerging nationalist movements opposed to colonialism. Indeed, some writers go so far as to depict the 1920 rebellion in terms of ethnic pride in race, blood and history, and some passionate love of liberty that is allegedly characteristic of Bedouins (Ireland, 1937, p. 144).

Many attempts have been made by the leaders of the rebellion to promote an ideological perception lauding their persons and actions. For instance, the father of the Abdullah Fayyad, a historian who has written extensively on the uprising, was himself politically involved in the events (Fayyad, 1975, p. 266). Once the 1920 insurrection and the events leading up to it were cast in nationalist and highly moralized terms, sustained efforts were made by various agents to confer as much weight and importance as possible to the role played by this or that group or personality. This rewriting process was intensified after the inception of the Iraqi state, since claims to crucial roles in the rebellion which had supposedly given birth to the state also meant moral claims for better access and promotion to high political positions in the administration.

For instance, Fariq al-Mizhir al-Fir'oun, who took part in the events and later wrote about them, has tried to emphasize what he saw as the unique, distinct and leading role played by chieftains of his own tribe, al-Fatla. Al-Fir'oun portrayed his tribe leaders as the sole heroes of the 'independence revolution' (al-Fir'oun 1952, p.7). By contrast, Ali al-Bazirgan, a recognized 'nationalist' leader from Baghdad, tried with equal enthusiasm to repudiate al-Fir'oun's accounts, dismissing many of the documents referred to by the latter as merely subjective pretensions (al-Bazirgan, 1954, p.7). Contrary to al-Fir'oun, al-Bazirgan strove to demonstrate the leading, and specifically intellectual, role played by the Baghdad elite, especially certain personalities including, of course, himself. He described these elites as 'the thinking powerhouse' and 'mastermind' of the 1920 'revolution'.

Iraqi historians like Mohammed Mahdi al-Basir and Mohammed Khairuldin al-Umari had, earlier, extolled the outstanding role played by political parties in triggering the revolution. Al-Basir, himself from a Shi'ite background, highlighted the role of the al-'Ahd (Covenant Association) and the *Haras al-Istiqlal* (Guards of Independence) Party in Baghdad (a number of prominent Shi'ite personalities were active in this party). By contrast, al-Umari, a Sunni Mosulite, attempted to underline the role of the Covenant Association branch in Mosul, paying high tribute to their 'patriotic exploits' for the country and its independence (al-Basir 1924; al-Umari 1925).

Other writers, especially those of a Shi'ite background, credited prominent Shi'ite clerics of the holy shrine cities as having played the most outstanding role, both intellectually and morally, in these events. Prominent among these clerics are the great mujtahid, al-Shirazi, based at the time in Karbala, and other Shi'ite *mujtahids*, such as Mohammed al-Sadr, in Baghdad.

Such interpretations have seriously undermined the process of understanding the aspects, be they negative or positive, of the evolution of the Iraqi 'state' and the role of tribes in this process. Commenting on these interpretations, the Iraqi sociologist Ali al-Wardi's, says, 'they have done well in the sphere of instructing the new generations on nationalism but such interpretations will not work in the field of scientific research' (al-Wardi 1977, p. 342).

The historian Abdul-Razzak al-Hasani tried to quiz some of the leading protagonists of tribal rebellions in order to prove that the events had been purely local in character; his point was acknowledged by most chieftains and notables, including Muhsin Abu Tabikh and various others. Al-Hasani said that he had written his book and carried out his investigation to show that the Iraqi revolt was a local occurrence, which had nothing to do with the great Arab revolution, and that the 'revolution' was fuelled by what the insurrectionists had put into it in terms of money, military equipment, and other resources (al-Hasani, 1935, p. 145).

The central theme that runs through al-Hasani's entire work is that the root cause of the revolution is the pursuit of political independence. He suggests that the 1920 insurrection was an independence revolution staged specifically by the Euphrates inhabitants and was therefore a Euphrates revolt. In his view, it would have become an Iraqi revolution had it not been for the lack of participation by many tribes in other regions, above all by Sunni tribes like the Dulaim and others (al-Hasani 1935, p. 56).

The assumption that the prime concern of the rebellious tribal chieftains was Iraqi independence contradicts not only the realities of tribal political culture, imagination or behaviour at that moment, but also runs counter to the actual sequence of events before this upheaval. In particular, this assumption is inconsistent with the fact that the British had already acknowledged and 'authorized' the creation of an Arab state in Iraq before the uprising broke out. Thus, al-Hasani's account uncritically accepts all the versions put forward by rebellious chieftains, especially later ones.

There is a third interpretation that attributes the 1920 revolt to conspiracies organized by hostile foreign powers. Some British intelligence officers like Major Bray attributed tribal revolts to German, Kemalist Turkish or Soviet machinations (Attiya 1988, p. 462), but the British Foreign Office did not agree with the logic of this analysis and the conspiracy theory as a whole was dismissed as groundless in later research. Equally unsuccessful was the conspiracy explanation adopted by Colonel Wilson, Deputy High Commissioner in Iraq. Wilson blamed Sharifian officers and the Arab government in Syria under the short-lived reign of King Faisal I for the alleged attempt to establish a federal Arab state incorporating Iraq, Syria, and the entire Fertile Crescent. In his book on Wilson, John Marlow tries to substantiate this explanation. He says large quantities of money and arms were supplied by Iraqi 'Ahd (The Covenant) officers and Syria to the rebels in the mid-Euphrates, especially to Karbala and Najaf. He does not, however, present any convincing evidence or sufficient factual data to prove the supposedly considerable magnitude of such aid.

The British Occupation of Ottoman Iraq

Let us now examine the British occupation of Iraq, its limits and impact on tribes and tribal positions and behaviour.

Less than one year into World War I and shortly after Turkey's declaration of war alongside Germany and the Axis, British forces based in India landed in Basrah which, after the battle of Shu'aiba, fell on 15 April 1915. Within two months the city of Umara followed suit. The British forces captured the entire Faw-Umara-Nasiriya triangle. Having consolidated their positions in the occupied cities, the British forces advanced in late 1915 towards Kut. However, due to a host of military factors, the British expeditionary force was not only halted in its hitherto successful advance but also encircled by the Turkish armies to eventually surrender unconditionally on 29 April 1916 (Longrigg 1953, p. 30).

This setback could, potentially, have had grave consequences for the future of British policy in the region (Cm. also al-Nafisi, Abdulla 1973, p. 107 and Yapp 1987, p. 517). A decision was soon taken to prepare for a thrust towards Baghdad. Newly appointed Commander General S. Maude ordered his troops to cross the southern bank of the Tigris. British troops were able to steadily drive the Turkish forces out of most areas south of Baghdad, which was finally captured on 11 March 1917. Before the armistice in November 1918 British forces had reached the southern approaches to the city of Mosul. Thus, along with the provinces of Baghdad and Basrah, the province of Mosul had come under British occupation.

Until the end of the World War I, significant areas that were administratively part of the three provinces were not under the jurisdiction of the British. These included the mountainous region inhabited by Kurds along the Iranian and Turkish borders, the mid-Euphrates area extending from the south of Baghdad to Nasiriya, and the two Shi'ite cities of Najaf and Karbala (Marr 1985, p. 33).

The British understood the problematic reality of their slender hold on the mid-Euphrates when they soon recognized that the area was the centre of a substantial grain-growing region irrigated by the Euphrates canals and thus could by no means be neglected (Sir Cox 1927, p. 517). The need for food supplies to the population and the army became so urgent in late 1917, in particular, that the Euphrates Basin acquired an ever-increasing significance. Accordingly, British political officers were sent to Karbala and Kufa in the Shamia district bordering Najaf and Hilla (Bell 1927, Vol. II, p. 518).

The Tribes' Shifting Political Loyalties

During World War I, tribal chieftains sided differently with either of the two warring parties. Some cultivated close relations with the British, whereas others decided it was wiser to maintain links with the Turks. The decisive criteria in these alignments were, firstly, the history of those sheikhs' and chieftains' past exchanges with the authorities and the resulting 'balance-sheet' of these transactions at the moment; secondly, and more importantly, the politico-economic benefits expected from alignment with either party. Finally, the concerned agents had their own considerations of expediency and the existing balance of forces. In fact, it is difficult to escape the conclusion that maximum personal advantages sought by various sheikhs were the ultimate consideration that determined the actual positions taken by various tribes.

For instance, the sheikhs or chieftains whose interests and influence had been previously damaged by the Ottoman authorities were mostly prepared to befriend the British forces. Simultaneously, sheikhs and chieftains who were under pressure caused by rivalry with equals over status, authority, and power would usually side with the party opposed to their contenders' patron. Moreover, for the tribes settled near towns, major communication lines and important rivers had a kind of expedient contingency that would promptly induce them to offer their loyalty to the dominant party at the time or gamble on the winner of the game. A shift in loyalties followed the siege of Kut and the subsequent surrender of British forces. Badr al-Rumaidh, chieftain of Bani Malik, Abdullah and Abdul-Karim, sons of Sheikh Falih al-Sa'doun, as well as other clan leaders who had cosy or neutral relations with the British army, swiftly reneged to collaborate with the Turks (Arab Bulletin, no. 81, p. 79f). However, most of these same sheikhs back-pedalled with the advance of British forces towards Baghdad.

As a significant political force, the majority of tribal chieftains were, therefore, acting in their own interests. In many cases, each sheikh was seeking the support of one side or the other mainly to promote his own cause of capturing more land and attaining wider influence (al-Jawahiri 1978, p. 288).

On the other hand, most urban groups remained passive towards the Turkish forces, and refrained from alignment with the Ottomans against the British. Even the nascent groups of local 'nationalists' only paid lip service to the question of *jihad,* or holy war. Hatred of the Turkish regime and its mismanagement as well as the hope of a better deal with the British, especially for the notables, merchants and landowners, and the expected improvement of the country's infrastructure were the people's main concerns. Such a pattern was, of course, not exclusive to Iraq. The Ottoman rulers in Egypt, for example, had failed completely to incite and pit the Egyptians against the British. The Turks were simply incapable of getting the tribes to secure unified and effective mobilization to fight the British forces (Yapp 1987, p. 272) much less to act in nationalist interests. The tribal army which was hastily knocked together under the aegis of the Turkish officers, soon disintegrated after the Turkish defeat at the battle of Shu'aiba in 1915. Blamed by the Turks for this defeat, some of the local tribes, including the Muntafiq clans, vented their anger at this unfair treatment by attacking the retreating Turkish troops on the banks of the Hammar marsh and killing and looting the vanquished Turks (al-Nafisi 1973, p. 90).

The policy apparently pursued by Britain was to offer support in proportion with the actual influence exerted by the respective sheikh over his tribesmen in terms of maintaining order and discipline. This policy had become a direct factor in enhancing or lowering the status of many tribal chieftains, city notables and other personalities. When settling disputes over land ownership and rights, the British would more often than not side with the sheikhs and tribesmen who were the real users of land rather than with landowners and leading sheikhs who claimed to hold title deeds (Haldane 1922, p. 23). Chieftains, sheikhs and notables aspiring for local influence and power like Talib al-Naqib in Basrah, al-Kammuna and others in Najaf and in other areas were disappointed by the British plans to assume direct rule of the occupied territories. In addition, in the two shrine cities of Karbala and Najaf the local civil and religious elites were appalled by British intolerance of an autonomous enclave within the occupied territories despite repeated assurances to respect the freedom of the holy sites (Attiya 1988, p. 298).

In sum, apart from economic and political advantages of the moment, there was no consistent logic to which side tribal chieftains aligned.

Sociopolitical Fragmentation and the Reality of Nationalistic Consciousness and Practices During the War

Until the plebiscite held by the British authorities in 1918 on the form of future government in Iraq, no nationalist consciousness and practice was evident. There was no indigenous political movement so there was no group which could raise a voice against the war, question its sense and purpose or oppose drawing any of Iraq's provinces and their inhabitants into the carnage. There was no one group that could recruit people to a clearly defined nationalist platform.

The nascent 'nationalist' groups in Iraq had, in general, four characteristics. First, they were mostly branches in the provinces set up on the instructions of, or initiated by, associations and parties established in Istanbul, Egypt or Syria, or simply a bland duplication of such initiatives. Second, membership was essentially from an elitist and wealthy background rarely incorporating 'common people'. Third, these groups had no clearly defined programmes apart from general ideas lacking a coherent vision of the relationship between authority and people, or the nature of the desired political and economic system and the ways to attain the set goals. Fourth, these associations were organized on the basis of patronage and contest relations between a few groups of limited numbers of individuals.

The inability of the local elites to engage in making common cause before 1914, and their breaking into sectionalism by primordial loyalties, made it difficult to produce a unified and unifying leadership.

Unrelatedness, a general antipathy to each other and a structural lack of homogeneity characterized the political existence of the local elites, at least those who attempted to engage in constructing the politics of nationalism. This may explain the failure of 'nationalist' groups to conduct any concerted action. In reality, neither the Shi'ite clergy nor the urban elites of Baghdad, Basrah and Mosul acted as a more or less unified nationalist movement, let alone arose in a joint action. Even during and immediately after British occupation, there is no evidence that joint action was undertaken by the existing local elites, or the public, either between provinces or within any of them. Furthermore, there is no indication of what may be described as unifying nationalist action triggered by the military occupation of Iraq. The years between 1914 and 1918 were merely characterized by very limited, and largely spontaneous, oppositional attitudes against the Ottomans and in lesser degree against the British. It is difficult to dismiss British intelligence reports that even news of Sharif Hussein's revolt in Hijaz in 1916 against the Turks was received with little enthusiasm, let alone with support by tribal sheikhs or tribesmen in the various regions of Iraq (Arab Bulletin no. 20, p. 235). As a result, the most common feature of local political action was a continuing lack of nationalist political consciousness and widespread positions stemming from purely local loyalties and interests, whether in urban centres, Shi'ite holy shrines or tribal areas (Cm. Attyia 1988).

Changing Attitudes Towards the British Occupation

As well as total political apathy on the part of the common people, there also existed a natural fear of becoming war victims, and there was general complacency at the possibility of the annihilation of the Turkish forces and the end of Ottoman domination. There is no doubt that broad manifestations of resignation to British occupation and collaboration by many tribal chieftains, individuals and town people with the expedition forces were among the political realities of the period.

Even the somewhat spirited response by the inhabitants of Najaf and Karbala to the call for Jihad made by the Porte, and the subsequent joining of the Turkish forces heading to Shuʻaiba to fight the British, soon evaporated with the swift defeat of the Turkish forces. Combined with the strained relations between the Shiʻites and the Turkish government, this defeat immediately resulted in general resentment and aversion by the population against the Turkish authorities and led to the withdrawal of most volunteers, including some Shiʻite clergymen, and their return home.

A new streak of nationalist discourse began to emerge after 1917 under the influence of external factors. Among these factors was: the 1917 declaration of General Maude, in which the British government defined its occupation of the country in terms of the liberation of the people of Mesopotamia from the Turks, and also President Wilson's speech at the League of Nations in 1918, particularly his 12th point on the right of the peoples in the defeated empire to self-determination. British representatives saw the spirit of these principles as gradually permeating the East (Sir Cox 1927, p. 522). Equally important was the 1916 Anglo-French declaration that gave the subjects of the Ottoman Empire the right to self-government and statehood. In this context, these external factors stimulated and encouraged some elites to put forward their demands.

Students of the 1920 revolt usually refer to certain socio-political events shortly before its eruption as the precursors or causes for the insurrection in the mid-Euphrates. Particular mention is made of the events that took place in the city of Najaf in 1917.[9] They are usually painted in the nationalist colours of an independence struggle, and no attempt is made to elaborate on local contexts and actual causes (al-Jubouri 1978, al-Mahbuba 1353H).

The Tribal Uprising of 1920

The series of events that formed the uprising were ignited by the arrest of Sha'lan Abu al-Jon, Sheikh of the Zawalim clan from Bani Hajim tribe, in late June 1920, because he refused to pay taxes to the occupation authority. Together with other sheikhs who subsequently rebelled, Abu al-Jon was contracted by the British to dig a canal; he was to act as a foreman of his own tribesmen. Many chieftains disdained working with their own tribesmen under the supervision of the British.

Abu al-Jon's arrest enraged his tribal kin to storm the police station where he was incarcerated, and they killed a number of policemen and set him free. He soon incited his tribesmen not to serve 'the infidel enemy who hates the Arabs and Islam' (al-Hasani 1935, p. 56). Nationalist writers like Mohammed Mahdi al-Basir, Abdulla Fayyad and others sought to dismiss the circumstantial and specific economic issue involved in the arrest of Abu al-Jon, a local leader not known for any political activism either before or, indeed, after the end of the insurrections.

Sheikh Ali al-Sharqi, who was a contemporary of many leaders in the revolt, wrote on the question of Abu al-Jon and his arrest emphasizing that it was a purely local case and that his 'revolutionary' actions were neither premeditated nor planned. The general norm on managing disputes between the mid-Euphrates tribes and the occupation authority was to seek peaceful settlements rather than raising arms (Quoted in al-Wardi 1977, p. 233).

In any event, within a few days after the outbreak of fighting, military mobilization was in full swing on both sides. On the British side, military units were rapidly assembled to relieve the small garrisons scattered in the area against possible encirclement and annihilation by the rebellious tribes. On the tribal side, there was frequent mobilization to inflict maximum damage on the British forces and capture as much military and material spoils as possible. These battles assumed the classical tribal pattern of hit-and-run. The insurgent tribesmen were highly successful in taking advantage of the mistakes made by the military authorities and of the reduced presence of British forces in their localities.

Within two weeks thousands of armed tribesmen and hundreds of British troops were deployed in the small theatre of Rumaitha (Haldane 1922, p. 75). On July 23 the British command decided to mobilize and dispatch its forces to al-Kifil. The aim was to prevent the al-Hindiya barrage from falling into tribal hands and to check repeated British retreats, which, according to British judgment, encouraged tribes to expand their revolt. However, rebels were able to encircle the British forces advancing from al-Rustam between Hilla and al-

Kifil, and engaged them in a fierce battle which left scores of casualties on both sides. The insurrectionists from al-Fatla, al-'Awabid, al-Hamidat and other clans captured large quantities of light arms and some military hardware. Tribesmen from al-Fatla, al-Ziad, al-Khaza'il, al-'Awabid and al-Ibrahim clans captured the al-Hindiya barrage and the village of Twaireej. Tribal warriors were poised to seize Hilla, which was encircled by al-Jubour, Albu Sultan, Khafaja, al-Yasar and some al-Fatla warriors (al-Hasani 1935, p. 90). That battle was the most successful episode in the revolt and it brought a great bounty of spoils. That is why it had become the theme of wide publicity rendering revolt against the British extremely attractive, at least to the tribesmen.

On August 17 the Karbala-based grand *mujtahid* Mirza Muhammad Taqi al-Shirazi died. There was intensive pressure by powerful members of the religious elite around the new great *mujtahid* Sheikh al-Sharia al-Asfahani to accept the reconciliatory letter sent by Sir Arnold Wilson upon al-Shirazi's death. Counter clerical pressures dissuaded al-Asfahani from reconciliation and negotiation with the British. Some tribal sheikhs, especially those who were already restive, lauded this position, while other chieftains showed dissatisfaction because confrontation disregarded the welfare of neutral sheikhs (Haldane 1922, p. 333–5).

In mid-November the British forces captured Kufa, relieving its garrison after months of siege. Finally, on 20 November, Najaf, 'the key to the mid-Euphrates', fell to the British when a city delegation signed the terms of surrender. Apart from a number of people who fled to Syria or beyond, the majority of leaders gave themselves up to the British. They were kept behind bars for few months and released when King Faisal was crowned.

Nationalism in the Discourse of the Shi'ite *Ulema*

Though the *ulema* were among the first social actors to use the term 'the Iraqi nation' in 1920, the polity they envisaged was left largely undefined, with only the ruler at the helm specifically defined as Muslim. That Muslim, the would-be ruler of Iraq, was the son of the Sharif of Mecca. Shi'ite *ulema* never suggested nor sanctioned a local figure, whether of a Sunni or a Shi'ite background. Nor did they envisage a Shi'ite political system, or purposefully seek to cooperate with other religious or secular forces to make a feasible common cause.

The fuqaha in Najaf and Karbala largely maintained traditions of political non-involvement just as the Shi'ite tribes were totally immersed in their own tribal world with all its traditional rituals and values. The tribes responded to the call of religion when it served and suited them and their values. The religious leaders, particularly the strategic core around the great mujtahid, were in an embarrassing dilemma as a result of the political burdens they were unexpectedly required to shoulder. On the one hand, it was important for them to assert their moral and spiritual role in all matters concerning the Shi'ites, including also the demands and grievances of the mid-Euphrates tribal sheikhs. Commitment or non-commitment by the clerical core had a direct moral and political impact on their authority and status. When clan chiefs and rebellious tribes were pressing their radical claims, non-involvement on the part of these strategic elites who, in theory at least, were held in high esteem by the Shi'ites, meant the possible erosion of that symbolic capital accumulated over the centuries. On the other hand, clerics were unfamiliar with ways of leading broad tribal movements or conducting militant revolts against modern, powerful military machinery. Moreover, the emphasis on seeking a peaceful way to attain the desired goals was a crucial element in the thinking of prominent clerics.

As attested by the situation in the holy cities of Karbala and Najaf, there was no unified leadership to synchronize actions and lend them purpose. On the tribal front, there was also no outstanding and unifying leader. This was intrinsically inherent in tribal structures.

British occupation created a favourable climate for the development of a new language with elements of an alternative political culture. The political idiom of the mujtahids in Karbala and Najaf was not pan-Arabist, but rather Islamic suffused with new concept of nationhood. For instance, the mujtahid al-Shirazi referred in some of his letters written during 1920 to 'the oppressed Iraqi nation', 'the pressured Iraqi milieu', etc. The Shi'ite *ulema*, al-Shirazi in particular, introduced such terms as 'Iraqis' and 'the Iraqi nation' into the clerical and secular political discourse of the time.

Factionalism, Localism and the Tribal Uprising

Tribes and clans living in other regions showed no solidarity with the rebellious tribes of the mid-Euphrates. In fact, a passive attitude was prevalent in most of the areas beyond the mid-Euphrates. Cases of tribal rebellion against the British outside this region were of a traditional character and confined to certain localities.

In addition, not all the Shi'ite tribes in the mid-Euphrates region were fighting the British forces. There were some clans that offered actual and explicit backing to the British. For instance, the al-Fatla clan, led by Muzzier al-Fir'oun, helped the 200-strong British garrison retreat from Abu Sikhair. Khayoun al-Ubaid, head of the 'Abbouda clan which was one of the most powerful of al-Shatra, went out of his way to calm the restless clans and acted as a mediator between some of them and the British authority. He emphatically refused to take part in any armed actions against the British.

Other collateral rebellions in regions like Kirkuk and Rawandouz had their own purely local motives and considerations. More often than not, every clan fought within its territory, some against rival clans (Longrigg 1953, p. 442). There were no indicators in major Iraqi cities like Basrah, Baghdad, and Mosul signalling that events in the mid-Euphrates could radically affect these cities' living conditions and hence elicit effective solidarity with the insurgents. Other predominantly Shi'ite regions like Kut, Gharraf, Umara and Muntafiq or southern towns and areas along the Tigris up to Baghdad as well as known Shi'ite tribes like Bani Lam, Rabia', 'Abbouda, al-'Izairij and Hussainat, not to mention important Shi'ite tribes within the Muntafiq confederation, showed no real signs of solidarity or communality of purpose and action with the rebels. Indeed, some urban notables, especially in Basrah, were hostile to the movement.

Lack of wide involvement in the tribal rebellions has been attributed to British bribes to the Tigris-based clans. This may apply in certain cases, but does not make a strong enough argument to explain the passive attitude by broad social groups towards armed political struggle which was, allegedly, of a strategic, nationalist character. Lack of unity between Shi'ite tribesmen themselves should be explained by the social, economic and political conditions under which the various actors perceived and defined their interests.

Let us take urban political parties. The al-'Ahd 'Party', for example, failed to incorporate the tribal uprising into nationalist strategic actions, or expand its territorial scope or to politically engage wider sections of the population. An attempt of sorts was made by the Haras al-Istiqlal Party in 1919 to extend a cooperative hand across the communal divide. Aspects of the party platform underlined the need for Iraqi national unity irrespective of religion and sectarian affiliation. The initiators of such calls may have been the first generation of the Iraqi political elites to develop nationalist identity beyond traditional fragmentation. However, al-Haras failed to translate this doctrine into reality. Like other outfits, this party did not and could not represent the whole gamut of heterogeneous social group forces.

British Plans for the Governance of Iraq

Until the occupation of Baghdad in 1917 there were no elaborate plans regarding the form of government in Iraq. A specific plan was drawn up to observe the right of the indigenous population to have their own domestic government (Busch 1984, p. 54).

In late 1917 and early 1918, the British government opted for the establishment of an Arab government in Iraq with as broad a popular base as possible among the population. A plebiscite to sound out the Iraqi views on the country's future was held.

The very idea of the poll stimulated local elites in Baghdad and other cities to become actively involved in national politics. Political activity by Shi'ite and Sunni Arab elites in some cities, above all Baghdad, become more frequent. Most local elites were now keen on having a place in the emerging central power.

The plebiscite held in the provinces of Baghdad, Mosul and Basrah posed three questions: first, whether the inhabitants wanted a unified Arab state extending from the northern border of the Mosul province to the Persian Gulf under British supervision; second, whether they wished to have the envisaged state headed by an Arab prince or Sharif; third, if so, who they would want as head of that state.

The mere fact of putting these questions to the various segments of Iraq's inhabitants helped to develop an entirely different level of political consciousness and practice. The political culture and imagination of both the elites and the populace began to take on a new appearance. Never before had such a poll been held. Abdul-Rahman al-Naqib, the head of the Qadiriya Sufi order in Baghdad, admitted that this was the first time ever that the people were being asked directly about the form of government and the ruler they wished to have. The plebiscite provided an intensive opportunity to mobilize political-minded people in an organized movement (Bell 1927).

On the other hand, what responses to the plebiscite questions could be expected from the populace? The segmented nature of political consciousness determined by local interests, and consequently, the total lack of any sense of common identity, precluded a general response of a unified national character. A telling example is what happened at a meeting held in Najaf by leading religious and tribal figures from the Middle Euphrates areas to arrive at a decision. One group voiced unity with Iran (including the viewpoints of prominent *ulemas*); another demanded a non-Arab prince. A third advocated direct British rule. A fourth demanded a republican system and a fifth was for an Arab prince. The participants were, however, unanimous on the question of maintaining British protection from Mosul to the Persian Gulf (al-Nafisi 1973, p. 119) .

Sir Arnold Wilson apparently urged his political officers to highlight views supporting his own vision on direct British rule. After the Anglo-French declaration of 1918, and the inception of an Arab government in Syria under Prince Faisal, the option of having an Arab prince or ruler for Iraq gained ground.Within one year – 1919 – parties and associations were being energetically established and re-established. Sir Arnold Wilson conveyed an accurate picture to his superiors when he pointed out in a telegram that apart from Baghdad, Karbala and Najaf, the population of Mesopotamia was unanimous on the need for British rule (Marlow 1967, p. 197).

In early 1920, the British government considered Prince Abdullah, Sharif Hussein's son, as a potential ruler for the country. It also considered possible shifts in the public opinion on this issue. Indeed, in a circular dated 17 June 1920, the British government issued instructions to convene a general congress of elected delegates. The congress was to be preceded by an election law, working out the related modalities, defining the constituencies and preparing the electoral registers (al-Hasani 1935, p. 53). On 20 July 1920, shortly before the outbreak of the tribal uprising, a decision was taken to install an Arab government in Iraq and have an Arab state council, an Arab head of government, a representative assembly freely elected by the population and a basic law for this state and other arrangements. It is, therefore, difficult to regard these steps as the outcome of a 'national independence revolution'.

Nevertheless, bitterness and frustration was felt by scores of dismissed civil servants and military officers because of what they perceived as British tardiness in introducing the desired national structures. These people were mostly Sunnis of Turkish, Arab and Kurdish backgrounds. There were, on the other hand, a very limited number of indigenous civil servants employed in the British-run administration.In August 1920 there were only 20 indigenous civil servants in high administrative posts accounting for less than 4 per cent (Ireland, 1937, p.146). The British civil administration insisted that the shortage of qualified Iraqis was the reason for not employing more indigenous civil servants, an argument which, of course, was difficult to dispute. Another reason often quoted was the inefficiency of former civil servants and military personnel who otherwise could still not be assimilated without building up the country's administrative apparatus and an army that would absorb them. According to Yassin al-Hashimi, a high-ranking officer and prominent politician at the time, this attitude antagonized some pro-British Iraqi officers enough to make them change their position and oppose the British Mandate (quoted in Attiya 1988, p. 387). This opposition further intensified when many officers found themselves replaced in Syria where Syrian officers were increasingly demanding that Syria be for the Syrians and priority be given to Syrians in military posts (Haldane 1922, p. 26). The bulk of the 15,000 Iraqi civil servants and officers who had served in the Ottoman government returned from captivity. It was those functionaries who first launched and led a movement opposed to the Wilson administration in Baghdad (al-Wardi 1977, p. 92).

The Politico-economic Considerations of the Tribal Insurrection

The armed action of the uprising was concentrated in a geographically contiguous area whose inhabitants were predominantly co-religionists. Their motives, however, were not always the same. Although there were common factors and motives revolving on economic interests and political status, their points of reference were divergent.

In the cases of many tribal leaders, opposition to the British was determined by the support the latter got from rival sheikhs with whom disputes over land or status was acute. Such antagonism had precedence in the rivalries of the Ottoman era.

Abdul-Wahid al-Haj Suker, a leader invariably described as a trailblazer and commander in the military actions of the uprising, disliked the British because, according to 'Alwan al-Yasiri, they appointed a peer of Suker's on an equal level of leadership, and they opposed his persistent efforts to seize the land of his own tribesmen and kinsmen in Rak al-Haswa district and other places of the Mishkhab region (Attiya 1954, p. 166).

Muhsin Abu Tabikh, another prominent leader of the insurrection, was locked in a prolonged dispute with Sha'lan al-Salman, head of the Khaza'il tribe, over land in the Ghammas district in Diwaniya. A third leader of the uprising, Marzouq al-'Awad, was challenging his cousin Abdul-Hamza al-'Ifrit's claims to land in the al-Salahiya district in Shamia. Hadi Zuwain was on a collision course against the al-'Abouda clan over land and orchids in the al-Ja'ara district in Abu Sukhair. The dispute between Mizhir al-Far'oun and his sons, Sartib and Fariq, from al-Fatla tribe, was so bitter that Sartib was killed by one of his brothers. 'Alwan al-Yasiri himself disputed with his brothers, especially Sayyid Jawad, and with Abdul-Sada al-Gisad, a clan leader, over taxes and land. 'Abadi al-Hussein contested claims by Hassan al-Shamkhi, head of Bani Hassan al-Jarrah, to land and water near the al-Mahannawiya river. These cases are only a fraction of those reported by Waddai al-Attiya who himself admitted that land and tax disputes quoted by him were 'only the tip of the iceberg' (Attyia 1954, p. 166f).

It may well be inferred from all this that the logic of rivalries, driven by economic interests and considerations of status and political influence, played a crucial role in the events. Commercial agriculture in Iraq went through a spectacular growth in the wake of land registration laws and the partial liberalization of private property. Suffice it to mention here that farming land expanded from about 125,000 donums in 1860 to 1.6 million donums (400,000 hectares) in 1913 (Yapp 1987, p. 15). Nevertheless, war had a disastrous impact on the middle and north of Iraq. The population of these regions had to bear the brunt of sustaining the Ottoman war effort over a prolonged period of time. By contrast, the southern region of Iraq enjoyed relative prosperity as trade continued with India and considerable employment opportunities were being created by the British forces reconstructing the Basrah port and building railways, roads, bridges, electricity and water plants. The tribal sheikhs reaped great benefits from these developments, virtually controlling the movement of a major part of the labour force and of some essential supplies like meat (Arab Bulletin no. 72, p. 491; Yapp 1987, p. 213).

But once the war ended, all tax breaks granted by the colonial administration were terminated. Government offices were drawing up plans to boost, in kind or cash, revenues from taxes, especially so when Great Britain sought to reduce the cost of its presence in Iraq. Targeted in this connection were, above all, regions that were major food producers like the Middle Euphrates where rice, dates and grain produce had considerably expanded, in addition to regions that had not been taxed before or were out of the reach of the central government. Steps were taken in earnest to enforce political and administrative control on the remaining regions of Iraq. In light of their experience in Basrah, the British saw agrarian taxation as the best means of political control. It was generally believed that the tribes themselves regarded tax collection as a distinct sign of the presence of the central government and of submission to it. In addition, the agricultural crops in the Middle Euphrates region would feed the army from local sources at a very low cost.

Accordingly, in 1919, certain Euphrates tribes like Bani Huchaim in Rumaitha (where the tribal insurrection is said to have started) began to pay heavy taxes for the first time ever (Ireland 1937, pp. 118, 248).

Disparities in political status and economic benefits, between pro-government city notables and sheikhs on the one hand and many mid-Euphrates chieftains on the other, were too large to go unnoticed by the latter. Tribes in this area were already extremely sensitive to the distribution of economic and political resources and the possible change in power relations. Among the paramount sheikhs who benefited from cooperation with the British were Fahad ibn Hidhal of the 'Aniza tribe, 'Ajil Pasha Samarmand of the Zubaid tribe, al-Amir Mohammed al-Sayhud, chief of the Bani Rabi'a tribe and Falih al-Sayhud and 'Uraibi bin Wadi, prominent sheikhs of the Albu Mohammed tribe. With British backing they enhanced their land properties, personal power and privileges. Most got actively involved in discouraging or preventing the revolt from spilling over into their territories, and actually assisted the British in crushing it.

While by dint of British policy, big chieftains augmented their material endowment and symbolic capital, middle and junior chieftains harboured a sense of deprivation and denial of future opportunities for themselves. The latter's sense of loss was accentuated by the irony that while their region, the Middle Euphrates, was gaining more economic significance, most of its chieftains and leaders were politically marginalized. Benefiting from the early cooperation with the British, pro-government tribal chieftains pursued a strategic policy of furthering their own power and status to increase their following. As a result, other minor sheikhs of the region became extremely sensitive towards such big sheikhs, and were profoundly disturbed by the consequent disparity in the matrix of tribal socio-economic-political stratification. As Waterbury notes on similar cases, 'any slight shifts in the balance of power do not go undetected' (Waterbury 1970, p. 65).

With regard to the settlement of land disputes and claims, many British military and civilian governors adopted a largely expedient policy, generally supporting sheikhs of clans whose members were actually deprived of land. However, overall British policy was in favour of the more powerful tribal chieftains (Batatu 1978, p. 123) to the detriment of the middle and small categories.

Fahad bin Hidhal, for example, was publicizing his name as the first authority in mid- Euphrates affairs. In his many conversations with Sir Cox, Bell and other British officials, he elaborated on his plans for the future, and insisted that 'in all tribal matters Sir Cox should rely on Hidhal's advice and for the rest he should seek counsel with Naqib and two other old turbaned worthies' (Bell 1927, p. 567). The British saw support for the big sheikhs as the most convenient way of enforcing order and serving the smooth running of military business, despite their awareness that those sheikhs were concerned with securing their own interests at the expense of their tribesmen. This paradox put the British face to face with a bewildering dilemma (Haldane 1922, p. 31). They opted for promoting the interests of the powerful sheikhs giving less consideration to the interests of small sheikhs and notables.Among medium land owners there were also '*sayyids*', like Hadi Zuain, 'Alwan Sayyid Abbas, 'Alwan al-Yasiri, Nour al-Yasiri, Hadi al-Mugotar and Muhsin Abu Tabikh. It is interesting to note that most members of the latter category joined the club of big landowners. At this point, General Haldane and Bell were among the most influential officials who acknowledged that the maltreatment received by some clan sheikhs and the shoddy work of tactless and inexperienced political officers like Major Daly, the governor of Diwaniya, had led to some chieftains being given vast areas of land and fixed allowances, and had ignited resentment against the British by other sheikhs. In predominantly Shi'ite towns like Kut and Umara, British policy, especially the policy led by Henry Dobbs who was in charge of the revenues department, was guided by political expediency. Dobbs saw the way to maintaining British rule in supporting powerful members of leading tribal houses and big landowners rather than the smaller cultivators, quite contrary to the intention of other officials like Colonel Stephen Longrigg (Haj, 1997, pp. 28–31).

As a result, the privileges heaped on the more powerful segment aroused not only considerable apprehension and envy but also ill feeling in the Middle Euphrates, provoking local sheikhs into political action in order to redress the imbalance. Moreover, being ignorant of the actual military power of the British at that time, those sheikhs exaggerated their own strength in their traditional tribal way, counting on the weakness of the British and their inability to subdue the rebellious tribes. On the other hand, the British lacked, as Bell repeatedly points out in her letters, information about the Euphrates tribes and their chaotic confusion.

Actually, until late 1917 the British had not dispatched any political officers to major Euphrates towns like Simawa, Shamiya and Hilla. Only after the disturbances in Najaf in the fall of 1917 did they open their eyes to the importance of the region as provisions provider and a hotbed of increasingly effective and hostile Turkish propaganda (Arab Bulletin, no. 85, p. 117). Another lure for rebellion was the traditional raid-loot-and-run which drove some tribes to attack government offices. A strong catalyst for revolt among ordinary tribesmen was, thus, the anticipated capture of the spoils of war.

These differences, interests and tensions were, however, cast in an ideological mould which simultaneously activated the values of loyalty to the clan and its leader and evoked the values of Islam and the Muslims' heroic exploits in their historical battles against 'the infidels'. In this situation of profound political uncertainty, the respective chieftains realized that to strike here and now meant access to more wealth, authority and power even outside their immediate regions.

In this atmosphere tribal chieftains and *sayyids*, especially in the areas adjacent to the Shamia canal, a tributary from Euphrates, engaged in active anti-British mobilization when their farm incomes declined. This decline was blamed on British mismanagement of water distribution in the Shamia and Hilla canals, which harmed those leaders and did not benefit tribes around the Hilla canal. But while the Euphrates chieftains and *sayyids* had strained relations with the British, the political officers of the colonial administration operating in the regions bordering the Middle Euphrates saw those groups as rebellious, arrogant individuals who were gleeful at the absence of government authority.

In mid-1917 the British political officer in a southern mid-Euphrates town wrote a remarkable report which clearly pointed out some of these tensions. He said those people were aware that the British authorities would inevitably enforce the collection of government revenues but they were trying to put off this day of reckoning as far as possible. The report predicted no difficulties against tax collection in full within two years (Arab Bulletin no. 63, p. 283f).

To be sure, there was an increase in tax revenues collected from the tribes, though this was not as easy as predicted by the report. Income tax in Muntafiq, for instance, increased manifold – from five rupees per head in 1916 to five shillings in 1919. The revenues collected from the three Shi'ite counties of Muntafiq, Diwaniya and Shamia accounted for 25 per cent of the total contributed by 14 such counties. In general, while revenues collected in 1918 were, on average, double the amount collected in 1911, in 1920 these revenues, excluding those paid by the railways, were 3.3 times the amount collected under Turkish rule in 1911 (Ireland 1937, p. pp. 118, 145). Tax evasion through bribery or force was no longer as easy as it had been in previous times.

To sum up the large tribal picture we may safely conclude that while the big landowners, tribal sheikhs, and Kurdish aghas did not take part in the 1920 insurrection, the majority of sheikhs with medium and small landed estates in the Hindiya, Shamia, Abu Sukhair and beyond, did. They formed 'the backbone of the anti-British movement' (Batatu 1978, p. 82).

The 1920 uprising was neither a peasant nor a big landlord revolt. It was an emotive and violent response by Middle Euphrates Shi'ite elites against British attempts to integrate the Middle Euphrates, politically and economically, into the rest of Iraq. This integrative process involved selective patronage extended to narrow segments of prominent tribal chieftains and city notables, without due regard to other segments that were, thus, politically marginalized. The 1920 revolt was also a reaction against the full-scale colonial taxation imposed on land and crops.

Thus the basic assumption behind the uprising was to alter the terms of inclusion of the Euphrates tribal collectivities into the emerging central power, in particular to claim a greater share of power, wealth and prestige.

A resultant paradox of the 1920 uprising is that direct economic and political interests were realized by the Euphrates elites and leaders more rapidly, while the elaboration of an explicit idiom expressing these interests lagged behind. By mixing their tribal and religious cultural symbols with nationalist discourse, this generation of Euphrates elites wanted to take advantage of the gap between British-declared intentions and actual practices on the ground, in order to enhance their politico-economic status or at least strike a balance with pro-government sheikhs.

The Idiom of Nationalism versus Particularism

What then does the 1920 uprising and the years before it tell us about the connection between tribal political culture and behaviour and nationalist political culture and behaviour? In particular, how does tribe as socio-political formation articulate and mobilize differentiated cultural traditions of kinship to refer to nationalism as a political ideology which indicates a specific way of structuring social life, and a historical framework of socio-political organization? The following is an attempt to answer these questions in the framework of the 1920 uprising.

Hidden Nationalism or Strategic Particularism?

A significant part of the answer is to define the meaning of tribe and tribalism in the agrarian epoch under consideration, and juxtapose it on that of nation and nationalism. On the basis of their Middle Eastern studies, various anthropologists define tribe in terms of lineage; others add territorial distinction and political unity under chieftains; an ideology of common descent is also added (Tapper, 1991, p.52f). Tribes are also conceived of as subsistence units, synonymous with nomadism and pastoralism. In political and cultural terms they are treated as an actual static social structure or as a residue value system.

The tribal form, however, is a constructed mechanism of references for the creation and mobilization of social identity and political loyalty. Any diminution of an existing tribal structure as a result of, for instance, the rise of large-scale political and economic structures (such as modern standing armies, bureaucracy, economic organization), is seen as a decline in the operation of the tribal mechanisms of social identity and political loyalty. Yet, in some instances, the tribe as a referential framework for social identity and political loyalty has endured in urban settings. This is despite the fact that large-scale structures have weakened the tribe as a socio-economic organization (Cm. Tibi, 1991, p.128). The interrelations between tribal social formations, ecological environment and central power are important aspects in any definition of tribe and tribalism. According to this view, we see tribes as a form of social organization and social reproduction, which mediates the control and distribution of scarce resources, manages processes of social reproduction through kinship bonds and loyalties and confers on its members a structure to regulate the socioeconomic and political interaction with other social formations anchored in sect, religion, city or other larger configurations.

By contrast, nationalism as an ideology is imagined in terms of 'a bounded horizontal community, a bounded totality, beyond immediate experience of place, and beyond which lie other nations' (Anderson 1983, pp. 15f, 19). Upon this premise, nationalism, then, constitutes a negation of tribal ideology or the structure of tribalism that I have described above. Essentially, tribalism cannot support 'large-scale political structures with their own resources' ... or 'handle internal political affairs beyond what could be provided by segmentary opposition' (Barified 1983, p. 166). While factionalism, segmented loyalties and small scale are inherent in tribalism as the Iraqi context shows, nationalist ideology connotes, as Michael Billig points out, that 'people, place and state should be bounded in unity' (Billig 1995, pp. 74, 77). Moreover, unlike tribal ideology, nationalism as an ideology is concerned with 'continuity and homogeneity encompassing diversity' (Handlar 1988, p. 6). While nationalism may invent nations where they do not exist, the inner structural limitations of tribalism make it highly unimaginable for tribal political formations to be transformed into nationalism. Not only theoretically, but also empirically, nationalism and tribalism are divergent modes of lifestyles and value systems, and, most importantly in the context of this study, divergent modes of political culture and organization.

Divergence notwithstanding, tribalism and nationalism may indeed overlap on some points. Representatives of divergent cultural and political formations may easily borrow from the ideological discourse of the other, once the appeal of that discourse is discovered. Tribal politics might, in such a vein, benefit from and manipulate the ideological discourse of nationalism at the same time as nationalist ideology may employ tribal values.

Three considerations may further serve to distinguish between tribalism and nationalism: First, they differ by the nature of the mechanisms of mobilisation of identity formation and political loyalty, as well as by the scale and duration of mobilisation. Unlike tribalism, nationalism provides extended possibilities for more fluid mobilisation by operating with anonymous individuals. Second, they differ in nature and in the level of territorial diffusion and social composition. To survive beyond the territorial and ideational limitations of tribalism larger-scale socio-political organisations must, at least theoretically, deny any association with the tribes and define themselves in terms that override particularism and segmented loyalties and identities. It is true that people who belong to nations also have local allegiances, but the question is whether people who have local allegiances do maintain feelings of national belonging as defined by their political culture, collective action and modes of political organization. In the 'successive' nation-states, group, communal components and status-groups are usually re-contextualised through the unfolding of various functional social subsystems, mainly the political system. Third, an additional, basic and more systematic difference between nationalism and tribalism is that while tribalism involves mostly face-to-face interaction between constituent members of a total tribal system, national society generally involves people who need not know each other personally and may constitute parts of differentiated social subsystems. Within the framework of national politics and action the question of who performs that action seems to be less important than the question of the nature of this action itself. This is mostly because nationalist performance, unlike the tribal one, is abstracted from individuals who perform it. As a result, nationalism makes up an associative system of social particulars that is not identical with the particularism from which it is composed. The implication of this observation bears directly on the problem of the large scale of the political action. In particular, participation in nationalist action is not based on any segmentary group membership or a system of pre-set primordial attributes. No practical or a priori genealogical limitation (primordial qualities of lineage, status, clan or household) can be set to hinder social movements from combining their action.

In conclusion, during the period under consideration, nationalism was not a socially relevant idea either among the urban elites (the official and embryonic intelligentsia in Baghdad, Mosul or Basrah) or among village tribal leaders or clerical notables. It did not appear to be socially coherent and/or a way for widely based interests to be articulated. Hence, what characterized the political culture and behaviour of that time was factionalism and localized response strategies embedded in the immediate interests of the actors. At any rate, nationalism, nationalist framework of collective action and nationalist identity have to be invented as a binding force and a collective generation of identity and strategies in a constructed meaning that transcends tribal imagination.

The Misinterpretation of Locally Particularist Histories as a Master Nationalist History

When tribal military operations are directed against foreign powers or conquerors, they can readily be given a more romantic aura as revolutionary projects defending historical rights of existence, irrespective of the actual character, causes and scale of such projects. The 1920 uprising indicates that the tribes received decisive ideological backing from religious leaders who traditionally were held to be above tribal feuds. Clerical leaders, in turn, had their own interests in such backing. When clerical resources were applied in tribal mobilization, anti-British tribal military operations, based on the traditional hit-and-run tactics, acquired a new appearance. Instead of being what they really are, namely, irregular, intermittent, short-term, brief and swift attacks, they were projected as a series of continuous, dense, intensive, connected and systematic revolutionary actions.

In modern times, nationalist historiography, in concert with the popular and international condemnation of colonialism, confers additional colour on such actions, depicting them in terms of nationalism and anti-colonialism, i.e. manifestations of the revolutionary temperament of all the indigenous people. In this process, nationalist historians, both 'focalise' and 'transvaluate' events of revolutionary acts directed against the foreign presence. They focalise such events by 'the process of progressive denudiation of local incidents and disputes of their particulars of context and aggregating, thereby narrowing, their concrete richness'. Such transvaluation is achieved by means of 'assimilating particulars to a larger, collective, more enduring, and therefore less context-bound, causes or interest' (Tambiah, S. J. as quoted in Appadurai 1997, p. 11). Agents who played an active part in tribal revolutionary operations against the British in 1920, and originally viewed their uprising as acts particular to local traditions of resistance and revolt, have then claimed in retrospect that actually they were fighting for the cause of all Iraqi people, for the Islamic and Arab virtuous rights, for the ancestral past, and, by extension, for the creation of the Iraqi State. Nationalist historians have persistently depicted the tribal uprising in nationalist terms, regarding it as a nationalist act conducted by the revolutionary tribal forces with an aim to put an end to British plans to make Iraq just another colony of their empire.

References

Arabic

al-'Azawi, Abbas, *Tarikh al-Iraq bayn Ihtilalayn* (The History of Iraq Between the Two Occupations), Baghdad, *Sharikat al-tijara almahduda*, volumes 7 and 8, 1955.

al-Basir, Mohammed Mahdi, *Tarikh al Qadhiya al'Iraqiya* (History of the Iraqi Question), two volumes, Baghdad, 1924.

al-Bazirgan, Ali, *al Waqa'iq al Haqiqiya fi al Thawara al 'Iraqiya* (Facts and Realities of the Iraqi Revolution), Baghdad, 1954.

Al-Fir'oun, Mizhir, *al Haqa'iq al-Nasi'a fi al Thawrah al Iraqiya Senat 1920 wa Nata'ijiha* (The Clear Facts of the 1920 Iraqi Revolution and its Consequences), Baghdad, al-najah lil tibaa, 1952.

al-Hasani, Abdul-Razzak, *Tarikh al Thawra al Iraqiya* (History of the Iraqi Revolution), Sydon, 1935.

al-Jawahiri, 'Imad Ahmad, *Tarikh Mushkilat Al Aradhi fi al Iraq* (History of land tenure in Iraq), Baghdad, Wizarat al-thaqafa wal funun, 1978.

al-Jubouri, Kamil, Salman, *Safahat min Muthekkarat Sa'id Kamal al Din, Ahad Rijal al-Thawra al Iraqiya 1920*, (Papers from the Memoirs of Sa'id Kamal al-Din, A leading Figure in the 1920 Iraqi Revolution), Baghdad, al-Ani Publishers, 1978.

al-Mahbuba, Ja'far Baqir, *Madhi al Najaf wa Hadhiriha* (Najaf, Past and Present), Sydon, 1953.

al-Nafisi, Abdullah, *Al Shi'a fi Tarikh al Iraq* (The Shi'is in the History of Iraq), Beirut Dar al-Nahar, 1971.

al-Umari, Mohammed Khairuldin, *Tarikh Muqaddirat al Iraq al Siyasiya* (Iraq, Political History), Baghdad, 1925.

al-Wardi, Ali, *Lamahat ijtima'iya min tarikh al-Iraq al-hadith* (Social Aspects of Iraq's Modern History), Baghdad, al-Shaab Publishing House, volume 5, 1977.

al-Za'im, Abbas Ali, *Al Thawra al 'Iraqiya* (The Iraqi Revolution), Baghdad, 1950.

Attiya, Ghassan, *al-Iraq, Takwin al-Dawla* (Iraq, State Formation) *1908–1921*, trans. Ata Abdul-Wahab, London, 1988.

Attiya, Wadye, *Tarikh al Diwaniya, Qadiman wa Hadithan* (History of the Diwaniya, Past and Present), Najaf, al-haidarja, 1954.

Fayyad, Abdullah, *al-Thawra al-Iraqyia al-kubra 1920* (The Iraqi Great Revolution of 1920), Baghdad, Dar al Salam Publishers, 1975.

Kotolov, L. N., *Thawrat al-'ishrin al-taharuriya fi al-Iraq* (The 1920 Liberation Revolution in Iraq) translated by Abdul-Wahid Karam, Baghdad, 1971.

English

Arab Bulletin 1986, *Bulletin of the Arab Bureau in Cairo*, 1916–1919, Archive Editions, Vol. I, II, III, IV. Redwood Burn LTD, Trowbridge.

Anderson, Benedict, *Imagined Communities*. London: Verso, 1983.

Appadurai, Arjun, *Modernity at Large: Cultural Dimensions of Globalization*, Minneapolis and London: University of Minnesota Press, 1997 (1996).

Barified, Thomas J., 'Tribe and State Relations: The Inner Asian Perspective' in Khoury, Philip S. and Kostiner, Joseph (eds.), *Tribes and State Formation in the Middle East*. London: I.B. Tauris, 1991.

Batatu, Hanna, *The Old Social Classes and the Revolutionary Movements in Iraq*. Princeton: Princeton University Press. 1978.

Beck, Lois, 'Tribes and State Formation in the Middle East' in Khoury, Philip S. and Kostiner, Joseph (eds.), *Tribes and State Formation in the Middle East*. London: I.B. Tauris, 1991.

Bell, D. B. E. (ed.), *The Letters of Gertrude Bell*. Harmondsworth, Penguin, 1927.

Billig, Michael, *Banal Nationalism*. London: Sage, 1995.

Bourdieu, Pierre, *The Logic of Practice*. Stanford: Stanford University Press, 1990.

Busch, Briton C., *Britain, India and the Arabs 1914/1921*. London: 1971.

Cox, Sir Percy, 'Historical Summary' in Bell, D. B. E. (ed.), *The Letters of Gertrude Bell*, New York: Harmondsworth, Penguin, 1927.

Haj, Samira, *The Making of Iraq, 1900-1963, Capital, Power, and Ideology*, New York, Albany, NY: State University of New York, 1997.

Haldane, A. L., *The Insurrection in Mesopotamia, 1920*, Edinburgh, 1922.

Handler, Richard, *Nationalism and the Politics of Culture in Quebec*. Madison: University of Wisconsin Press, 1988.

Hart, David M., 'The Tribes in Modern Morocco: Two Case Studies' in Gellner, Ernest and Micaud, Charles (eds.), *Arabs and Berbers*. London: Duckworth, 1972.

Ireland, W., *Iraq, A Study in Political Development*. London, 1937.

Longrigg, S. H., *Iraq, 1900 to 1950, A Political, Social and Economic History*. London: Oxford University Press, 1953.

Marlow, John, *Late Victorian, The Life of Sir Arnold Talbot Wilson*. London, 1967.

Moberly, F. J., *The Campaigns in Mesopotamia*, Vols I, II and III, London, 1924.

Marr, Phebe, *The Modern History of Iraq*, Boulder, London: Westview, 1985.

Richards, Alan and Waterbury John, *A Political Economy of the Middle East*, San Fransisco and Oxford: Westview Press, 1990 (1979).

Sluglett, M. F. and Sluglett, 'Sunnis and Shi'is Revisited: Sectarianism and Ethnicity in Authoritarian Iraq' in Hopwood, D., Ishow, Habib and Kozcinowski Thomas (eds) *Iraq: Power and Society*. Reading: Ithaca Press, 1993.

Sluglett, Peter, *Britain in Iraq*. London: Ithaca Press, 1976.

Tapper, Richard, 'Introduction' in Tapper, Richard (ed.), *The Conflict of Tribe and State in Iran and Afghanistan*, London: Croom Helm and New York: St. Martin's Press, 1983.

—— 'Anthropologists, Historians, and Tribespeople on Tribe and State Formation in the Middle East' in Khoury, Philip S. and Kostiner, Joseph (eds.), *Tribes and State Formation in the Middle East*. London: I.B. Tauris, 1991.

Tibi, Bassam, 'Old Tribes and Imposed Nation-States in the Modern Middle East' in Khoury, Philip and Costiner Joseph (eds.) *Tribes and State Formation in the Middle East*. London: I.B. Tauris, 1991.

Waterbury, John, *The Commander of the Faithful*. London: Weidenfeld and Nicolson, 1970.

Wiarda, Howard J., 'Toward a Non-ethnic Theory of Development: Alternative Conceptions from the Third World', in Wiarda, Howard J. (ed) *New Directions in Comparative Politics.* Boulder and London: Westview, 1985.

Wicker, Hans-Rudolf , 'Introduction: Theorizing Ethnicity and Nationalism' in Wicker, Hans-Rudolf (ed), *Rethinking Nationalism and Ethnicity: The Struggle for Meaning and Order in Europe.* Durham: Berg, 1997.

Yapp, M. Y., *The Making of the Modern Near East, 1792–1923.* London and NY: Longman, 1987.

Contributors

Pierre Bonte is Research Director at the Centre National de la Recherche Scientifique (CNRS) in Paris. He holds two PhDs for his work on Saharan societies. He is author and co-author of several works relating to the Arab and Muslim world. These include *La Tribu* (1991), *Le Mariage* (1994), *Le Sacrifice* (1999) and *La Politique* (2001). He was also co-author of the *Dictionnaire de l'anthropologie et de l'ethnologie* (1991).

Kenneth Brown was born in 1936, and earned his PhD in Islamic Studies from the University of California, Los Angeles (UCLA). He was a Fellow of the Committee for the Comparative Study of New Nations at the University of Chicago and is currently editor of *Méditerranées*, a bi-annual review published in Paris. His publications include *People of Salé, The Social History of a Moroccan City (1830–1930)*, and various articles on Berber poetry, Muslim cities, social change in Tunisia and the Israel-Palestine region.

Martin van Bruinessen is Professor of Comparative Religious Studies at Utrecht University and the International Institute for the Study of Islam in the Modern World (ISIM) in Leiden. He is the author of *Agha, Shaikh and State: Social and Political Structures of Kurdistan*, and has written numerous articles on the Kurds.

Edouard Conte is Research Professor of Anthropology at the French National Centre for Scientific Research (CNRS) and a member of the Laboratoire d'Anthropologie Sociale at the Collège de France in Paris. His publications in the field of Arab studies include *al-Ansab, La quête des origines:Anthropologie historique de la société tribale arabe* (Paris, MSH, 1991), *Emirs et présidents* and *Figures de la parenté et politique dans le monde arabe.*

Hosham Dawod is a researcher at the French National Centre for Scientific Research (CNRS) and a member of the Centre d'Etudes Interdisciplinaires des Faits Religieux. He is preparing a PhD in social anthropology. He has written widely on Middle Eastern societies, including *Ethnicité et pouvoirs au Moyen-Orient, Le cas kurde, La société traditionnelle kurde* and *Tribalisme et pouvoir en Irak.*

Toby Dodge taught Middle Eastern Politics and International Relations at the School of Oriental and African Studies (SOAS), University of London. He is currently a Research Fellow at the Royal Institute of International Affairs (RIIA) in London, where he is working on the effects of war and sanctions on Iraqi society. He is completing a PhD at SOAS on the concerns of state-society relations in Iraq from 1914–1932.

Nelida Fuccaro is a lecturer in Modern Middle Eastern History at the Institute of Arab and Islamic Studies, University of Exeter. She is the author of *The Other Kurds: Yazidis in Colonial Iraq* (London, IB Tauris, 1999). She is currently researching the urban history of the Persian Gulf.

Faleh A. Jabar was born in Baghdad in 1946. He holds a PhD in Sociology and is a Visiting Fellow at Birkbeck College, University of London. He has published widely on Iraq, including *Religious Thought in Iraq* (1985); *The Classical Roots of the Theory of Alienation* (Beirut 1989); *State and Civil Society in Iraq* (Cairo, 1994); *Nationalism: Malady or Antidote?* (London, 1995); and *The Impossible Democracy* (Beirut, 1999). He has also edited *Post-Marxism and the Middle East* (London 1997) and *Ayatollahs, Sufis and Ideologues* (London, 2001), and has translated three volumes of Karl Marx's *Das Kapital* (Moscow, 1985–9).

Thair Karim earned his PhD in Economic History from Moscow University. He teaches History and Social Science at Vilunda Gymnasium, Stockholm. His publications include a host of essays for *An-Nahj, al-Tariq* and *al-Thaqafa al-Jadida.*

Madhawi al-Rasheed is a senior lecturer in social anthropology at King's College, London. Her current research looks at Arab migration to Britain and issues concerning ethnic and religious minorities in London. She writes widely on Saudi Arabia and is the author of *Politics in an Arabian Oasis* (1991), and *The Construction of Ethnicity: Iraqi Assyrian Christians in London* (1998).

Farian Sabahi is a Visiting Fellow at the Graduate Institute for International Studies in Geneva. After earning her Ph.D. from London University's School of Oriental and African Studies, she spent one year as a post-doctoral Fellow for Iranian Studies at Bologna University. She has published a book on the Shahsevan tribes (in Italian) as well as several articles in English and Italian journals. Her PhD dissertation will be published in Switzerland in 2001.

Keiko Sakai is a researcher at the Institute of Developing Economies at the University of Durham. Her publications include *Ten Years with Sanctions* (S. Fukuda ed.), *Politics, Economy and Sanctions in Persian Gulf States in a Changing Environment*, (IDE, Chiba, 2001); and (in Japanese) *Nationalism and Islam* (IDE, 2001).

Glossary

English	Arabic	Transliteration
A		
abtar	أبتر	amputated (with no sons)
ahkam al-nikah	أحكام النكاح	marriage codes
akhlat	أخلاط	cardinal humours
'ahd	عهد	contract, covenant
ahl al-bayt	أهل البيت	house
ahl al-ibil (ahlil-bil)	أهل الإبل	the people of the camel
ahrar (sing. hurr)	أحرار (حرّ)	noble (also: free)
akh (pl. ikhwan)	أخ (إخوان)	brother
albu (al)	ألبو (آل)	sub-clan, family
amir	أمير	prince, commander
amir al-mu'minin	أمير المؤمنين	commander of the faithful
'ammiya	عامية	social system in Lebanon
'amm (pl. 'amam)	عم (أعمام)	father's brother
anfusana	أنفسنا	ourselves
ansab	أنساب	genealogies
ansab al-'alam	أنساب الأعلام	genealogy of human world
'aqirat	عقيرة	slaughter-beast
'asaba	عصابة	solidarity group
'asabiyya (pl. 'asabiyyat)	عصبية (عصبيات)	solidarity (ies)
asbab (sing. sabab)	أسباب (سبب)	aspects (also causes, factors)
'asha'ir (sing. 'ashira)	عشائر (عشيرة)	clan or tribe
ashraf (sing. sharif)	أشراف (شريف)	descendents of the Prophet, also: noble
asliyyun	أصليون	rooted
awlad al-'amm	أولاد العمّ	patrilateral cousins

314

English	Arabic	Transliteration
'ayd (al-Kabir)	العيد (الكبير)	Muslim festival (after pilgrimage to Mecca)
'aylaqat al-dam	علاقات الدم	blood relations
azef (Berber)	ازف (بربر)	customary law
B		
banu-l-'amm	بنو العم	patrilateral cousins
badal	بدل	substitute, exchange (in marriage)
badawa	بداوة	nomadism
badu	بدو	nomads
batin	باطن	internal
batn (part of a tribe)	بطن	belly
bay'a	بيعة	allegiance
bayraq (pl. bayariq)	بيرق (بيارق)	tribal banners or flags
bayt	بيت	family, house
bayt al-mal	بيت المال	central treasury
bdh' (istibdha')	بضع (استبضاع)	man requires his wife to cohabit a nobler person to beget a son for him of noble stock (pre-Islamic)
baldiyyin	بلديين	original inhabitants of the city (Morocco)
Brutistant	بروتستانت	Protestant
bunuwwa	بنوه (ابن)	establish a relation of filiation with a child (derived from ibn: son)
D		
da'i (v. idda'a)	داعي (ادعَاء)	claimant
dam (pl. dima')	دم (دماء)	blood
dakhil (or dakheel)	داخل (دخيل)	he who enters
dawla	دولة	state, taking turns
dira	ديرة	tribal camping or pastures or domain
diya	دية	blood money
E		
ekhtiar (Persian)	اختيار	the freedom of choice
emirate	إمارة	principality

English	Arabic	Transliteration
F		
fakhidh (pl. afkhadh)	فخذ (أفخاذ)	thigh
fasad	فساد	collapse, corruption
fasila	فصيلة	lower part of the leg (large household)
fasl	فصل	segmentation, compensation paid in settlement of disputes
fenda	فندة	breast (sub-tribe section, Iraq)
filalih (hirratha)	فلاليح (حراثة)	peasants (land tillers)
firash	فراش	literally bed, or wife, concubine
firqa	فرقة	team (sub-tribe section, Iraq)
fitna	فتنة	chaos
G		
ghariba	غريبة	female stranger
ghar'ib	غريب	stranger
glawi	قلاوي	regional notable (Moroccan)
H		
hadhar	حضر	urban dwellers
hadhara	حضارة	civilization
hadhari	حضري	urban
hajin	هجين	child of a slave mother
hamula (pl. hamulat)	حمولة (حمولات)	clan or sub-clan, or lineage
harka wa mahalla	حركة ومحلة	annual expeditions (Morocco)
hayba	هيبة	awe
haydh	حيض	source of pollution
hayy	حي	clan
hella	هلّة	emiral camp
hilf (muhalafa)	حلف (محالفة)	political alliance
hurma	حرمة	women (literally: forbidden)
husa	هوسة (عامية عراقية)	tribal war chanting, also chaos
I		
ibn	ابن	son
ibn khal	ابن خال	son of mother's brother
ikha' (see: mu'akhat)	إخاء (مؤاخاة)	confusion, mixing
ikhtilat	اختلاط	social organization

English	Arabic	Transliteration
ijtima'	اجتماع	principality (see Emarate)
imara	إمارة	sub-tribal structure (Iraq)
'imara	عمارة	absorption into another agnatic
indimaj	اندماج	unit
intisab	انتساب	affiliation
iqrar	إقرار	adoption, confirmation
ista'bba	استأب	(derived from: abb=father) recognize someone as father
istalhaqa	استلحق	to adjoin
J		
jar	جار	neighbour
jar thul-qurba	جار ذو القربى	a relative
jash (jahsh) (Kurish)	(جاش (جحش) (كردية	donkey
jad	جَد	grandfather, ancestor
jihad	جهاد	holy war
jihat	جهات	quarters
jiwar	جوار	neighbourhood, co-residence
K		
kadu khuda (Persian)	(كادو خودا (فارسية	headman
kafa'a	كفاءة	parity between spouses
Kathulik	كاثوليك	catholic
khal (pl. akhwal)	(خال (أخوال	mother's brother
khan (Persian)	(خان (فارسية	leader
khudhairi	(خضيري (عامية عراقية	vegetable growers
khums	خُمس	fifth, religious tax
kitba	كتبة	documented, written
kubra	كبرى	superior
L		
laff (or leff)	(اللَف (اللَف	the attached, the connected, a form of tribal alliance
lahma	لحمة	meat
laqab	لقب	title, tribal name
laqit	لقيط	child found
Latin	لاتين	Latin
luhma	لُحمة	kinship bond

English	Arabic	Transliteration
M		
mahr	مهر	bride wealth
majhul	مجهول	unknown
makhzan	مخزن	central power, dynastic state (Moroccon)
malak tawus	ملك طاووس	Peacock Angel
mawla	مولى	freedman
mawali	موالي	dependents
mi'dan	معدان (عامية عراقية)	marsh dwellers (Iraq)
mithaq	ميثاق	proclaimed pact
mizaj	مزاج	temperament
mu'imm	مُعِمّ	one's paternal ascendants
mu'amma	مُعامّة	pact of agnatic cousinship, cousin-hood
mu'akhat	مؤاخاة	brotherhood
mujtahid	مجتهد	clerical jurisprudent
mukhwa	مخوة	(a variation of mu'akhat)
mukhwil	مخول	one's maternal ascendants
mulk	ملك	political power
mulla	ملا	cleric
muqawiloon	مقاولون	contracotrs
musahara (see: sihr)	مصاهرة (صهر)	designating affinity
mustana'un	مصطنعون	artificial
muta'ammun (see:mu'amma)	متعامون	cousinhood
N		
naqil	ناقل	relocated
nasab (pl. ansab)	نسب (أنساب)	affinity, agnatic descent, lineage, filiation, origin
nasab abawi	نسب أبوي	patrilineal descent
nasib	نسيب	agnate or brother in law
nikah	نكاح	marriage
nisba	نسبة	cognatic kinship, also origin
nisba 'uliya	نسبة عليا	higher kinship
niswan (colloquial of Nissa')	نسوان (نساء)	women
nu'ra (or Na'ra)	نُعرة (نَعرة)	group susceptibility

English	Arabic	Transliteration
Q		
qabila	قبيلة	tribe
qaraba	قرابة	kinship, proximity, propinquity
qa'id	قائد	leader
qayed (see Glawi)	قايد	regional notable
R		
rahim (pl. arham)	رَحم (أرحام)	uterus
ridha'a	رضاعة	suckling
riyasa	رياسة	chieftainship
S		
sadr	صدر	breast (tribal section)
sahih	صحيح	correct
sarkal (or sirkal)	سركال (عامية عراقية)	village head (Iraq)
sayba (also: siba)	ساية (سيبة)	tribal domain, dissidence (Morocco)
sayyid	سيّد	noble (see: Ashraf)
sha'ab	شعب	small tribe (also: people)
shari'a	شريعة	Islamic law
shawiya	شاوية (عامية عراقية)	sheep breeders
shajarat al-nasab (see: ansab)	شجرة النسب (أنساب)	tree of lineage
shajarat al-ansab (plural)	شجرة الأنساب	
sheikh	شيخ	tribal chief
sheikh al-mashayikh	شيخ المشايخ	chief of chieftains
shu'ubiya	شعوبية	non-Arab or anti-Arab movement
sihr	صهر	affinal, the affine
silsilat al-nasab	سلسلة النسب	chains of lineage
silat	صلة	relationship
silat al-raham	صلة الرحم	uterine relationships
shigharr	شغار	exchange of daughters by fathers in mutual marriage
soff (see: laff)	الصَف	dual alliances
sunna	السُنّة	Prophet's Muhammad tradition
T		
tabbana	تبنّى	to adopt, take as a son

English	Arabic	Transliteration
tabbani	تبنَي	filial adoption
tadhamur	تذامر	defence of family honour
taqbilt (Berber)	تقبيلت (بربر)	tribe (qabila)
tarikh	تاريخ	history
tazawwuj (zawaj)	تزاوج	marriage
ta'ifa	طائفة	confessional faction
talib	طالب	he who requests, request
tawa'if	طوائف	confessional factions
tha'r	ثأر	retaliation
U		
'ulama'	علماء	doctors of religion
umma	أمة	community (of brothers in faith)
'umran	عمران	civilization
'umumiya	عمومية	mutual protection pact
'unuq	عنق	neck (sub-tribe section)
'urf	عرف	customary law
V		
vilayat (Turkish)	ولاية	province
W		
wahm	وهم	illusion
Walad	ولد	boy, son
Weli	ولي	tutor
Wali	والي	governor
Wilaya	ولاية	province
Y		
Yadkhulu	يدخلوا	enter into
Yaqta'u	يقطعوا	cut, sever
Z		
Zanqa	زنقة	tributaries
Zawaya	زوايا	sufi lodges
'na	زنى	fornication

Index

Abbas, 'Alwan Sayyid, 301
Abbas, Shah, 168
Abd al-Muttalib, 24
Abdulhamid II, Sultan, 171, 236
Abdullah, Prince, of Iran, 297
Abdulmajid, Sultan, 168, 172
Abu Bakr, 25-6
Abu al-Jon, Sha'lan, 292
Abu Tabikh, Muhsin, 298, 301
Abu Talib, 24
Adiyaman, Tahir, 174
Ahmad 'Ayda, 60-3
Ahmad uld Mhamed, 60
Ali, Hasan, 141
Ali, Mohammad, 227
al-Ali, Salah Omar, 87
Alwan, Hamid, 152, 157
Amin, Idi, 122
Antara, 27
Aquino, B., 123
Arsuzi, Zaki, 91
Arif, Abdul Rahman, 140
al-Asfahani, al-Sharia, Sheikh, 293
al-Attiya, Waddai, 299
al-'Awad, Marzouq, 298
Ayache, G., 207
Ayish, Muhammad, 84
Aziz, Tariq, 81, 141
al-'Azzawi, 'Abbas, 137

Badie, Bertrand 114
Bahmanbegi, Muhammad, 238-42, 245-8
al-Bakr, Ahmad Hassan, 84-7 passim, 120,
    140-1, 144, 146
Barified, Thomas J., 304
Barry, Naomi, 245-6
Barzani, Mulla, 173
Barzinji, Mahmud, Sheikh, 185
al-Basir, Mohammed Mahdi, 285, 292
Batatu, Hanna, 84, 272-3
al-Bazirgan, Ali, 285
Beck, Lois, 236
Bédoucha, G., 16, 29, 40, 43
Bell, Gertrude, 265-6, 300-1
Berque, J., 206
Bhutto, Z., 123
Billig, Michael, 304
bin Hidhal, Fahad, 300
bin Ihda, Sidi 'Azza, 208
bin Wadi, Uraibi, 300
Bokassa, J.B., 122
Bourqia, R., 207, 209
Bray, Major, 286
Bucak, Fayik, 171
Bucak, Mehmet Celal, 171
Bucak, Sedat Edip, 171
Bucak, Serhat, 171
Burke, E., 210

Chelhod, J., 63

Cigar, N., 207-8
Cole, D.P., 41
Combs-Schilling, M.E., 59
Conte, E., 56
Cornwallis, Kinahan, 262, 271-2
Cox, Sir Percy, 284, 300

Daly, Major, 301
al-Dawod, Ibrahim, 140
al-Dawud, Dawud, 192, 195-6, 198
Della Vida, G. Levi, 207
Dobbs, Sir Henry, 261-2, 265, 271-2, 301
Doutte, E., 206
Dresch, P., 19, 32, 40-2
al-Dulaimi, Mazlum, 99, 152, 157
Dumont, Louis, 57
Dunhill, J.W., 246-7
Durkheim, Emile, 83, 206

Eickelman, D., 206
Ellow, Agha Petros, 197-8
Evans-Pritchard, E., 206

Faisal, King, 139-40, 186, 286, 293
Fayyad, Abdullah, 284, 292
Fernea, Robert, 77-8
al-Fir'oun, Mizhir, 285, 295, 298
Foucault, Michel, 262
Friedman, Jonathan, 112

Gagon, Glen, 238-40
Garibaldi, Giuseppe, 267
Geertz, C., 206, 209
Geertz, H., 206
Gellner, Ernest, 57-8, 187, 206
Ghaydan, Sa'dun, 144
al-Gisad, Abdul-Sada, 298
Gizar, Nazim, 84
ibb, John, 263

Gluckman, M., 206
Godelier, Maurice, 112
Goldziher, I., 18, 20-1
Grady, H.F., 239
Granqvist, H., 26-8
Guessous, M., 207

Haddad, Na'im, 141
al-Hadithi, Murtadha, 87
al-Hajj Sawwad, 35
Haldane, General, 301
Hamid, 'Abdul, Sultan, 187
Hammadi, Sa'dun, 143
Hammoudi, A., 58, 207
Hamu Shiru, 191-9 *passim*
Hamza, 25
Handlar, Richard, 304
Hart, D., 206
al-Hasan, Watban, 86
al-Hasani, Abdul-Razzak, 286
al-Hashimi, Yassin, 297
Haskani, Khalaf, Sheikh, 192, 196
Hassan, Ibrahim, 120
Hassan II, King, 60
Henninger, J., 42
Héritier, F., 22
al-Hiba ibn Shaykh Ma' al-'Aynayn,
    Shaykh, 60
Holt, V., 266-7
al-Hussein, 'Abadi, 298
Hussein, Adnan, 84
Husayn, Ahmad, 145
Hussein, Saddam, 81-2, 87-8, 111-15,
    120-1, 124, 137, 141-9 *passim*, 156, 284
Hussein, Sharif, 290
Hussein, Uday, 87-8, 122, 158

Ibn Abdul Wahhab, Mohammad, 221, 228
Ibn Abdullah, Turki, 225-6
Ibn Dawas, Dahham, 220

Ibn Hadhdhal, Fahad Beg, 268
Ibn Haritha, Zayd, 21-8 *passim*
Ibn Hidhal, Fahad, 300
Ibn Khaldun, 50-64 *passim*,
    72-3, 83, 207, 218-19
Ibn Manzur, 20-1, 27
Ibn Mijland, Jaid, 268
Ibn Muamar, Uthman, 220
Ibn Rashid, Mohammad, 229
Ibn Salman, Ibrahim, 220
Ibn Saud, Abdul Aziz, 226, 230
Ibn Saud, Mohammad, 221-2
Ibn Suwait, 265
Ibn Zamil, Zayd, 220
Ibn Zayd, Usama, 23, 26
Ibrahim, Barzan, 141
Ibrahim, 'Izzat, 144, 146
Ibrahim, son of Muhammad the Prophet,
    25
Ibrahim Pasha, 225
al-'Ifrit, Abdul Hamza, 298
al-Isfahani, Abu al-Faraj, 27

Ja'far, 25
Jamous, R., 58, 206
Jassim, Latif, 152
Jaussen, A., 40
al-Jawahiri, 'Imad Ahmad, 288
al-Jazi', Khashan, 268
al-Juburi, Mash'an, 152, 157

al-Kammuna, 289
Kamal, Mustafa, 267
Khairallah, Adnan, 141
al-Khawjah, Rashid, 140
Khidr, Sheikh, 196
Kotolov, L.N., 284

Lane, E.W., 20
Laroui, A., 207

Lawrence, T.E., 284
Layard, Henry, 198
Layne, Linda L., 262-3
Leach, Edmund, 112
Leveau, R., 207
Longrigg, Stephen, 301

Madelung, W., 25
Mahmud, Sheikh, 266-7
Mahmud II, Sultan, 168
al-Majid, Ali Hassan, 87, 91, 100, 120, 141
al-Majid, Hussain Kamel, 87, 121, 123, 158
al-Majid, Rokan Ghafour, 91, 95
al-Majid, Saddam Kamel, 87
al-Ma'jun, 'Azzarah, 269
Malik, Imam, 30
Mansur, Malek, 238
Mariya the Copt, 25
Marlow, John, 286
al-Mashhadani, Muhammad Jasim, 137, 156
Maude, S., 287, 291
Medhet Pasha, 73, 75, 262
al-Mijlad, Jazza', 268
Montagne, R., 206
Monteil, V., 56
Morgan, L.H., 16
Morsy, M., 58
al-Mugotar, Hadi, 301
Muhammad the Prophet, 21-6, 38, 54
Muhsin, Jabbar, 90
Mukhaylif, Omar, 145
Mukhlis, Mawlud, 139
Mukhtar uld Hamidun, 53
Mylles, C.C., 264

al-Naqib, Abdul-Rahman, 296
al-Naqib, Talib, 289
al-Nayif, Abdul Razzaq, 140
Noel, Major, 185

Pascon, P., 207
Peters, E., 15, 21, 28, 41-2, 206
Planhol, X. de, 167
Proksch, O., 18

Qaraqulla, 'Abd al-Karim, 198
Qashqai brothers, 248
Qassim, General, 80, 82
Qaylan, Awlad, 62
Ramadhan, Taha Yasin, 81, 144
al-Rashid, Sheikh, 218
Rashiq, H., 207
Rassam, Hormuzd, 198
al-Rawi, Ibrahim, 140
al-Rawi, Jamil, 140
Razmara, Ali, 239
Reza Pahlavi, Muhammad, 250
Reza Shah, Muhammad, 237
Rosen, L., 206
Rousseau, Jean-Jacques, 260
al-Rumaidh, Badr, 288

Sa'id Beg, 196, 199
al-Sadr, Mohammed, 285
Said, Edward, 18
al-Sa'id, Nuri, 80, 143
Salih, Muhammad, 145
Salim, S.M., 32-5
al-Salman, Sha'lan, 298
Samarmand, 'Ajil Pasha, 300
al-Sayhud, al-Amir Mohammed, 300
al-Sayhud, Falih, 300
Serjeant, R.B., 38
al-Shaalan, Sheikh, 218
Shabandar, Samira, 124
Shaker, Sa'dun, 141
·l-Shamkhi, Hassan, 298
  ⁀harqi, Ali, Sheikh, 292

Sharaf Khan, 167, 170
al-Shaykh Ibrahim al-Samarrai, Yusuf, 137
Shihab, Hammad, 84
al-Shirazi, Mirza Muhammad Taqi, 285, 293-4
Shryock, A., 43
Sluglett, Peter, 272-3
Smith, Robertson, 115
Smith, W.R., 18-19, 39
Steppat, F., 38
Suker, Abdul-Wahid al-Haj, 298
Sulaiman, Ali, 265, 270-1
Sulaybi, Sa'id, 140

Tabari, Abu Ja'far Muhammad ibn Jarir, 25
Takriti, Barzan, 158
Takriti, Hardan, 87, 140-1
Tambiah, S.J., 306
Tapper, Richard, 235
Tozy, M., 59, 207, 209
Truman, Harry, 239
Tulfah, Adnan, 84, 87, 120, 124
Tulfah, Khairallah, 120
Tulfah, Sabha, 123
Tulfah, Sajida, 120, 123

al-Ubaid, Khayoun, 295
Ubayda, 25
al-Umari, Mohammed Khairuldin, 285

Varlet, Henri, 246-7

al-Wardi, Ali, 285
Warne, William E., 239
Waterbury, John, 207, 300
Watt, W.M., 21-2, 25
Wellhausen, J., 17-19, 22, 39, 41, 206-7
Westermarck, E., 206
Wilken, G.A., 18

Wilson, Sir Arnold, 284, 293, 297
Wilson, A.T., 262–3
Wilson, Colonel, 286
Wilson, Woodrow, 291
Wright, S.A., 241–2, 248–9

Yahya, Tahir, 140
al-Yasiri, 'Alwan, 298, 301
al-Yasiri, Nour, 301
Yetts, L.M., 270

Zaynab, wife of Muhammad the Prophet,
    21–3, 28
Zeki Pasha, 172
Zhadija bint Khuwaylid ibn Asad, 23–4
Zuain, Hadi, 301